Practical Writing

A Process Approach to Business and Technical Communication

Carol Niederlander

St. Louis Community College at Forest Park

David Kvernes

Southern Illinois University at Carbondale

Sam Sutherland

McDonnell Douglas Astronautics Company

Holt, Rinehart and Winston
New York   Chicago   San Francisco   Philadelphia
Montreal   Toronto   London   Sydney   Tokyo
Mexico City   Rio de Janeiro   Madrid

for Nicholas and Rebecca
for Anton and Benjamin
for Nancy

Library of Congress Cataloging-in-Publication Data

Niederlander, Carol.
  Practical writing.

  Includes index.
  1. Business report writing.   2. Technical writing.
I. Kvernes, David.   II. Sutherland, Sam.   III. Title.
HF5719.N54   1986   808'.066651   85-27039

ISBN 0-03-071111-8

Address correspondence to:
383 Madison Avenue
New York, NY 10017

CBS COLLEGE PUBLISHING
Holt, Rinehart and Winston
The Dryden Press
Saunders College Publishing

Acknowledgments are on page 430.

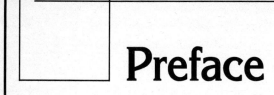

Preface

This textbook is intended for undergraduate students in what are usually called technical writing courses but that we prefer to call courses in practical writing. We hope it will be useful to students in classes composed of majors from a variety of disciplines: science, technology, business, health, social science, and education—in short, all majors that lead students into careers that require them to produce practical, as opposed to expressive, writing. Of course, people from almost every professional field, including liberal arts, at some time need to produce practical writing; the funding for many arts projects is secured by writing a proposal, a very practical form of writing indeed.

The three authors, one a community college teacher, one a university teacher, and one a writer in industry, draw upon a broad range of experience in the practice and teaching of practical writing. Thus the text reflects an understanding of the needs of teachers in a variety of settings and of what is required of writers in business and industry today.

We see this textbook as unique in two important ways: (1) it uses a process approach in all chapters that deal with the production of a form of practical writing, and (2) it describes practical writing as writing that addresses real-world problems and emphasizes the importance of defining a problem before composing.

Research on the process of writing indicates that there are many ways in which writing is produced. There is little agreement about what the steps or stages actually are or in what order they tend to occur or should occur. For the kind of writing done in regular composition courses, this lack of consensus may reflect the actual state of affairs; that is, different students follow different writing processes, with varying degrees of effectiveness.

Yet we feel that for technical or practical writing, it is possible to describe more precisely than for expressive writing a number of stages through which good practical writers proceed in composing. This is possible because practical writing deals with problems and the search for solutions to them. This practical orientation places less emphasis on invention or "finding the subject" and more on designing a response to a clearly limited situation in the real world, and on presenting it in a commonly accepted form. Though we believe an efficient sequence of stages for practical writing can be determined, we recognize that the process is also cumulative and recursive: each step in the process is not simply completed and never reconsidered, but instead, frequent return to earlier stages can take place.

We have divided the process of producing a finished document into seven stages and have described these stages in detail in Chapter 2, which is intended to provide an overview of the sequence for students. We have then used the seven stages to teach the forms of practical writing covered in the chapters that follow. Thus students are led through the process of producing most of the forms of writing they are likely to encounter on the job. We believe that our thoroughgoing application of the process approach is unique and will prove helpful both to students as they write and to teachers as they teach.

Furthermore, in this textbook all practical writing is seen as a problem-solving activity, and the process always begins with the definition of the problem. In the world of business, government, and industry, no one writes simply for the pleasure of it or for practice, as in a composition course; there is always a pragmatic reason for writing that can be defined in one sense or another as the need to solve a problem. This problem-oriented starting point for the process of writing is, we believe, the second unique feature of our text.

In addition, each chapter has been preceded by an abstract and followed by a recapitulation of main points. We have also supplied a set of exercises at the end of each chapter, some suitable for use in class and some to be done outside class. Instructors will no doubt want to supplement these exercises with some of their own, but those supplied in the text should prove especially useful to beginning teachers.

The careful reader will also note that our treatment of library research and field research—the latter including interviewing, observing, and using questionnaires—is especially thorough. Since research skills are commonly taught in second-semester college composition courses such as the kind of course for which this book is intended, no assumptions about students' previous library work have been made; and all skills, from using a card catalog to evaluating sources, are explained. The book does assume, however, that students using the text have completed a first semester of freshman composition and have therefore gained some familiarity with the basic modes of rhetoric, such as narration, description, and argument, and with the form of an essay.

Students who use this text should first learn the principles of the seven stages of practical writing through reading Chapter 2 and then apply their understanding by producing some of the forms of writing explained in the ensuing chapters. During the course of the semester, they should also learn to collect data for their work—by conducting library and field research—and to create and incorporate simple graphics in their documents. Some instructors may choose to end the semester by giving students the opportunity to present one of their reports orally, according to instructions given in Chapter 14. Since few classes will have the time to review every form of writing explained in this text, choices appropriate to the needs of particular groups of students will often have to be made. However, students who learn the concepts involved in the process of practical writing should, by the conclusion of the semester, be able to produce almost any form of practical writing they may need.

Finally, we would like to acknowledge the help of a number of people who helped us to produce this text: the reference librarians at St. Louis Community College at Forest Park, especially Carol Shahriary for her help in reviewing the library chapter and for permission to cite reference works from her library handout "How to Research Employers"; Ruth Bauner, education librarian at Southern Illinois University, for critiquing the library chapter; Jim Hoelscher, for testing a number of chapters in his classes and providing helpful critiques; Dan Landiss and Bill Muckler for advice about technical subjects; the students in technical report writing classes at Southern Illinois University, St. Louis Community College at Forest Park and Florissant Valley, and at St. Louis University; and to our reviewers: Lynn Beene, The University of New Mexico; Tom Colonnese, Northern Arizona University; Rick Eden, The University of New Mexico; Esther Gloe, University of Southern Colorado; Keith Hamon, University of Houston—Victoria; Joyce Hicks, Valparaiso University; Martha Hiestand, Syracuse University; Catherine McCue, Framingham State College; Louis Murphy, Bucks County Community College; and Robert Utterback, Owens Technical College

St. Louis   C. N.
December 1985   D. K.
          S. S.

Contents

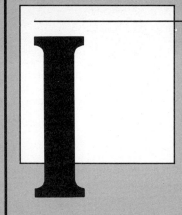

Introductory Principles

1 An Introduction to Practical Writing

Abstract

This book provides instruction in practical writing, the sort of writing you will do on the job. What is usually called technical writing is only one part of it. Job-related writing differs from that which you may have done in high school and freshman composition in its greater emphasis on a practical purpose, attention to audience, use of graphic aids, conveyance of a single meaning, and value as a record. Practical writing is a craft that can be learned by those who approach it systematically and practice it conscientiously. Since its purpose is to communicate, clarity and simplicity are its hallmarks.

This book is intended to help you write better on the job. Since many of you, as future college graduates, will in time become managers, you can expect to do a good deal of writing on the job, whatever that job may be. The course you are currently taking might be called Technical Writing, Report Writing, Composition for Engineers, or a variation of one of those titles, but the kind of writing this book teaches goes beyond topics associated with science and technology to include all work-related writing. That is why we have left the word *technical* out of the title even though many of the suggested assignments have to do with technical subjects.

What makes this practical writing different from most of the work you may have done in a regular freshman composition course is not the *subject* of the writing but the *purpose*. Any subject, from cabbages to computers, can be treated in a practical or a nonpractical way. It is the purpose that determines how you will treat it. The writing you do in a regular composition course certainly has a practical value, but it is practical in a quite

3

different way. It may enable you to do a variety of things: to give expression to feelings, to learn more about a particular subject, to write more effective essay exams, or to respond to what you read and observe. All these purposes are valuable, yet most have little direct bearing on the world you will enter once you graduate. The writing taught in this book, on the other hand, nearly always reflects a job-related task: applying for a position, summarizing the results of a meeting, evaluating a site for a new building, or drawing up a set of instructions.

The differences between these two approaches to a subject may be seen in the following two accounts of the process of planting cucumbers—a humble but useful task. The first is from a long poem, appropriately titled "The Task," by the eighteenth-century writer William Cowper. The second is from a how-to-do-it book on gardening. Cowper's purpose is to celebrate the joys of a life of retirement in the country. Not the least of those joys, according to the poet, is growing cucumbers.

> The seed selected wisely, plump and smooth
> And glossy, he commits to pots of size
> Diminutive, well filled with well prepared
> And fruitful soil, that has been treasured long,
> And drank no moisture from the dripping clouds.
> These on the warm and genial earth that hides
> The smoking manure and o'erspreads it all,
> He places lightly, and as time subdues
> The rage of fermentation, plunges deep
> In the soft medium, till they stand immersed.
> Then rise the tender germs upstarting quick
> And spreading wide their spongy lobes, at first
> Pale, wan, and livid, but assuming soon,
> If fanned by balmy and nutritious air
> Strained through the friendly mats, a vivid green.

Note how little specific information is given and how many questions are left unanswered if one is looking for actual advice on gardening: how deep the seeds should be planted, how far apart, and so on. Obviously that is not the poet's purpose. Yet many evaluative terms, such as *genial earth* and *balmy and nutritious air*, convey the poet's positive, even joyful, attitude toward the task.

Contrast that passage with the instructions in a recent book on vegetable gardening:

How To Plant Gherkin Cucumbers

Choose a loamy, well-drained garden site with plenty of humus, compost, and, if possible, well-rotted manure.

Plant in hills about two feet apart to allow plenty of room for growth.

Place a layer of compost or manure on the bottom of each hole before setting the seed.

Plant four or five seeds in each hill, pressing them less than an inch into the ground.

When the seedlings are about six inches tall, choose the three strongest vines and pinch out all the others. Three vines will produce enough for a normal family.

Gherkins are prolific and, if picked regularly, they will produce throughout the season.

The content is remarkably similar to that in the poem, but the manner is quite different, and the manner is determined by the writer's purpose: to tell you, as briefly and clearly as possible, how to plant and prune cucumbers. No words betray the writer's feelings about this simple task, though it is certainly not made to sound unpleasant. The tone is neutral and objective, for the writer is obviously intent on making the steps as clear and simple as possible. The goal is to help you produce a successful crop of cucumbers.

This kind of writing can be called *practical*, and when applied to most white-collar jobs, it can also be called *professional*. These terms cover all the writing you will need to do on the job, including what is usually called *technical*. It differs from the writing you might have done in a regular composition course in five important ways. It has a practical purpose, is directed to a specific audience, makes use of graphic aids, conveys a single meaning, and has value as a record of the activities of an organization.

Practical Purpose

First and most important, practical writing has a purpose that reflects the sorts of tasks done in business, industry, and government. You will no longer be telling a professor all you know about an assigned subject, a subject the professor usually knows better than you do. Rather you will be communicating information that is new to someone who needs to know it in order to do a job or make a decision. You become the expert on the subject and your reader truly needs what you can supply. Hence you must write clearly and simply. Furthermore, you will not tell *all* you know about the subject but will select from that body of knowledge only what you think the reader needs. Enabling a reader to do a job quickly is an important part of being practical.

Direction to a Specific Audience

Second, the writing you will do on the job, and thus the kind taught in this book, will usually be directed to a clearly defined audience. Your purpose helps you determine who the reader is. Knowing first of all what you want done, you can decide who is best able to do it or ought to do it. If it involves a decision about company investments, your reader might be an accountant in the finance department. If the problem is a labor dispute, your audience might be a shop supervisor or all the truck drivers assigned to local deliveries. Often, of course, you don't get to decide who your readers are; they are simply given to you along with the writing task. Once you know who the readers are, you must find out as much about them as possible so you will know how formal or informal you should be, how much background to supply, and what level of technicality is best. Defining the reader carefully makes your writing task easier and your success more certain.

Use of Graphic Aids

Graphic aids are a third mark of good practical writing. Notice how Figure 1.1 uses space—the length of the bars—as well as numbers, words, and a drawing to get its message across. This is a simple chart, yet if you were to put the same information into prose, you would need nearly as much space and the information would be much harder to grasp.

Other purposes call for other forms of graphic aids: Tables present even more specific information than that shown in Figure 1.1 in even less space; line graphs are unsurpassed for showing trends; and a picture's superiority to words is captured in a familiar saying.

However, different readers require different approaches. Figure 1.2 combines a table and a graph to convey a unified message to a reader who will study them no matter how commonplace their presentation. In Figure 1.1, by contrast, the writer has added a drawing of a school building in order to catch the reader's attention. The bar chart (Figure 1.1) is intended for readers whose interest needs to be aroused; the table and graph (Figure 1.2) are directed to more specialized readers who make a point of keeping abreast of some specific economic indicators. In Figure 1.2 little attempt is made to catch the reader's attention or to make the presentation "interesting." Good writers are very conscious of the need to appeal to different kinds of readers, and carefully planned graphic aids can help them do it.

Conveying a Single Meaning

Good practical writing differs from the writing you might have done in other composition courses in a fourth way: it conveys a single meaning. Gone is the literary aim of conveying several meanings simultaneously, an aim that helps produce the richness and complexity of much prose fiction and some essays. And it carefully excludes those unintended double meanings that are present when our writing is misunderstood. Practical

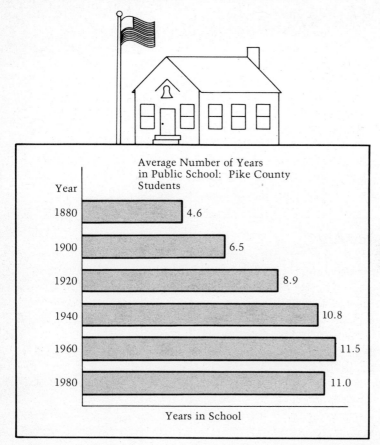

Figure 1.1   A Bar Chart

writers strive to avoid being misunderstood when, for example, they give instructions on how to mix chemical spray for lawns or how to shut off a machine when an emergency arises. Their readers can't afford to make a mistake. That is why companies try out their instruction sheets on a test audience to detect any omissions or double meanings.

Importance as a Record

A final distinguishing quality of practical writing is that it is often preserved, or kept on file, far longer than the writing you do in school or the letters you may get from home. It becomes part of an elaborate record of your company's business dealings or internal functioning. On occasion it may even become part of a legal proceeding; much more often it is used to reconstruct events months or even years later, sometimes long after you have left the position you held when it was written. Therefore it is impor-

Plus & Minus® USN & WR WEEKLY INDEX OF BUSINESS ACTIVITY

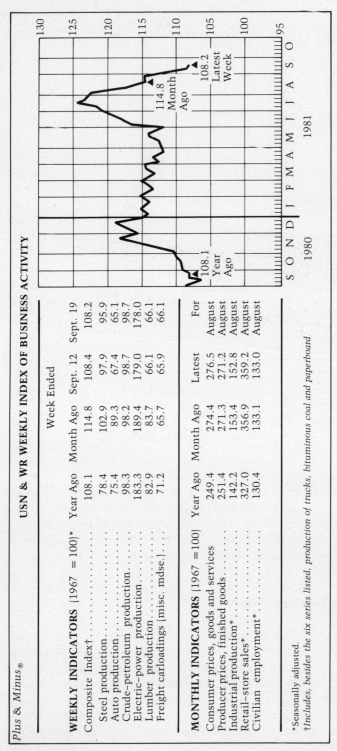

WEEKLY INDICATORS (1967 =100)*	Year Ago	Week Ended Month Ago	Sept. 12	Sept. 19
Composite Index†	108.1	114.8	108.4	108.2
Steel production	78.4	102.9	97.9	95.9
Auto production	75.4	89.3	67.4	65.1
Crude–petroleum production	98.3	98.2	98.7	98.7
Electric–power production	183.3	189.4	179.0	178.0
Lumber production	82.9	83.7	66.1	66.1
Freight carloadings (misc. mdse.)	71.2	65.7	65.9	66.1

MONTHLY INDICATORS (1967 =100)	Year Ago	Month Ago	Latest	For
Consumer prices, goods and services . .	249.4	274.4	276.5	August
Producer prices, finished goods	251.4	271.3	271.2	August
Industrial production*	142.2	153.4	152.8	August
Retail–store sales*	327.0	356.9	359.2	August
Civilian employment*	130.4	133.1	133.0	August

*Seasonally adjusted.
†Includes, besides the six series listed, production of trucks, bituminous coal and paperboard

Figure 1.2 A Table and Line Graph

Reprinted from U.S. News & World Report, October 5, 1981. Copyright © 1981, U.S. News & World Report, Inc.

tant that you write clearly and objectively, check the accuracy of the information, provide background to the problem at hand, and make clear the positions of you the writer, all the readers, and others who may be mentioned in the document. The function of letters and memos as records of events or deliberations also makes it important that they be dated.

Advice to Practical Writers

Most of us find writing hard work. We put it off as long as we can and often don't feel satisfied when we have finished a letter, memo, or report. The eighteenth-century essayist and dictionary-maker Samuel Johnson once said, "No one but a blockhead would write but for hire" (money). Perhaps he felt that way because he depended on writing for his bread and butter—and he enjoyed eating very much. Yet writing doesn't have to be so difficult. Practical writing is a craft, not a mysterious art. One doesn't have to be an inspired genius to turn out a good piece of writing. To learn to write does, however, require proper guidance, a systematic method— and practice. Your instructor and this textbook should supply you with the guidance and the method; it is up to you to give yourself the practice.

If you approach each writing task confidently, follow the advice of your teacher and this text about how to plan the paper, gather the material, organize it, and write a draft, and finally, are willing to rewrite it at least once, but more often if necessary, you will find writing easier than you may have thought it to be.

We talked earlier about the ways practical writing differs from the writing you did in high school or in other college courses. Yet it is also true that in some important ways it is similar. In both, the organization must be clear and logical; the paragraphs unified; and the grammar, punctuation, and spelling correct. In addition, the further you advance in your profession the more you will be required to write to laypeople with less special training than you. You must therefore know how to use the kind of clear, common language that is characteristic of most good writing, in or out of college. Clarity and simplicity should also mark your graphic aids and the appearance of your reports.

Producing high-quality practical writing, then, requires you to combine the skills you have learned in your writing courses thus far with new skills, particularly applicable to science, business, and technology, which you will learn in this course. Your aim will be to convey information effectively so that your readers can do their jobs well. When you have done that, you also will have functioned well in your role as a practical writer.

2 The Process of Practical Writing

Abstract

The process of writing a document with a practical purpose can be divided into seven stages, some of which you may omit when carrying out simple writing tasks. The stages that precede your writing of a first draft are (1) defining the problem and purpose, (2) analyzing the audience, (3) collecting the data, and (4) designing the document. Those that follow the crucial stage, (5) drafting the document, are (6) revising and editing and (7) producing the finished document. Experienced writers find that in practice they don't finish each stage completely before moving on to the next but frequently must go back to earlier stages as new ideas and new ways of expressing ideas occur to them.

Have you thought about how you produce a piece of writing? When you sit down to write a term paper or an essay for an English class, do you have a method, a series of steps you always follow? You may not have given the subject much thought, but very likely you usually follow the same pattern, with minor variations depending on the assignment and the subject. Sometimes the method works well, sometimes not so well.

It is important for you to be aware that you have a method or process for writing, since knowing how you now do it will help you discover how that process can be improved. The first exercise at the end of this chapter asks you to describe your current method of planning and writing an essay or report. Even if your instructor does not specifically ask you to do this exercise, you will find it worth your time. Very likely you will be surprised at some of the things you discover about the way you now carry out a typical writing assignment. This text offers an alternative method.

In this chapter we will describe a set of seven stages that experience has shown will work for most of the practical writing you will do in the course you may now be taking and in your career once you graduate. You will not need to use all these stages for every writing task you face, and with experience you may find it works best to alter the order or work on several stages simultaneously. Here are the seven stages:

- Defining the problem and purpose
- Determining the audience
- Collecting the data
- Designing the document: Organization, graphics, and style
- Drafting the document
- Reviewing and reworking the document
- Producing the finished document

A memo reminding a co-worker of a meeting may easily be written without reference to the entire list, although the chapter on memo writing will make clear why attention to problem and purpose, even in memo writing, is important, and the same may be true of routine reports that answer a prescribed set of questions, such as a machinery failure report. Conventional form or company policy may answer most if not all of your questions about how to proceed in those cases. But for other, less routine tasks, our set of stages will provide a useful pattern for you to follow as you plan and write a letter, proposal, or research report. We have organized the chapters that teach you how to produce a particular form of practical writing such as the abstract, the description of a mechanism, or the formal report around this set of stages. Thus you will be able to see clearly how they can be applied to the typical tasks you will face as a writer in business or industry.

Although the stages are presented in a fixed order, the actual process of planning, writing, and revising does not, for most writers, consist of a simple straightforward set of self-enclosed tasks. That is why we call them *stages* instead of *steps*. The word *steps* implies a rigid sequence of tasks, each of which is completed once and for all before you go on to the next. Most experienced writers, however, say they are constantly revising as they proceed, moving backward and forward among these stages. Late in their work on a document they may revise the introductory elements, the graphic aids, or one of the other elements when later discoveries reveal a better way of formulating them. Thus the actual process involves frequent backtracking to earlier stages as new ideas come to mind or new, more effective ways of organizing become apparent. The recursive nature of the process of practical writing is pictured in Figure 2.1.

Note that a writer may return all the way to the earliest stages from the revising and editing stage as well as from intermediate stages. And, although the chart doesn't reflect it, writers are sometimes at work on several stages simultaneously.

Some of the recursiveness, the "doubling back" in the process,

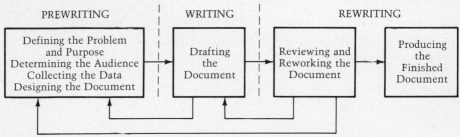

Figure 2.1   The Process of Practical Writing

occurs because writing is often a process of discovery as well as a process of presenting ideas you already have in mind. Don't shut the mind to those discoveries triggered by the act of writing itself.

Nevertheless, although writing does help you discover new ideas and new ways of expressing them, in practical writing discovery as the sole method of finding your subject and direction is not likely to work very well. Although you may sometimes change your plan and will probably add new examples and alter details as you write, your purpose will generally require you to stick to the main points of your plan. For writers in business and the professions, finding a subject and material to support that subject are usually not the biggest problem; knowing *how* to say what they want and knowing what to leave out are bigger problems.

In this book we have provided a set of guidelines, our seven writing stages, which will help you determine the purpose, audience, and design of your document before you begin a first draft. The stages that follow the writing of the draft will help to ensure that you produce a piece of writing that is professional in all respects.

Stage 1: Defining the Problem and Purpose

Defining the problem and purpose are closely related, and you may be tempted to see them as a single task, but it usually works best to deal with them separately.

Defining the Problem

You may not think of writing as a problem-solving activity, but most practical writing can be viewed that way. In business and industry, writing is produced to solve a variety of problems, or to provide at least one step toward their solution. An engineering firm may have produced a new surveying device, and a manual must be written to explain to customers how to use it. The manual will solve the problem of the lack of personal instructions for customers. In another instance, the manager of a department store may have been informed of an increase in shoplifting in the store and wants to call a meeting of the sales staff to discuss the problem. The immediate writing problem is to inform the sales staff of the meeting. This, of course, will not solve the problem of shoplifting, but the first step is simply to bring the staff together.

You may, in the past, have thought of your writing problems as simply "my history and composition teachers' demands that I write a term paper or a personal essay." That's not what we mean by *problem* here. We are referring instead to a real-world *situation* that creates the need for a letter, memo, report, manual, or some other kind of document. When you set out to produce any kind of practical writing, you should always start with a problem situation since that is how your writing tasks must be addressed once you take a job. Businesses and industrial firms are pragmatic institutions; the people who run them don't feel they or the workers under them can afford to spend time in speculation or in finding out new information simply for the pleasure of it. Writing with no practical application in mind is an important and valuable activity, but it is generally restricted to research centers, certain college courses, and one's leisure time.

One confusing fact about practical writing tasks is that they involve not one problem but two: The problem "out there" that causes people to begin looking for a solution and the problem of how best to carry out the writing that will help implement that solution. In this chapter the term *problem* refers to the first kind, that which motivates you to start the process of producing a piece of writing. In the series of stages that lead to the production of a piece of writing, defining the problem comes first because that definition will ensure that you know why you are writing. It will also direct you to the heart of the problem, set limits to the task, and move you toward a solution. As a writer you ought to be involved in the discussions that lead to a definition of a problem and the outline of a solution since you are the one charged with the task of solving the writing problem that follows.

Focusing on a problem will help you understand the reason for producing a document and will suggest what should be included, what left out, and to whom it should be addressed. Since a problem situation is the logical starting point, most of the chapters in this text begin by listing some typical problems—situations that create the need for the kinds of writing discussed in those chapters.

Once you have been confronted by a problem, either on the job or in the classroom, your first task will be to define it in a way that makes it clear both to you and to your readers. If you fail to provide an accurate definition, and hence address your writing to an aspect of the situation that is not the real problem, the writing will miss its mark. In the case of the surveying equipment mentioned earlier, the problem is that customers who buy it can't operate it without instructions, and since they are many and live at a distance, the instructions can't be given in person by the makers of the equipment. An instruction manual therefore appears to be the best remedy. If you mistakenly assume that what the customers need is an understanding of the theory of surveying, you might produce a manual that gives a thorough grounding in the science of surveying but neglects to provide step-by-step instructions on how to operate the equipment. A little theory might enable the customers to operate it better, but what they most need to know is how to set up the surveying device, how to adjust the eyepiece, and so on.

Sometimes solving a problem requires dividing it into parts and producing writing to help solve each part—and eventually the entire problem. In the shoplifting situation described earlier, we can see how four pieces of writing might be required. Initially the problem might be defined in this way: Shoplifting has recently risen to an unacceptable level. To determine the extent of this problem, a supervisor in the stockroom might be assigned to write an objective description of the amount of shoplifting based upon the amount of recorded sales and the flow of goods from the stockroom. With this report in hand, the store manager will be ready to call a meeting to discuss the problem. A second document, a memo, will be needed to announce the meeting. As a result of the meeting, a third document might be written proposing actions to be taken by store personnel to combat the shoplifting. Finally, these proposed actions, once approved by management, might be written up in a fourth document—a set of guidelines for detecting and dealing with shoplifters, to be distributed to personnel on the sales floor.

This text cannot provide step-by-step instructions in how to define business or technical problems—a complex and difficult task that cannot be pinned down with a set of rules or guidelines. Defining and solving problems require a good knowledge of the subject at hand and a good portion of common sense as well as persistence in pursuing a solution. Your major course work and your experience on the job will supply some of what you need, and your lifelong habit of observing and drawing inferences will provide still more. There are, in addition, books and articles that provide good advice, such as Linda Flower's *Problem-Solving Strategies for Writing*, 1985, and Richard Young, Alton Becker, and Kenneth Pike's *Rhetoric: Discovery and Change*, 1970, both published by Harcourt Brace Jovanovich.

Determining the Purpose

After defining the problem your next task is to determine your purpose. The purpose should follow from the definition of the problem, and in general, it will be to overcome the problem or to take one step in that direction. Not all solutions require that you write. If it is a matter of getting subcontracted parts delivered on time so there are no delays in production, you may simply need to *talk* to the supervisor in your own receiving warehouse. That is the person in charge of receiving the parts when they arrive by truck (always on time, as you have discovered by investigation) and forwarding them to the production department. Or you may need to modify your agreement with the subcontractor to move up the delivery date to a day earlier each week. You might do this by writing a letter, but sometimes you can do it better in person or on the phone, and often more quickly as well.

But since this book is about writing, our advice covers those situations when you find you need to write. In the case just described, you may decide that the best course is to write a letter to the subcontractor proposing a change in the contract. Modifying the contract itself will take more writing, but once the subcontracted parts begin arriving one day earlier, your purpose will have been accomplished.

Most of the exercises in this book attempt to simulate the practical tasks you will face once you begin full-time work by suggesting a practical purpose for each piece of writing or asking you to formulate a purpose yourself.

In all cases the basic question you must ask is this: What do I want to happen as a result of my writing the document? A memo announcing a meeting must give place, time, and purpose of the meeting; persons invited; and the originator of the memo in case anyone has questions. Including these points should result in all those who are asked getting to the appointed place on time and in a reasonably agreeable frame of mind. If that happens, the memo will have accomplished its purpose—to inform its readers of the essential facts about the meeting. As letters and reports address more complex problems, determining and carrying out the purpose gets progressively more difficult.

Your definitions of problem and purpose should be used to help plan the first draft, but they should also be stated at the beginning of the document, even if it is a relatively brief memo. For example, a department manager in an accounting firm might begin a memo to subordinates in the following way:

> Many of you are confused about when the newly adopted Professional Evaluation System will be put into effect. The purpose of this memo is to set forth the timetable for starting that system.

In longer documents, such as investigative reports and proposals, separate sections labeled *Problem* and *Purpose* may be incorporated into the introduction. If stating the problem and purpose seems to make your opening too explicit, remember that in practical writing it is better to err in that direction than in the opposite.

Stage 2: Determining the Audience

Once you have defined the problem and purpose, you must determine your audience. In other words you must decide who ought to receive your written message and, on the basis of it, take the action needed to solve the problem.

On the other hand, like the problem itself, your audience may already be defined for you. If the problem has to do with the budget and there is a budget committee set up to handle matters of that sort, the first thing needed is a memo to all members calling a meeting of the committee. At another time your supervisor may tell you to submit a trip report after your two-day visit to a branch office. And routine weekly and monthly reports usually have a clearly defined audience built into the report form.

Once you have identified your audience, find out as much as you can about that person or group in order to tailor what you say to their knowledge and needs. Even if you don't know precisely who your readers will be, determining their approximate level of knowledge and interest will enable you to do a better job of getting your message across.

Questions About the Readers

Asking yourself a series of questions about your readers will help you decide what to say and how to say it. The following questions should help you determine their needs.

- *How well versed are they in the subject?* By finding out the field and level of their academic training, their occupational title and years on the job, and their position in the managerial hierarchy, and by looking at any letters or reports they may have written, you can get a fair idea of their technical expertise. Generally, your co-workers and workers in a department similar to yours but in another company will have technical knowledge comparable to yours. Top managerial officials usually lack specialized expertise but have a general knowledge of the areas their companies deal with. Hourly workers tend to have a practical knowledge of a very narrow part of a company's activities.
- *How much do they know about the particular situation or context?* If your readers have already become involved in the problem, or if they are your co-workers, they will probably know the situation well. If not, you will need to provide background to bring them up to date. Generally, the further the readers are from you the less they are likely to know about the context of your problem. They may be distant in the company hierarchy, in an unrelated department, or completely outside your organization. A broad general audience almost always requires background to make them aware of the context.
- *What is their general level of understanding?* It may seem insulting to consider this factor, but some writing situations require that you do. Technical manuals for military equipment may require you to write at an eighth-grade reading level, and a textbook in health science for sixth-graders would certainly have to consider this factor.
- *How interested are they in what you have to say?* Generally readers in business and industry are interested since your writing relates in some way to their jobs, although there are levels of interest even among these

readers, depending on their level of responsibility for the problem and their role in solving it. In general, upper-level managers can be expected to be highly interested in matters of policy but are often not concerned about details; lower-level workers may want to know precisely what they must do on a project but may be little concerned about the philosophy behind it. Readers with little built-in interest must often be persuaded to read attentively; if you direct a report to readers who haven't asked for it, you may need to make a special effort to arouse their interest.

- *How much detail do the readers require?* Here the amount of expertise, the level of familiarity with the situation, and the part to be played by the readers in the solution will determine how much detail you need to include. What to include and what to leave out is often a difficult decision, since what will bore some readers is absolutely essential to others. Often you can provide a general summary at the beginning for top executives and then a detailed discussion in the body of the report for those who will carry out the project. An account of molecular structure in a textbook for students of advanced college physics will require much more detail and of a different sort from that in an article on the same subject for readers of *Science Digest*.
- *What do the readers particularly like or dislike?* To answer this question you will probably need to know the readers by name, so this question can not easily be applied to a broad audience. If you are addressing a report to your supervisor and you know this person likes brevity, make the report shorter rather than longer. If the reader likes statistical support for each point in a proposal, be sure to look for statistics when you do your research.

By applying these questions to your potential readers, you should be able to draw up a profile that will make writing the report easier and the report itself more effective. Obviously, if you know the readers personally you can simply ask them what you should include in the report and what form it should take.

Multiple Readerships

However, your report will often be read by more than one kind of reader. In these cases it is important that you determine the kinds of readers you have and how they differ in knowledge and interest. If, for example, you are submitting a proposal for a waste disposal contract to a mayor and a city council, you must keep several audiences in mind. First, of course, are the city council members who will vote on whether to accept or reject your proposal. They are usually lay people of above-average intelligence who may have a general knowledge of waste disposal but little technical knowledge. A second audience may be the city engineer or a group of experts in city government who are technically expert in waste disposal methods and in finance. They will read your proposal very carefully and will probably make a recommendation to the council. A third audience might be a reporter who will read the report and quote from it in an article for the general public. All these audiences are important and all must be kept in mind as you write. Some parts should be directed mainly to the technical and financial experts in city government. The introduction and conclusion, which highlight the proposal's main ideas and make a persuasive appeal, might be directed to the city council and the public. A graphic illustration showing the report, its various parts, and the probable readers of each part is shown in Figure 2.2.

You may have to reach several kinds of readers in one document even in writing you do while a student. Suppose you are asked by the officers of your student engineering society to draw up a report on job opportunities and salaries in your branch of engineering. The audience will include not just members of the society, who have already decided to become engineers, but also other students who have yet to choose a major and perhaps the advisers in your college's placement office. Students already committed to the field will simply want the facts relating to their branch. Those who have not yet chosen a major and the advisers would probably want some comparisons with opportunities and salaries in other branches of engineering as well. Yet these three groups, different as they are, are probably closer in background and interest than the audiences for the proposal on waste disposal described earlier.

Most writers find it easiest to report information in the order in which they discovered it and to write it in the special terms that are most familiar to them. But that method usually doesn't meet the needs of readers. It takes a special effort to put yourself in the place of your readers and

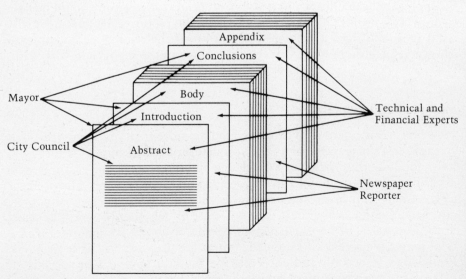

Figure 2.2   Interactions Between a Report and Its Multiple Readers

try to imagine their needs, for what is clear to you will not necessarily be clear to them and what interests you may not interest them.

It is also important to distinguish primary readers from secondary ones, usually on the basis of responsibility or influence. In the case of the city waste proposal, the most influencial readers will probably be the financial and technical experts in city government. They will read all of the report carefully but especially the supporting data in the body and the statistics in the appendix. The mayor and city council, who have the most responsibility, may read only the abstract, introduction, and conclusion, and although they must make the final decision, they will put great weight on the recommendations of their technical experts. Hence those experts make up the primary audience, the mayor and council the secondary audience, and the news reporters the third. As later chapters will make clear, each writing situation requires a separate analysis of audience. The city waste disposal case is an example of the kind of analysis you might have to make in an administrative job.

Stage 3: Collecting the Data

Your purpose and audience determine what you need to say, and that in turn determines the amount and kind of information you must gather. This section will give you some general advice about collecting data for a piece of writing. More detailed advice is given in the chapters on specific forms of documents and in Chapters 6 and 7 on library research and field research. You may be engaged in gathering information from the very beginning of your project to the final revision. You will need a certain amount of data initially to define the problem and purpose, and while making your final revision you may discover the need for one last piece of supporting evidence.

It may surprise you to hear this, but as an expert in the field in which you will be hired, you may know all you need to know about a subject without doing any research. It might simply be a matter of sitting down and taking thought. If that is the case, listing is a good technique for calling up information or plans of action from your experience. Always begin by putting in writing the points you know or can recall from memory.

A second method is to gather ideas from your fellow workers. Conversation is the easiest and most commonly used method; carefully planned interviews may work better if you don't know the person well or the amount of material you hope to get is significant. Brainstorming is also a productive method of gathering ideas from others. A group of people get together and throw out ideas on a particular subject with no effort made to criticize or limit contributions in any way. All ideas are simply listed as offered and only later are they gone over with a critical eye to select the most useful ones. This method works well partly because the exchange of ideas in a group is mutually stimulating.

Some problems may require you to locate printed sources of information in your office, your company library, or a large research library. Still other methods of gathering information fall under the heading of field research: site visits to observe your subject in operation, interviews with authorities outside your company, and oral surveys and questionnaires. Chapter 6 tells you how to find information in a library and Chapter 7 how to conduct field research.

Getting the information down in written form, however sketchy, as you gather it is essential if your report is more than a page or two long. Specific statistical information should be written down no matter how short the document will be. Advice on how to take notes is given in Chapter 6.

Limit your collection of data to those aspects of your subject that purpose and audience tell you are essential, and narrow your search as rapidly as you can. Set aside a certain amount of time for gathering data, and when that time has been used up in well-managed research move on to the next stage. If gaps in your data become obvious in later stages, you can return to this stage and fill those gaps. Most writing in business and industry is carried out under more difficult time constraints than writing in school. It is therefore good practice to impose a definite time schedule on the various stages of your work, and that includes collecting data. Students must also meet deadlines, and one of their commonest mistakes is to spend too much time on reasearch and too little on subsequent stages, especially writing, revising, and editing.

Stage 4: Designing the Document

Once you have gathered all the data you need, you may think it is time to plunge into the first draft. But wait a moment. Before you begin you need to decide what form your document will take and how the information in it will be organized. By "form" we mean one of the standard forms, such as memo, letter, formal report, or one of the other standard patterns that practical writing can assume. These conventional forms have evolved out of the experience of many writers over many years. As a result, convention, or standard practice, will determine the basic shape of much that you write on the job. Conventional forms save time and energy both for the writer and the reader since they provide a pattern for the writer to follow and they fulfill the expectations of readers in business and industry, most of whom are accustomed to finding written material in certain patterns. For example, a busy executive reading a proposal to expand the company's market for a small product into new territory looks for a concise summary of main points since this person does not have time to read all of the 40-page report. Putting those main points into an introudctory summary makes good sense and is one standard method of organizing the beginning of a business report. The discussion of abstracts in Chapter 11 explains this technique in detail. In another instance a parent putting together a new toy for a child needs the steps laid out clearly. Experience has shown that it works best to begin each step or instructon with an imperative verb ("Insert tabs in slots A and B") and to place all the steps in a list with warnings emphasized and explanatory notes subordinated. How to write a set of instructions is explained in Chapter 10.

Your choice of a form does not mean that your letters or reports must conform to a single, rigid set of guidelines. For each writing task you must adapt the basic form you have chosen to fit the purpose and audience you are addressing. In some cases you will probably find it necessary to depart from the standard forms completely. Yet in most cases your first decision will be to choose a form; your second will be to decide how to design the shape of the data within the document so that it fits your purpose and audience.

The rest of this section will discuss things you must consider in choosing a form and the ways you can adapt the form to fit your readers' needs. It will also discuss some general principles of organization that will supplement the information in Appendix D, "Outlining."

Choosing the Form

In your introductory college course in composition you were probably shown how to organize a general purpose essay: Begin with an introductory paragraph that provides background and states a thesis; develop that thesis in a series of paragraphs, limiting each paragraph to one important idea; and close with a restatement of main points in a concluding paragraph. One common form based on this model is the five-paragraph theme consisting of an introduction, three body paragraphs, and a conclusion. Some of the principles that lie behind this kind of organization also lie behind the forms used in practical writing, but the forms described in great detail in succeeding chapters are designed to fulfill more specific practical functions than those fulfilled by the five-paragraph theme.

The table of contents of this book lists some of the basic forms available to you. In practice these general forms can be further subdivided into a seemingly infinite number of subforms: letter of inquiry, claim letter, trip report, machinery breakdown report, progress report, test report, and a host of others.

Although the existence of conventional forms makes your task easier, conventions do vary from company to company and from industry to industry. Therefore you must learn to adapt the basic forms presented in this text to a variety of problems and settings. When you begin your first full-time job, become acquainted with your company's correspondence or communication manual. Most companies have one. It will tell you how letters and many standard reports are to be laid out, and in addition, will usually contain sample letters and reports using your firm's letterhead or memo form. These manuals may discuss such subjects as amount of prefatory material, use of headings, and ways of presenting conclusions and recommendations. Readers in your company as well as regular clients will have certain expectations about how a report is going to be organized. It is your responsibility to fulfill those expectations while at the same time making certain you convey exactly the message you need to convey.

Sometimes the choice of a form is made for you. For instance, when you are applying for a job, the advertisement listing the position may ask that you send a résumé and application letter. Once you are employed, if your job requires you to submit routine reports each month, the company may supply a form that must simply be filled out. Even when you must make the choice yourself, that choice is often easy. For example, if you need to inform fellow workers of a meeting of the personnel committee and must do it in writing, a memo is obviously called for.

Other situations are more complex, however, and the decision is more difficult. If, for example, a good client of your company asks for a description of your financial management service—advice on how to manage the financial side of a business more efficiently—how would you respond? Your company might have a pamphlet or booklet already made up to fulfill requests of this sort; you need only send it to your client with a brief cover letter. Lacking that, you might consider several alternatives. You might send a long business letter in standard paragraphs or an informal report containing lists, headings, and other earmarks of a business report but incorporated into a letter. You might make up a free-standing report and mail it with a cover letter. Finally, you might consider having a pamphlet or booklet printed, since you remember having received a similar request last month and were faced then with the same choices you face now. If you decide on the last alternative, but don't want to make a good client wait, you may decide to send an informal letter report and at the same time to begin work on the booklet. In a month, when your booklet is finished, you won't have to reconsider the choice of a form for your answer each time a request is received.

Even when a conventional form such as a formal report is called for, you must make some decisions about how it is to be organized. A formal proposal must be organized differently from an investigative report or a feasibility study. The models in Chapter 12 illustrate several of the ways the parts of a formal report can be designed. If you are writing a letter of application for a job, you can consult the models in Chapter 5, but the kind of job you seek may call for some carefully planned variations from the standard format. Some general principles for planning those variations are provided in the next section.

Organizing the Information

One basic rule for organizing a document in the absence of any conventional order is to consider your readers' needs as nearly as you can determine them. If you know that some of your readers are busy managers but that others, not so busy, need lots of detailed information, you can accommodate both groups by providing an introductory summary and then giving full details in the body. If your readers are unfamiliar with the subject of your report, provide plenty of background first; if they are familiar with it, go directly to the presentation of new material.

A second basic rule is to organize longer documents by first giving an overview of the main ideas in the text—summarizing both the content and the organizational plan. Then make that organization explicit in the rest of the document. One method of carrying out this rule in short reports is to state the main points in the first paragraph and to use headings or topic sentences to introduce each main idea in the body of the report. If your report is longer than about eight pages, a table of contents is also useful, especially if it matches the headings used in the text.

As to the actual sequence of material in the document, decide, on the basis of your purpose and audience, which of several alternatives will work best. If you know all readers won't read the report all the way through, *order of importance* may be a good organizing principle. This principle, embodied in what is called the *top-down* or *pyramid* method of organization, is the most effective way to organize a majority of business and technical reports. It enables readers who are not experts to read the first few paragraphs and know they are getting the most important points. Figure 2.3 illustrates the method for both long and short reports.

In business correspondence two basic patterns of organization, called *direct* and *indirect order*, will fit nearly all letter-writing situations. If the letter brings good news, direct order is called for since the main point, the good news, is placed first. If the letter brings bad news, it is usually best to precede that news with an opening that conveys a positive attitude—that is, indirect order.

For some purposes the best method of organization is obvious. If you are describing a process or giving instructions, chronological order is called for. If you are describing a mechanism, an area of land, or a city neighborhood, spatial organization may work best.

Appendix D, "Outlining," gives detailed instructions on how to put your organizational plans in writing. If your document will be longer than one page, a written outline or some other written plan should be prepared before you attempt a first draft. The chapters in this text covering each form give detailed information about organizing those forms.

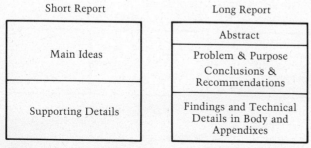

Figure 2.3 The Top-Down Method of Organization

Considering Graphic Aids

The important point of this section is to remember to do as the title asks: Consider using graphic aids. Since they are part of the design of a document, it is good to consider them at this stage. A good graphic aid and your supporting commentary can convey the central idea of a whole section, and in addition, a graphic aid always changes the appearance of a document, usually for the better. Chapter 8 provides detailed instructions on how and when to use the various kinds.

In looking over the data you have gathered, spend a few moments thinking about which sets of information or which ideas could better be presented in graphic form than in writing. If you have much precise statistical data to convey, consider using a table; if you must describe and interpret a trend, consider using a line graph; if you must describe storm damage to a beach house, consider using a photograph.

Those of us who are print oriented, and that includes most teachers and students in colleges, tend to overlook the opportunities and advantages of graphic aids. They are ignored in most writing courses, and even though we may see photographs, tables, and charts in newspapers and textbooks, we somehow consider them someone else's province. It is easier to stick to one medium: print. In addition, we may be intimidated by the feeling that it takes special skills—artistic talent or mathematical ability—to do a passable job. A photograph, for example, must first be snapped, then developed, and finally fitted into the text. In short, we can always think of reasons not to use graphic aids, but as Chapter 8 will make clear, there are many more reasons to include them.

Graphic aids do require some special skills if they are to be done well, but help is available. Chapter 8 provides models that can be modified to fit a variety of situations, and classmates or friends may have had courses in design or mechanical drawing and be willing to give help or advice. If after graduation you work for a large company, you can get help from a graphic aids or design department. And since businesses are tuned in to the advantages of graphic aids, you can usually find co-workers who are able to help you.

The main points in the document design stage are summarized in Figure 2.4. Even within this stage some doubling back may occur, since the choice of a graphic aid may cause you to revise the organization or even to reconsider the basic form of the document.

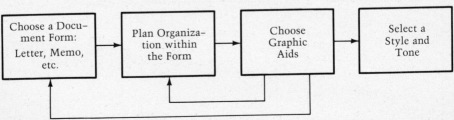

Figure 2.4   Steps in the Design of a Document

Selecting an Appropriate Style and Tone

Knowing your purpose and audience will enable you to choose the proper style and tone for your document. By *style* we mean the *way* something is written as distinguished from its content. It is determined by such things as your choice of words and the structure and arrangement of phrases and sentences. A style can be simple or complex, formal or informal; it can also be described in a number of other ways. By *tone* we mean the attitude toward the subject or reader (or both) conveyed by a piece of writing. Thus the tone can be approving or disapproving, firm or conciliatory, emotional or objective, warm or cold. It is impossible to distinguish style from tone completely since style is an important determiner of tone.

Contrary to what you may have heard, or the impression you may have gained by reading a few samples, all business and technical writing is not cast in a single impersonal, objective style—nor should it be. No longer do writers of letters and reports carefully exclude all use of *you* and *I* or put all their verbs in passive voice, if they ever did. The style and tone should vary as widely as the purpose and audience vary.

Here are two pieces of writing that differ rather widely in both purpose and audience, and hence they differ also in style and tone. The first, from a book called *Rules of the Road*, gives information and advice about driving on public roads. Its purpose is to inform but also to instruct and persuade and the audience includes all adults who are eligible for a driver's license. This passage gives directions to expressway drivers who feel tired.

> Stop driving when you feel drowsy. Don't try to fight it. Pull off the highway at the first rest stop or service area. If you merely feel tired, a cup of coffee and a bit of stretching may be enough to help you stay awake. But if you feel really sleepy, get off the highway and take a nap.

Contrast this passage with the following paragraph from a journal for specialists in the study of birds. Here the purpose is to convey the results of a study of red-shouldered hawks in Arizona. Thus its purpose is to inform and to provide the basis for further study, and its audience is narrow: those with a fairly good scientific knowledge of birds. Here are the opening sentences of the concluding paragraph of the article.

> Finally, in attempting to determine the origin of the Red-shouldered Hawks that have occurred in Arizona, and thus to provide insight on various ecological aspects of this species' life history, I recognize the value of collected specimens. If no *specimens* were in existence, comparison with the feathers collected would not have been possible. Basing subspecific identification solely on the photo (Figure 1), might have left unquestioned the possibility that the trapped bird could be an eastern migrant *(B. l. lineatus)*, and not necessarily a western vagrant *(B. l. elegans)*.

Both passages fit their purposes and audiences well. The first is in a simple style, its chief characteristics being familiar words and short, simple sentences. The tone of the passage is friendly and informal; the writer uses personal pronouns and conveys to readers a sense of concern for their welfare.

The second passage, on the other hand, uses many unfamiliar words and longer, more complex sentences. Terms such as *ecological aspects* and *subspecific identification* are probably not familiar to average adult readers in the special senses intended here, and the distinction between *migrant* and *vagrant* would probably escape them. Also, the abbreviated Latin names for subspecies would certainly mean little to most of the public. Yet bird specialists would either know the meanings of those terms or know where to look them up. The tone of this passage is objective and relatively impersonal, despite the use of the personal pronoun *I*. The aim is to convey scientific conclusions as clearly and directly as possible to a special audience, and the writer does it successfully.

The writers of these two passages obviously had purpose and audience in mind when they chose their styles and tones. As these two passages also illustrate, all writing *has* a style and conveys a tone or attitude regardless of its simplicity or complexity.

The point is that you need to choose the style and tone for each piece of writing you do according to your purpose and audience. Appendix A, "Style," provides a detailed discussion of the elements of style and shows how you can achieve a variety of styles and tones in your writing.

Stage 5: Drafting the Document

This stage includes all you need to do to produce a first draft. The advice given here applies mainly to the writing of a long document since that is the biggest challenge. Many of the points can be skipped if you are writing a short memo or report since the conditions for writing will then be quite different.

Setting the Stage

Your first task is to make careful preparations so that you give yourself the best chance to get your ideas down in a coherent form. Set aside a block of time long enough to enable you to continue writing until the draft is finished, or if the document will be too long for that, until you have written a significant part of it. Set this time aside far enough ahead of the deadline so that you can let the first draft lie dormant for at least a day before you revise and edit it. The reason you should do as much as possible at one sitting is that once you have begun writing you will find it gets easier with each succeeding paragraph, especially if you have prepared yourself in the ways described in the earlier stages. In this respect writing can be compared to pumping water: It take strenuous effort to get the water to flow freely, but once it begins to flow it isn't difficult to keep it going.

Next, if you have a choice, pick a comfortable place, preferably the place where you have done your best writing in the past, a place free of distractions. Gather about you all the materials you will need for the task: pencils or pens, a pad of wide-spaced paper, or if you compose at the typewriter, a good supply of plain bond paper. Some writers go through an elaborate ritual before they begin to write; they sharpen not just one pencil but a half dozen, they adjust the lamp just so, and they put on their most comfortable jacket. Do similar things if you must, but it is good to wean yourself from these practices as soon as you can, since once you take a job you will often be forced to write under less than perfect conditions. Do all you can to avoid interruptions; they make writing much more difficult.

When you have all your materials at hand, review your notes and the outline for the section where you plan to begin. Get clearly in mind your main points for that section and the order of those points. They will have been decided when you designed the document in stage 4. All these preparations will help you overcome writer's block, the paralysis some writers suffer when they face a blank page.

Writing the Draft

Begin writing the first main section of the document or the part you know best and feel most comfortable about. This beginning point will probably not be the introduction, since that is better left until after the first draft of the main body is finished and you know exactly what you are introducing. The reason for starting where you are most confident should be obvious: to give yourself the best chance of beginning successfully.

The writing of a first draft can be thought of as the creative part of the writing task; in the next stage, revising and editing, you switch roles to that of a critic of your own work. In writing the first draft you must concentrate on the ideas, not on the form of sentences or their correctness, and you must give free rein to your creative abilities. You have enough natural ability to get ideas down in reasonably correct sentences; depend on that ability as you write the first draft. The important thing is to get your ideas on paper in a form that provides a fairly good draft to revise and edit. As you compose the first draft, be sure to skip spaces if you do it in longhand or double-space if you type. If you have prepared well and if you stick to the task, you will find that one idea will lead naturally to another. Continuity within the draft is usually much better if you do it this way than if you were to revise each sentence laboriously as you go along. You will discover that many of your sentences can be left just as they are, though of course many will require revision or have to be cut out completely. To repeat, in writing the first draft concentrate on content; don't worry too much about sentence structure, grammar, punctuation, or spelling. Those things will be taken care of in revision and editing.

As you write you may discover new ideas or think of better ways to organize the document than you came up with in the design stage. This is less likely to happen in practical writing than in writing essays, and it is even less likely to happen if you have planned carefully. But the act of writing is a powerful stimulant to the mind, and you should not dismiss immediately new ideas that come to you as you write. If you can incorporate them into the first draft, do so. If you can't, make a note of the new ideas or new structures on scratch paper and consider them when you revise.

As you write the first draft, note the places where documentation is needed and include in the text as much information as necessary to enable you to put in the documentation later. Put in parentheses the author's name and the page number of the original document at the place in your text where the documentaiton must go. In the editing stage you can put the documentation in final form.

A Word About Word Processing

If you have a personal computer or access to one through your school, we encourage you to use word processing to draft. Computers with a word-processing software program act as glorified typewriters and can simplify and make less tedious many of the technical aspects of writing.

Once you learn a word-processing program—which can take from about an hour to several days, depending on the complexity of the program—you will be able to take advantage of several features of word processing that make drafting easier. First, you can draft rapidly, letting your mind work freely in phrasing sentences and expressing your thoughts. If you have already planned the document, you can follow the plan and write with little hesitation. You don't need to worry about wording because it will be simple to make changes later. A second advantage of word processing is that a writer using it can afford to be more creative and spontaneous and to take more risks with writing. If a sentence or section turns out to be inappropriate or unusable, it can be removed with one electronic "swipe" of the delete key. Finally, if you can learn to draft *at the computer*, instead of drafting by hand and recopying it into the computer, you will save additional time. There is no need to make two "first" drafts, and you can print out a paper copy of your draft if you like, to look over before revising.

Setting the Draft Aside

Finish the first draft as quickly as you can, in one sitting if possible, in two or more if the document is long. Once finished, this draft will provide you with a tangible piece of work, a thing separate from your mind, to work on after you have let it lie dormant for a day or more. Writing is a marvelous means of objectifying ideas that would otherwise remain more or less subjective in your mind. You may have noticed that it is easier to revise someone else's writing than your own, since you approach it from the outside, objectively. A similar, though not identical, situation is created when you set aside your first draft for a day or more. The longer you let it lie the further it is separated from you, in an intellectual sense, and the more objective you can be about it. Separation from it gives you a new perspective on it, enabling you to see weaknesses you wouldn't otherwise notice and making it possible for you to deal with it in a firmly critical way.

Put the completed draft away, and if possible, put it out of your mind for a day or longer. Actually, it won't escape from your subconscious mind even though you may have banished it from your conscious mind. In a process psychologists call *incubation* the ideas you have been working on so intensively will continue to be worked on in your subconscious mind. When you take up the draft again you may discover that the unconscious working of the mind has produced a new and better solution to the problem you have addressed, or at least a better way of expressing some of your ideas.

Stage 6: Reviewing and Reworking the Document

Most composition textbooks that view writing as a process assign only one step to reworking the first draft. We ask you to do it in two steps: first, revising the content and structure, and second, editing for correctness of expression. Many inexperienced writers think of revision as chiefly a matter of cutting out repetitious passages and unnecessary words; finding better words to replace inappropriate ones; and correcting errors in grammar, spelling, and punctuation. These tasks are important but not so important as reworking the ideas themselves and the way they are arranged, or in other words revising the content and structure. Since revision is so important, we ask you to do it separately from editing for correctness.

Revising

When you take up your first draft after setting it aside for a time, read it in the light of your definitions of the problem, purpose, and audience arrived at in stages 1 and 2. Looking at these definitions, ask yourself two questions about each. First, have your notions about what is the true problem, purpose, or audience changed since those definitions were formulated days, or even weeks, earlier? If the work involved in collecting data, designing the document, and writing the first draft has given you new insights into the nature of the problem, prompting you unconsciously to address a problem different from the original one, you must explicitly change your definition and make certain the draft addresses that new view of the problem throughout. Apply the same analysis and action to the purpose and audience.

If, on the other hand, you are satisfied that your original definitions still hold, then ask yourself the second question: Does the draft conform to those original definitions? You may find that neither the problem nor the purpose is clearly set forth in the opening paragraph, even though you have defined them well in the planning stages. That may mean that a problem and purpose statement needs to be added to the introduction. In light of your definition of the audience, a number of questions might be asked: Have I said enough, too much, or too little, given the audience's probable knowledge of the problem and interest in it? Will the readers be able to take the action I want them to take or do they need more information in order to act? Are more examples needed to make difficult points clear? Would more graphic aids help? Have I made sufficient use of headings, and are they well stated and in parallel form?

You should also check the accuracy of your facts if any of them now look suspect. Is your logic weak, and are there any gaps in the line of your reasoning? Are there digressions that need to be cut out? In considering all these things, ignore matters of style and correctness for the moment; concentrate exclusively on the content and its structure.

In marking up your first draft you will see why you were asked to use wide-spaced theme paper or to double-space if you type—and to leave ample margins on all sides. All that space is extremely useful as you cut and slash, add and detract. Like some writers, you may find it convenient to have scissors and paste handy to cut out and relocate whole paragraphs that are well written and useful but in the wrong place. Since what results is not a final draft, don't worry about appearance but do make certain your corrections are legible.

If you draft your document at a computer, this stage will be much easier. Most word-processing programs allow you to move words, sentences, paragraphs, or even larger blocks of writing to any position you choose within a piece of writing. The task is carried out electronically and immediately with no need to cut and paste. This advantage of word processing is so great that it more than compensates for the time it takes to learn a word-processing program. In fact, many people who use word processing say they would simply be unwilling to revise as extensively as they do with word processing because manual revision, involving extensive retyping, is so time-consuming. Using word processing can provide an incentive to revise, since the results are good and the procedure is simple. Nevertheless, a word-processing program cannot usually tell you *what* to revise, replace, or remove. That is your job as a writer.

If you have time before the deadline, lay the draft aside again before beginning to edit. You probably need a rest.

Editing

Once you are certain about the content and organization of your document, you are ready to edit it. This stage involves checking for ways to improve the phrasing, word choice, grammar, spelling, and punctuation in order to make your writing concise, comprehensible, and correct. A writing handbook and dictionary are useful tools at this stage, and no conscientious writer should be without either of them. Appendixes A and B in this book provide handbook information; a dictionary should be part of your basic college equipment.

Help from others is especially useful at this stage because an objective eye is needed. After you have done your best to put the writing into shape, ask a co-worker to read your draft and mark errors or make suggestions for improvements in the points just noted. Then look up the corrections yourself in your handbook or dictionary.

One other useful technique is to read your final draft aloud, listening for ways to improve the phrasing, transitions, word choice, and punctuation. Things that often go undetected when you read silently become obvious when you read aloud. Reading aloud forces you to proceed slowly and provides a sort of outside perspective on your writing.

Here is a list of points to look for as you edit:

- *Sentences:* Are they varied in length and structure, not all long or all short? Short sentences are useful to emphasize a point, but they must stand in contrast to longer sentences if they are to fulfill that function. Are there any fragments or run-on sentences?
- *Grammar:* Do verbs agree in number with subjects, and are you consistent in your use of past, present, and future tenses? Don't shift from one tense to another without a clear and logical reason. Do pronouns agree with the nouns they stand for?
- *Word choice and phrasing:* Here is where reading aloud will help you most, for it is much easier to "hear" an incorrect or weak word choice than to "see" it. Look, also, for ways to make the writing concise by cutting out repetitive or roundabout expressions.
- *Spelling:* Mark not only the words you are certain are misspelled but those you are simply suspicious of as well. Have your friend also mark misspelled words, but look up correct spellings yourself.
- *Punctuation:* Check for missing, inaccurate, or unneeded punctuation. Appendix B gives brief but useful advice on this subject.

In doing the editing you will again see why we urged you to double-space your drafts, whether you write in longhand or type. The space between lines as well as the ample margins provides lots of room to write in your changes. At this stage you must also put your documentation in final form for the typist. See Appendix E for advice on how to document.

Stage 7: Producing the Finished Document

How a document looks is much more important to readers in business and industry than to those in college. Your teacher may be willing to accept assignments that are handwritten on sheets of lined theme paper, though it is best to type all papers because typing greatly improves readability. If your teacher doesn't specify the format, you should take the initiative to find out what is expected.

In business and industry you seldom have a choice. Content and organization are still the major considerations, as they are in college, but appearance is also extremely important. Handwritten business letters or reports submitted on theme paper are simply not acceptable. Each piece of writing you produce on the job, aside from memos on trivial subjects, should be letter perfect and should conform to your company's requirements in format and appearance. All the writing you do reflects your image to your supervisors and co-workers, and each letter and report sent out under your name reflects your company's image as well. Fortunately, given these more stringent requirements and expectations, businesses usually provide the equipment and help you need to produce professional-looking documents. Secretaries are employed to do most of the typing, often using word-processing systems, though you are still responsible for the content and correctness of everything you write. You are provided with professionally printed letterhead stationery and memo forms, and you often have access to the services of design departments.

One further source of help is the company correspondence or communication manual, which was mentioned as a help in designing a document. It usually provides detailed instructions on how to capitalize and punctuate, how to arrange headings, and how to handle a host of other details. Models show how your letters and reports are expected to look; those provided in this text approximate the practices of a wide range of companies.

Obviously, you can't expect to match in your course assignments the professional appearance of commercially produced documents, but you can prepare yourself to meet those standards by giving thought to the appearance of all the assignments you submit. Here are some specific suggestions about producing the finished document.

1. In laying out the physical dimensions of a letter or report, use wide margins and leave ample white space between sections. Paper is still relatively cheap, and the improvement in both comprehensibility and appearance is well worth taking the extra space. You should also consider using color on graphic aids and including foldouts or transparent overlays. The chapter on graphics supplies more detailed suggestions.

2. If someone does the typing for you, submit a clear copy with corrections marked clearly and unambiguously. Provide a note about format if the copy you submit doesn't look the way you want the finished document to look. Be sure to finish the final draft far enough ahead of the deadline so that your typist can do a careful job.

3. If you type it yourself, use a good typewriter ribbon and clean the keys if some spaces within the letters are filled with ink. Try to keep erasures to a minimum and retype pages that get soiled with fingermarks or too many erasures. Electric typewriters produce even-looking copy, but a manual typewriter in good condition produces acceptable results.

4. When assembling a report, make certain all the pages are numbered and in proper order.

5. If the report is more than about ten pages long, provide some kind of

binding, since paper clips and staples become ineffective at about that length. The appearance of a report of that length is also improved if you supply a cover.

6. Proofread the typed document carefully, preferably with the help of a friend or co-worker. If one of you reads aloud from the finished copy while the other checks it against the manuscript, few errors will escape detection.

Conclusion

The steps described in this chapter provide a set of guidelines that you can draw on in planning and carrying out any practical writing assignment. They form the framework for the discussion of each of the common forms of business and technical writing discussed in the chapters that follow. The advice given for each stage can be applied to most of the tasks you may face. More detailed and specific advice about each form is given in the chapters on the letter, the abstract, and a number of other forms. The chapter on graphic aids, the two on gathering information, and the appendixes, on the other hand, provide help in writing all the forms covered in this text and do not use the process approach except in isolated sections.

Key Points in The Chapter

1. This chapter describes seven stages in the process of practical writing:
   Defining the problem and purpose
   Determining the audience
   Collecting the data
   Designing the document: organization, graphics, and style
   Drafting the document
   Reviewing and reworking the document
   Producing the finished document
2. The stages in the process are not always completed in one operation or in a set order. Experienced writers often return to earlier stages as new ideas or new ways of expressing them come to mind.
3. The writing of a first draft is more efficient and successful if the document is carefully planned.
4. A first draft, even when well planned, is almost never satisfactory. Revising and editing are essential to finishing a writing task.
5. Appearance is more important in business and technical writing than in writing done in school.

Exercises

1. Describe your usual method of planning, writing, and revising an essay or report for a college class. How long before a paper is due do you begin work,

what kind of plan or outline do you use, where and how do you write the essay, and what sorts of things do you change when you revise? Add any other details you think are important to a description of your own writing process.

2. Describe a situation that has been a source of difficulty for you recently. It can be a problem at work, in the dormitory, on the athletic field, or in your family. Describe the background, crucial issue, and people involved, putting each point of your analysis in writing. Then frame a brief definition of the problem as if it were the beginning of a report to your work supervisor or to another appropriate person.

3. Think back to your least successful course last term. Define the problem associated with that course, isolating if you can the crucial issue. Was a solution to the problem within your control?

4. Imagine yourself ready to graduate and therefore ready to look for a job in your field. First list your qualifications and put in writing an analysis of your situation. Then compare your analysis with that found in the section on the résumé and job application letter in Chapter 5. Obviously, the search for a job might be considered an opportunity, not a problem.

5. Find and bring to class two short articles from a magazine or newspaper or a brief brochure. Don't bring an ordinary news story. Be prepared to read parts of the articles in class and to describe the purpose, audience, style, and tone of each.

6. Identify a problem that exists on campus or at your place of work. Describe the problem in a paragraph, identifying the crucial issue or issues and the two or three most important people or groups involved.

7. For sample passages 1, 2, and 3 describe the purpose, audience, style, and tone.

NICOTINE, *NICK oh teen* or *NICK oh tin* (chemical formula $C_{10}H_{14}N_2$), is a colorless, oily, transparent vegetable chemical compound of the type called an *alkaloid*. It has a hot and bitter taste. It is found in small quantities in the leaves, roots, and seeds of the tobacco plant. It can also be made synthetically.

The quantity of nicotine in most tobaccos ranges from 2 to 7 per cent. Turkish tobacco has practically no nicotine. Good Havana tobacco contains little of it. Nicotine is most abundant in cheaper and domestic varieties. The amount of nicotine in the tobacco from which cigars, cigarettes, or pipe tobacco may be made is not the same as the amount in the finished product.

Nicotine is exceedingly poisonous. In a pure state, even a small quantity will cause vomiting, great weakness, rapid but weak pulse, and possibly collapse or even death. Tobacco varies in its effect. Nicotine harms some persons less than others. But physicians generally agree that use of tobacco in any form is not wise for young people. Overuse of tobacco may cause nausea, indigestion, and heart disturbances.

Nicotine is valuable as an insecticide. Physicians sometimes use nicotine compounds to treat tetanus and strychnine poisoning.   A. K. REYNOLDS
See also TOBACCO (Effects of Using Tobacco).

Sample Passage 1

A CHECK LIST FOR YOUR MECHANIC

The final, and most important, examination of a used car should be made by an experienced and reliable mechanic. The check list below covers most of the places where trouble is likely to occur —or already has. The potential buyer should go over the check list with the mechanic before and after commissioning the work: before, in order to make clear the extent of the examination and to fix the charge for the service; afterward, to pin down needed repairs and probable trouble spots:

Under the hood

1. Loose or worn belts
2. Worn or leaking hoses
3. Radiator leaks
4. Engine cracks or leaks
5. Ignition timing
6. Spark-plug examination
7. Cylinder compression
8. Carburetor examination
9. Crankcase ventilation valve
10. Exhaust-system damage
11. Clutch-pedal free play
12. Oil level and condition
13. Battery voltage and electrolyte level
14. Brake-cylinder fluid level
15. Alternator efficiency
16. Brake-pedal travel and free play
17. Air-conditioning system

On the lift

1. Axle damage or leaks
2. Drive-shaft lubricant leaks
3. Transmission-oil leaks
4. Exhaust-system damage
5. Shock-absorber damage or leaks
6. Ball-joint play
7. Steering play
8. Brake-fluid leaks
9. Brake-lining wear
10. Gas-tank damage and leaks
11. Underbody corrosion

Wheels and tires

1. Wheel alignment and balance
2. Tire condition

Sample Passage 2

That's a fish?! Looks more like a rock! A moss-covered rock. What's the point of a fish looking like a rock?

Well, for one thing, it's a great way to get food without working at it.

The spotted scorpion fish just nestles down close to rocks. It waits right there—on a muddy or grassy bottom, or on a coral reef. Then when a smaller fish or crustacean (kruh-STAY-shun) comes along—*gulp*— it's gobbled up.

Looking like a rock works like a charm for the scorpion fish. So does its ability to change color. It can make itself look like things around it. It hides so well it's very hard to see—even though some scorpion fish grow to be 18 inches (46 cm) long. *Cirri (SEER-y)*—small growths—cover its body, especially the head. They look so plantlike that small fish might even try to get close enough for a nibble—*oops*, too late: That was *not* a seaweed on a rock! The scorpion fish has a big mouth—a great help in the pounce-and-gobble game.

Sample Passage 3

II

Letters and Memos

3 Writing a Business Letter

Abstract

Business letters are still an important means of communicating with those outside one's organization, despite the increased use of the telephone, since they provide an authoritative record of any interchange. They are used for an extremely wide range of purposes, from arranging a meeting to selling goods, but most have the additional purpose of creating or maintaining good will. To create good will it is important to convey a positive tone and to keep the reader's needs in the forefront. One of two basic designs will fit most letter-writing situations: The direct approach is used when the main message is good news; the indirect approach, when the message is unfavorable. Great care must be taken to ensure that the finished appearance of a letter is professional and the contents free of errors.

No matter what field you enter after graduation, the fact that you will have a college education means that you will very likely need to write letters. In fact, letters are the commonest kind of writing done by college-trained people in business and industry. They come in two kinds: ordinary business letters, which might be called *outside letters* since they are sent to people outside your organization, and inside letters, called *memorandums* or *memos*, which are sent to those within your organization. Memos will be covered in Chapter 4.

Although most business letters follow the same general pattern, they are used for a wide variety of purposes. This versatility makes them an important part of your company's day-to-day business, and it is therefore important that you learn to write them well. There are several additional reasons. First, letters are a personal means of communication, and thus they reflect your image more directly than other kinds of writing; and since they go to people outside your company or organization, they reflect your company's image as well. Second, as the cost of labor has gone up, they have become more expensive to produce and send. Estimates of the average cost of writing and sending a business letter, including all hidden costs, vary from $7 to $10, so the need for making each letter do its job well is great. Finally, of all the practical writing you will do, business letters are the best means of creating and maintaining good will since they allow you, in a limited way, to express feelings as well as facts and opinions. This advantage, which makes it possible to use business letters to substitute for personal visits, also makes them more difficult to write since letters lack many of the elements that make face-to-face meetings so effective—gestures, eye contact, variations in tone of voice, immediate responses from the listener, and the adjustments that those responses make possible. In writing letters you must make up for the lack of these ways to convey your message by more careful use of the written word alone. That is part of the challenge in writing them.

Defining the Problem and Purpose

As a device for solving problems in business and industry, the letter has been partly superseded by the telephone. Each time a problem arises that calls for communication with someone outside your company, you should ask yourself if it might more easily be solved by a phone call. The speed with which you can communicate, the immediate response from the listener, and often the lower cost as well, make the telephone a better choice in many situations. More recently the letter has also been affected by the use of computers, word processors, and electronic mail. These devices have already changed the routine in many offices, moving them closer to the so-called electronic office, but the exact direction these developments may take is still uncertain. Computers and word processors still call on people to do the writing, and electronic mail brings a difference mainly in method of delivery, not in the nature of the letter itself.

For many purposes the letter is still superior. It enables you to get in touch with people whom social or business customs wouldn't allow you to call on the telephone; it gives you more time to consider your words carefully and to revise or omit a wrong phrase; likewise, it gives the receiver of your letter more time to consider an answer carefully. Finally, it provides a written record that is authenticated with a signature and thereby reduces the chances for error or slips in memory and provides a firmer basis for action by the receiver.

Defining the Problem

Here are some problem situations that might be solved by the writing of a business letter:

- Your engineering society has decided to invite a nationally known expert on satellite communication to speak at its annual Engineering Day ceremonies, and you have been asked to make the invitation.
- A local appliance dealer has not, in your opinion, fulfilled the provisions of the warranty on a newly purchased refrigerator that has broken down. A brochure that came with the refrigerator suggests that you get in touch with the manufacturer.
- Your company is thinking of offering a new financial management service to farm implement dealers, but you need to know more about the need for such a service. An officer in your company suggests the name of an expert in another city.
- A company report is being sent to six individuals for six slightly different reasons. Each of the six needs to be told why he or she is getting the report and what action needs to be taken on the basis of it.
- The secretary of the local Boy Scouts organization has been asked by the other officers to convey the thanks of the Boy Scouts to a local church that has provided space, at a small charge, for the scouts' annual banquet.
- You are the owner of a dry-cleaning shop and have a policy that goods left more than 90 days can be sold to cover the expense of cleaning. This policy is stated on the customer's claim ticket. A once-faithful customer has left some clothing for 90 days on which the cleaning bill is nearly $25. What action should you take?

The list could go on and on. Often the situation does not pose a problem in the usual sense but might better be viewed as an opportunity to provide new business for a company or simply to create good will. In the fifth case in the list, the need to convey thanks is not a problem in the usual sense, but failure to send a letter would be, at the least, discourteous and, as a practical matter, would make the church less willing to offer its meeting room to the scout troop for its banquet next year.

In all the cases listed here, considerable thought has already gone into defining the problem. In the first a committee of the engineering society has met to draw up plans for this year's Engineering Day. Someone has brought up the need for a keynote speaker, and at the suggestion of the faculty advisor, the committee has agreed to invite an expert on satellite communication. As president of the society, you have been asked to make the invitation. You choose a letter as the best means for several obvious reasons: You don't know the expert personally, you want to give this person, in writing, all the facts needed to make the decision, you want to give enough time to decide, and you want to include some carefully thought-out sentences of persuasion. A letter enables you to do all these things. Once the expert accepts, that part of your Engineering Day "problem" will be solved.

The problem in the last situation lies in getting the customer to pick up the dry cleaning as soon as possible but at the same time retaining his or her good will and hence future business. You would like to avoid selling the clothing, since that would require a certain amount of time and paper work, and it would certainly alienate the customer, who might eventually find out about it.

In all other cases, with the possible exception of the inquiry about financial management services for farm implement dealers, a letter clearly seems the best means of moving toward a solution. In that one situation a phone call might provide answers to your questions more efficiently, especially if the officer who suggested the expert knows him or her well.

Defining the Purpose

After defining the problem and deciding that a letter is the best means of carrying out a solution, you need to define the purpose of the letter. Often your definition of the problem, as in most of the cases analyzed here, carries with it a well-defined purpose for the letter. The purpose in the first case is to make the invitation and to provide enough information to enable the expert to make a decision without writing or calling for more details. Implied in making the invitation is the need to persuade as well as simply to present facts about the proposed engagement, such as date, place, and length of the speech.

In the second case you decide to write a letter of complaint to the manufacturer of the refrigerator. The purpose will be to get the company to fulfill the provisions of the warranty, which usually means to get the refrigerator repaired or replaced at no cost to you. If the situation has become a vexing one and you have built up a great deal of hostility, you might be tempted, as one purpose of the letter, to unleash your anger. That may make you feel better for the moment, but it won't help to accomplish the other, more central purpose of the letter. If, on reading the first draft of the letter, you see that a good deal of anger has crept into it, you can try again later when you have cooled off a bit.

In the fourth case the purposes are strongly implied by the statement of the problem: to tell the receivers of the report why they are getting the report and what they are expected to do. A third purpose, which is common to most business letters, should also be included: to create good will. In every letter sent out by a company, whether the letter brings good news or bad, the writer should strive to create or maintain good will for the company. When writing as an individual, you should also attempt to create good will, since it makes life pleasanter for the reader, and as a practical matter, it makes it more likely you will accomplish your other purposes.

In the case of the clothing left at the dry cleaners, the purpose will be to get the customer to pick up the clothing and still feel good will toward your firm so that he or she will continue to be a good customer. An important purpose may be to avoid losing money, but that is not the first purpose addressed nor the only one. Were that the *only* concern, selling the clothing without notifying the customer would do the job. On the other hand, writing a letter will do the customer a favor by reminding him or her of the clothing, which has apparently been forgotten, and it may also mean additional business from that customer in the future. The threat to sell the clothing if it is not picked up should thus be mentioned but in as unthreatening a way as possible.

Analyzing the Audience

The audience for a letter is different from that of most other kinds of practical writing since it is usually one person who can be identified by name. If your identification of problem and purpose hasn't enabled you to single out the person or group that should receive your letter, that task should be taken care of now. You may discover that the receiver should be a company legal officer or personnel officer, but don't stop there. Find out, if you can, the *name* of the person by looking it up in a business directory, annual report, or previous correspondence on the issue. Additional advice about using directories to research a company is given in Chapter 5. Your letter will get a more favorable response if you can find the full name and title of the person addressed.

The fact that the audience for a letter is usually one person whom you know by name and title makes it easier to fit what you have to say to the audience. These facts will tell you the person's level in the company and specialty. Unless you or a co-worker knows the addressee personally, it is usually difficult to find out more about the person, and fortunately it is usually not necessary to do so. If you do, however, it will be easier to fit what you have to say to that person's needs, level of knowledge, and special likes and dislikes.

Your analysis of the reader needn't attempt to cover all aspects of the person; rather it should cover only those things that touch the question at hand, including your relationship to the reader. In the first case described at the beginning of the chapter, the situation doesn't involve the expert's knowledge of satellite communications directly; that is assumed. For purposes of the letter you need only keep in mind that the expert is an important person in the field, is probably a busy person, and by virtue of position and experience, is in a sense above you. These facts will help you decide that the letter should be written four to six months before the date of the lecture, that the tone should be fairly formal but courteous and straightforward, that the letter should contain all the information the expert will need to make a decision (so as not to waste this person's time in getting further information), and that there should be no attempt at humor or excessive friendliness. Neither your knowledge of communication nor the expert's is an issue, and you don't need to know personal likes and dislikes, unless they might affect arrangements for the talk. For example, the expert may strongly dislike speaking in the morning. Yet for idiosyncrasies such as this, it is usually up to the person invited to let you know of any special conditions that might affect the arrangements.

In the case of the refrigerator that has broken down, you will probably be writing to a customer service department and will therefore have little chance of finding the name of a person to address the complaint to; nor is it necessary to do so. You can simply assume that the person who will answer your letter is a human being, is well aware that he or she represents the company, has considerable experience in dealing with letters such as yours, and knows the details of the warranty extremely well. It is therefore important to treat the reader of your letter as a representative of the company but also as a human being. That means you should be businesslike but courteous. It will do no good to vent your anger or make extreme charges. You are more likely to get satisfaction by writing in a calm, businesslike way, describing the refusal by the local dealer to remedy the situation and citing the facts of the warranty that you think apply.

The reader of the letter from the dry-cleaning establishment may be known to the writer, but if not, certain assumptions can and should be made. The customer brought in the clothing fully intending to pick it up and pay the cost of cleaning. Either the clothing has been forgotten outright or the customer has moved away and failed to pick it up before leaving. A less likely possibility is that the customer is temporarily short of cash and intends to pick up the clothing later. In any of these cases, a reminder should produce the hoped-for results; there is no need to make a dire threat. The customer can be assumed to be an ordinary, decent person who will respond to a courteously worded reminder.

In these examples the analysis of the audience depends more on common sense than on careful research or clever detective work. At times it might be useful to write out a profile of those aspects of the reader that relate to the situation at hand, but generally you can simply keep the points in mind as you write the letter. The technique applied in these three cases can easily be applied to the others described at the beginning of the chapter. The sample letter of complaint (Figure 3.11) illustrates these principles well.

Collecting the Data

Since letters usually, though not always, deal with one aspect of a relatively short-term issue, they don't involve the kind and amount of research or experimentation required for a technical or business report. If the letter is one in a continuing exchange of letters, look up in your files earlier letters on the issue. That will give you good background as well as supply many facts you may need in order to write your letter.

If there has been no previous correspondence, you must take a different approach. Consider the third case cited earlier. The letter of inquiry about a financial management service for farm implement dealers will, at the suggestion of an officer in your company, be addressed to a professor of agricultural economics at a university in another city. What data must you collect in order to write an effective letter of inquiry?

First, you must find the full name, title, and address of the expert. The officer who suggested this person may have corresponded with him or her and thus would have this information. Otherwise, a college catalog for the school or a directory of scholars in the field would yield the information.

Next you must frame questions that will elicit the information your company needs. Interviews with one or two local implement dealers and with one or two local bankers who make loans to farmers and implement dealers would yield a great deal of information. Research in farm newspapers or periodicals and the trade journal for implement dealers would also be extremely helpful. A final method might be to arrange a brainstorming session with co-workers to solicit questions for the letter. How to make up a letter of inquiry is discussed near the end of this chapter.

Collecting data for the letter to the refrigerator manufacturer would consist mainly of getting out the warranty and other printed material that came with it. These would give you the address of the department to which your letter should be sent as well as all details related to the warranty that you might need to cite. You would, in addition, need to look up the date you bought the refrigerator, recall when it broke down, and summarize the facts surrounding your treatment by the local dealer. With this material at hand, you will be ready to design the letter.

Each kind of letter requires a different approach to the collection of data, but with these samples in mind, and by the exercise of common sense, this stage should present few problems.

Designing the Letter

In organizing the content of your letter you must first ask yourself how the reader will react to the message it conveys. If the reader will see the message as good news, or at worst neutral, you should use a *direct approach*, in which the main point of the letter is given first. If the reader is likely to see the message as bad news, use the *indirect approach*; that is, delay the telling of the bad news until you have prepared the reader by giving some of the background to it. It is fairly easy to classify all business letter situations according to the approach required.

The Direct Approach

This approach divides the message of a letter into three parts, an arrangement that doesn't necessarily match the paragraphing.

- *Opening:* Announce the subject and at the same time make a positive beginning by giving the good or neutral news.
- *Supporting information:* Describe how a decision was made, explain the implications of a decision or situation, describe how a plan will be carried out, or provide any other necessary details.
- *Closing:* Use this section to tell the readers what they must do, offer to provide more information, or simply make a personal comment that ends the letter on a positive note.

The direct approach should be used in the letter of thanks to a local church from a scout troop, the fifth situation listed at the beginning of the chapter. The message is good news and shouldn't be postponed. The *opening* should say "thank you" and make clear what organization is sending thanks and the occasion for it. The *middle* section might say something about the success of the annual banquet and praise the facilities provided by the church. The closing can repeat the thanks in different words and praise the church for its public-spirited attitude. The final version of this letter is illustrated in Figure 3.5.

The Indirect Approach

This approach recognizes the fact that bad news is generally received with less disappointment if some of the reasons for it are presented before the news itself. Nevertheless, the news should be given clearly and firmly; it would only irritate a reader to imply by your opening that you might be bringing good news only to dash those hopes later in the letter. You must carefully guard against misleading the reader. Maintain a consistent tone throughout the letter, be clear and honest, and take the trouble to supply a full explanation of the decision or condition at issue. The indirect approach has four parts:

- *Opening:* Provide a brief, positive beginning that announces the subject of the letter.
- *Lead-in:* Supply some of the reasons for or background to the negative main message.
- *Main message:* Give the bad news firmly and clearly but as tactfully as possible. Add additional reasons, if any exist, and develop this most important section of the letter by explaining the implications of the main idea.
- *Closing:* End on a positive note by offering whatever help you can or by suggesting a course of action the reader might take to remedy the situation.

The letter to a customer who has left clothing at the dry cleaners requires an indirect approach. The main message—the customer must claim the clothing within a reasonable length of time or it will be sold to cover expenses—should not be set forth in the *opening* paragraph. Rather the writer should find a way to begin positively and at the same time simply state the subject of the letter: The clothing has been left for 90 days. By mentioning that the reader has been a good customer, the writer can express thanks for past business. The *lead-in* to the main message can then state the policy and note that it is written on the claim check. If that is done, the *main message* does not have to be stated directly but need only be implied. The letter writer should assume that the customer will come in soon and should suggest a way to get the job done if the customer simply can't find the time: Have a friend do it. The closing should be positive. Express hope that the customer will come in soon and will make use of the company's services in the future.

Choosing a Style

Business letters have long been characterized by a style that many now consider stilted, unnecessarily impersonal, and full of clichés. Companies are paying large amounts of money to get their people to unlearn these conventions, so you will have a head start if you take care not to adopt them in the first place. Here are some typical stilted phrases and suggested revisions:

Stilted phrases	*Revisions*
Enclosed please find . . .	I have enclosed . . .
In accordance with our phone conversation of May 9 . . .	As we agreed May 9 on the phone . . .
As per your request, replacement parts have been forwarded . . .	We have sent replacement parts as you requested . . .

Write as you would in an informal essay; be friendly, simple, and to the point. Use personal pronouns if they seem natural, as in the preceding revisions, and avoid borrowing passages word for word from letters you might find in the files or in a textbook. You can usually make a letter shorter, clearer, and friendlier if you use your own phrasing rather than someone else's. Remember that the level of formality should fit your reader, but readers at all levels now expect to be treated more as fellow human beings than as units in a faceless bureaucracy.

The advice to keep your writing simple applies to sentences and paragraphs as well as words. It is best to keep all three relatively short. Sentences should average from 15 to 20 words, though it is important to vary the length from sentence to sentence to avoid monotony. Since other elements besides sentence length affect clarity, short sentences do not ensure clarity, but consistently long sentences will ensure difficulty in reading.

Paragraphs should also be shorter, on the average, than those in essays and reports. Eight to ten lines should be the maximum length, and very short paragraphs, some as short as one line, are acceptable in letters, especially at the beginning and end.

Words needn't be short if they are familiar, but short ones are generally more familiar than long ones. The best advice is to fit your word choice to your readers; if they are experts in your field, use the technical language of your field. For all other readers use language that can be comprehended by laypeople. Since you often don't know the level of expertise of your readers and can't be certain who will read your letters in addition to the primary addressee, it is best to aim your writing at the non-expert.

The style as well as content of a letter should reflect your desire to see things from the reader's point of view. Rather than speaking of how a proposed action will benefit you or cause you difficulties, point out ways that the action will help the reader. You should also suggest ways to make that action easier for the reader to carry out. A courteous, concerned, and helpful attitude should characterize all business letters, especially when touchy issues are discussed, as in answers to letters of complaint or those that ask a favor.

This readiness to see things from the reader's point of view can best be expressed by using the second person pronoun *you* more frequently than *I* or *we* and by choosing words that carry positive connotations rather than negative ones. The first draft of the letter to the dry-cleaning customer (Figure 3.1) is weak because it neglects to consider the reader's point of view. The second version (Figure 3.2) is much better; notice the number of *you*'s in the second in contrast to those in the first.

Drafting the Letter

Once you have identified the purpose of the letter, collected the information, and worked out a design for ordering it, the writing of a first draft should be fairly easy since you will be well prepared and most letters are short. Keep the reader's point of view in mind. As with all first drafts, however, the important thing is to get your ideas in writing so that you will have a draft to revise. Don't worry about grammar, spelling, punctuation, or word choice on this draft. Many writers surprise themselves with the amount of writing they produce in a first draft that needs no revision at all.

Aside from complete and accurate factual information, the most important element in any letter is the tone or attitude conveyed by it. The tone should be positive and courteous yet businesslike. If you are not satisfied with the tone of your opening sentence, which is often a difficult one to write, don't struggle with it at this point as long as it contains the information you want it to carry. You are better able to modify the tone when you come back to it. Following the suggestions for either the direct or the indirect approach should help you to establish the right one on the first draft.

Figure 3.1 is a first draft of the letter to the dry-cleaning customer.

Dear Ms. Benson:

Last year you left goods with us for cleaning that have been ready for you since October 20, 1984.

We regret the need to remind you of our policy, which is stated in bold print on your claim ticket, that all goods must be claimed within 90 days of the promised date, or they may be forfeited to us for sale in lieu of payment. This procedure is necessary if we are to recover expenses incurred during the process of our services. We sincerely hope that this will not become necessary.

If you can't claim your clothing yourself, please arrange to have someone else do it. Be certain that your claim ticket is presented at the pickup time. We will not release your goods without it. Part of the reason we take the trouble to write is that the bill is so large—$25.

We hope you will take care of this matter soon, since overdue garments take up valuable space on our storage racks.

Figure 3.1 A First Draft of a Letter

The writer is too much concerned about his or her own problems and comes across as abrupt and negative if not downright rude. The draft contains more references to the writer than the customer and it begins and ends on a negative note. The details about the size of the bill and the overcrowded storage racks are especially self-centered.

This draft needs a great deal of revision before it can fulfill its purposes well. One of those purposes should be to retain the good will of the customer; sending this draft of the letter would doubtless mean the loss of it.

Reviewing and Reworking the Letter

Although letters must often be turned out on short notice, it is always essential to make a careful revision of a first draft. As noted in Chapter 2 the revision should be done in two stages: First look at content and then at form, which includes grammar and mechanics as well as layout.

Comparing the first draft of the letter from the dry-cleaning firm with the designs outlined in stage 4 reveals some clear discrepancies. If you were writing the letter you would first determine that it is a bad news letter since it tells the reader that she may forfeit her goods if she doesn't claim them soon. (It might happen that the reader is simply absentminded; has wondered from time to time what happened to three sweaters, two suits, and winter scarf; and will be pleasantly surprised to learn that they are safe at the cleaners—but that is highly unlikely.)

The draft clearly does not use the indirect approach as it should. It does announce the subject in the opening paragraph, but it doesn't begin on a positive note and it presents the bad news more bluntly than necessary. The same is true of the instructions in paragraph three. Finally, it doesn't end positively but rather emphasizes the inconvenience the delay is causing the writer. Not only must some parts be revised but also new sentences must be added to improve the tone.

Figure 3.2 is a revision that remedies most of the problems with the opening and closing and the tone, even though it still contains a number of errors.

The last points to be considered in a revision are the mechanics of the body of the letter—grammar, spelling, punctuation—and the word choice. These points have been corrected by hand on the version that follows, along with a few changes in word choice that improve the style and meaning. The copy shown in Figure 3.3 is ready for final typing.

The changes in spelling and punctuation make the letter more correct; those in word choice are more important since they make the meaning clearer and improve the tone. The removal of the word *sincerely* from each of the first two paragraphs actually makes the letter sound more sincere since these words seem a substitute for sincerity. The phrase *in bold print* was removed because it gave the impression that the reader was incapable of seeing what should be obvious. Finally, the restoration of *not* to the second paragraph avoids a serious mistake in meaning resulting from a simple typographical error. Figure 3.7 shows the letter in finished form.

Producing the Finished Letter

Getting the body of a letter written properly is the most difficult part of the task. Putting the letter in an appropriate format and ensuring that all the necessary parts are included is easier, but it is equally important since appearance is the first thing a reader notices. Sloppy letter form can turn a successfully written message into a letter that fails. Make it professional in appearance and inviting to read by providing a proper format.

Type all business letters on good quality bond paper that is 8½ by 11

Dear Ms. Benson:

 We wish to thank you for your patronage and sincerly hope that our services have been satisfactory. Perhaps you have forgoten that you left garmets with us for cleaning. They have been ready for you since October 20 1984 which is shortly after you brought them in.

 We regret the need to remind you of our policy, which is stated in bold print on your claim ticket, that all goods must be claimed within 90 days of the promised date, or they may be forfeited to us for sale in lieu of payment. This procedure is necessary if we are to recover expenses incurred during the process of our services. We sincerely hope that this will become necessary.

 If it is inconvenint for you to claim your goods personally, Perhaps you could arrange to have someone else do it for you? Please be certain that your claim ticket is presented at the time of pickup as we cannot release your goods without it. The amount due is $25.

 We look forward to seeing you soon, and hope to be of service to you again in the near future.

Figure 3.2 A Revised Draft of a Letter

inches. Never send a handwritten business letter, and avoid typewriters with cursive or other odd sorts of type faces. If the company you work for has letterhead stationery, and it very likely will, use it. Leave margins of at least an inch all around and larger ones if the message is brief. Center the body just above the middle of the page, single-space within paragraphs, and double-space between them. Get your letter onto one page if at all possible; that makes it easier for everyone, especially your reader. Letter reports that customarily run more than one page are discussed in Chapter 4.

 The business letter is a highly conventional form; that is, many of the decisions to be made about the parts of a letter and their layout are dictated by custom. Most companies have a correspondence manual that describes in great detail how letters and other communications should be

Dear Ms. Benson:

We wish to thank you for your patronage and ~~sincerly~~ hope that our services have been satisfactory. Perhaps you have forgot*t*en that you left gar*n*mets with us for cleaning. They have been ready for you since October 20, 1984, which is shortly after you brought them in.

We regret the need to remind you of our policy, which is stated ~~in bold print~~ on your claim ticket, that all goods must be claimed within 90 days of the promised date, or they may be forfeited to us for sale in lieu of payment. This procedure is necessary if we are to recover expenses incurred *while providing* ~~during the process of~~ our services. We ~~sincerely~~ hope that this will *not* become necessary.

If it is inconveni*e*nt for you to claim your goods personally, *p*erhaps you could arrange to have someone else do it for you. Please be certain that your claim ticket is presented at the time of pickup *since* ~~as~~ we cannot release your goods without it. The amount due is $25.

We look forward to seeing you soon, and hope to be of service to you again in the near future.

Figure 3.3   A Revised and Edited Draft of a Letter

arranged. Follow the manual carefully, since companies are properly concerned about their public image and departures from prescribed formats are not tolerated. The conventions described in this chapter cover most of the variations found in business correspondence. The format of a letter consists of its parts, or *elements*, and the *layout* of those elements on the page.

The Elements of a Letter

A typical business letter almost always contains six regular elements; it may also contain one or more additional elements, depending on the kind of letter being written. The six regular elements are heading, inside address, salutation, body, complimentary close, and signature. Their placement on the page in the three most common layouts is shown in Figures 3.5, 3.6, and 3.8.

Heading   Most companies supply printed letterhead stationery similar to that pictured in Figure 3.12. You need only add the date directly below. If your stationery has no printed heading, make up your own but include only your address and the date, not your name:

```
1715 North Carico Street
Evansville, IN  47715
March 19, 1986
```

Either spell out the name of the state or use the official abbreviation recommended by the postal service. A list is provided in Figure 3.4.

Inside Address   On the left margin in all layouts appears the inside address, spaced down from the heading so that the letter seems balanced

Alabama	AL	Montana	MT
Alaska	AK	Nebraska	NE
Arizona	AZ	Nevada	NV
Arkansas	AR	New Hampshire	NH
California	CA	New Jersey	NJ
Colorado	CO	New Mexico	NM
Connecticut	CT	New York	NY
Delaware	DE	North Carolina	NC
District of Columbia	DC	North Dakota	ND
Florida	FL	Ohio	OH
Georgia	GA	Oklahoma	OK
Guam	GU	Oregon	OR
Hawaii	HI	Pennsylvania	PA
Idaho	ID	Puerto Rico	PR
Illinois	IL	Rhode Island	RI
Indiana	IN	South Carolina	SC
Iowa	IA	South Dakota	SD
Kansas	KS	Tennessee	TN
Kentucky	KY	Texas	TX
Louisiana	LA	Utah	UT
Maine	ME	Vermont	VT
Maryland	MD	Virginia	VA
Massachusetts	MA	Virgin Islands	VI
Michigan	MI	Washington	WA
Minnesota	MN	West Virginia	WV
Mississippi	MS	Wisconsin	WI
Missouri	MO	Wyoming	WY

Figure 3.4   State Abbreviations Prescribed by the Postal Service

on the page. Always try to find the name of the person you are writing to rather than using a title such as Personnel Director. Sometimes, however, that can't be avoided. A few titles, such as Ms., Mr., and Dr., should be abbreviated, but most, such as Lieutenant and Attorney General, should be written out. A good desk dictionary provides full information about titles and abbreviations of titles.

Salutation   We call people "Dear" in the salutation even though we probably don't know them. That is one of the oddest conventional details in a letter, if one stops to think about it. Yet its oddity is not noticed; it seems odd only if it is missing. One of the advantages of knowing the name of the reader is that it is easier to write the salutation with a name rather than simply a title. However, if you can't find the name of your reader, use *Dear Sir or Madam* or some other nonsexist greeting. It sometimes works to identify the group the reader belongs to: *Dear Homeowner*, *Dear Customer*, or a similar name. A colon follows the salutation. If you are a good friend of the person addressed, you can use the first name and follow it with a comma. The salutation is omitted in the simplified layout.

Body   This most important element in any letter is described in all the stages preceding this one.

Complimentary Close   This is a conventional friendly word or phrase that comes just above the signature. The most common are *Sincerely, Sincerely yours, Yours truly,* and *Cordially.* If you know the reader well you can use the more friendly *Warmest regards. Cordially* used to be considered an especially friendly closing, but many companies now use it in addressing readers they are not acquainted with. *Respectfully* is now beginning to sound rather more humble than our notions of equality permit; it fits best in a military or other tightly structured organization. Most readers pay little attention to the complimentary close but notice if it is missing, except in a letter using the simplified layout.

Signature   You should sign all your letters unless they are part of a mass mailing. Using a stamp or having a secretary sign for you may make little difference in routine correspondence, but most readers like to feel they have been given your personal attention. Your signature lets the reader know you stand behind what is said, and it tells precisely who should get the reply. Sometimes the company's name in full capitals appears above the signature, indicating that you are a representative of the company. Below the signature should appear your name typed in full followed by your title. This enables the receiver to read your name easily in case you should write like a medical doctor or a celebrity.

Other Elements in a Letter In addition to the six regular elements, several others might be used. Even if you may rarely or never use some of these, it is good to know what they mean. All appear below the signature.

Identifying Initials If someone types letters for you, your initials should appear in capitals followed by the typist's in lower case.

RJD:dr (or) RJD/dr

Enclosure If you include documents, brochures, or other material with a letter, note that fact in a notation below the identifying initials. Several forms are used:

Enclosure: Map of Snowmass area

Enclosure

If more than one item is enclosed, you can name both items or include the number in parentheses:

Enclosures (2)

Courtesy Copies When carbon or photocopies of your letters are sent to readers other than the addressee, you should notify the addressee:

cc: Mr. Jonathan Edwards
     Ms. Janet Flanery

Postscript This is an additional sentence or two introduced by the letters *P.S.* and added below the signature. In personal letters, it is used when the writer didn't think of something in time to include it in the body. In more formal correspondence, however, postscripts are usually planned additions intended to draw attention to an idea or to serve as a final reminder in a sales letter. They should not be used in ordinary business letters.

Second Page Heading If a letter runs to more than one page, provide a heading at the top of the second page containing the name of the addressee, the page number, and the date. Use plain bond paper, not letterhead stationery, for additional pages.

Mr. James T. Mason
page 2
October 14, 1986

Choosing a Layout

Most business letters are arranged in one of three layouts, which are given the traditional names *full block, modified block,* and *simplified.* We prefer to call them *full left, balanced,* and *simplified,* since these terms describe more accurately their appearance. These three layouts are illustrated in Figures 3.5, 3.6, 3.7, and 3.8. Note the margins, spacing, and punctuation in each. The first two are acceptable in any business letter; the last is a new layout used only in routine letters.

Full left layout is usually used with letterhead stationery. Its simplicity has made it the most popular current format in spite of making the

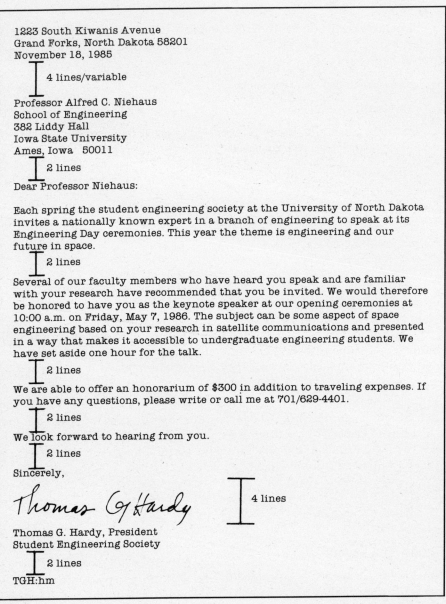

1223 South Kiwanis Avenue
Grand Forks, North Dakota 58201
November 18, 1985

    4 lines/variable

Professor Alfred C. Niehaus
School of Engineering
382 Liddy Hall
Iowa State University
Ames, Iowa   50011

    2 lines

Dear Professor Niehaus:

Each spring the student engineering society at the University of North Dakota invites a nationally known expert in a branch of engineering to speak at its Engineering Day ceremonies. This year the theme is engineering and our future in space.

    2 lines

Several of our faculty members who have heard you speak and are familiar with your research have recommended that you be invited. We would therefore be honored to have you as the keynote speaker at our opening ceremonies at 10:00 a.m. on Friday, May 7, 1986. The subject can be some aspect of space engineering based on your research in satellite communications and presented in a way that makes it accessible to undergraduate engineering students. We have set aside one hour for the talk.

    2 lines

We are able to offer an honorarium of $300 in addition to traveling expenses. If you have any questions, please write or call me at 701/629-4401.

    2 lines

We look forward to hearing from you.

    2 lines

Sincerely,

Thomas G Hardy   4 lines

Thomas G. Hardy, President
Student Engineering Society

    2 lines

TGH:hm

Figure 3.5   Full Left Layout

```
                                    1722 West 29th Street
                                    Modesto, California  95351
                                    May 2, 1986


Mr. John F. Hines, Chairman
Church Council
Oak Street Methodist Church
921 West Oak Street
Modesto, California  98310

Dear Mr. Hines:

The members of Boy Scout Troop #44 of the Cherokee Region want to thank
you and the others on the church council at Oak Street Methodist Church for
letting us use your church's assembly hall for our annual banquet on April 27.
A check for $20 is enclosed to cover the agreed-upon fee.

As you have probably heard, the banquet was the best ever and the best
attended, since more than 125 scouts and parents were there. We found all the
facilities we needed both for the dinner and the program that followed. The
caterers told us yours is the best-equipped kitchen they have worked in this
year.

We trust that our cleanup crew left the assembly hall and kitchen as clean and
orderly as we found it. If we should need the assembly hall in the future, we
hope that our request will be as cordially received as it was this year.

                                    Sincerely,

                                    William F. Hofstra

                                    William F. Hofstra
                                    Assistant Troop Leader
```

Figure 3.6   Balanced Layout

page look unbalanced. The advantage is that the typist does not have to make tab settings, since all is flush with the left margin.

In the *balanced layout* the sender's address and the date are placed to the right of the center of the page and the complimentary close and signature are aligned with them just below the body. The placement of these elements gives a balanced appearance to the page. Paragraphs are sometimes indented, as shown in Figure 3.7, but more often not.

The *simplified layout* is gaining acceptance for routine business letters, especially those sent to a company or department in which no single person can be identified as the receiver of the letter. It is identical to full left except that it has no salutation and no complimentary close. It avoids the problem of how to address the reader when no proper name can be found, and it conveys the impression that the letter is devoted strictly to business. It works well for order letters, letters of inquiry and complaint,

EMERALD CLEANERS
1744 South Harvard Ave.
Tempe, Arizona 85281

January 22, 1985

Ms. Jeanine Benson
1542 Jackson Blvd.
Tempe, Arizona 85281

Dear Ms. Benson:

   We wish to thank you for your patronage and hope that our services
have been satisfactory. Perhaps you have forgotten that you left garments
with us for cleaning. They have been ready for you since October 20, 1984,
which is shortly after you brought them in.

   We regret the need to remind you of our policy, which is stated on your
claim ticket, that all goods must be claimed within 90 days of the promised
date or they may be forfeited to us for sale in lieu of payment. This procedure
is necessary if we are to recover expenses incurred while providing our
services. We hope that this will not become necessary.

   If it is inconvenient for you to claim your goods personally, perhaps you
could arrange to have someone else do it for you. Please be certain your claim
ticket is presented at the time of pickup since we cannot release your goods
without it. The amount due is $25.

   We look forward to seeing you soon and hope to be of service to you again
in the near future.

Sincerely,

Harry Sorheim

Harry Sorheim
Proprietor

HS/rb

Figure 3.7   Balanced Layout with Indented Paragraphs

or any routine letter when the name of the reader isn't known. A subject
line is usually placed between the inside address and the body of the letter.
Subject lines are also used with either of the other two layouts, but not
often. They are placed either two spaces above or two spaces below the
salutation.

   Be prepared for a number of variations on the layouts described here
in the letters you may receive once you have taken a job. The variations
are especially common in sales letters, where the departures from the
usual formats are calculated to catch your attention. Most business correspondence, however, still adheres rather closely to one or another of
these three layouts.

722 West Seventh Street
San Angelo, TX 76903
January 20, 1986

Parts Department
J. T. Solomon Brothers, Inc.
9045 Terrace Avenue
Houston, TX 77020

Subject: Order for backhoe repair parts

Please send us the following parts for a Solomon Bros. backhoe, model 24D, and
listed in parts catalog 1985SB421:

Part No.	Part Name	Price
SA22341	Scoop-arm linkage yoke	1 at $37.50
CL2452	Clutch liner	1 at 24.80
CLP425	Clutch pedal arm	1 at 14.50
		$76.80

Can your parts delivery service get these to us by February 2? If it will take
longer, please give us a phone call. Also, please figure tax and delivery charges
and include the total in next month's bill.

Jackson Evers

Jackson Evers
Citrus Construction Company

JE/bn

Figure 3.8 Simplified Layout

Types of Letters

Since the types of letters you might be called on to write are many, it is
impossible to describe and illustrate all of them here. The general principles set forth in the process stages of this chapter will enable you to handle
most letter-writing tasks competently. This final section of the chapter,
however, provides samples of four common types of letters: inquiry,
answer to inquiry, complaint, and answer to complaint. In addition, the
job application letter is described in Chapter 5 and the transmittal letter
in Chapters 12 and 13.

Letter of Inquiry If you need information that can't be found in
your company files or in a library, a letter of inquiry may be the best way
to obtain it. You need to have a fair idea of what you want in order to
make the inquiry specific; you also need to find out what person or organization is likely to have the information. Getting these two kinds of

information requires some research, but you will already have done a good amount of it in order to determine that the information you need cannot be found locally. Your research may also give you leads to the best person or organization to ask.

In the third situation described at the beginning of the chapter, your company is looking for information on a financial management service for farm implement dealers. Your questioning of others in your company yields a suggestion to get in touch with an expert in another city. In this case you decide that a letter of inquiry has several advantages over a phone call:

- It gives the respondent time to look up answers to the questions.
- It puts the questions in writing and hence makes misunderstanding less likely.
- It gives you a chance to make up a few carefully worded sentences about your need for the information and thus increases the chances of getting a thorough answer.

Inquiry letters can be either solicited or unsolicited, and these should use the direct and indirect approaches, respectively. Most solicited letters of inquiry come in response to advertisements offering brochures or information about a product or service. Since the companies making these offers hope to make sales as a result of the inquiries, they welcome them. The letters requesting information are good news letters and can be brief:

> Please send me the brochure entitled "Ten Dynamic Ideas for Making Money in Real Estate" and the description of your home-study course in real estate selling, which was advertised in the March 28 issue of the New York Times Magazine.

Unsolicited letters require more careful planning. The writer is asking a favor, since the respondent has little to gain beyond the gratitude of the questioner. The beginning should therefore prepare the way for the request by identifying the writer and the subject of the inquiry. It is also a good idea to tell why you need information and why you have written to that person or company, an opening that enables you to offer some mild praise—the company is a leader in the field or the person is a well-known expert in it.

Then introduce the questions themselves with a courteously worded request. The questions should be carefully phrased and specific. General information on any subject can be found in a library; what you need is specific information that you couldn't find anywhere else. Don't ask for "any information you may have on . . . " or similar blanket questions. Put the questions in a numbered list. That will encourage the respondent to reply in the order they are presented and to give a separate response to each. Avoid questions that require much research or a lengthy answer and also those that may infringe on commercial secrets. Don't put the receiver of the letter in the position of having to refuse to answer.

The last paragraph should contain a brief expression of appreciation for whatever help the reader can give and an offer to do a favor in return, if that is a plausible offer. For example, if you are writing a report on the subject, you might offer to send a copy of it. You should also assure the reader that he or she will be cited in any report that might result.

Figure 3.9, which grew out of one of the problems described at the beginning of the chapter, reflects a number of these points.

Answer to Letter of Inquiry   Since this is a good news letter, you can be direct and as brief as adequate answers will allow you to be. Being direct does not mean being curt or unfriendly. It never costs anything to be courteous, even though you may be busy or see no benefit to you in answering.

Begin by referring to the questioner's letter and making clear any limitations on your answers. Then answer the questions in the order they were asked, fully but not at great length. One page is as much as you should be expected to write in answer to a set of well-phrased, specific questions. If you have a brochure or other printed matter that answers one of the questions, simply enclose it. If you know of a good article or book on the subject, refer the questioner to it. After writing your answers, close with a friendly statement such as "I hope my answers provide the information you need" and then offer additional help if you feel disposed to. Figure 3.10 is an answer to the letter of inquiry in Figure 3.9.

Letter of Complaint   You are as likely to write this kind of letter as a private citizen as on the job, so it's a useful skill to acquire. It is sometimes called a *claim letter.* In writing it be sure to adopt a courteous tone, however angry you may be, and include all the facts necessary to enable the reader to make a judgment. Your purpose is to persuade the reader to rectify the problem at no cost to you, and your chances of accomplishing that are greatly increased if you do those two things.

The organization of the letter tends to follow a narrative pattern because your main task is to describe the sequence of events that led up to your writing. After you have introduced the subject, either in a subject line or in the opening sentence, the narrative should be presented in enough detail to make clear why you believe you have a legitimate complaint.

In the last paragraph lay out what you feel is a fair settlement of the complaint or the action you want the reader of the letter to take.

The sample letter in Figure 3.11 follows this pattern well. The subject line states the subject and includes a careful identification of the product in question. The first two paragraphs are narrative, the third explains why the writer thinks the warranty should apply, and the last calls for action by the manufacturer.

HASKINS AND BEYERS
Public Accountants
1919 Oak Ridge Way
Cedar Falls, Iowa 50613

May 26, 1986

Professor Lewis H. Sneed
School of Agriculture
University of Illinois
Urbana, Illinois 61801

Dear Professor Sneed:

We are a public accounting firm in an agricultural area that has severe economic problems among both farmers and those who provide services to them. One of the hardest hit groups has been implement dealers, who have seen little movement of their inventories of expensive farm equipment and who have been unable to collect on debts owed by hard-pressed farmers. We feel the implement dealers in this part of Iowa need help in managing their finances, and we are thinking of offering a financial management service directed to their needs.

Before proceeding further, however, we need answers to several questions. Since you are a specialist in problems of capital investment, debt, and cash flow in agriculture, we thought you could provide us with authoritative replies. We have three specific questions:

1. In your opinion, are the financial problems of farm implement dealers in the Midwest severe enough to make them willing to pay for a service that will help them solve those problems?

2. In what specific areas are farm implement dealers most in need of financial advice: inventory management, cash flow, credit to farmers, relations with local banks, or other areas?

3. Do you know of any financial management software packages that would provide help to farm implement dealers?

Any help you can give us in answering these questions will be appreciated; if you have any advice to offer us, apart from what you might say in answer to these questions, we will be happy to receive it.

We look forward to hearing from you.

Sincerely,

Randall C. Beyers

Randall C. Beyers, Partner

RCB/nb

Figure 3.9   A Letter of Inquiry

School of Agriculture
Landkammer Hall
University of Illinois
Urbana, IL 61801
June 2, 1986

Mr. Randall C. Beyers, Partner
Haskins and Beyers
1919 Oak Ridge Way
Cedar Falls, Iowa 50432

Dear Mr. Beyers:

Your plan to offer financial advice to farm implement dealers, which you describe in your letter of May 26, would fill a real need. Judging from the experience of several who have tried it, however, I think you will have to work hard at it to make it succeed. Here are my answers to your questions.

1. Although many implement dealers need financial advice, most would find it hard to justify paying for the service. I think they would be wise to seek help from a firm such as yours, but they need to be convinced it is worth the price. You should consider printing a persuasive description of your services and, in addition, make plans to sell the service personally.

2. In my opinion, the areas where they most need help, and where a firm like yours can provide it, are record keeping (a basic function that is often handled badly), inventory management, and cash flow. Most implement dealers have too much money tied up in inventory, and as a result, they frequently have liquidity problems.

3. The best software package I know of is Datamag's program #CB425, which is sold under the name "Financial Pro." The others I know of are either extremely complex or require equipment not likely to be owned by a small business such as an implement dealership.

I hope these answers are useful to you. My general advice is that there is a need for the service, but your success will depend upon the effectiveness of your advertising and the talents of your staff; do you have staff members skilled in the areas suggested above?

I wish you success in your venture should you decide to undertake it; let me know if I can be of any further help.

Sincerely,

Lewis H. Sneed

Lewis H. Sneed
Professor, Agricultural Economics

Figure 3.10   Answer to a Letter of Inquiry

906 West Linden Street
Worthington, MN 56187
April 11, 1985

Customer Relations Department
Electro Products Corporation
1040 Industrial Drive
Chicago, IL 60601

Subject: Repairs to Electro Refrigerator, Model 27.5, Serial #12641B

On March 20 of this year, I bought an Electro model 27.5 refrigerator-freezer
from Lee Appliance in Worthington, Minnesota. Just two weeks later, on April
2, I called Lee Appliance and asked them to send a repairman out since the
refrigerator and freezer were not cooling properly. The repairman diagnosed
the problem as a malfunctioning compressor and repaired it that day.

I assumed that the cost of the repairs was covered by the warranty, which
clearly states that parts and labor are covered for 12 months unless the damage
occurs through negligence or as a result of repair work done by unauthorized
repair personnel. However, a week later a bill arrived in the mail for $94.50
with no mention of the warranty. When I called the dealer, he said the
repairman had noticed that the refrigerator had been moved into the kitchen
from the utility room where he had installed it two weeks earlier. The dealer
claims that moving the refrigerator was the probable cause of the compressor's
failure and refuses to honor the warranty.

In moving the refrigerator, I had the help of my brother-in-law, and the total
distance of the move was about nine feet. The warranty says nothing about
moving the refrigerator.

The brochure that came with the refrigerator says that you want owners to be
satisfied and that if any problems arise with a dealer, to get in touch with you.
I have not yet paid the bill, since I feel the warranty covers the repair work. I
would appreciate your clearing this up with Lee Appliance and letting me
know of your action.

Gunnar Larson

Gunnar Larson

Figure 3.11   Letter of Complaint in Simplified Layout

Letter of Adjustment   A letter in answer to a complaint can either
grant the complainant's request or refuse it. Thus it will be either a good
news or a bad news letter and should be organized accordingly. If you
grant the request, your task is easy, since you need only express regret for
the cause of the complaint, explain what is being done to rectify it, and
close with a positive statement that is aimed at retaining the good will of
the customer.

If you must say no, the task is much more difficult. Your purpose
should be to explain the reasons for the denial in a rational way so that
the reader will accept them as reasonable. Since the reader will be skepti-
cal, if not genuinely upset, your chances of success are limited, but you
must try. Use the four steps of the indirect approach.

- The first part of the letter should set a positive tone by finding some-thing that is not negative in the situation. Some companies want to know when things go wrong with their products, or seem to go wrong, and hence thank the customer for reporting the problem. You may express regret, but if you have decided that your company is not at fault, there is no need to apologize.
- Next, give your explanation of what went wrong, making clear why you believe your company is not at fault. In doing this, avoid accusing the customer of ignorance or lack of skill. Simply say something like "Apparently the escape valve was not in the full 'off' position" rather than "You forgot to turn off the escape valve, as the instructions tell you to." Don't make this part too brief. The fact that you spend some time explaining what has gone wrong will help to convince the reader that you are concerned. A full explanation may also help the reader to avoid the problem in the future or to remedy it if it does happen again.
- Make clear that the request is being denied, if that is not clear from the explanation in the preceding section. Usually it is best to state the denial explicitly, but state it as tactfully as you can and tie it to your explanation of the cause of the problem.
- Close on a positive note by suggesting another course of action that might solve the problem for the reader, by partially granting the request if that is possible, or by making some positive statement.

Figure 3.12 is a positive answer to the letter of complaint in Figure 3.11. It gives the good news in the opening paragraph, explains why the writer's request is being granted in the second, and then explains what may have caused the refrigerator to malfunction. The letter closes with an offer to provide help in the future should the writer need it.

A negative reply to the same letter of complaint appears in Figure 3.13. A negative answer is called for since the facts are somewhat differ-ent. In this case the dealer is able to explain the cause of the refrigerator's failure, since the repairman reported that the compressor was struck by a floor electrical outlet when the refrigerator was moved. Even though the cause had been explained to the customer, he had omitted that fact from his letter of complaint. The writer of the negative reply, however, doesn't accuse the customer of leaving out an important fact, but simply repeats the repairman's explanation. The letter begins and ends positively and, in the middle section, makes clear in a tactful way why the warranty doesn't apply.

Key Points in the Chapter

1. Business letters are brief, written messages sent to readers outside one's own organization.
2. Since letters reflect your image as well as the image of your organi-zation, both the content and appearance should be carefully attended to.

```
                    ELECTRO PRODUCTS CORPORATION
                          1040 Industrial Drive
                         Chicago, Illinois  60601

                     Customer Relations Department


April 16, 1985


Mr. Gunnar Larson
906 West Linden Street
Worthington, Minnesota  56187

Dear Mr. Larson:

We regret the problems your new Electro model 27.5 refrigerator may have
caused you. Because we want owners of our products to be satisfied owners, we
have written to Lee Appliance directing them to cancel the bill for $94.50,
which they sent you on March 26.

Moving the refrigerator may have been the cause of the compressor's failure,
as the dealer says, but we have no way of verifying that claim. We have
therefore reimbursed the dealer from our warranty fund so you won't have to
pay the bill.

It sometimes happens that a block of wood or an electrical floor outlet that is
raised above the surface of the floor will press against the compressor as the
refrigerator is moved, causing a break in the compressor's connecting line. The
repairman thinks that happened in your case. As noted above, we cannot
verify the cause but we urge you to be certain to avoid any floor obstructions
should you move the refrigerator in the future.

We hope your new Electro refrigerator gives you good service for many years.
If we can help you in any way in the future, please don't hestitate to write.

Sincerely,

ELECTRO PRODUCTS CORPORATION

James P Willey

James P. Willey
Customer Relations Director

JPW:hy
```

Figure 3.12   A Positive Reply to a Letter of Complaint

3. The telephone has taken over some of the functions formerly handled
   by letters, but the letter is still one of the most important means of
   communication between organizations.
4. Important letters should be prepared by using all seven stages in the
   composing process.

ELECTRO PRODUCTS CORPORATION
1040 Industrial Drive
Chicago, Illinois 60601

Customer Relations Department

April 16, 1985

Mr. Gunnar Larson
906 West Linden Street
Worthington, Minnesota 56187

Dear Mr. Larson:

We regret the problems your Electro model 27.5 refrigerator has caused you and thank you for writing to us about them. We want the owners of our products to be satisfied and have no way of knowing when things need attention unless they tell us.

The warranty on your refrigerator does cover parts and labor for 12 months, as you state in your letter, except in cases of negligence or unauthorized repair. As you also point out, the refrigerator was moved from one room to another shortly after you bought it. The repairman at Lee Appliance who serviced it reports that the refrigerator had been pushed up against a raised floor outlet hard enough so that the compressor housing was cracked and the connecting line broken. He pointed this out to you after the repairs were made. Perhaps he should also have made clear that hitting an obstruction constitutes negligence, and for that reason the warranty doesn't apply. We make our refrigerators strong enough to operate reliably for many years, but we cannot prevent accidental damage of the sort your refrigerator sustained. We urge you to be certain to avoid any floor obstructions should you move the refrigerator in the future.

We hope your Electro refrigerator gives you good service for many years. If we can help you in any way in the future, please don't hesitate to write.

Sincerely,

ELECTRO PRODUCTS CORPORATION

James P. Willey

James P. Willey
Director, Customer Relations

JPW:hy

Figure 3.13   A Negative Reply to a Letter of Complaint

5. Since letters enable writers to express themselves more personally than most other forms of practical writing, managing the tone is one of the letter writer's most important tasks.
6. Use the direct approach in letters whose main message is good news

or, at worst, neutral; use the indirect approach if the main message is bad news.

7. Avoid stilted, impersonal, and cliché-ridden language in letters; instead write naturally and informally, making free use of personal pronouns.
8. Write the draft of a letter at one sitting and check for the accuracy of the facts and appropriateness of the tone in revising.
9. Many elements in a letter are prescribed by convention, and the arrangement of those elements should follow one of several conventional layouts.
10. Since letters are judged first on their appearance and then on content, it is important that they be professional looking.

Exercises

1. Pick a campus service that has recently failed to perform as you think it should—registration office, laundry room, or a service at the student center. Find out who is in charge of the one you pick and write a letter of complaint, but don't mail it before checking with your instructor.
2. Imagine yourself the person written to in exercise 1; write a letter of adjustment addressed to the complainer. You could also exchange your letter of complaint with a classmate and write a letter of adjustment in answer to it.
3. Write a letter inviting someone to come and speak to a club or organization you belong to. Be certain to include all the details needed to enable the reader to make a decision without having to request more information.
4. Write a letter to a professor asking for information on the subject of your long report in this class. Make your purpose clear and tell him or her exactly what information you need. Put the questions in list form.
5. Write a letter to a private firm asking for a brochure or information on the subject of a hobby of yours. Since the firm may have a chance to sell a product, they should be willing to answer your letter promptly without your telling them your purpose, but include it if it will make the inquiry clearer.
6. Write a letter of inquiry or complaint strictly from your point of view (I-centered), not the reader's. Exchange letters with a classmate and translate his or her I-centered letter into a letter that reflects the reader's point of view (you-centered).

4 Writing Memorandums and Informal Reports

Abstract

Memos are brief, written messages, ranging in length from a few lines to several pages and addressed to others within one's own organization. They often serve the same purposes as business letters but their format is simpler, the tone is less formal, and the content is more directly focused on the business at hand. In writing longer and more complex memos, all seven stages of the writing process are useful. Informal reports are often written in memo form, but they are usually longer than the typical memo; they can also take the form of letters or be completed by filling out printed forms. There are many kinds of informal reports, including the progress report, the incident report, the trip report, and the recommendation report.

When writing a message to someone within your company or organization, use the memorandum form. The term *memorandum* originally referred to "an informal record of something that one wishes to remember or preserve for future use; a note to help or jog the memory" (*Webster's Unabridged Dictionary*, 3rd ed.). This first definition reflects only one of the memorandum's many current uses. Its broader use in business and industry nowadays is reflected in its more recent definition: "a usually brief informal communication typically written for interoffice circulation on paper headed *memorandum*." The memorandum, or memo, is useful when you need to communicate with someone in your organization but speaking face to face or telephoning won't do. It can reach a number of people simultaneously and provides a written record that is easily referred to and preserved. It can also be useful without being circulated—you may write a memo to yourself simply to save something "for the record." This is the purpose reflected in the first definition quoted.

As a college graduate on the job you will very likely produce more memos than any other kind of writing, and hundreds may cross your desk in a year. They are the commonest form of written communication in an organization since they can serve a wide variety of purposes, from calling a routine meeting to issuing an informal report.

The memo is similar to the business letter in a number of ways, but because it stays within the organization, it differs in several ways as well.

- The format is simpler, as illustrated in Figure 4.1.
- The tone is often less formal since the writer may know the reader well.
- Less time and effort are given to creating a positive image and good will, since both reader and writer belong to the same organization.

Memos should, of course, be friendly, courteous, and tactful, since they reflect the writer's image. These qualities are also important because memos are often circulated later to people other than the original addressees. Once a memo has been sent out, the writer has little control over it, and therefore it is safest to be tactful and diplomatic even though it might feel good to express your feelings candidly. How often have memos, written in the heat of momentary strong feeling, come back to haunt a writer weeks or months later? Some people would say you should never put in writing anything you wouldn't want read in court.

Since writers often know their readers well, memos are usually devoted strictly to the business at hand, and hence they can, on occasion, be extremely short—even two or three lines of text, as in this example:

> The departmental Policy Committee will meet at 2:00 p.m., Wednesday, June 2, in the conference room, A212. Guidelines for annual personnel evaluations will be discussed.

Conciseness is a virtue in memos. As with business letters, it pays to keep them to less than a page, since memos of one page are more likely to be read than longer ones. Yet it should not be said that they must always be a page or less; you should say concisely what needs to be said, and if it comes to more than a page, so be it. Brevity in itself is no virtue if it forces you to say less than needs to be said or to say it badly.

This chapter will cover typical kinds of memos first, then take up the informal report, which includes both the memo report and the letter report. All seven stages in the writing process are usually involved in the writing of memos.

Defining the Problem and Purpose

Except when writing a memo so brief and routine that the problem and purpose are obvious, it is good to spend some time first getting these two elements clearly defined before attempting to gather data or make an outline.

Defining the Problem

Memos can often be used to solve the same kinds of problems as those listed for the letter, even though they are addressed to someone within your organization, not outside it. Here are some other problem situations that might call for a memo:

- As chairperson of your department's recreation committee you are aware that if the annual fall picnic is to be a success it must be planned.
- As teachers of composition, you and a colleague require that students in your classes type all their papers, but you have discovered that the department's typing room is open only part of each school day and never at night. This is true in spite of the fact that there are several night classes scheduled.
- Someone in your department has been honored by a civic organization; you think the person should be congratulated and all members of the department should know about the honor.
- As director of the counseling office in a large company, you have noticed that many managers and shop supervisors cannot recognize psychological problems among their workers until those problems are far advanced, and they don't know where to find help for them once the problems are recognized.

In the first situation, the problem is how best to set up plans for the picnic. A logical first step is to seek help from the recreation committee in your department. A meeting needs to be called, and the most efficient means is a memo to each of the six members. Of course, that memo won't completely solve the problem, since like most problems, this one requires several steps; calling a meeting is only the first step.

In the second situation the problem has arisen because the typing room is open too few hours to serve the needs of all the students in composition classes, including night-school students. It may be that those who set up the current schedule were unaware of the needs of all students, or it may be that they had no money to hire more workers to supervise the room for longer hours. The problem also involves discovering exactly who has the authority to make the needed changes in the schedule. Once that person has been identified, a memo drawing attention to the problem is a good first step.

The need to congratulate a fellow worker presents a fairly simple problem—one might better call it a pleasant opportunity. The fourth, however, is more complex and difficult. The managers and supervisors need to be taught how to identify psychological problems and also to be told where help can be obtained. As director of the counseling office you might consider offering a set of training sessions. However, the sessions would take participants away from their jobs for a time and would be difficult to schedule. Managers might, on the other hand, be asked to read a book from the company library on common psychological problems among workers, but you recognize that some would read it and some wouldn't. Even if all were to read the book, only half the problem would be solved since they would still not know where to refer patients. A carefully written memo might do the job.

Identifying the Purpose

Having decided that a memo would provide the means of carrying out a solution to your problem, or at least a first step toward it, you must decide exactly what you want to accomplish—in other words, you must determine your purpose. To illustrate this stage, let's look at the first and second cases since they are good examples of a simple, routine memo and a more complex one.

Your purpose in the memo to the recreation committee is to get all the members to the meeting on time and prepared to discuss plans for the picnic. That means it must make clear the date, time, and place of the meeting, as well as the agenda. If all members of the committee do, in fact, get there on time and are ready to contribute, you will have accomplished your purpose. Writing this memo is chiefly a matter of remembering to include all the necessary details. Here is the text of an actual memo, a rather informal one, that failed to accomplish its purpose because it omitted some important pieces of information.

To: Office staff

From: Marie

Date: June 21, 1985

Subject: Birthday party for Jean

Another birthday for Jean has arrived, and we're putting together a surprise gathering. Bring a snack to share. We'll meet at my house. RSVP at 445-7835. See you there!

The heading identifies the sender, the receivers, the date it was sent, and the subject, but a second memo had to be sent to correct the omission of the date and time of the party and to give the full address of the writer.

The more complex situation, the one about hours of operation of the typing room, calls for a message that has two purposes: to convince someone with authority to take action to increase the number of hours the room is open and to suggest a plan for that expansion. To carry out the first purpose successfully you must first acquaint the reader with the situation and then make a convincing case that the hours ought to be expanded. Thus the main purpose is to persuade the reader to act in a certain way. To carry out the second purpose—to offer a plan for the expansion—will help to fulfill the first, since it will suggest how it might be done.

Analyzing the Audience

The audience for a memo is always someone within your organization. That fact, which accounts for most of the differences between letters and memos, means you can come to the point more quickly and need only include details related to the business at hand. A memo *can* include more than the business at hand if the message is personal, if there is a strong need to create good will, or if you are attempting to persuade someone to adopt a certain policy. A friendly offer of additional help or some other gesture of good will is often a good way to close a memo.

The fact that the primary readers of memos are always within your organization doesn't mean they should all be treated alike. Sometimes your reader will be an expert in your own field and sometimes not, and hence your level of technicality must be adjusted to fit. At times the reader will be high in the organization, at times your equal, and at other times below you in the company hierarchy. That may determine how formal or informal you should be, since generally you should be more formal in writing to those above and below you than to your equals. The short memo inviting fellow workers to a birthday party, quoted earlier, was obviously sent to equals, and the writer probably felt even freer to be informal since the subject was not related to business.

When writing to those who are distant from you in a large organization, the situation is similar to that for a regular business letter. Then it is often necessary to make an effort to create or maintain good will; and since you are writing to someone you may never have met, it is necessary to be more formal than with those you know well. The memo in Figure 4.4 reflects this situation well.

The cases of the recreation committee chairperson and the teachers seeking longer hours for the typing room present somewhat different problems in audience analysis. The committee chairperson can provide all the information needed to call the meeting without worrying very much about fitting it to the audience. The message will be brief and factual, the situation routine, and the readers of the memo are all well known to the writer.

The teachers, on the other hand, must first identify the person who has the authority to change the hours and then learn something about that person, if they aren't already acquainted, in order to plan the best method of persuasion. It turns out that they know the man personally, and that makes their task easier than it would have been had they been forced to direct the memo to someone they knew only by title. They know he is concerned about providing good services to students but also with keeping the departmental budget balanced and the equipment in the typing room safe. They also decide that he may not know precisely the hours the typing room is currently open, and hence they need to provide background on the present schedule. Finally, since the chairperson is in the same department they are, they realize that there is little need to spend time creating or maintaining good will. The memo can stick to the business at hand.

Collecting the Data

Most of what was said about collecting data for letters in Chapter 3 applies to memos as well. Since they are a form of business correspondence, all the important ones should be kept on file. Files are therefore a good source of information on issues of continuing interest. Much of the information in memos is factual and of short-term interest, but that does not reduce the importance of carefully checking the accuracy and completeness of the facts. Put yourself in the position of your readers and ask what they will need to know in order to fulfill the purpose of the memo. Err on the side of too much information rather than too little. In the brief text of a memo quoted earlier, calling a meeting of a departmental policy committee, the writer, sensing that some might not know what was meant by *conference room*, included the number, A212, as well.

The two memos we have been planning pose quite different problems in data collection. The first, which calls a committee meeting, requires very little; the other, a great deal. To schedule the recreation committee meeting you might need to find out if the conference room is free at the time you plan to hold the meeting. If it isn't, a different meeting place or a different time must be chosen.

The teachers who are concerned about the hours of operation of the typing room will need to collect data of two sorts: first, information about the current hours of operation and the number of student workers who are assigned to the room, and second, information about the availability of funds to hire more student workers to staff the typing room during expanded hours. They might also want to gather opinions from other teachers about the adequacy of the current schedule.

Designing the Memo

As the samples on the following pages make clear, memos have a simpler form than letters. In large companies and governmental agencies, more elaborate formats than a simple TO, FROM, DATE, and SUBJECT may be used, but those four parts plus the text are sufficient for most. To make the writer's task even easier, most companies provide printed memo forms that list the elements in the heading and provide space for the text that follows. Figure 4.3 is an example.

In designing memos longer than a paragraph or two, a four-part organization generally works well: (1) heading information, (2) problem and purpose, (3) development, and (4) conclusion.

Filling in the Heading

The heading above the text usually contains four elements, as shown in this sample:

TO: Muriel Oates, Advertising Manager

FROM: Wilson Goodbeck, Vice President for Finance *WG*

DATE: 8 July 1985

SUBJECT: Revised Deadlines for Submitting Quarterly Revenue Data

Since the information in the heading, especially the subject line, is part of the message, write out the heading in your first draft. Include full names or first initial and last name followed by titles, unless you are well acquainted with the reader and the memo is on an unimportant subject.

Stating the Problem and Purpose

Unless the memo is brief or the problem and purpose obvious, these two elements should be stated explicitly at the beginning. The *subject line* can announce both and should certainly mention at least one of them. It should be a noun phrase, not a complete sentence, and should say something about the subject, not simply name it. It is best to limit it to one line, though two lines are acceptable. In a memo to a department head asking for more open hours for the department's typewriting room, the subject line should not simply say "Typewriting Room" or even "Open Hours for Typewriting Room." It fulfills its purpose much better if it states the problem, as in "Lack of Sufficient Open Times for Typewriting Room," or the purpose, as in "Proposal for Additional Open Hours for Typewriting Room."

The opening sentence of the text should repeat the problem and purpose and, if the memo is short, begin the development. In the sample about the typewriting room, the opening lines of the text were "It seems to us that the typewriting room is not open enough hours this semester; we suggest an expanded schedule that will fit the needs of our students better than the current one." The rest of the memo presents reasons for thinking the current hours too few and proposes a new schedule. Here is another opening section from an actual memo that does an excellent job of stating the problem and purpose:

> There has been some confusion about whether the self-documentation section of the Faculty Evaluation System is to be submitted for the current evaluation period. This memorandum is to confirm that this section is to be submitted for the 1981-82 evaluation cycle.

Of all the memos we have been planning in this chapter, the one on psychological counseling requires the most careful design. The subject line can state both the subject and the purpose and at least imply the problem:

> SUBJECT: Identifying Psychological Problems Among Workers; Procedures for Securing Emergency and Routine Help

The opening paragraph spells out the problem more fully and repeats the two purposes as well. Here is a draft of the opening paragraph:

> During this calendar year, with its predictable periods of personal and job-related stress, I want to remind you of the resources available to you should you need assistance in responding to psychological emergencies. Pressures are commonly generated by anxieties related to job performance, desire for promotion, working conditions, relations with fellow workers, and difficulties at home. Many employees who could benefit from counseling assistance also need encouragement in seeking such help. The following information may help you to identify people with psychological difficulties and help them to receive the assistance they may need.

The first part outlines the problem well; the last sentence states the two purposes explicitly. Figure 4.4 shows the memo in finished form.

Developing the Body of the Memo

In brief memos, little more may be required than is supplied by the opening sentences. A few precise facts about date, place, and subject are sufficient for calling a meeting, as has already been illustrated. Only longer, more complex memos require some thought in their development.

In the memo about the hours of operation of the typing room, the development will consist mainly of describing the current schedule, proposing a new one, and providing support for the changes. Keep the readers in mind as you plan the body of the memo. If they are familiar with the situation, you needn't provide much background and can concentrate on what is new. If the problem is being brought to their attention for the first time, a good deal of background may be needed. In the typing room memo, a brief listing of the current hours of operation is all that is necessary. Most of the body of the memo can be devoted to offering reasons for providing more hours and to proposing a new schedule.

Concluding the Memo

In a brief memo, no conclusion is necessary; whatever action the reader is expected to take may simply be stated early or implied by the facts. In a memo that calls a meeting, the announcement itself, along with the listing of time and place, implies "please be there." To say it would only annoy the reader. In a longer memo, however, it is usually wise to spell out the actions expected of the reader. Here is the conclusion of the typing-room memo; it puts the call to action in the form of a question and closes with a sentence of persuasion:

> Is it possible to hire enough work-study students to keep the typewriting room open more consistently during all school hours? This is an important service to students and seems to us to merit support from our department, in particular.

A conclusion can also include an offer of additional help, an expression of willingness to answer questions, or a simple statement of good will.

Choosing a Style and Tone

Your choice of style and tone in a memo should depend mainly on who is your reader and what is your purpose. The more familiar you are with the reader and the less serious the purpose, the more informal the style can be. The memo inviting a co-worker to a birthday party belongs at the informal extreme; the one addressed to supervisors on the subject of psychological counseling, on the other hand, calls for a rather formal style. The style should also reflect your awareness that a wider audience than is specifically addressed might read the memo. This awareness should limit any attempts to be cleverly humorous or ironic or to express strong personal opinions. It should also encourage you to write to as broad an audience as you can, limiting the number of highly technical words while still saying what you need to say. The more your memo has to do with issues of permanent interest, the more likely it is to be read by a number of readers far into the future. Choose your style accordingly.

Whether your style is formal or informal, however, you should use short sentences, short paragraphs, and familiar words. Avoid technical terms when writing to a lay audience and avoid jargon in all memos. Your style should be simple and concise, as in the samples in this chapter, but it should not be telegraphic: Always write in complete sentences. Headings can make the style more concise by serving the same purpose as transitional sentences between sections.

Drafting the Memo

Drafting a brief memo requires nothing more than putting the necessary facts into a few sentences. A memo calling a meeting can be readied for typing in a minute or two. A longer memo requires the same kind of attention as the drafting of a business letter. The outline you prepared in the design phase should make the drafting of the body relatively easy.

Write the draft at one sitting and don't worry about punctuation and other mechanical matters; concentrate on getting the facts and ideas down on paper as quickly as possible and in the proper order. If time allows, set the draft aside before revising.

Revising and Editing the Draft

As with all other documents, it is best to revise the draft of a memo in two stages: Look at the content first, and then edit for correctness. Check to make certain all the facts needed by the reader are included and look again at the outline or list of main points to be certain the parts are in proper sequence. Now is the time to cut out, add, or rearrange sections if you see that those changes will fulfill your purpose better or improve the continuity.

In *editing*, follow the advice given for this stage in the preparation of the business letter. Being letter perfect is probably less important with memos than with letters, but your co-workers will think more highly of you if you set a high standard of correctness for yourself. Memos may be the only means some of those above you may have to form an impression of you; make certain that impression is a positive one.

Here is a first draft of the typing-room memo with editing changes entered in ink. Since the organization was well planned in the design stage, the contents of the first draft do not need to be rearranged.

To: Robert Makowitz, chairperson, English Department

From: Don Peterson and Janet Meis, Instructors

Date: January 10, 1985

Subject: Proposal for Additional Open Hours for Typing Room

It seems to us that the Humanities Division typing room is not open enough hours this semester; we therefore suggest an expanded schedule that will fit the needs of our students better than the current one.

Currently, the typing room is open 9:00 to 3:00 on Monday, Wednesday, and Friday and 9:00 to 11:00 and 2:00 to 3:00 on Tuesday and Thursday. This means that there are no times at which most night students can use the typing room. In addition, the gap from 11:00 to 2:00 on Tuesday and Thursday seems too long. Both of us require that students type their papers for our composition courses, so it's important to us that our students have access to typewriters. Three other instructors, all of whom teach night classes, feel that open hours in the evening are especially important since most of their students aren't on campus during the day.

~~If possible,~~ *w*e'd like to see the room open 9:00 to 9:00 *on* Monday, Tuesday, Wednesday, and Thursday and 9:00 to 4:00 on Friday. Is it possible to hire enough work-study students to keep the typing room open during these expanded hours? This is an important service to students and ~~seems~~ *seems* to us to merit support from our department, in particular.

Producing the Finished Memo

Most companies supply printed memo forms on either whole or half sheets. Use those printed forms unless the memo is very informal or it must be reproduced by ditto or mimeograph. Figure 4.3 is an example of a printed memo form. Company correspondence manuals usually give instructions on the format of memos as well as letters. Follow those instructions. If your company has no printed memo forms, type in the words that would normally be printed by using any of the styles shown in Figure 4.1.

All memos should be typed except the least important and most informal. As with letters, always double-space between elements in the heading and between paragraphs; single-space within paragraphs. If you use headings within the text, be sure they are consistent in form and uni-

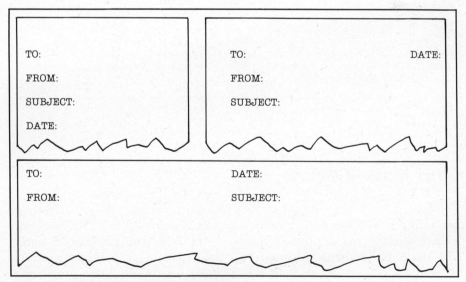

Figure 4.1   Formats for Memo Headings

formly spaced. Proofread the finished copy and initial it next to your name on the FROM line. No signature is needed, but some writers sign their names at the bottom or after their names on the FROM line instead of initialing it. A signature or initial lets the reader know that you have given the memo careful attention. Initialing also shows that if someone else prepared the memo for you, you have read it and approved its contents.

Figure 4.2 is a finished version of the typing-room memo, incorporating all the corrections made in the revision stage.

To: Robert Makowitz, Chairperson, English Department
                        DP   *JM*
From: Don Peterson and Janet Meis, Instructors

Date: January 10, 1985

Subject: Proposal for Additional Open Hours for Typing Room

It seems to us that the Humanities Division typing room is not open enough hours this semester; we therefore suggest an expanded schedule that will fit the needs of our students better than the current one.

Currently, the typing room is open 9:00 to 3:00 on Monday, Wednesday, and Friday and 9:00 to 11:00 and 2:00 to 3:00 on Tuesday and Thursday. This means that there are no times at which most night students can use the typing room. In addition, the gap from 11:00 to 2:00 on Tuesday and Thursday seems too long. Both of us require that students type their papers for our composition courses, so it's important to us that our students have access to typewriters. Three other instructors, all of whom teach night classes, feel that open hours in the evening are especially important since most of their students aren't on campus during the day.

We'd like to see the room open 9:00 to 9:00 on Monday, Tuesday, Wednesday, and Thursday and 9:00 to 4:00 on Friday. Is it possible to hire enough work-study students to keep the typing room open during these expanded hours? This is an important service to students and seems to us to merit support from our department, in particular.

Figure 4.2   A Memo in Finished Form

Other Kinds of Memos

The two memos reproduced in this section illustrate several variations not found in the samples presented earlier. Figure 4.3 is a fairly routine memo written on a printed memo form with the company's name and room for routing information—the latter in case copies need to be sent to readers other than those listed on the TO line. Sometimes routing information for additional copies is given below the body at

INTRA-COMPANY CORRESPONDENCE

TO: DEPARTMENT SECTION HEADS   ROUTE TO:

FROM: MEDICAL SERVICES

DATE: FEBRUARY 2, 1986

FILE: RED CROSS BLOOD DRIVE

SUBJECT: RESCHEDULING OF BLOOD DRIVE DUE TO INCLEMENT WEATHER

      Emerson's annual blood drive has been temporarily cancelled this coming Friday, February 4, 1986, due to the recent snowstorm that hit the St. Louis area.

      The blood drive has been rescheduled for Friday, February 18, 1986, between 8:30 A.M. and 2:30 P.M. in the main auditorium. Your continued participation in the blood drive is greatly appreciated by the American Red Cross and Emerson's Engineering and Space Division.

Figure 4.3 A Memo Using a Printed Company Form
Emerson Electric Co., Electronics & Space Division, St. Louis, Mo.

the left margin, using the letters *cc* for "courtesy copy," as in this sample:

> cc: Vice President for Public Relations
>   Personnel Director

Note the use of a good will statement at the end of the memo.

Figure 4.4 is longer than most memos because it treats an important subject and provides a great deal of detail; it gives advice that will be useful to a large number of people over a long period of time. Note the use of headings, subheadings, and lists to make important information stand out.

Informal Reports

Reports are generally about something that has already happened, though not always. The term *report* implies reporting, or carrying back, news about something—a construction project, an experiment, an accident, a trip, or almost anything of practical value. Generally, reports should be factual, and in the case of an accident report, where the document could be used in legal proceedings, the contents must be strictly factual. Reports can include speculation or opinion if those statements are clearly identi-

Wilson Machine Tool Company

Counseling Center

October 2, 1985

M E M O R A N D U M

TO: All Wilson Department Heads and Supervisors

FROM: Clifford E. Hatch, Director, Counseling Center

SUBJECT: Procedure for securing assistance with psychological emergencies
          and routine psychological consultation

During this calendar year, with its predictable periods of personal and job-related stress, I want to remind you of the resources available to you should you need assistance in responding to psychological emergencies. Pressures are commonly generated by anxieties related to job performance, desire for promotion, working conditions, relations with fellow workers, and difficulties at home. Many employees who can benefit from counseling assistance also need encouragement in seeking such help. The following information may be helpful to you in identifying people with psychological difficulties and in helping them to receive the assistance they may need. The three major types of psychological disturbances and their main symptoms are listed so that you may more readily identify someone with severe psychological distress and seek consultation or make a referral.

Mood Disorders

Mania: Unusual energy, talkativeness, grandiosity, inability to sleep,
        aggressiveness, or combativeness.

Depression: Sadness, crying, withdrawal, suicidal thinking or attempts, or
        loss of energy or interest in work.

Thought Disorders

Paranoia: Suspiciousness; organized belief systems, often that one is being
        watched or in danger of being harmed.
Schizophrenia: Bizarre thoughts or actions, illogical thought patterns.

Situational Disorders

Unusually severe stress from excessive change, death of a loved one, pressure to perform; an abrupt change in work assignment or breakup of a personal relationship producing strong states of fear, anxiety, anger, helplessness, depression, frustration, or impulsive decisions to leave town or to attempt suicide.

24-Hour Psychological Emergency. To secure assistance when a person is threatening suicide or homicide, or whose actions severely frighten or disturb others, phone 622-3531 (Safenet). Ask for the Wilson Company's "Go-Out Crisis Intervention Team" to return your call. Leave your name, location, and phone number. The Go-Out Team will be alerted by telephone page and will return your call. If appropriate, the Go-Out Team will come to the location of the person in need of assistance. If for any reason you have difficulty reaching the Go-Out Team, phone 622-4141, "The Network," a county-wide crisis service operated by Sanborn County Community Mental Health Center.

Telephone Consultation. For psychological information and advice or for
assistance in arranging a referral, phone 772-5321, the Wilson Counseling
Center, open from 8:00 a.m. to 5:00 p.m., and ask for the "Counselor-on-Duty."
If you need information or advice in the evening or on a weekend, use the same
procedure as for an emergency; i.e., phone 622-3531 (Safenet), leave your name
and phone number, and ask for the Go-Out Team to call you.

Counseling Agencies. Listed below are the names and phone numbers of some
of the company and community mental health resources:

Alcohol Resource Center	622-4413
Ambulance (Medical Emergency)	622-6621
Crisis Go-Out Team	622-3531
Sanborn County Mental Health Center	622-4511
Network	622-4141
Wilson Clinical Center	772-7810
Wilson Counseling Center	772-5321
Safenet	622-3531
Women's Center (also Domestic Abuse Center)	622-4352

We continue to seek ways in which we can more effectively respond to the
mental health concerns of the company community. If you have any questions
about the above emergency procedures, or suggestions about ways in which we
might more effectively serve you, I invite you to contact me at your
convenience.

Figure 4.4 A Memo Using Headings and Lists

fied as such. The opinion of an expert in any field is valuable and carries
great weight when decisions are to be made. Reports can range from brief,
routine reports written as memos or on printed forms to fairly complex
accounts of long investigations laid out in a highly structured form called
the *formal report*. The rest of this chapter will deal with several kinds of
informal reports; formal reports will be covered in Chapter 12.

All reports are intended to keep others informed about activities so
that those requiring cooperation can be carried out efficiently. Since everything one does in an organization is related to the activities of others, constant communication is essential. Assembly line supervisors fill out production or progress reports; managers compile these and pass the
information on in more complex reports to planners, who need to know
what has been done in order to draw up a report that sets forth what needs
to be done in the future.

Informal reports are not easy to define since they come in so many
different forms and can cover so many subjects. Generally they range from
a page in length to four or five pages, and they share many of the characteristics of the memos shown in the first part of this chapter, which means
they can range from very informal to quite formal in language and format.
Most deal with things that occur routinely, such as monthly production
or the meeting of committees, or with things planned or expected, such as
a trip to a branch office or a search for a new vice president. On the other
hand, a few deal with unexpected and unplanned events such as accidents,
crimes, machine breakdowns, or wildcat strikes.

The wide variety of situations reported leads quite naturally to a wide variety of forms in the reporting of them. Many organizations try to standardize the reports their employees write by making up printed forms for a variety of situations from accidents to weekly sales. They may also specify how reports in memo form or letter form should look. When you begin to work for a company you should learn, early on, how they want your reports laid out. Some organizations, however, don't provide models or other guidance, and many decisions about both form and content are left up to you. The rest of this chapter will provide some general guidelines for writing informal reports and then will discuss the progress report as a typical example.

Organizing an Informal Report

Like the memo structure suggested in the first part of this chapter, and like many other kinds of documents, the informal report can be divided into a beginning, a middle, and an end. The *beginning* may describe the problem and purpose, as in an ordinary memo, but generally it also provides whatever background is needed, explains the period of time covered, or identifies the place and time of the event—an accident, for example.

The middle, or *development* section, should contain such things as the instrument readings and results in a test report, the narrative of events in a dispute on the shop floor, or the things observed on a trip. *Findings* is another good term for what goes into this section in many reports.

The end, or *conclusion*, contains evaluations of the events or things reported in the middle section or, generally, the conclusions reached. If recommendations for further action are called for, they would come here as well.

The Progress Report

A common kind of informal report is one written to tell others how well a project is proceeding. Called a *progress report*, it can vary from a simple form to be filled out to an elaborate formal report on a large project involving millions of dollars. Many, however, are written as memo or letter reports.

Progress reports come in two kinds, *occasional* and *periodic*. An occasional report is usually the only progress report on a project and is written in response to a special request. Your instructor may ask for an occasional progress report on your research project in the course you may now be taking. A periodic report, as its name implies, is one of a series of reports on a long-term project written at regular intervals, such as monthly or quarterly. Both kinds identify the project clearly and summarize progress on it to the date of the report or during a stated interval. This information is extremely useful to supervisors in planning the work of their departments, since to plan effectively they must know what has been accomplished. They particularly want to know if a project is on schedule or not. This planning purpose is the most important one, but a second purpose is to make those working on a project aware of where it stands. The report can thus serve to inspire greater efforts to meet a deadline or to get the project back on schedule.

In drawing up a progress report, it is extremely important for the writer to be factual and objective, since the temptation is sometimes great to make the report more favorable than the facts warrant. This practice obviously undercuts its purpose since it gives those in charge a false notion of where a project stands. Furthermore, such distortions will probably be exposed when the next progress report is due or the project's completion date arrives. Thus they gain the false reporter only a temporary period of grace.

Most progress reports can be organized into five sections: (1) introduction, (2) work completed, (3) problems encountered, (4) work remaining, (5) conclusions, and if called for, recommendations.

Introduction   In a letter or memo report of a page or two, the opening paragraph should clearly identify the project and give a summary of its current status, stating whether it is on schedule or behind.

Work Completed   This section is likely to be the longest since it is the most important. The writer's most difficult decision is how much detail to include. No hard rule can be set down. If it is a periodic report covering one week of work, you can probably include more details, without its getting out of hand, than in a report that covers three months. Earlier reports on the same or similar projects and an acquaintance with the exact function of the report will help you decide how detailed you should be.

Problems Encountered   Supervisors want to know about the major problems, not the day-to-day ones. This information will give them at least a partial explanation for any delays and may enable them to provide help in overcoming them. This section could be combined with the description of the work completed, since it is in the past or present that problems exist. The future is the realm of promise. Don't make this section a kind of list of excuses for having fallen behind schedule. Single out the real and crucial problems and provide enough detail to convince your reader that they indeed exist.

Work Remaining   Include here the chief tasks remaining and the schedule you hope to follow in completing them. If the readers know the project well, they will know what remains to be done and this section can hit only the high points or be omitted entirely.

Conclusions and Recommendations   This section is a good place for the writer to provide his or her estimate of the project's progress. The conclusions may repeat and expand on the summary given in the introduction, or they may introduce entirely new matters. They should follow clearly from the facts presented in the earlier sections. If one of the conclusions is that changes ought to be made in project plans—deadlines revised or new techniques used—those changes should be described in a set of recommendations.

This plan of organization follows a roughly chronological pattern. For most progress reports that pattern makes good sense, but sometimes it might be better to consider the major parts of a large project separately and cover each part chronologically.

Figure 4.5 is an example of a progress report in memo form. Note that it begins with a section not normally found in a progress report—an informal, personal note explaining why the report was put in writing rather than given orally. The report uses headings to mark the major divisions and makes one recommendation to compensate for the delay in construction.

This progress report has four parts: (1) an opening summary, (2) work completed, (3) work remaining, and (4) conclusions and recommendations. The description of the chief problem encountered—the delay in plumbing work—is combined with the discussion of work completed. Both work completed and work remaining are presented in lists to make the separate elements easier to pick out.

Other Kinds of Informal Reports

As noted earlier, informal reports can be written on virtually any subject of practical value to an organization. Among the typical kinds, in addition to the progress report, are the trip, accident, inspection, test, audit, and recommendation reports. If you keep in mind the purpose of any report you may be assigned, as well as the advice given at the beginning of this chapter, you can produce an effective report on any subject. The company you work for may have its own guidelines for preparing some of the types listed earlier. If not, check the files for copies of reports on these subjects written by others in the company. For some kinds, printed forms may be available to simplify your reporting task.

Key Points in the Chapter

1. Memos are brief, written messages similar to letters but addressed to readers within an organization, not outside it.
2. The format of memos is simpler than that of letters, the tone is usually less formal, and less space is given to creating and maintaining good will.
3. Memos can range in length from a few lines to several pages. It is good to limit them to a page or less, when possible.

To: Robyn McCourt, President, Sewanee Photo Club

From: Stephen Batchelor, Darkroom Committee Chair *SB*

Date: October 22, 1985

Subject: Progress on construction of photo darkroom

You asked that I give a report on construction progress at our next meeting on October 25. Since I will be out of town that night, I am submitting the report in writing. At the meeting you can read from it as much as you see fit.

Summary

Construction work on the darkroom is proceeding on schedule in all areas except plumbing work, which is being done by Peabody Plumbers, a local company. It now looks as though they will not be finished with the plumbing till November 6, two weeks behind schedule. That means the finishing work on floors and walls will be delayed and the whole project won't be finished till November 10. This is the earliest we can hope to finish even if club members put in extra hours of work after November 6.

Work Completed

- The layout of the room was designed and equipment chosen and ordered by September 22.
- The construction space was cleared and walls roughed in by October 12. All work to this point was done by club members.
- Electrical work by Paoli Electric was finished by October 17 except details that must await the installation of print-drying equipment and wallboard.
- Plumbing work was begun on October 18 but was stopped on the 20th with less than 20 percent of it completed. The stoppage was caused by the need to shift workers back to two other projects being completed by the contractor. They have promised to resume work on November 1 and to finish it by the 4th.

Work Remaining

- Plumbing: 80 percent of work remains to be done.
- Electrical: Installation of wall sockets and hookup of print-drying machine.
- Finishing work on walls and floors.
- Installation of cabinets and equipment other than print-drying machine.

Conclusions and Recommendation

If the plumbing work is finished by November 4, as promised, club members should be able to finish the remaining tasks by November 10.

I recommend that to be on the safe side, we reschedule our ribbon cutting and open house from November 12 to November 19.

Figure 4.5   A Progress Report

4. Brief, routine memos can be prepared quickly at one sitting; longer, more important ones should be prepared by using all seven stages in the writing process.
5. Memos of more than about one-half page can use headings to indicate major sections.
6. Informal reports are often a kind of extended memo, but they can also be written as letters or on printed forms.
7. Informal reports serve an extremely wide variety of purposes that cannot easily be served by regular memos or letters, on the one hand, or by formal reports, on the other.

Exercises

1. Write a memo to the president of a club or other organization you belong to suggesting changes in the way meetings are conducted, new ideas for club programs, or ways to gain new members.
2. Find a memo of moderate length in your club's or student organization's files. Rewrite it so that it conforms to the suggestions in this chapter for statement of problem, purpose, and message.
3. Some teachers prefer to have semiformal messages from students conveyed to them in memos. These messages could include reasons for an absence or late paper, proposal of a topic for a paper, or a request for additional time to finish a long report. Ask your instructor if he or she would like you to write memos on subjects such as these.
4. Write an informal report to a current or former employer suggesting ways to improve the method you were taught to carry out your duties. First describe how you currently do the job, evaluate that method, and then propose changes in a list of recommendations.
5. Write an informal progress report on the work you have done toward completion of your long report in this class. Address it to your instructor.
6. Assume you work for a large corporation, such as a bank, hospital, or government agency. One of the employees you supervise, Laura Hamilton, has suddenly begun doing what you consider to be substandard work, although her previous performance has been satisfactory. You confront Laura with the problem, but she doesn't respond. You discuss the situation with your own boss, Malcom Jackoway. He asks you to write him a memo, describing Laura's behavior, in case he must eventually fire her. Write the memo to Jackoway, objectively describing Laura's deteriorating performance on the job.

5 Writing Letters of Application and Résumés

Abstract

A letter of application requests consideration for a job. A résumé presents an applicant's work and educational history. Since only a small percentage of job applicants receive interviews, having the ability to write a good letter and résumé is extremely important. Before drafting, you should gather information about each company to which you apply so you can address yourself to its particular needs; you will also need to gather information about yourself. In your letter, name the position you want, present your main qualifications, and ask for an interview. In your résumé, present your educational and work experience, add some personal information, and provide a list of references. After revising the content of your work, decide which letter format to use and select a good layout for the sections of your résumé. Edit both carefully; both must be 100 percent correct in spelling, grammar, and punctuation. Neatness and clarity are also very important in the final document.

Two of the most important pieces of writing you may ever produce are the letter of application and résumé. A letter of application is a business letter requesting consideration for a specific job or for work in a particular area of employment. The résumé—also referred to as a *data sheet* or *curriculum vitae*—is a highly organized presentation of your work and educational background. Lack of a good letter and résumé may seriously limit your job prospects, but an excellent letter and résumé may give you the edge you need to succeed in obtaining an interview. Competition for jobs is rigorous in nearly every field, and even in fields with many openings, job candidates find themselves fighting for the best positions.

Every time you submit a letter of application and résumé, you are in effect entering a writing contest. Only the best win an interview. You should also realize that executives or personnel managers who appraise job applications are to some extent looking for reasons to throw applications away. A single job advertisement today may produce over a hundred responses, but of that number only about 10 percent will be interviewed; therefore, about 90 percent are doomed in advance to be discarded. Though some applications will be rejected because their writers clearly do not meet the minimum job qualifications, others will be eliminated in the first round of review simply because they fail to present the applicant well: The letter and résumé may be poorly worded, ungrammatical, incomplete, too skimpy, too long, or too disorganized. When a great number of people compete for a single position, an employer need consider only those who present themselves effectively.

Your job in writing a letter of application and résumé is to make sure you are among those seriously considered for an opening and not among those routinely rejected. Writing a good letter and résumé is more difficult than it may sound. The task presents a considerable challenge, involving in-depth audience and self-analysis; attention to organization, layout, and headings; and meticulous proofreading of the final copy. Yet once you have produced a résumé, you have a basic document you can continue to modify and update for the rest of your career, and your first letter of application can serve as a model for others. Since most professionals today do not remain with a single employer throughout their careers, there is a good chance that you will use your skills in writing a letter and résumé over and over.

Although some people trust a professional employment service to produce their résumés, we do not recommend this practice. Professionally written résumés too often have a "canned" look and are sometimes noticeably standardized in appearance. Such a document is not likely to impress an employer. In addition, though a résumé can be duplicated and sent to a number of prospective employers, the letter of application that introduces it should be tailored to address the concerns of each organization to which you apply. An employment service will not produce all the different letters you will need, so it is important that you know how to write them yourself.

The purpose of this chapter is to teach you to do an excellent job of producing these two critical documents. Writing a good letter of application and résumé will involve attention to all seven stages in the process of practical writing.

Defining the Problem and Purpose

The problem you face in writing a letter of application and résumé is usually quite clear: You want a job. However, you may also write such a letter in other closely related situations, such as when you want an internship or when you want to advance to another position within an organization. The appropriate first step in many of these situations is to submit a letter and résumé to a personnel manager, supervisor, or screening committee. Your ultimate purpose in writing is to get a position, of course, but the immediate reason for writing a letter and résumé is *to obtain an interview*. Since this is a book mainly about writing—not speaking—this chapter is devoted to teaching you how to write a good letter of application and résumé, but a few tips on how to conduct yourself in an interview are included at the end of this chapter.

Determining the Audience

Before even planning a draft, you should find out all you can about the organizations and individuals to whom you plan to send letters and résumés. This is a step often omitted by job applicants, but this omission is also a major reason why many letters are rejected. An organization will hire you in order to meet *its needs*, not yours. Therefore, find out as much as possible about the organization. A description of the kind of work you would like is meaningless to employers unless you can also make clear exactly how you will help them solve their problems.

Information about large organizations is relatively easy to find, but information about small, local concerns is more difficult to locate. Nevertheless, some information about both kinds of institutions can often be found in even small college libraries. A reference librarian can help you, but first you yourself should check some of the following sources.

Telephone Books

The white pages of telephone books will provide the name, address, telephone number, and number of locations of an organization. The size of the organization may be judged from the number of departments listed or from the number of locations. The yellow pages of telephone books can also be useful by providing an idea of the competition facing a company in a given area. Company ads also often describe hours, services, and products.

Local Chambers of Commerce

You can sometimes find information about local hard-to-research organizations through your chamber of commerce. The telephone number of your chamber of commerce can be found in the telephone directory.

Better Business Bureau

When researching a small company, a call to your local Better Business Bureau will let you know whether or not complaints have been made against the organization.

The Company Itself

If an organization is fairly large, it may have a public relations department that can provide you with brochures and information about the company.

Company Annual Reports

Many college libraries maintain a file of annual reports produced by large local and national publicly owned businesses. You can find information about the size, holdings, interests, and general concerns of an organization through its annual report.

Periodicals and Newspapers

Large or unusual companies may be the subject of articles published in various magazines and newspapers. To find particular articles, you will need to use newspaper and periodical indexes, many of which are described in Chapter 6 on library research. Of particular use in researching companies is the *Business Periodicals Index.* This index is arranged by subject and gives article title, author, periodical title, volume, pages, and date. If a company you are researching has been discussed in an article in a business periodical, it will be listed in this index under the company's name. You can also use this index to find out the important issues and the competitive situation in the general area you are researching.

Reference Works

A number of standard reference works can help you find at least a minimum of information about an organization—and sometimes much more. The books discussed in this section should lead you to names, addresses, and phone numbers of companies; products or services; names of subsidiaries, branches, or plants; names of officers, directors, and managers; numbers of employees; and financial details. Many of the works provide Standard Industrial Classification (SIC) numbers. These SIC numbers are numeric categories established by the U.S. Department of Commerce to identify all industries. Every corporation and type of business is assigned at least one industry SIC number. Many have more than one. The list of SIC numbers tells you the kinds of work a company is engaged in. A list of SIC numbers and corresponding industries appears in the front of Dun and Bradstreet's *Million Dollar Directory.*

Directory of Corporate Affiliations This annual publication lists parent companies and their divisions and subsidiaries and provides address, telephone number, type of business, top corporate officers, approximate sales, number of employees, and more.

Fairchild's Financial Manual of Retail Stores This manual provides information about general merchandising chains, discount chains, mail order firms, drugstores, food stores, shoe stores, and so on. Over 475 firms are listed. The manual provides company name, address, and telephone number; officers and directors; business activities; number of stores; financial data; acquisitions; and divisions and subsidiaries. Use the index in the back of the book for the page number of the retail store you are researching.

Million Dollar Directory This very useful reference work consists of three volumes: Volume I, companies with a net worth of $1,200,000 or more; Volume II, companies with a net worth of $800,000 to $1,200,000; Volume III, companies with a net worth of $500,000 to $800,000. Each volume lists companies in three ways: alphabetically, numerically by SIC number, and geographically. The geographic listing might be particularly valuable to students looking for the names of companies in a particular region of the country. The directory gives the company's name, address, and telephone number; annual sales to the nearest million; number of employees; lines of business; names and titles of principals and directors; and division names with lines of business, SIC numbers, and import and export information. Each volume has an index to all three volumes.

Billion Dollar Directory This publication lists corporations with a net worth of a billion dollars or more and provides the same kind of information given in the *Million Dollar Directory*.

Standard & Poor's Corporate Descriptions This six-volume collection lists more than 6,300 of the largest companies and provides background reports, plant locations, subsidiaries, securities, annual earnings, and number of employees. It is arranged alphabetically.

Other Reference Works There are also other reference works with similar information about particular kinds of companies, such as the *Standard Directory of Advertisers*. Your reference librarian can help you find the best directories for the kinds of businesses you are researching. There are also local business directories for all metropolitan areas. Students in St. Louis, Missouri, for example, can refer to *Large Employers of Metro St. Louis*, published by the Regional Commerce and Growth Association; the *Missouri Directory of Manufacturing and Mining*; or *Contacts Influential: St. Louis*. Check with your reference librarian for the titles of similar works describing organizations in your area.

Guides to Research

There are also general guides to researching business information. Three that may help you are *Where to Find Business Information: A Worldwide Guide for Everyone Who Needs the Answers to Business Questions*, by David M. Brownstone; *Business Information Sources*, by Lorna M. Daniells; and *How to Find Information About Companies*, published by Washington Researchers. These sources will give you the titles of additional sources of information—not the information itself.

Collecting the Data

If you have used the library and other resources to find information about the company for which you wish to work, you have already begun collecting the necessary data for your letter of application and résumé. However, in addition to gathering data about prospective employers, you will need to collect information about yourself. Therefore, before proceeding further, you need to take stock—as honestly and objectively as possible. The information you will need falls into three general categories: educational experience, work experience, and personal information. You will use some of this information in your letter of application and some in your résumé—both of which will be discussed in detail in the next section. But for now, simply gather and organize the information described in the next three subsections.

Education

Your educational experience will show a prospective employer that you have completed at least the minimal educational requirements for a position, but you can use the education section of your résumé to show much more. By adding related information, you highlight aptitudes and experiences that show you are different from the typical applicant. It is important to make yourself stand out from the other candidates, all possessing the same basic credentials.

Begin by listing the correct name and address of each school you have attended, beginning with high school. Add the inclusive years of your attendance—for example, *September 1983–June 1984.* You should cite months as well as years when indicating time spent in military or trade schools, but you can cite years alone when listing high school and college education.

After getting down these basics, consider adding the following kinds of information to each section:

- *High school:* Try to recall what made you special. Was your grade point average high? Did you receive any honors or awards? What extracurricular activities did you engage in? What leadership positions did you obtain? What special educational workshops or programs did you attend? What special or extra courses did you elect to take?
- *College:* Consider all the previous questions and also the following: What percentage of your college expenses did you earn yourself? What scholarships or fellowships did you win? What awards were you nominated for? What special skills did you learn, in addition to those typically learned by students in your field of study?
- *Military schools:* Many people continue their education in the military.

Whether through formal instruction or through on-the-job training, what additional skills did you learn in the military?
- *Trade schools:* Begin by listing certificates or awards obtained. Consider also describing specific technical skills you acquired or naming equipment you can operate.

Work Experiences

In collecting data about your work experiences, you may have to consult notes, employers, and telephone directories to gather all the information you will need. For every place you have ever worked, write out the following information:

- Inclusive dates of employment
- Full name and address of the organization employing you
- Your job title or position
- A list of your major responsibilities, duties, or accomplishments
- The name of your immediate supervisor

Personal Data

Although educational and work experiences are the two most important parts of any job application, personal experiences also play a part. The details you provide in this section of your résumé should portray you as a well-rounded and stable person, someone willing and able to get along with others and interested in some areas outside the concerns of work. If you were choosing people to interview, and possibly work with, wouldn't you prefer to hire someone interesting and likeable as well as competent? A letter of application and résumé will be read by another person, not a computer. The personal information you provide should make you sound like a human being to this reader. In collecting personal information for your job application, consider the following categories:

- Personal interests, such as sailing, stamp collecting, or gourmet cooking
- Athletic activities, both individual and group
- Clubs and organizations to which you belong
- Travel experiences and years lived abroad
- Fluency in languages, written or spoken
- Any special aptitudes
- Awards and honors
- Certifications
- Height and weight—especially for jobs requiring physical labor
- Birthdate
- State of health
- Marital status and number of children
- Professional memberships and affiliations
- Military service: years spent, training, and rank upon discharge

This list is not exhaustive; there are other things you might wish to let an employer know about you. As you consider what to include, ask yourself whether or not the detail will help to make you stand out from all the other candidates with the same minimum qualifications as yourself.

Designing the Document

The letter of application and résumé are nearly always sent together to a prospective employer and are often thought of as a single unit, since they present some of the same information and reinforce one another. They are separate documents with entirely different designs, however, and will be discussed separately in this section.

Designing the Letter of Application

The letter of application for a job usually is sent to a specific reader, requesting consideration for a particular position. The only exception to this general rule occurs when a job applicant responds to an advertisement that conceals the name and address of the organization offering the position, or when an applicant sends a bulk mailing of letters and résumés to organizations around the country. The return on such "blanket" mailings is generally extremely poor, however; therefore, this chapter will describe how to write a good letter of application to a specific organization. Such a letter cannot be duplicated and sent to a number of firms. It must be designed for a particular institution.

The design of such a letter includes three sections, usually drafted as three separate paragraphs. In these three sections you must

- Name the exact position you seek.
- Present your main qualifications for the job and try in a few sentences to explain what distinguishes you from your competition and what you can do for the organization.
- Ask directly for an interview.

Further discussion of these three divisions, including examples of specific wording, appears in the "Drafting the Document" section of this chapter. However, keeping this three-part outline in mind will help you when you draft.

Designing the Résumé

A résumé includes four basic sections, but their order of presentation can vary:

- Your educational experiences, listed in *reverse* chronological order
- Your work experiences, listed in *reverse* chronological order

- Personal information about yourself
- A list of references

The general rule to follow in writing a résumé is to put your best foot forward in terms of ordering the contents. This means that you should lead with your best credentials for a particular position. When applying for a job for which your education best qualifies you, begin your résumé with that section; if, on the other hand, your work experiences best qualify you for a job, begin with that. The choice of design is up to you. Some people write two different résumés—one leading with work and one with education—and send the appropriate one to each organization to which they apply.

The third part of your résumé should contain whatever personal information you have chosen to include. Previously recommended résumé designs placed this section first, directly beneath the heading, but this practice is changing, and for good reason. Although an employer may want to know something about your personal life, your marital status and hobbies are really the least important things about you as an employee. Therefore they should be described later.

The fourth section of the résumé is the list of references. A list of three persons is recommended.

Drafting the Document

You now know the three main sections of a letter of application and should have chosen a basic approach—work or education section first— for your résumé. With your notes about yourself and about the company to which you are applying in front of you, you will be ready to draft your documents. As you write, concentrate on content and wording, rather than layout and the use of headings. You can make decisions about these matters when you review and revise your draft.

Although the letter of application will appear before the résumé when read by an employer, we suggest that you reverse the order and draft the résumé first. Since in the letter you will often refer to the résumé, it makes sense to write that document first, so you will know clearly what you refer to in your letter.

Drafting the Résumé

A résumé is a highly organized but brief piece of technical writing. Its purpose is to highlight your major qualifications for a job in such a way as to make it easy for an employer to see and understand your strengths as a job applicant. You should make every word count. If your résumé is too long, too detailed, or too difficult to read and understand, it may well be discarded. On the other hand, you should not omit truly important details. Include all critical information about yourself. Before you complete a final draft of your résumé, you will probably revise, edit, and retype several times, but the time spent will be worth the effort. Unlike the letter of application, the résumé is a standard document and can be duplicated and sent to various employers, so you may use it many times.

A résumé must be short. Employers do not have the time to pore over lengthy and long-winded documents. In "Designing an Advertisement for Yourself" (*Money*, January 1974) Caroline Donnelley quotes executive recruiter Peter Lauer of Chicago, who flatly stated, "I don't spend more than 15 seconds on a résumé." This may sound unfair, but it is not uncommon.

The résumé of a graduating student should fill one typed page but be no longer than two pages. The résumé of a mid-career executive should fill no more than three pages. The better organized and designed your résumé is, the better your chances of being seriously considered for an interview.

Although brevity, appearance, and the organization of a résumé are very important, concentrate at this stage, as suggested previously, on selecting and wording information. During revision you can add and delete, experiment with various placements of headings, decide what lettering to use, and handle other such considerations. At the conclusion of this section, three sample résumés appear. They will give you some idea of possibilities in layout to consider as you move into reviewing and revising.

The Heading   The heading of your résumé must contain your name (including middle initial or full middle name), address, and home telephone number. You may also wish to include your work telephone number and the date of the completed résumé. These elements should be arranged neatly and attractively across the top of the page. Some people center their name under the opening phrase "Résumé of . . . " or "Vita of. . . . " In writing the word *résumé*, either omit the accent marks over each *e* or add them by hand (as in *résumé*). American typewriters usually do not have the right key to add a proper accent mark; the apostrophe doesn't have the right slant.

The Career Objective Statement   Some employment counselors recommend beginning your résumé with a statement of your career objective. The best such statements are brief and simple, such as "I am seeking a management trainee position in the manufacturing industry." If you choose to write a career objective, avoid lofty, pretentious language and sweeping statements such as "I desire a challenging position in a dynamic company with state-of-the-art capabilities." This sort of statement doesn't really tell an employer anything about you and succeeds mainly in making you sound like an egotist.

Those who advise against including any career objective statement in a résumé argue that it can only limit your opportunities. If your objective statement is too general it is useless, and if it is too specific it may give an employer the impression that you would accept only a narrow range of positions, when in fact you might consider other possibilities.

The choice of whether or not to state a career objective in your résumé is up to you, but in general it seems best to omit it.

Educational Experience The first major section in the résumé of most students describes education, since this is generally the student's strongest asset. Of course, if your work experiences better qualify you for a particular job, lead with that.

In the education section, list all the schools you have ever attended, *beginning* with the school you now attend and working back to your high school. Do not list your grade school. Professionals in mid-career often omit mention of their high school education, unless they attended a particularly prestigious high school. The high school education of an applicant who has completed college and advanced in a career is of little interest to an employer.

Along with the name and address of each school you have attended, cite the inclusive years of your attendance and add a statement summarizing the work you completed. After the high school section you might write "Graduate" or "Completed G.E.D." If you did not receive a high school diploma or its equivalent, it is better to omit mention of high school and to cite only your college degree. For colleges from which you did not obtain a degree, state the number of hours you accumulated and your grade point average, if it was good. A good grade point average is generally considered to be one of 3.0 or above on a 4.0 scale.

You can also add other relevant information to this section. Options include major coursework completed, special electives taken, or particular skills learned. Do *not* list courses like English Composition 101 or College Algebra 101 since these are courses commonly taken by every student. Think of things that make you different from others with your degree.

In addition, students in some fields should list particular skills that employers will want to know about. For example, data processing students should list computer languages they have mastered. In selecting information, think in terms of the employer's needs as well as of your own special competencies.

Work Experience Work experience is always a major selling point, even if the work is not related to the job for which you are applying. Having worked shows you have initiative and stability and that you can handle responsibility. You should list all work experience, as a rule, again working backward from your most recent or present work to your first job. If you have never worked for a salary you can cite volunteer work.

For each job you have held, provide inclusive dates of employment and the name and address of the company employing you. Indicate also which jobs were held part time. We suggest you add an additional two, or possibly four, other kinds of information:

- Your job title or a word describing your position
- Your responsibilities, duties, or accomplishments
- The name of your immediate supervisor
- Your reason for leaving

The first two items on this list are worth including in any résumé. The name of your supervisor is not always important, and you may know that the person is no longer with the company, so inclusion of this information is optional. Some employers indicate that they wish to know why employees have left previous positions; whether or not you include this information is up to you.

You may want to consider dividing your work experience into two separate sections: Related Work Experience and Nonrelated Work Experience. If you have worked at a number of different kinds of jobs, this division can help employers see easily the things in which they are most interested.

If you have worked at a number of nonrelated, part-time jobs, you do not need to include them all on your résumé. Try, however, to cite some activity—either work or schooling—to account for what you did with your time since you graduated from high school. Indicating only the years of these activities—not the months—in your chronology can help you deal with periods of time when you were, in fact, neither employed nor in school.

Finally, since the purpose of a résumé is to highlight your accomplishments, you should consider describing advances you made while employed at one particular organization. People who hold a job for a number of years seldom stay at the same level of employment. Show your career growth within an organization by citing the dates of your promotions and the changes in your responsibilities. Figure 5.1 shows how this can be done on a résumé.

Personal Details   What personal details you include are entirely up to you, and occasionally this section is omitted altogether, although we advise you to include it. You may choose to present your personal information in narrative form (in a brief paragraph) or to list it in the way you have presented other information in your résumé. If you would like to explain something unusual about yourself, such as that you are a woman returning to work after a period of raising children, you may wish to place this information in the personal details section and to use a narrative approach. Review the list of personal information you wrote about yourself while collecting data for ideas about what to include in this section of your résumé.

Throughout this and other sections, use only information that will be seen as positive by your employer. You should *never* lie, as this would

---

Résumé
of
Joe C. Simmons
5070 DeGiverville
(314) 862-7867   St. Louis, MO   63112   October 19, 1982

Employment History

1966-Present   Federal Reserve Bank of St. Louis, St. Louis, MO
               Check Department, Check Processing Division

       1978 - Promoted to Manager, Evening Shift

               Under my direction productivity on the Evening Shift improved
               25%, making it the most productive of the three shifts.

       1975 - Promoted to Administrative Assistant

               Appointed chairman of the Operations Improvement Committee,
               responsible for developing and implementing numerous
               operational changes.

       1972 - Promoted to General Supervisor, Evening Shift

               Responsible for supervision of 35 full-time and 35 part-time
               employees.

       1970 - Promoted to Supervisor

               Responsible for supervision of clerks performing various
               phases of the check-processing operation.

       1966 - Employed as Mail Clerk

               Held various other clerical positions within the department;
               given more responsible clerical assignments as skills improved.

Figure 5.1   Section of Résumé Showing Promotions

be grounds for immediate dismissal, but you do not need to include negative information about yourself. If, for example, your health is only fair,
do not mention your state of health. If you have five children and you
think your employer might think your parental obligations would interfere with your work, don't mention your children in your résumé. Do
include your birthdate, but don't specify your age. If you do, your résumé
will be out of date as soon as you have another birthday.

Once you have an interview, you may be asked pointed questions
about your marriage, health, and ability to handle various problems that
may affect your performance. At that time you must be prepared to
answer all questions fully, but it is often easier to explain problems in
person than to discuss them in your résumé.

Finally, do not indicate your race, religion, sex, or political affiliation, except as part of a description of organizations in which you are active or by which you were employed. Stating such things may be seen by some employers as unprofessional or as an attempt to curry favor. Other companies actually discard all applications with such information in order to avoid accusations of prejudice or possible lawsuits. The *Equal Educational Opportunity and Equal Pay Compliance Handbook* specifies kinds of questions that employers may not ask on applications forms; these questions include anything concerning race, sex, religion, or type of citizenship. Most employers also do not wish to solicit such information through résumés, since considering this kind of information in selecting an employee is illegal—unless it can be proved that the information has a direct bearing on the job.

As with the section on work, you may wish to subdivide your section on personal details. Headings such as PERSONAL INFORMATION, MILITARY EXPERIENCE, PROFESSIONAL AFFILIATIONS, PROFESSIONAL ACTIVITES, CERTIFICATES HELD, or AWARDS AND HONORS can be used to announce each section.

List of References   The final section of your résumé deals with references. The best people to use as references are teachers and former employers. You may also list as character references people such as your minister or coach, but the best references are those who can testify to your competency in a work or work-related situation. *Never* list relatives or personal friends unless they also happen to be your teachers or employers. Also, never list a name unless the person has agreed beforehand to act as a reference. If someone you want to list as a reference hesitates upon being asked, don't use that person; list as references only people you can count on. For each reference, provide name, professional title, place of employment, and business address. Consider providing each reference's telephone number.

There is also an alternative way to handle references. Instead of listing references on your résumé, simply write "References Available on Request" at the bottom. Many employment counselors advise this approach. It saves space on the résumé and generally guarantees that your references will be contacted only by employers seriously interested in hiring you.

Figures 5.2 through 5.4 are complete résumés. Evaluate them in light of the suggestions made in this section.

Drafting the Letter of Application

Whenever possible, address your letter of application to a *particular person.* If you are not answering a blind ad, use the resources described in Determining the Audience to find the correct name and business title of the person within an organization to whom you should apply. Draft the body of the letter in three sections.

Résumé of
David Frederick Hamilton
4138 Flad Avenue
St. Louis, MO 63110
(314)772-9876

OBJECTIVE

I am interested in a position as an engineer within a company specializing in the development of microcomputers.

EDUCATION

1980–1984   University of Missouri at Rolla, Rolla, MO 63145
Received Bachelor of Science degree in Electrical and Electronic Engineering

Graduated Cum Laude
Member Tau Beta Pi, National Engineering Honor Society, and Eta Kappa Nu, National Electrical Engineering Society; Corresponding Secretary for the latter

1976–1980   McKinley High School, St. Louis, MO 63110
Graduate, top 10% of class.

WORK EXPERIENCE

1982–1984   University of Missouri at Rolla
Position: Electrical Engineering Aide, part time
Duties: Operated a thin film deposition unit in a microelectronics lab

1981   Jay's Records
1198 Penn Street, Rolla, MO 63145
Position: Record Salesman and Clerk, part time
Duties: Sold, stocked, and ordered records and tapes, especially jazz and folk music

PERSONAL DETAILS

Date of Birth: September 12, 1961   Health: Excellent

Single   Hobbies: Backpacking
                                                                              Rockclimbing
Second language: German   Collecting jazz records
                            Reading: Excellent   Playing guitar
                            Speaking: Fair   Building computers

REFERENCES AVAILABLE ON REQUEST.

Figure 5.2   Standard Résumé

Data Sheet of
DALE M. ADAMS
3077 Knox Avenue
St. Louis, MO 63139

(314) 644-2299   January 20, 1982

EDUCATION

1980-present   St. Louis Community College at Forest Park, St. Louis, MO
               63110
               I will receive my Associate of Science Degree in Mechanical
               Engineering Technology in May 1982. My cumulative grade
               point average is 3.76 of 4.00.

               Major Courses: Hydraulics Pneumatics
                                Energy Conversion
                                Mechanical Design I and II
                                Report Writing

1978-1979   St. Louis University, St. Louis, MO 63110

               Major Courses: Calculus I and II
                                University Physics
                                Chemistry I and II

1974-1978   Southwest High School, St. Louis, MO 63139
               I graduated in June 1978.

WORK EXPERIENCE

1980-present   Part time during school
               St. Louis Community College at Forest Park
               5600 Oakland Avenue, St. Louis, MO   63110

               Position: Student Assistant, Mechanical Engineering Lab
               Duties: I am responsible for setting up experiments and
               demonstrations, for designing and manufacturing projects for
               class activities, and for drafting revisions of existing project
               drawings.

1978-present   Part time during school, full time during summer
               Bayer's Garden Shops
               3401 Hampton Avenue, St. Louis, MO 63139

               Position: Salesman/Gardener
               Duties: I am responsible for the sale and care of shrubbery and
               tropical plants, for trouble-shooting ailments of plants, and for
               the sale of chemical products. Business is seasonal, so I put in
               extensive overtime during peak business periods.

<u>PERSONAL DETAILS</u>

I am a 21-year-old single male in excellent health. My hobbies include motorcycling, archery, hunting, and carpentry. I am willing to travel and to relocate.

<u>REFERENCES AVAILABLE ON REQUEST</u>

Figure 5.3 Data Sheet

Janet E. Solomon
1409 East Sixth Street
St. Louis, MO   63104

Home: (314) 647-5099
Work: (314) 644-9763

EDUCATION:
1982-1984

St. Louis Community College at Forest Park,
5600 Oakland Avenue, St. Louis, Missouri 63110.
I will complete my Associate Degree in Data Processing
in June 1984. My grade point average is 3.3 of 4.0.

Relevant Courses:

COBOL
Fortran
RPG
Computer Concepts
Logical Methods

1978-1982

University City High School
7401 Balson, University City, MO 63130
Graduated June 1980, 31st in a class of 206.

WORK EXPERIENCE:
1982-Present

Position: Lab Assistant, part-time
St. Louis Community College at Forest Park
Computer Center
5600 Oakland Avenue, St. Louis, Missouri 63110.

Responsibilities: Monitoring Hewlett Packard 5000,
orienting students to the IBM 370 using CICS operating
system and the Apple Nestar system, assisting in general
debugging and program problem solving.

1981-Present

Position: waitress, part-time
Cheshire Inn and Lodge
6306 Clayton Road, Clayton, Missouri 63117

ACHIEVEMENTS:	Dean's List four consecutive semesters.
	Data Processing Management Association 1983 Scholarship Award.
	Member of Phi Theta Kappa Honor Society.
ACTIVITIES:	President, Student Chapter, Data Processing Management Association—Forest Park.
	Contributor to college newspaper, *The Scene.*
PERSONAL DATA:	Date of Birth: January 20, 1964 Health: Excellent Marital Status: Married, one child Interests: sailing scuba diving chess creative writing playing guitar
REFERENCES:	Ms. Diane Young Chairperson, Data Processing Department St. Louis Community College at Forest Park 5600 Oakland Avenue, St. Louis, Missouri 63110.
	Mr. David Daniel Professor, Data Processing Department St. Louis Community College at Forest Park 5600 Oakland Avenue, St. Louis, Missouri 63110.
	Mr. George F. Williams General Manager, Cheshire Inn 6306 Clayton Road, Clayton, Missouri 63117.

Figure 5.4   Extended Résumé

First Section   Begin by stating clearly the exact position for which you are applying or the kind of job you want. If you are responding to a particular advertisement, you might open by referring to it. Consider also using the "name" opening, in which you name the person who informed you of the open position or encouraged you to apply. Be careful with this approach, however. Always ask the individual involved for permission to use his or her name, and don't use a name unless you are sure the individual you are referring to is well respected within the organization.

Conclude the first section by stating directly what you feel to be your best overall qualification for the job, usually either your education or work experience, although both could apply equally. Be positive. Use the "you" approach and state your qualification in terms of the organization's interests, not your own. Here are three sample first sections.

Please consider my qualifications for the position of library technical assistant in your audiovisual department. I am already familiar with your extensive collection of films, tapes, recordings, and artworks; my experience with them comes from personal use, my work as a teaching assistant in the Normandy School District, and my coursework in the Library Technical Assistant Program at St. Louis Community College.

Jane Williams, a maintenance engineer in your Offshore Division, has informed me of your opening for a maintenance manager. I would like you to consider me as a candidate for this position. I have majored in engineering management at the New Jersey Institute of Technology and have also completed extensive coursework in mechanical engineering. I feel confident I could be an asset to your organization.

Please consider my qualifications for the position of programmer with McDonnell Douglas Information Systems Group. I understand McDonnell Douglas is always searching for individuals with a broadly based education in data processing. My four years of study at Washington University have given me experience working with a variety of commercial languages, and my duties as a computer lab assistant have enabled me to develop systems programming skills.

Second Section   Your aim throughout your letter and résumé should be to distinguish yourself from your competition, most of whom will possess the same basic credentials. In the second section of your letter of application, follow the advice of W. Dean Ferres, lecturer to students at New York University, and "position" yourself as an applicant.

"Positioning," a technique practiced in advertising, is emphasizing a product's strongest points for a particular section of the market. In this case, the product you must promote is yourself. The market is your potential employer.

Look over the notes you made in collecting data for your letter and résumé and determine the things that make you *unique*, that separate you from your competitors. Your special appeal might be that you are consistently a high achiever, that you are particularly good at dealing with people, or that you have an unusual amount of practical work experience. Other positions might stress your ability to speak several languages, your strong mathematical ability, or your unusual creativity.

In choosing a position to emphasize, remember that (1) it must help show that you can meet the organization's needs, and (2) it must be objectively verifiable. For example, don't say you are creative unless you can add evidence, either in the letter or résumé, to support your claim.

This section of your letter is likely to be the longest. The examples that follow continue the three letters begun in the first section.

I will receive my Associate's Degree in Applied Science as a Library Technical Assistant from St. Louis Community College at Florissant Valley this June. I also have technical film knowledge and experience gained from working for the Fotomat Corporation. In addition, I am a certified religion teacher through the Paul VI Institute. My seven years of classroom experience have shown me the value of audiovisual materials as integral teaching tools and as aesthetic works.

I will receive my Bachelor of Science in Engineering Management in May of 1986. My coursework has included 30 hours of mechanical engineering, including all basic mechanical engineering courses. As part of my management curriculum, I have completed courses in accounting, computer programming, and economics. I have also completed a design project in computer integrated manufacturing. In addition, my hobby of restoring classic automobiles has further enhanced my practical understanding of machine design and operation.

I will complete my Bachelor of Science Degree in Computer Science this June. In addition to 48 hours of data processing coursework, I have completed 21 hours of business-related courses. I have also been independently studying the field of robotics, an area in which I understand McDonnell Douglas is becoming increasingly involved.

Third Section   In the final section of your letter of application, ask directly for an interview. This is the purpose of the letter and should be stated clearly. If you have not already done so, you may also wish to indicate when you will be available for work and whether or not you are willing to relocate. Be sure to explain how the company can contact you, and refer to your enclosed résumé, which contains your address and telephone number. The following examples of third sections finish the three letters begun earlier.

May I request an interview to discuss this position and my qualifications? I can be reached at home by telephone anytime after 2:30 p.m. My telephone number and address can be found at the top of the enclosed résumé. Thank you for your consideration of my application.

May I have an interview with you to discuss this position? I can be available immediately, and I am willing to relocate. My telephone number and address are on the enclosed data sheet. I look forward to hearing from you.

I would very much appreciate the opportunity to discuss with you my qualifications for a position at McDonnell Douglas. May I have the privilege of an interview? The enclosed résumé includes both my work telephone number, where I can be reached Monday, Wednesday, and Friday from 2:00 to 6:00 p.m., and my home telephone number. I am available at your convenience.

The Closing   Probably the best way to close a letter of application is to use the conventional "Sincerely yours." Be conservative in this matter. Under no circumstances close with anything other than a standard closing phrase. Finishing with something like "Best Wishes" won't advance your employment prospects.

Two complete letters of application follow (Figures 5.5 and 5.6). Evaluate them in terms of the suggestions made in this section.

Reviewing and Reworking the Document

The previous examples of letters and résumés provide models for you to follow in making decisions about the layout and lettering of your work. In drafting, you were asked to concentrate mainly on selection and wording of the content. Now look at your drafts to choose a final format and to edit your documents. *The final copy of your letter of application and résumé should be 100 percent perfect in spelling, grammar, and punctua-*

8911 Drexel Drive
St. Louis, MO 63110
February 16, 1985

Mr. John Ross
Director of Personnel
Anheuser-Busch Companies, Inc.
One Busch Place
St. Louis, MO 63118

Dear Mr. Ross:

The manager of Employee Records, Mr. James Ryan, has told me that you have
an open position for a secretary in your Employee Relations Department. I
would appreciate your consideration of my qualifications for the opening. I am
presently working as a secretary for the marketing and communications
manager of Anheuser-Busch Employees' Credit Union and have seven years
secretarial experience with Mobil Oil Corporation. I am also a certified Wang
word-processing operator.

I understand that you are looking for an experienced secretary who also has
good organizational skills. I believe I have the qualities you want. When I was
employed by Mobil Oil Corporation, I helped plan many of the district's
meetings and was responsible for arranging speaking engagements for the
district manager with various civic organizations of St. Louis city and county.
I also helped organize and implement the first credit card program for the
credit union where I am presently employed.

I have explained my basic experience and qualifications, but there are
undoubtedly details you would like to have clarified. May I do so in an
interview? My address and telephone number for both work and home are
provided at the top of my enclosed résumé. I would be pleased to hear from you
at any time.

Sincerely yours,

May E. Harris

May E. Harris

Enclosure

Figure 5.5   Letter of Application

tion. Any error in such routine concerns could result in your letter and
résumé being discarded.

Revising the Letter of Application

Choose a letter format. Your letter of application may be written in full
left or balanced layout. However, a letter of application is a personal letter, written from one individual to another, and the balanced layout provides a more personal appearance than the highly businesslike full left
form. See Figures 5.5 and 5.6 to compare the two formats.

```
                                    1028 Manor Drive
                                    St. Louis, MO  63132
                                    February 27, 1985


Ms. Betty Pollard
Personnel Director
Northwestern Bank and Trust Company
1500 St. Louis Ave.
St. Louis, MO  63102

Dear Ms. Pollard:

I would like you to consider my qualifications for the position of computer
programmer in your Data Processing Department. I have been studying
computer programming at St. Louis Community College at Florissant Valley for
several semesters and expect to receive an Associate's Degree in May 1985.

During my time at Florissant Valley, I have studied COBOL I and II, RPG, and
BASIC programming languages. We use the HP 2000 computer, which I
understand you use in your company.

While I've been studying, I've also been working full time and raising a family.
I've been employed at Packaging Corporation of America for seven years and
have a good record as a machinist there. I am especially proud of the fact that
in those years I have missed only two days of work. More details about my
education and work experience are provided in the enclosed résumé.

May I have an interview with you to discuss my qualifications further? I am
available at your convenience at the phone number listed on my résumé.

                                    Sincerely yours,


                                    Kevin F. McClain


Enclosure
```

Figure 5.6   Letter of Application

In evaluating the content of your letter, reread the instructions given in the designing and drafting sections of this chapter. Also, read your letter *aloud* to check the flow of the sentences and the "sound" of the letter in general. If you stumble as you read a section, the problem may be a poorly written sentence.

After you have chosen a form, ask yourself the following specific questions:

- Are all three necessary sections of the letter included?
- Is the information in the "positioning" section perhaps too specific, including information that would be better presented in the résumé?
- Is the tone of the letter appropriate: friendly, confident, reasonable?
- Is the letter 100 percent correct in spelling, grammar, and punctuation?

Revising the Résumé

Evaluate the draft of your résumé in terms of its appearance and design. You have a number of things to consider.

- *Types of headings:*   You may choose ALL CAPITALS
                           Initial Capital Letters
                           <u>ALL CAPITALS
                           UNDERLINED</u>
                           <u>Initial Capitals Under-
                           lined.</u>

- *Placement of headings:*   You may choose
                              to center headings on the page
                              to place headings at the left margin
                              to create an original design.

- *Placement of information:*   You may place your information any-where on the page. You may center blocks of information, or place them to the left or right. Experiment with different patterns and choose what looks best to you. You will need to *type* various drafts to see the differences.

- *White space:*   Avoid a cluttered look. A good résumé includes plenty of white space around each section. Don't crowd sections. If your one-page résumé is crowded and you don't want to eliminate information, go to two pages.

- *Amount of information:*   Your résumé, if you are a student, should be no more than two pages long, and one page is best. However, it also should not be *less* than one full page long. If your résumé is only half a page, go back to your notes and select other items to include. A résumé with too much detail may need cutting, but one with too little needs "beefing up."

Now ask yourself the following specific questions:

- Are items in both the work and education sections listed in *reverse* chronological order?
- Are the inclusive years for work and education easy to see?
- Have you given the complete address for each place of employment?
- Have you cited the job title and duties for each position you have held?
- Have you double-checked *all* items of grammar, spelling, or punctuation about which you were unsure? Don't fail to take the time to do this!

Producing the Finished Document

When you have worked out the wording, layout, and headings for your letter and résumé, you will be ready to produce the finished copies. This is no time to skimp or save money. Choose a good quality paper—not onion skin, erasable bond, or duplicating paper. Paper with a visible watermark is best. Although white paper is always acceptable, you may want to consider using paper with a soft color: very pale yellow, tan, green, gray, or blue. Do not use pink—it may not convey the desired businesslike impression. Type your résumé with a new typewriter ribbon, for a high-quality appearance.

If you duplicate copies of your résumé, use only a copier that produces clear, dark copies, or have copies made professionally at a copying service. You can also have your résumé professionally typeset and printed for a nominal fee. Companies in nearly every college town offer such services, and the final look can be very good, but it is not necessary to have your résumé professionally typeset. A good typed copy is just as acceptable. Your letter, of course, cannot be typeset and duplicated, as each letter of application should be unique.

However you choose to prepare your final copy, use the same kind of paper and same typewriter face for both your letter and résumé. The two will appear together as a unit and will look best if they are similar.

Examine the following sets of letters of application and résumés (Figures 5.7 to 5.10). Look especially at how each writer has attempted to communicate his or her best points in light of the needs of the organization addressed. Notice which details appear in the letter, which in the résumé, and how the two documents reinforce one another. Note that although the documents vary in layout and design, each letter contains the three essential points mentioned in "Designing the Document," and each résumé includes the four standard sections—divided differently—described in the same section. A final section about interviewing ends the chapter.

The Interview

If your letter of application and résumé are successful, you will be granted an interview. Your interview will go better if you prepare for it.

Nearly everyone feels nervous when going for an interview. Even the most experienced professionals often get jittery. However, feeling nervous doesn't mean you can't do a good job at the interview. Knowing how to handle it makes all the difference. The following list of suggestions should help you.

1. Try to find out even more about the organization offering you the interview than you did when you wrote your letter of application. If possible, find out more about the duties of the position for which you

4908-D Brittany Court
Bridgeton, MO 63044
October 17, 1985

Ms. Joy Donahue
Personnel Director
St. Louis Federal Savings and Loan Association
401 N. Lindbergh Boulevard
St. Louis, MO 63141

Dear Ms. Donahue:

I would like you to consider my qualifications for the position of electronic technician with your association. I understand that you are looking for someone with a strong background in an on-line computer system, and my two years at St. Louis Community College have given me experience in this area.

I will receive my Associate's Degree in Electronic Engineering Technology with a Specialization in Microprocessors in May of 1986. My courses in programming and circuit analysis have enabled me to trouble-shoot and repair any type of system, including the Olivetti computer system, which I understand your association uses. The enclosed data sheet provides additional details about my education and work experiences.

May I have an interview with you to further discuss my qualifications? I can be reached at the address and telephone number provided on my data sheet.

Yours sincerely,

Timothy L. Brooks

Timothy L. Brooks

Enclosure

Figure 5.7 Letter of Application

TIMOTHY L. BROOKS
4908-D Brittany Court
(314) 291-0419   Bridgeton, MO 63044   October 17, 1984

OBJECTIVE

I am seeking a position as an electronic technician at a firm that either uses computers in their business or deals in the production of computers.

EDUCATION

1984–Present   St. Louis Community College at Forest Park
               5600 Oakland Ave., St. Louis, MO 63110
               Major: Electronic Engineering Technology
               Minor: Specialization in Microprocessors
               Relevant Coursework:
                   Circuits I and II
                   Microprocessors: Applications and Interfacing

113

Electronics: Devices and Communications
Technical Algebra through Calculus
Physics
Useful Courses/Special Electives:
Introduction to Business Administration
Technical Report Writing
Electronic Drafting
Computer Graphics
GPA: 3.85 of 4.00
Will Graduate in May 1986

1980-1982   Lower Richland High School
Hopkins, SC 29061
Useful Courses:
Computer Programming
College Prep Calculus
College Prep Analytics
GPA: 3.87 of 4.00
Honor Graduate, 6th in class

EMPLOYMENT

1984-Present Shoney's Inc., Florissant MO, a restaurant
part time   Job Title: Cook
Duties: Prepare food to order and clean workroom and kitchen.
Supervisor: John Kilcullen, Mgr.

1983-1984   Quickheet Oil Co., Hazelwood, MO, an oil distributor
Job Title: File Clerk
Duties: Updated files of old and inactive customers
Supervisor: Jim Majewski, Accountant

1982-1983   Weaver's Electric Co., Hopkins, SC, a privately owned electric
service
Job Title: Apprentice Electrician
Duties: Wired residential homes and rewired old homes
Supervisor: Eddie Weaver, Owner-Operator

PERSONAL DETAILS

Health: Excellent, 185 lbs., 6 ft.
Hobbies: Fishing, hunting, tennis
Interests: Electronics/Microprocessors, robotics

REFERENCES

Available on request

Figure 5.8   Résumé to Accompany Letter of Application in Figure 5.7

Room # 217, University Hall
825 Good Hope
Cape Girardeau, MO 63701
February 10, 1985

Mr. Ken Cohen
Cohen, O'Connell, and Senturia
335 S. Meramec
Clayton, MO 63105

Dear Mr. Cohen:

I am writing to apply for a position in your company this summer. I am interested in any job or internship that might enhance my knowledge of advertising and public relations and make use of my education and work experience to serve your company.

In May I will complete my sophomore year at Southeast Missouri State University, where I am majoring in advertising/public relations and minoring in English. During these two years, I have completed most of my general requirements and a number of courses in my major. I particularly enjoy writing and have maintained straight A's in my college writing courses.

Most of my work experience in advertising, however, was gained at Clayton High School, where I was the business manager of the school's newspaper, *Clamo,* and responsible for all business aspects of the paper, from selling ads to proofreading finished ad copy.

I have additional sales experience gained from a job as a theatre concessionaire, and clerical experience gained from my work as a typist and receptionist for the Continuing Education Department at Forest Park Community College last summer. Finally, I am cooperative, friendly, and extremely interested in learning more about advertising and public relations.

May I have an interview to talk with you about working for your company? I will be available for work after May 15. You can reach me now at my college address or at home in Clayton between March 9 and March 16, my spring break. Both addresses and telephone numbers are provided on the enclosed résumé. I look forward to hearing from you.

Sincerely yours,

Rebecca F. Fitzgerald

Rebecca B. Fitzgerald

Enclosure

Figure 5.9 Letter of Application

REBECCA B. FITZGERALD

College: Room 217, University Hall   Home: 6870 San Bonita
         825 Good Hope   Clayton, MO 63105
         Cape Girardeau, MO 63701   (314) 721-8282
         (314) 644-0891

EDUCATION

1983-1985   Southeast Missouri State University
            Cape Girardeau, MO 63701
            MAJOR: Mass Communications/Advertising
            MINOR: English
            Relevant courses completed:
            Marketing, Advanced Magazine Production, Newswriting, Survey
            of Mass Communications, Business and Ethics, Lettering I,
            Design Foundations, Drawing I, Composition I & II

            Assistant Editor and Poetry Editor of *Journey,* student literary
            magazine; responsible for choosing copy, proofreading, lay-out,
            paste-up, and managing staff

Summer 1984   St. Louis Community College at Forest Park
              St. Louis, MO 63110
              Completed seven elective credits

1979-1983   Clayton High School, Clayton, MO 63105
              Graduate, 1983
              Business Manager of *Clamo,* student newspaper
                  Duties: sold ads; billed and collected fees; supervised ad
                  staff; produced ads from rough copy or verbal
                  instructions; laid out and pasted up ads

September 1982-   St. Louis Art Museum, St. Louis, MO 63110
December 1982   Selected for High School Visual Arts Seminar
                  Studied art history through a review of the museum's
                  collection

WORK EXPERIENCE

August 1984   St. Louis Community College at Forest Park
              5600 Oakland Avenue, St. Louis, MO 63110
              Clerk/typist, Continuing Education
              Duties: answered phones, typed, proofread schedules, assisted
              students in filling out forms
              Supervisor: Dean Mary Ann Cook

April 1983-   Tivoli Theatre, University City, MO 63130
August 1983   Concessionaire
              Duties: sold concessions; operated cash register; took
              inventory; did general upkeep; closed theatre
              Supervisor: Melissa Green

March 1983-   St. Louis Art Museum, St. Louis, MO 63110
April 1983   Worked in 6-week program with preschool art classes
              Duties: assisted teacher; supervised children and assisted them
              with their art projects; kept storeroom
              Supervisor: Veronica Jenke

```
August 1982-    Shady Oak Theatre, Clayton, MO  63105
April 1983      Concessionnaire
                Duties:  same as at Tivoli Theatre
                Supervisor:  Mr. B. Graham Fidler
```

PERSONAL DETAILS

```
Birthdate:      September 11, 1965     Health: Excellent
Affiliations:   Sigma Tau Delta, National English Honor Society
                    Active in fund raising and publicity; worked on *The Deltan*,
                    the society's literary magazine
                Society of Collegiate Journalists, Print Journalism Section
                Member, St. Louis Art Museum

Typing skills:  Approximately 50 words/minute; experienced user of the
                Magic Window word-processing program on the Apple IIe

Interests:      Art and art history, music, writing
```

REFERENCES

```
Alexandra Bellos
Assistant Director, Education Division
St. Louis Art Museum
St. Louis, MO  63110
(314) 721-0067

Mary Ann Cook
Dean of Continuing Education
St. Louis Community College at Forest Park
St. Louis, MO  63110
(314) 644-9175

Dr. John Bierk
Department of English
Southeast Missouri State University
Cape Girardeau, MO  63701
(314) 651-2000
```

Figure 5.10   Résumé to Accompany Letter of Application in Figure 5.9

are applying. The more you know about the organization, the more you will impress your interviewers.

2. Be sure you know the exact location of the organization. It might even be a good idea to go to the site beforehand to check on the parking arrangements if you plan to drive. This may keep you from feeling nervous and harried on the day of your interview; you'll feel more relaxed if you are already familiar with the surroundings.

3. Dress appropriately. You do not have to dress in expensive clothes, but be neat and well groomed. Dress on the conservative side. Men should wear a suit or trousers and sports jacket and a shirt and tie.

Women are advised to wear a dress or suit. Applicants should avoid wearing excessive perfume, aftershave lotion, makeup, or jewelry. Look like you're going to work, not to a party.

4. Be ready for the paperwork often involved. Bring a pen, notepad, and copy of your résumé. Know your social security number.

5. Go to your interview alone. Bringing a friend or relative will make you seem weak and dependent.

6. Arrive at least ten minutes early. If you are feeling particularly nervous, close your eyes, sit back, and breathe deeply and evenly. Imagine yourself as a very capable, calm person who will be a great asset to this organization.

7. When you enter the room for the interview, introduce yourself and be ready to shake hands. Make your handshake firm and friendly. Smile. Remain standing until you are invited to sit down.

8. Sit comfortably but erectly. Maintain eye contact with your interviewer. Avoid distracting behavior such as glancing at the ceiling or out of the window. Don't hunch, tap your fingers, or swing your legs.

9. Answer each question promptly, courteously, and briefly. You should avoid mumbled one-word answers, of course, but it is probably even more important not to ramble on and on. Speak clearly in a normal tone of voice. Don't lecture.

10. Show enthusiasm for the job! Don't be "cool" about your interest in the open position. Explain why you are interested in the organization and, more importantly, what you can do for the company.

11. Maintain a positive attitude. Don't apologize, complain, or dwell on any past failure. *Never* criticize or attack past employers.

12. If you have not been told about the salary for a position, you can ask toward the end of the interview what the typical salary might be.

13. You may well be asked at the conclusion of the interview if you have any questions. It is a good idea to come prepared with one or two intelligent questions. Your research will help you think of some.

14. You may also be asked to summarize your own strengths and weaknesses. Prepare for this by deciding beforehand what you will say. When it comes to weaknesses, try to name something that might also be seen as an advantage. For instance, you might say, "I have not had direct work experience in this area, but it is the area I most want to learn, so I would value the opportunity greatly."

15. When the interview is over, thank the interviewer. You will probably be expected to shake hands again. Let the interviewer know that you are hoping to hear further about the job.

The sign of a really professional interviewee is that he or she will send a follow-up letter of thanks to the interviewer, expressing gratitude for the interview and a continued interest in working for the organization. Such a letter need be no longer than a paragraph or two, but it makes an impression and keeps your name in the interviewer's mind.

Finally, if you get a job, internship, or promotion, don't forget to write additional letters of thanks to those who wrote references for you. It is the decent thing to do, and you may need them again in the future.

Key Points in the Chapter

1. The purpose of a letter of application and résumé is to obtain an interview for a job.
2. Find out all you can about each company to which you apply because an organization will hire you to meet *its* needs—not yours.
3. In both your letter and résumé attempt to point out what makes you *different* from other applicants.
4. In the résumé, lead with your strongest points and conclude with those least relevant.
5. In both the education and work experience sections of your résumé, use *reverse* chronological order; it's what you've done recently that counts the most.
6. Keep both the letter and résumé brief; ideally, a letter should be one page and a résumé one or two pages.
7. Make both letter and résumé 100 percent perfect in spelling, grammar, and punctuation, as these are routine matters that anyone with enough time should be able to handle correctly.
8. Type the final copy of your résumé in dark ink on good-quality paper with no discernible smudges or erasures.
9. If you are offered an interview as a result of your letter and résumé, prepare for it beforehand; don't expect to "wing it."

Exercises

1. Choose an organization for which you would someday like to work. Using the reference works described in this chapter, write a one- or two-page memo report on the company, addressed to your instructor. Cite the organization's correct title in full, its address, telephone number, and the name of its president or director. Add the names of its leading officers and the director of personnel. Describe the major divisions of the organization, the number of employees, the approximate annual sales and profits (if applicable), and the products or services provided. Describe current trends or problems within the company. Finally, in a few sentences, explain what you feel to be the general state of the organization.
2. Making use of what you have found out through research in completing exercise 1, write a letter and résumé to the organization asking for a job after you graduate.
3. Write a three-paragraph letter of application to an organization for which you are currently qualified to work. Write also a one- or two-page résumé to accompany the letter of application.

III

Resources and Techniques

6 Gathering Information— Library Research

Abstract

A report writer should know how to use libraries. Productive use requires knowing what resources a library provides as well as how to find the titles of good sources of information, locate the sources in the library, evaluate them, and take good notes.

Professionals on the job write hundreds of letters, memos, and reports. They gather information for these documents either from primary sources—such as observations, interviews, surveys, and laboratory tests—or from secondary sources of information such as journal articles and books. A report writer may need information from both kinds of sources. The next chapter explains how to conduct standard kinds of field research to obtain first-hand information. This chapter will describe the variety of sources available in libraries and explain techniques that will make you an efficient library researcher. Using a library is one of the most valuable skills you will learn in college.

Before beginning, you should understand clearly what a library is. Although libraries are used by many people mainly as sources of leisure reading, a library is primarily a place to find *information*. Libraries collect and categorize data on every conceivable subject. The best libraries offer an overwhelming variety of facts and figures on a wide range of subjects; some of the data you find may not even be consistent. Various interpretations and opinions may be found because libraries do not censor material. *You* must always evaluate materials and use your own critical abilities to draw conclusions about subjects.

Before using a library, you should familiarize yourself with the various kinds of resources available. After that, you will be ready to begin a process of research that you will use over and over in gathering information: You must first use a reference aid to find the titles of possible sources of information, then locate the sources in the library, evaluate them, and take good notes.

Resources Available in Libraries

Libraries offer a great variety of sources of information. Books are one good source, but report writers also often need data from other sources, such as reference works, periodicals, newspapers, government publications, and a library's vertical file.

Books

Books are a major source of information and often form the largest part of a library's collection. However, obtaining information from books presents two problems. First, because of the time it takes to publish a book, information in book form is rarely less than one year out of date. Second, a book may present so much information on a subject that it takes considerable time to find the exact data needed.

Reference Works

Most books are written to be read through from beginning to end, for enjoyment or information. Reference works, however, are not written to be read from cover to cover. They are volumes of categorized information that you can consult when you need a particular piece of information.

Sometimes reference works are single volumes—as in the case of yearbooks and almanacs. Sometimes they are multivolume, as are many encyclopedias. Whatever their organization, length, or subject matter, reference works are usually housed together in a separate reference section of the library, and not along with other books.

There are many kinds of reference works. Six common types that might be of use to report writers are encyclopedias, dictionaries, bibliographies, directories, almanacs, and yearbooks.

Encyclopedias   Most people are familiar with multivolume general encyclopedias, which contain information about a variety of subjects. The articles in encyclopedias also often provide bibliographies, which are lists of additional sources of information about a subject.

Different general encyclopedias have different features and are organized differently. The *Encyclopedia Britannica*, probably the best-known general encyclopedia in the English language, provides extensive and detailed information. However, it features an unusual three-part organization of material: A "propaedia" addressing general subject areas such as anthropology or physics; a "macropaedia" of lengthy, definitive articles; and a "micropaedia" of short articles and references back to the macropaedia. Some librarians consider it to be the most difficult encyclopedia to use.

If you are looking for information about a subject that is new to you or by nature quite complex, you should consider reading about it first in a simpler encyclopedia such as the *World Book Encyclopedia*. This reference work is known as one of the best of its kind and offers cross-references as well as short bibliographies. General encyclopedias such as the *World Book* may not give you the kind of specific data you need for a college or professional report, but they can introduce you to a subject.

There are also many special encyclopedias that give much more detailed information than do the general encyclopedias. An excellent special encyclopedia for scientific subjects, for example, is the *McGraw Hill Encyclopedia of Science and Technology*. Ask a reference librarian about special encyclopedias in your field.

Dictionaries   Another standard reference work is the dictionary. Most people have used standard English-language desk dictionaries such as *Webster's New Collegiate Dictionary* or the *American Heritage Dictionary of the English Language*, each of which defines and describes over 150,000 words. However, the English-language dictionaries are only the tip of the iceberg.

You may benefit from consulting one of the special dictionaries. Many of these works provide not only definitions but also extensive discussions and even illustrations. Works such as the *Van Nostrand Rhinegold Dictionary of Business and Finance* and Weik's *Dictionary of Computers and Information Processing* are valuable reference tools.

Bibliographies   Bibliographies are lists of sources of information about a particular subject. A bibliography might include the titles of books, magazine articles, newspaper articles, reference works, reports, records, and films on a given topic.

Bibliographies exist for both broad and narrow subjects. Sample titles include the *Consumer Education Bibliography, Electronics: A Bibliographical Guide,* and *Bibliography on Suicide and Suicide Prevention*. There is even a *Bibliography on Bibliographies* that you can consult to find out if a bibliography has been published on a subject you are researching. If a bibliography has been compiled on your subject, much of your work may already be done for you. After examining the bibliography, you may need only to supplement it with information published since the date of the bibliography.

Some bibliographies are annotated. This means that after each listing, a short description of the work is given. An annotated bibliography is more useful than one that is not because you don't have to guess at the general contents of a work listed.

Directories   Directories provide lists of information about corporations, government agencies, schools, political movements, manufacturers, associations, and almost any kind of formal or informal organization within the United States. For example, through one directory, *Environment U.S.A.: A Guide To Agencies, People, and Resources*, you can find out what groups and individuals are active in environmental issues today. Another directory, *Civil Rights: A Current Guide to People, Organizations, and Events*, lists people and agencies that have provided civil rights leadership; it would give anyone researching this subject an excellent list of people and organizations to contact for information.

There are also directories to directories, such as the *Directory on Directories* and the *Guide to American Scientific and Technical Directories.* These guides tell you if a directory you need exists.

Of particular interest to students researching companies during job searches are the directories, such as the *Million Dollar Directory*, that describe American corporations. From these reference works, you can find such information as the names of company officers, company net worth, and number of employees. These directories are discussed at more length in the chapter on writing a letter of application and résumé, since you should research a company before requesting a job from it or appearing for an interview.

Almanacs   Almanacs are single volumes of information published yearly by a variety of organizations such as newspapers, private corporations, and professional associations. Almanacs have existed for centuries and were formerly devoted mainly to providing information about heavenly bodies and the weather. Today's almanacs still contain weather information, but they now include many additional facts and figures about such topics as politics, finance, and education.

The *World Almanac and Book of Facts* is one of the most frequently used almanacs today. It contains quantities of miscellaneous data and statistics for each year of its publication. Other well-known almanacs include the extremely useful *Statistical Abstracts of the United States* and the *Information Please Almanac*, which covers such subjects as sports and motion pictures, in addition to topics commonly found in almanacs.

Unfortunately, almanacs are not always clearly organized and can be difficult to use. No general index to almanacs exists. To use an almanac, you must look at the index and table of contents for each year of publication to see what the volume contains.

Yearbooks   Yearbooks are similar to almanacs in that they are published annually by various organizations and companies, but they are different in that they usually address particular subjects instead of offering miscellaneous information. Typical yearbooks include the *Yearbook of Agriculture*, published by the U.S. Department of Agriculture; the *Yearbook of International Trade Statistics*, published by the United Nations; and the *Aerospace Year Book*, published by Aerospace Industries Association of America. The information published in such yearbooks is likely to be quite technical and up to date.

Overviewing Reference Works Libraries stock more than the six kinds of reference works described here. An excellent way to get an idea of the reference works available in your field of study is to consult the classic reference index *Guide to Reference Books*, ninth edition, by Eugene Sheehy. Every college library owns a copy.

The guide is organized into five subject areas: general reference works, the humanities, the social sciences, history and area studies, and pure and applied sciences. Each of these areas is further divided and subdivided. For example, one division of the pure and applied sciences category is *agriculture*. A subdivision of that is *forestry*. The ninth edition lists ten reference books on the subject of forestry: one bibliography, one periodicals listing, one abstract journal, three dictionaries, three handbooks, and one yearbook.

No single library is likely to own all the reference books listed in Sheehy's *Guide*, but most libraries provide at least the standard works.

Periodicals

Publications issued at regular (but not usually daily) intervals throughout the year are referred to as *periodicals*, or sometimes, as *serials*. The number of periodicals published in English is tremendous and growing every year. Even small college libraries are likely to subscribe to hundreds.

Magazines and journals are both periodicals, but there are differences between the two. Magazines generally are written for a lay audience, whereas journals contain articles of interest to professionals working in their fields. The typical pagination of the two kinds of periodicals is also different. Magazines usually begin pagination anew with each issue; journals typically continue pagination throughout each volume year. The January issue begins with page 1, but the December issue may begin with page 999.

There are periodicals that address the information needs of almost every interest group. Criminal justice students, for example, may choose to read articles from these periodicals: *Corrections Magazine, Crime and Delinquency, Crime and Social Justice, Criminal Justice Newsletter, Federal Probation, Journal of Criminal Law and Criminology, Journal of Police Science Administration, Journal of Social Issues, Law and Contemporary Problems, Police Chief*, and the *Search and Seizure Bulletin*. These are only some of the titles pertinent to the corrections field.

Newspapers

The most up-to-the-minute information can be found in newspapers. Newspapers can provide the kind of current facts about contemporary events, people, and places that books and periodicals cannot. Libraries usually subscribe to several local newspapers as well as to a number of newspapers with national circulation, such as *The New York Times* and *The Wall Street Journal.* Most libraries also subscribe to a number of newspapers from foreign countries.

U.S. Government Publications

The U.S. government publishes an enormous number and variety of documents, some of interest to general readers and some written for experts. Specific and accurate data, especially pertaining to social science or technology, can be found in the reports, bulletins, pamphlets, and books produced by the government.

Most libraries receive at least some government documents, and some major libraries, referred to as *government depositories,* receive and house large numbers of these publications. Every major city has at least one library serving as a government depository, and many universities are government depositories.

Vertical File

The vertical file is a filing cabinet (or several filing cabinets) containing a miscellaneous collection of paper documents such as newspaper clippings, pamphlets, or mounted photographs that library personnel have clipped or received. Arrangement of materials roughly follows the subject headings used in the library's catalog of books. Vertical files are developed as extensively as time devoted to their maintenance allows.

Reference Aids

Knowing the kinds of information available in a library is of no help unless you also know how to *find* the titles of particular books, articles, and reports that provide the information you need. You certainly can't look through every source in the library, hoping to stumble on relevant material. In order to find the titles of work that will further your research, you need to learn how the reference librarian can help you and how to use reference aids.

The Reference Librarian

In every college library there is at least one person whose duty is to assist library users in finding information; this person is the reference librarian.

Large libraries employ many reference librarians, some of whom help students to use reference collections in specialized subject areas. It's up to you to decide on and narrow the subject of your research, but once you have done that, the reference librarian can assist by explaining how to use reference aids and by offering tips on little-known sources of information about your subject.

You should learn the names of your reference librarians and get to know the kinds of services they offer. They are extremely valuable members of the college community.

Catalogs

Most works available in a library are listed in its catalog. A library catalog contains the titles of its books, including reference works, as well as the titles of films, tapes, periodicals, and newspapers. After periodical listings, the dates of the issues owned are usually noted. For example, a catalog might follow the listing for *Psychology Today* with the entry "June '70–current," indicating that the library's collection begins with the June 1970 issue.

Catalogs list holdings in three ways: under author, title, and subject. By looking under your subject heading in a catalog, you can produce a list of all works in a library that pertain to your topic. You cannot, however, find magazine articles through a catalog because only titles of magazines—not titles of articles *within* magazines—are listed. To find the titles of magazine articles and the magazines they are in, you need to consult a periodical index, which is described later.

Until recently, nearly all catalogs were kept on 3- by 5-inch index cards, with at least three cards (author, title, and subject) for each work—except for works of fiction, which aren't classified by subject. However, because of the thousands of works now being published and because of developments in computer and microform technology, many libraries are changing the format of their catalogs. The basic catalog in most large libraries is still the card catalog, but in some institutions this is being replaced by catalogs on microfiche, microfilm, or computer. In still other libraries, the card catalog is "closed" at a certain point, and new acquisitions are placed in a computer catalog.

In spite of the fact that holdings in your library may someday be placed in computer or microform catalogs, it is still advisable to learn how to use the card catalog, since this should remain a major reference tool for years to come.

The Card Catalog   As explained earlier, most works in a library with a card catalog can be found on the author, title, or subject card, but the author card is the basic card in the catalog. Formerly, many libraries purchased author cards from the Library of Congress and created their own additional cards by adding typed-in lines at the top. Library of Congress cards are still in use in many libraries. Typical author, title, and subject Library of Congress cards are shown in Figure 6.1, with their most important features labeled.

As you can see, the three cards are exactly alike except that the title and subject cards bear typed additions. The following list explains each labeled part.

1. *Author:* The author's last name is always given first. If more than one author is listed, the order of names follows the order given on the book.

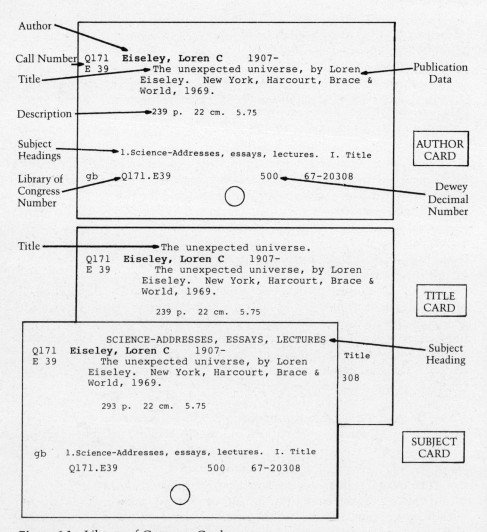

Figure 6.1   Library of Congress Cards

2. *Call number:* To the left of the author's name appears the call number. This number is added by librarians to the basic Library of Congress card and may be different from the Library of Congress classification number. The combination of letters and numbers indicates the location of the work in your library. *You must have the call number to find a work.*
3. *Title:* Remember that titles beginning with *a, an,* or *the* are filed according to the second word of the title. Thus, the title card for *The Unexpected Universe* would be found under *U.*
4. *Publication data:* Publication data explain when, where, and by whom a work is published.
5. *Description:* Some cards give rather detailed descriptions of works; others do not. The sample card informs you that the book has 239 pages and is 22 centimeters high.
6. *Subject headings:* The list of other subject headings tells you other headings under which the book is cataloged.
7. *Library of Congress classification number:* The Library of Congress number is a unique combination of letters and numbers that the Library of Congress assigns each book it catalogs. This classification system allows for the cataloging of books in thousands of subject categories.
8. *Dewey Decimal number:* The Dewey Decimal system is an older and simpler classification method. The Library of Congress assigns a Dewey Decimal number as an alternative to the Library of Congress number.

Other letters and numbers may appear on catalog cards, but these are of interest mainly to library personnel, not researchers. The initials *gb,* for example, which appear on the sample card, are merely the initials of the local librarian who prepared it.

Most works in the catalog are listed under author, title, and subject. Of course, you seldom know the titles or authors of books you need when you are doing research, so you will usually use the card catalog as a *subject index.* In doing so, you must be aware of a potential problem. Works you need may be cataloged under different subject headings from the ones you have in mind. For example, information about institutions that care for the terminally ill may be listed under *terminal care units,* or under *hospice,* which is a term not familiar to everyone.

A reference librarian can help you think of alternative subject headings when you are stumped; but there is also another source of help, the *Library of Congress Subject Headings,* a reference work that provides a list of all the headings currently used to classify library materials. If you cannot find any information about your subject under what seems to be a likely heading, look up the subject heading you are using in *Subject Headings.* It will direct you to the words used by the Library of Congress to classify information about your subject and also give you "see also" references, which refer you to additional subject headings under which you may find sources listed in the catalog. For example, if you look for information about black Americans in a card catalog by looking under the subject heading *Negroes,*you will find nothing. This is because the Library of Congress classifies all information about black Americans under the subject heading *Afro-Americans.* In addition to explaining this, the *Subject Headings* will also tell you other subject headings under which to look to find information about black Americans.

The Microfilm Catalog   Microfilm catalogs may contain less information about each work than do card catalogs, but they tell you all you need to find a work. A typical microfilm catalog entry, under the subject heading *Computer Crime,* is given in Figure 6.2.

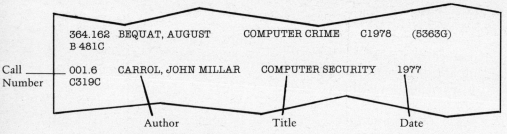

	364.162	BEQUAT, AUGUST	COMPUTER CRIME	C1978	(5363G)
	B 481C				
Call Number	001.6	CARROL, JOHN MILLAR	COMPUTER SECURITY	1977	
	C319C				
		Author	Title	Date	

Figure 6.2   Microfilm Catalog

The microfilm catalog tells you the call number, author, title, and copyright date of each work in the catalog. It may also give additional information.

Computer Catalogs   As mentioned earlier, many libraries are now storing their catalogs in computer data bases. Anyone wishing to use the computer catalog as an index may be able to go to an available computer terminal with a display screen, enter a subject heading, and then read on the screen a list of all the library's holdings on the entered subject. Entering a title or author in such a terminal would produce information about the work similar to what would be found on a Library of Congress catalog card.

Some libraries may make terminals with printout facilities available to students. With such a terminal, entering a subject heading would produce a computer printout of holdings that you could tear off and take with you. When holdings are simply displayed on a screen, of course, you must copy them down yourself. Computer catalogs are very new, and the future may see many more options. Library personnel will assist you in using whatever sort of terminals your library makes available.

Indexes

An index is a reference aid that guides you to specific information. Periodical and newspaper indexes guide you to particualr articles in magazines, journals, and newspapers. Indexes can be used almost like catalogs. You can look up information by author, subject, and sometimes by title. When you look up a subject such as *air pollution* in a periodical index for a certain year, you will find a list of articles about air pollution printed during that year, along with the names and issues of the periodicals that printed them. Periodical and newspaper indexes are the two most common kinds.

Periodical Indexes   The best-known index, and the one that directs you to articles within popular magazines, is the *Readers' Guide to Periodical Literature*, published by the H. W. Wilson Company, which also publishes several excellent special indexes to more professional publications. *Readers' Guide*, begun in 1901, has been published monthly or semimonthly ever since. Approximately 160 magazines are currently indexed in this guide. At the end of each year, the issues for the year are reprinted together in one volume.

When you use a particular volume of *Readers' Guide*, you will be directed only to information published during the time period covered in the volume. Therefore, to find articles published on a subject over a ten-year period, you would have to consult the successive volumes of *Readers' Guide*.

Readers' Guide is an author and subject index. This means that to find information, you could look under the name of the author of an article, if you know about an article or want to find out what a particular author has written during one year. However, most people use the guide as a subject index. Citations beneath a particular subject heading will provide you with a list of magazine articles on your topic.

Citations in *Readers' Guide* look like this:

Aging worker: asset—and liability.   J.L.
    Sheller.   il   U.S. News 90:76-7 My 4 '81

The citations make use of a combination of fully spelled-out words and abbreviations. Each citation begins with the title of the article. A *period* follows the end of the title. Thus the title of the cited article is "Aging worker: Asset—and Liability." Next the author's name (if one is given in the article) appears. The author of the sample article is J. L. Sheller. Initials, not first names, are used. A period follows the author's name.

Next you may see any of a number of abbreviations—all in *small* letters. A guide to all the abbreviations used in *Readers' Guide* is provided within the first few pages of every issue, but some commonly used abbreviations are *il* for illustrations, *por* for portraits, and *bibl* for bibliography.

After the abbreviations, the name of the magazine is presented, usually in abbreviated form. The full title of this magazine is *U.S. News and World Report.*

Following the title is a list of numbers. These numbers are the real key to the citation. You must correctly interpret the numbers to locate the article you want. Let's take a closer look at the numbers in the sample citation.

90:76–7 My 4 '81

The first number—90—is the *volume* number. It is followed by a colon. The volume number is the number that would be written on the spine of a bound volume of accumulated issues of the magazine. The number 90 here indicates that the magazine article you want is in the 90th bound volume of the magazine on the shelves of a library that keeps paper copies of the magazine. In a library that keeps microfilm copies, the number 90 will appear on the box within which the microfilm roll is kept.

Following the colon are the *page* numbers on which you will find the article. The sample article appears on pages 76 and 77. Sometimes the page numbers are presented like this: 33–35+. This means that the article runs from page 33 through page 35 and continues elsewhere in the magazine. Finally, the last letters and numbers indicate that the article appears in the May 4th, 1981, edition of the magazine.

Readers' Guide is not the only magazine index. Special indexes, such as the *Business Periodicals Index, Cumulative Index to Nursing Literature,* and *Public Affairs Information Service Bulletin (PAIS)* will direct you to articles published mainly in professional publications. These indexes typically index journal articles rather than magazine articles, although some of each are indexed in both the special indexes and *Readers' Guide.*

A special index may lead you to articles that are difficult to follow; how useful they are to you may depend on how much of your education in your field you have completed. The *Applied Science and Technology Index,* for example, will lead you to articles with titles such as "Application of Monolithic CMOS Switched-Capacitor Filters and Amplifiers for Signal Processing" as well as to simpler ones such as "Britain's Chip Technology is Profit for the U.S."

Newspaper Indexes   There are also indexes to newspapers. Indexes for nationally circulating newspapers, such as *The New York Times,* date back to before the turn of the century. Newspaper indexes are very similar to magazine indexes and can be used in much the same way. Guidelines within the indexes explain the citation forms used. Indexes to local newspapers also exist in most large cities.

Current news information may also be found in *Facts on File,* a weekly world news digest with a cumulative index, and through *NewsBank,* which provides microfiche copies of clippings from newspapers across the United States. *NewsBank* is a relatively new service, but more and more libraries now provide it. A reference librarian can show you how to use this special reference aid.

Guides to Government Documents   Although there are a number of catalogs and indexes to government documents, the major catalog is the *Monthly Catalog of United States Government Documents.* This catalog contains titles of government publications and instructions for how to obtain them. The *Monthly Catalog* is organized alphabetically by the government department or bureau responsible for the document. Publications may be listed under the Agricultural Department, Census Bureau, or Commerce Department, for example. In addition, an index is issued monthly along with the catalog, and at the end of each six month period a volume index is printed. This index allows you to look up publications by author, title, subject, series/report number, stock number, classification number, or title key word.

Also, a number of government offices that publish quantities of material provide lists of their publications. Some list only free publications; others list publications that can be purchased. If you send a letter to an office you think might publish useful information, you may be able to receive a list of that office's publications. You can get the addresses of government offices from directories.

A major reference book in the field of government publications is *Introduction to United States Public Documents* by Joseph Morehead. The government publications described in this book include congressional publications (such as bills and resolutions), court decisions, bureau reports, department reports, agricultural maps, technical reports, and many other kinds of government documents.

Computer Data Bases   The computer data base is a rapidly developing research tool. On-line computer systems are becoming expected resources in major libraries. There are now hundreds of available data bases containing references to millions of journal articles, books, newspaper articles, brochures, reports, and government documents.

Using a computer data base for research requires some training, and usually professional librarians conduct computer searches for students. The librarian establishes contact with a data base through a telephone coupler and then enters into the computer certain key words describing the kind of information desired. In a few moments, the computer responds with a printout sheet of titles of works published during the time period requested.

A computer terminal and coupler to the data base—which is not located in the library—are not extremely expensive and many libraries can afford them. There is a charge, however, each time the data base is consulted, and this must be borne by the library or the researcher.

Many data bases are now commonly available. These includes COM-

PENDEX (the Computerized Engineering Index), ERIC (the Educational Resources Information Center), and MEDLARS (the Medical Literature Analysis and Retrieval System). Most computer data bases correspond to printed indexes. COMPENDEX, for example, corresponds to the *Engineering Index*, and MEDLARS corresponds to *Index Medicus.* However, having information available in a data base is an advantage to a researcher. If your researching techniques are good, you can get more postings much more quickly through a computer than you can through a manual search through every volume of a particular index.

Research Strategy

You should now know many of the sources of information available in a library and how to locate information within these sources. However, you will probably seldom use all these sources in researching a particular subject. Also, the *order* in which you consult various sources of information should vary according to your subject, but here is a general strategy.

First, especially if your subject is unfamiliar to you, consider reading about your topic in a general encyclopedia to gain the background information you will need in order to follow more complicated discussions of the subject.

In researching a subject that is not especially current, the best strategy is probably to continue by checking the bibliographies to find out if a list of resources has already been compiled. Also, consult directories for the names of people and organizations from whom you might be able to obtain information. It is best to check directory listings early in your research so that you will have time to receive replies from out-of-town sources if you need to write for information.

Next, use indexes and your library's catalog to find titles of books and articles on your subject. Which reference aids you use first will depend on the nature of your subject. If your topic is clearly historical in nature or one that has been the subject of scholarly work, go immediately to the card catalog and hunt for the titles of books. The best of what has been written will probably appear in book form. However, if the subject is relatively current, your best bet may be to begin with the periodical indexes and indexes to government documents, which will direct you to recent information. This is also the time to consider requesting a computer search if that service is available. Finally, consider checking the vertical files.

Figure 6.3 summarizes this research strategy.

If your subject is very current, you may not be able to find any information in books or reference works. Your best strategy then will be to begin with periodical and government document indexes and then to check the vertical file. You may also need to use field research techniques to interview experts in the field about current developments.

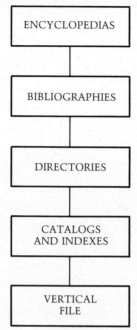

Figure 6.3   Research Strategy for Noncurrent Subject

Locating Your Materials in the Library

The first step in library research is to use research aids such as catalogs and indexes to produce a list of titles you believe will be useful. Such a list, when written in alphabetical order by the authors' last names, in conventional bibliographic form, is referred to as a preliminary bibliography. After you have compiled a preliminary bibliography, the next step is to acutally locate the works you need in your library or to arrange for the loan of a work from another library if your library doesn't own a copy.

Finding a Book

Books are the easiest works to find in a library. Libraries organize their books according to either the Dewey Decimal System or the Library of Congress (LC) system. The library's catalog provides you with the Dewey or LC classification number for every book. This number is added to the spine of each book, and the books are shelved in order within the library. The ends of each range of shelving bear placards identifying the inclusive numbers of books in that shelf.

The major divisions of the Library of Congress system, which is used in many large libraries, are given in Figure 6.4.

A	General works	M	Music
B	Philosophy and religion	N	Fine arts
C	History and auxiliary sciences	P	Language and literature
D	History and topography	Q	Science
E–F	America	R	Medicine
G	Geography	S	Agriculture
H	Social sciences	T	Technology
J	Political Science	U	Military science
K	Law	V	Naval science
L	Education	Z	Bibliography and library science

Figure 6.4 Library of Congress Classification System

Each heading in the Library of Congress system is further divided with letters and numbers to produce specific categories of study. For example, the Q (science) section is divided as shown in Figure 6.5.

The Dewey Decimal system classifies all information into one of ten major divisions. These ten divisions and their major subdivisions are shown in Figure 6.6.

A major purpose of both the Library of Congress and the Dewey systems is to bring books on the same subject together and in proximity to books on related subjects. By browsing through the shelves in one subject area, you may come across a number of helpful books.

You will find, however, that reference volumes are not shelved in order along with all other books in a library. They are kept together in a special section although they are placed in Dewey or Library of Congress order *within* that section. When you want to use the reference section, first find the precise classification number of the subject you are researching. Any library can give you a complete Dewey or Library of Congress classification chart, which you will need to find the number. When you go to the appropriate reference section, you will find there any dictionaries, directories, encyclopedias, and other reference works on your subject that are available in your library.

QA	Mathematics	QK	Botany
QB	Astronomy	QL	Zoology
QC	Physics	QM	Human Anatomy
QD	Chemistry	QP	Physiology
QE	Geology	QR	Bacteriology
QH	Natural History		

Figure 6.5 Q Division

000	**Generalities**	500	**Pure sciences**
010	Bibliography	510	Mathematics
020	Library & information sciences	520	Astronomy & allied sciences
030	General encyclopedic works	530	Physics
040		540	Chemistry & allied sciences
050	General serial publications	550	Sciences of earth & other worlds
060	General organizations & museology	560	Paleontology
070	Journalism, publishing, newspapers	570	Life sciences
080	General collections	580	Botanical sciences
090	Manuscripts & book rarities	590	Zoological sciences
100	**Philosophy & related disciplines**	**600**	**Technology (Applied sciences)**
110	Metaphysics	610	Medical sciences
120	Epistemology, causation, humankind	620	Engineering & allied operations
130	Paranormal phenomena & arts	630	Agriculture & related technologies
140	Specific philosophical viewpoints	640	Home economics & family living
150	Psychology	650	Management & auxiliary services
160	Logic	660	Chemical & related technologies
170	Ethics (Moral philosophy)	670	Manufactures
180	Ancient, medieval, Oriental	680	Manufacture for specific uses
190	Modern Western philosophy	690	Buildings
200	**Religion**	**700**	**The arts**
210	Natural religion	710	Civic & landscape art
220	Bible	720	Architecture
230	Christian theology	730	Plastic arts Sculpture
240	Christian moral & devotional	740	Drawing, decorative & minor arts
250	Local church & religious orders	750	Painting & paintings
260	Social & ecclesiastical theology	760	Graphic arts Prints
270	History & geography of church	770	Photography & photographs
280	Christian denominations & sects	780	Music
290	Other & comparative religions	790	Recreational & performing arts
300	**Social sciences**	**800**	**Literature (Belles-lettres)**
310	Statistics	810	American literature in English
320	Political science	820	English & Anglo-Saxon literatures
330	Economics	830	Literatures of Germanic languages
340	Law	840	Literatures of Romance languages
350	Public administration	850	Italian, Romanian, Rhaeto-Romanic
360	Social problems & services	860	Spanish & Portuguese literatures
370	Education	870	Italic literatures Latin
380	Commerce (Trade)	880	Hellenic literatures Greek
390	Customs, etiquette, folklore	890	Literatures of other languages
400	**Language**	**900**	**General geography & history**
410	Linguistics	910	General geography Travel
420	English & Anglo-Saxon languages	920	General biography & genealogy
430	Germanic languages German	930	General history of ancient world
440	Romance languages French	940	General history of Europe
450	Italian, Romanian, Rhaeto-Romanic	950	General history of Asia
460	Spanish & Portuguese languages	960	General history of Africa
470	Italic languages Latin	970	General history of North America
480	Hellenic Classical Greek	980	General history of South America
490	Other languages	990	General history of other areas

Figure 6.6 Dewey Decimal System

Finding a Magazine or Journal

Finding a periodical usually involves more work than finding a book. For one thing, if you have found the title of a book through your library's catalog, you know your library owns the work. However, although you may find an article and magazine title listed in an index provided by your library, the library may *not* subscribe to the magazine you need. There are thousands of periodicals, so no library can subscribe to them all.

Therefore, the first step in finding a magazine is to determine whether or not your library owns copies. This can be done by checking the catalog or your library's periodicals listing. If your magazine is listed, the library owns it. The catalog, and sometimes the periodicals listing, will also give you the call number for bound-volume copies. With the call number, you can go directly to the shelf and pull out the volume with the issue you need. The dates for each volume will appear on the spine.

However, many magazines are not kept in paper copies because they require too much self space. In many libraries, issues of periodicals are kept on microfilm. A reference librarian can show you how to locate the microfilm roll you need. To read a microfilm, you must take it to a microfilm reader, which displays an enlargement of the microfilm copy on a large screen. Usually at least one microfilm reader in a library will be constructed to provide paper copies of microfilm pages, usually for a small fee. A coin box attached to the microfilm reader activates the printout.

Periodicals also can be kept in other ways, and every library handles its collection differently. Current issues, for example, usually are kept separate from back issues, often in special shelving or in a browsing area. Sometimes magazines are kept in "hanging" shelving. You must check with a librarian or look for posted directions to learn your libarary's system.

Finding a Newspaper

Since newspapers disintegrate rapidly because of the low quality of the paper on which they are printed, only the most current editions of newspapers are kept in paper copy. These are either hung from wooden poles or folded in neat stacks or both. Back issues of newspapers are kept on microfilm or on microfiche, which is microfilm in card form instead of in rolls. The catalog will tell you which newspapers your library owns and how they are stored. Microfilm or microfiche readers or both are usually provided near the storage area for back copies.

Interlibrary Loans

Sometimes an index will have a title of an article that seems to be exactly what you want, but you find your college library does not subscribe to the magazine in which it appears. Or perhaps you have learned the title of a book you think will be useful, but you find your library doesn't own it. In these cases, you must try to arrange for an interlibrary loan. Usually, a book on interlibrary loan can be obtained within a week, and sometimes sooner. It is also possible to get copies of periodical articles from other libraries.

If you have any trouble finding a book or periodical, always ask a reference librarian for assistance. Also, be aware that the clerks at the library circulation desk are not likely to know all the resources, such as interlibrary loans, available to students. Don't give up on finding information until you have talked to one of the professional librarians.

Evaluating Your Sources

Once you find a magazine, book, or report that you think might be useful, you must decide whether or not the information provided is accurate enough to be worth using. Not all sources of information are equally valid or reliable. When you attempt to evaluate a text, you should take into account four aspects of the work: date of publication, documentation, bias, and professionalism.

Date of Publication

The date of publication has a great deal to do with how useful a work will be, especially for report writers, since they often require up-to-date information. In scientific fields, for example, new discoveries and inventions can quickly make recent data obsolete. Depending on the subject of a report, the copyright date of material may be relatively unimportant or the most critical feature of all. *You* must make the decision about whether or not the information from a particular source is current enough to bear quoting.

Documentation

One way to check for quality in a source is to check its documentation. Specific sources should be given for all data included. When an author writes something like "According to many leading authorities, the government's fiscal policy will lead to disaster"—but does not name those authorities—the information cannot be verified and may be worthless. Unfortunately, many popular magazines, even respected weeklies like *Time* and *Newsweek*, offer statistics and information without giving specific sources. This practice severely limits their use by serious writers. A professional or scholarly study will always give credit to sources of information, in the text or through footnotes.

Bias

Another problem you may encounter is bias. Some issues are highly controversial or political, and sometimes research is initiated mainly to support a previously held point of view. In such a case, any data not supporting the foregone conclusion may be ignored. You may not be aware that an issue you are researching is controversial, but if you find a great deal of conflicting data, you may have to do additional research to determine which authors are likely to be the most objective. Your instructors and biographical reference books may be able to acquaint you with the background and probable reliability of individual authors and studies. If you find out, for example, that an author is known for active involvement in the defense of nuclear energy production, that writer may not be the most reliable source of information about nuclear power plant hazards. At the very least, you will need to check additional sources.

Professionalism

As you research a topic, you should become more aware of the differences in style and purpose of different authors and publications. An article appearing in a popular magazine, for example, is likely to make more generalizations and to provide less specific information than one appearing in a professional journal. The purpose of the two pieces may be entirely different—one being written to entertain and the other to inform. The best professional work is well documented, well developed, logical, and objective.

In summary, when you undertake library research, you must remember that everything in print is not equally significant or valid and that it is not the business of the library to judge the information it provides. This is part of your job as researcher and writer. You are responsible for evaluating any source you locate and for including in your reports only the most reliable and valid information.

Taking Good Notes

After you have found the title of a work that looks promising, located the work, and evaluated it, you are ready to take notes. However, all your previous work will be useless unless you can take *good* notes. The suggestions that follow should make that job easier.

First, take your notes on note cards—not on random sheets of paper or in a spiral notebook. Using cards will make it simpler later on to organize your findings. It is easy to group cards with similar kinds of notes.

Second, make a bibliography (or "bib") card for each source you locate before you begin taking notes. A bib card is simply a notecard with all pertinent bibliographic information about a work. (Consult Appendix E for the correct bibliographic citation form for different kinds of sources.) You will use your bib cards when you write a bibliography for your report. Bib cards are also very useful when you need to go back to a work to consult it a second time because they give you all the information you need to find a source again. A typical bib card for a book, with all its sections noted, is shown in Figure 6.7.

A bib card resembles a simplified catalog card; you might think of it as a catalog card you can take with you. You should begin making up a bib card by writing the library call number of the work in the upper left-hand corner. In the center of the card write the bibliographic citation. Don't use any "shorthand" abbreviations, such as you may find in citations in indexes. The correct bibliographic citation form will make your card easier to read and will make it easier to write your bibliography later.

You will write only one bib card for every work you consult, but you may write many notecards from each source. Take notes about only one aspect or subtopic of your subject on each card. Make up a subject label for each notecard; this will be of great use to you later when you organize your notes. When you have completed your research, you can place the cards with the same subject labels in separate groups, as you would deal playing cards into different groups by suit. From these grouped notes you can then construct a tentative outline; in fact, when placed in a logical order on a table, the stacks of notecards form a physical outline before you.

A sample notecard with information taken from Barry Commoner's *Science and Survival* is shown in Figure 6.9. The entire passage from which the note was taken is shown first, in Figure 6.8.

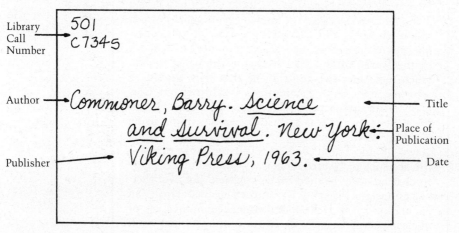

Figure 6.7 Bibliography Card

The Scientist's Role: Two Approaches

Since World War II scientists have become deeply concerned with public affairs. We are all acutely aware that our work, our ideas, and our daily activities impinge with a frightening immediacy on national politics, on international conflicts, on the planet's fate as a human habitation.

Scientists have tried to live with these responsibilities in a number of ways. Sometimes, in moments of impending crisis, we are aware only that the main outcome of science is that the planet has become a kind of colossal, lightly triggered time bomb. Then all we can do is to issue an anguished cry of warning. In calmer times we try to grapple with the seemingly endless problems of unraveling the tangle of nuclear physics, seismology, electronics, radiation biology, ecology, sociology, normal and pathological psychology, which, added to the crosscurrents of local, national, and international politics, has become the frightful chaos that goes under the disarming euphemism "public affairs."

Many scientists have studied the technology of the new issues and have mastered their vocabulary: megatonnage, micromicrocuries, threshold dose, and all the rest of the new technical terms. Nuclear physicists have struggled to learn the structure of the chromosome and how cows give milk. Biologists have returned to long-discarded text books of freshman physics.

Directly quoted section begins here.

A good deal of the scientist's concern for public issues may be generated by a sense of responsibility for the events which have converted nuclear energy from a laboratory experiment into the force which has almost alone molded the course of human events since 1945. It was a group of scientists who, fearful of the consequences of the possible development of nuclear weapons by the Nazis, conducted a strenuous campaign to convince the American government that they should be achieved in the United States first. As it turned out, Germany never succeeded in achieving an atomic bomb, and the Allies won the war against Germany without using it. Many of the scientists who worked on the United States atomic bomb were relieved to know that the threat which motivated them was gone and that the new force need never be used for destruction. But over their objections the weapon was turned against Japan, an enemy known to lack atomic arms. The human use of nuclear energy began with two explosions which took several hundred thousand lives; from this violent birth it has since grown into a destructive force of suicidal dimensions.

> I believe that it is largely the weight of this burden which has caused the scientific community, since the end of the war, to examine with great care the interactions between science and society, to define the scientist's responsibilities to society, and to seek useful ways to discharge them.

Figure 6.8   Passage from *Science and Survival*

At the top left-hand corner write your subject label. In the card shown, the subject label is *Origin of concern*. This might be an appropriate subtopic of a report on the growing concern of some scientists for the political implications of their discoveries. In the right-hand corner, write the name of the author. If you are consulting more than one book by a particular author, write the title of the book as well. Follow this with the page number of the book from which you took your notes. After that, add your notes.

Notes can be taken in one of three forms: a direct quotation, a paraphrase, or a summary. You can mix notes in all forms on one notecard, but if you do you must be careful to indicate by proper punctuation which is which. You must do this because when you look back over your notecards later on you may not be able to remember what you quoted directly and what you summarized.

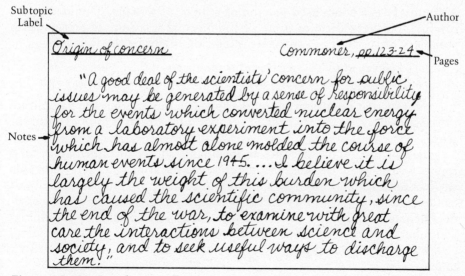

Figure 6.9   Notecard

Direct Quotations

The sample notecard contains a direct quotation, information taken word for word from a source. It is preceded by and ends with quotation marks. The sample direct quotation also contains an ellipsis, three spaced dots between two sections of the quotation. Their presence indicates that some material between the last word before the ellipsis and the first word after it has been omitted.

Paraphrases

To paraphrase is to rewrite material, more or less sentence by sentence, in your own words, simplifying and omitting irrelevant material as you work. The total length of a paraphrase might be nearly the same as the original, but it will be easier to follow and in your own words. A paraphrase of the direct quote on the sample notecard might read like this:

> Scientists' concern for public issues may have begun because of their sense of responsibility for what happened in the world after the atomic bomb was developed . . . this responsibility may have been the main reason why scientists after the war have begun to examine the relationship between science and society.

A report writer often has to translate complicated technical prose into language a manager or consumer can read. When you want to simplify such difficult material, but retain much of the original detail, the paraphrase technique can be especially useful.

Summaries

A summary is a condensed version of a piece of writing. The idea of the original, but very little or none of the original wording, is preserved. A summary of the Barry Commoner quotation might be the following:

> The concern of today's scientists for the effects of their work may stem from problems which followed their development of the atomic bomb.

Notice that no quotation marks appear around either the paraphrase or the summary. None are needed because no material is quoted word for word.

In conclusion, libraries are an invaluable source of information for a report writer. With the help of the reference librarians and reference aids such as catalogs and indexes, specific information on almost any subject can be found. Good library research requires time, however, and considerable patience, since a search for information often requires looking in a number of places under various subject headings. Nevertheless, learning to use your college library effectively will make research and writing much easier.

Key Points in the Chapter

1. Libraries contain many sources of information: books, encyclopedias, dictionaries, bibliographies, directories, almanacs, yearbooks, periodicals, newspapers, government publications, and the vertical file.
2. To find the best source of information on a subject, use catalogs and indexes and talk to the reference librarians.
3. Books in libraries may be found by their Library of Congress or Dewey Decimal system numbers.
4. To find a periodical article, first check to see if your library subscribes to the periodical and then locate the issue you need on the shelves or in microfilm copy.
5. Newspapers may be found in paper, microfiche, and microfilm forms.
6. When your library does not own a work you need, you may be able to get it through an interlibrary loan.
7. You are responsible for evaluating for accuracy and bias any material you include in a report.
8. Taking good notes requires you to write both bibliography cards and notecards.

Exercises

1. Produce a preliminary bibliography for a report about a problem in your field of study. Consider using the topic you have selected for your formal report. Include at least 10 bibliographic citations, among them at least one book, one magazine or journal article, and one newspaper article or government document. Be sure to alphabetize your bibliography by the authors' last names or by title when an author isn't named. See Appendix E, "Crediting Sources," for citation forms.
2. Photocopy a page of a journal article in your field of study. Produce one extended direct quote, one paraphrase, and one summary, from *different* sections of the page. Turn in the photocopy and your three kinds of notes.
3. Make an alphabetized list of all the journals and magazines your library owns that address topics in your field of study. To do this, go through your library's list of periodicals, write down likely titles, and then look at the periodicals. Cite only those that clearly pertain to your field.
4. If you are attending a community college or a four-year college with a fairly small library, make a list of all the encyclopedias, dictionaries, bibliographies, directories, almanacs, and yearbooks the library owns that address your field of study. If you are attending a university with a large library, restrict your list to two kinds of reference works.
5. Look up your field of study in Eugene Sheehy's *Guide To Reference Books*. Write the names of all major reference books for your field that are cited in the Sheehy work. Go to your library's catalog and find out which works your library owns. Report your findings to your instructor in a memo.

7 Gathering Information— Field Research

Abstract

Field research is the gathering of information from sources other than written ones. Of the many kinds of field research possible, this chapter deals with five. *Observation* of an object, person, or process enables a researcher to see things not included in published literature or in the testimony of an authority. *Interviews with experts* also supply information not found in a library and can, in addition, provide a synthesis of ideas that may not be available elsewhere. *Survey interviews* gather facts or opinions from a special group, such as salespeople or housekeepers, by means of face-to-face interviews or by telephone. *Questionnaires* accomplish the same end by means of a written set of questions distributed by mail. *Letters of inquiry* are especially useful when a few specific facts are needed and a particular person or organization is known to possess them. In all five methods the chances of success are increased by taking care in setting goals, choosing the audience, and framing questions.

Libraries contain an enormous amount of information on a wide range of subjects, yet they cannot supply all the information you may need in order to write a report on a specific, local topic. Consider these problems:

- A city council needs a recommendation for a site for a municipal swimming pool to be chosen from among five proposed sites.
- The bicycle paths on your campus are deteriorating and a proposal for an improved system of paths is needed.

- Workers in an office find themselves in each other's way as they attempt to carry out their duties; a proposal for a more efficient layout for the office is called for.
- English teachers need to know the amount and kind of writing done on the job by graduates in a particular field of study in order to make their courses more up to date and useful.

The library may supply some information on all these topics, but you must look elsewhere for much of it. In other words, you must do field research, which is simply research in sources other than printed ones. The kinds of field research covered in this chapter are

- Observations
- Interviews with experts
- Survey interviews
- Questionnaires
- Letters of inquiry

Observations

Often there is no substitute for examining the thing itself in order to write about it. For example, when studying the behavior of animals or small children who are unable to describe their actions, the researcher may find observation to be the only way to gather first-hand information.

Observation of a Person, Object, or Process

How a writer examines an object differs according to the object in question and the writer's purpose. If the project calls for writing a repair manual for a gasoline engine, the researcher, usually with the help of a technician, must not only examine the engine closely but also take it apart, put it together again, and become intimately familiar with all its quirks by running it under a variety of conditions. No matter what the object or process, it is important to take careful notes at the time of the observation. How to describe a mechanism after you have examined it is explained in great detail in Chapter 9, "Describing a Mechanism."

An *experiment* is a special kind of observation, one carried out under controlled conditions, as in a laboratory. The experimenter sets up the observation carefully in order to control all variables, makes exact measurements, and records results as fully and accurately as possible. Since techniques for carrying out experiments vary from field to field, you can best learn those techniques in your major course work.

Site Visit

A site visit, or field trip, is another kind of observation, made when a writer needs to observe a geographically located place such as a building, office space, or land area. For example, to describe the process of making road material from limestone, a visit to a limestone quarry is useful if not essential. Here are some suggestions for making a site visit successful:

- If the site is part of a business establishment or on private property, get permission for the visit and set up a time when you will be expected.
- Arrange for someone to meet you at the site, if that seems feasible. An explanation given by someone who knows the site or the process carried out there can be valuable.
- Come prepared to take notes. If you have a camera, take pictures so that you have a permanent record of the things observed.
- Make a rough drawing of the site, showing the arrangement of counters and machines in a work area or the lay of the land and location of trees on a building site. The sample notes at the end of this section contain an example.
- Arrange to return a second time if you need to see the process or place under different conditions or if you need to fill in details missed on the first visit.
- Immediately after the visit review your notes and fill in gaps from memory.
- Write a note thanking the owners of the site, if that seems appropriate.

Figure 7.1 is a sample set of notes taken on a visit to one of the proposed municipal swimming pool sites mentioned at the beginning of the chapter.

VISIT TO PROPOSED GRANTSBURG SWIMMING POOL SITE, 28th and Holland Ave.

May 3, 1984, 9:00 a.m.

The three-acre site lies west of Holland Ave. and south of 28th Street. Residential areas border it on the north and east, the Burlington Northern railroad tracks on the south, and a marshy area on the west.
Site is empty except for the remains of a brick warehouse adjacent to railroad tracks. Little cost or effort would be required to clear the site before beginning construction.

The site is relatively flat but falls away on the west edge to marshy land filled with cattails and other marsh vegetation. No trees grow on the site except for brushy, unplanned growth around the remains of the warehouse. Soil is claylike and well drained along the east side but appears to flood along west side in winter and early spring. The high water mark from spring rains is clearly visible east of the marsh. Filling would be required to make that part of the site usable.Soil tests by boring are needed to determine depth of water table under the site.

No city buses serve the adjacent streets. The closest bus stop is five blocks to the north on 23rd St. The site is accessible to vehicles only on the north (28th St.) and east (Holland Ave.) sides.

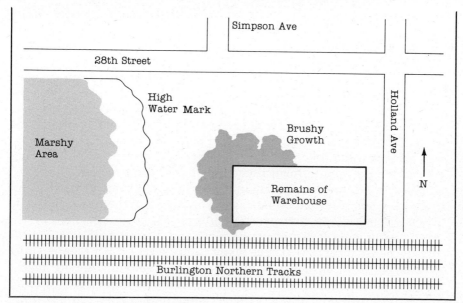

Figure 7.1   Notes Taken During a Site Visit

Interviews with Experts

Interviews with experts are an excellent source of information for several reasons. They enable a researcher to get information that is not available in published sources as well as information that might take weeks to search out in a library. An expert can also synthesize information for a researcher in a way that no published source can, and may even suggest new sources of information. A successful interview requires careful planning, execution, and follow-up.

Planning the Interview

An interviewer should never go into an interview cold, expecting the authority to direct it in a useful way. You will waste his or her time as well as yours. Employ as many of the following steps as you think useful:

- Have your goals for the interview clearly in mind by writing them out.
- Do some research on the topic before scheduling the interview. You need to know a fair amount about the subject in order to ask good questions, and the person interviewed will probably expect you to know what is easily available in published sources.
- Choose the authority in the light of what you want to learn. Sometimes the choice is easy, but frequently several people may seem, at first glance, to be equally good. Once you have chosen the person find out about his or her background. Most people, including experts, are happy

when they discover that people know about their work, and the information will help you frame good questions.

- Set up the interview by phone or by a personal visit. Letters are usually too slow and make the task of working out a time too cumbersome. Arrange the time and place at the interviewed person's convenience and ask for a specific amount of time—as much as you think you will need. Describe your project when making the appointment and indicate the kind of information needed by providing a sample question or two. That will enable the interviewed person to prepare.

    If you would like to record the interview on tape, ask at the time of making the appointment if you may use a tape recorder. A recorder enables you to capture all that an expert says, but some people become nervous when recorded on tape, and you may find them less willing to discuss sensitive or controversial subjects. Then, too, switching the machine on and off and changing tapes can distract both you and the person being interviewed. Yet many interviewers use a tape recorder whenever they can, since it cuts down the amount of note taking needed, if it doesn't eliminate it, and enables an interviewer to cover much more ground. However, the decision to use a tape recorder or not should always be left up to the interviewee.

- Make out a set of specific questions and put them in writing on 3-by-5-inch cards or in some other convenient form. General questions may, in a few situations, elicit the information you need, but usually specific questions produce better responses. If you are doing a report on Christmas buying habits, don't begin with a question such as "What do you think of this year's Christmas buying season?" You are more likely to get useful information with such questions as "What factors contributed to the increase in spending this year?" or "In what product areas was buying particularly heavy this year?"

- Arrange the questions in some logical order, but place the most important ones early enough so that you are certain to get to them. This is not a good time to save your best points for last.

Carrying Out the Interview

Careful preparation will go a long way toward reducing anxiety as you go into the interview. Consider the following tips about getting ready:

- Arrive on time and try to set a relaxed atmosphere by engaging in a short, pleasant conversation on a subject other than your project. Once you are both well settled, get to the business at hand.

- Begin by repeating the subject of your project and the kind of information you need; then ask your first prepared question. Be pleasant but direct. People being interviewed expect direct questions, since their purpose in agreeing to the interview is to help you.

- If an answer is a simple yes or no, follow it up with a "Why?" or "How can that be carried out?" or "What consequences do you expect?"

- Allow the authority to do most of the talking. Since you are there to collect information, restrain yourself from showing how much you know. If the speaker gets off the subject, steer the discussion back with another question from your prepared list.
- Don't be straitjacketed by your prepared questions. If answers lead in unexpected directions, follow them as long as they prove useful.
- Take notes in whatever shorthand form works best for you. Don't attempt to record everything the expert says; pick out what you think you can use. Take down enough to fix the main ideas; you can fill in more details immediately after the interview.
- Near the end of the interview, have the speaker clarify points about which you have questions. If you plan to quote, ask if you have the lines you plan to quote written correctly.
- Ask if there is another person who would be especially useful to your research and if there is published material that should not be over-looked. Ask your expert what questions you should have asked but didn't.
- Bring the interview to a close when the agreed-upon time is used up. If it seems appropriate, offer to give the person interviewed a copy of the report when it is finished. Thank your interviewee.

Following Up the Interview

As soon as possible after the interview, go over your notes and fill in from memory things you may need but failed to record. If the notes are difficult to read, recopy or type them after you have filled in the gaps.

Survey Interviews

A survey is a means of gathering information from a group of people, either a group that shares similar interests, such as students or construction workers, or a cross-section of the public. It may be conducted by face-to-face interviews, telephone, or questionnaire. Since questionnaires call for somewhat different methods from interviews, they are treated separately. The value of the information obtained in a survey depends on its *reliability*, that is, the degree to which the results reflect the truth. Reliability depends on how well your sample group represents the entire group of people involved in the issue you are studying, on the care with which the questions have been framed, and on the objectivity with which they are asked. Both factual information and opinions can be obtained by surveys.

Face-to-Face Interviews

Some of the steps suggested for an interview with an expert apply to the face-to-face survey interview as well: Frame a clear set of goals, do some preliminary research, determine the group to be interviewed, and then make up a set of questions.

For survey interviews, the questions must be worked out with great care since the time spent in each interview is usually no more than a few minutes. The number of questions must be low and the questions themselves short and capable of being answered briefly, in one word if possible. Since surveys are a kind of oral questionnaire, see the advice for drawing up questions in the section on the questionnaire that immediately follows. Questions requiring a "yes" or "no" answer or some other one-word response work best because they are most easily recorded and tabulated. In multiple-choice questions the choices should be limited to three, since four or five are difficult to remember when presented orally. Bring a clipboard with spaces marked to the right so that answers can be checked off or written in quickly. Figure 7.2, a sample survey question sheet, illustrates some of these points. The audience consists of bicyclists randomly

---

NORTHERN STATE COLLEGE BIKE PATH SYSTEM

1. How long have you ridden your bicycle on campus? years____

                        months____

2. Do you ride to school from a place of residence off campus? yes____ no____

3. Do you ride your bicycle between classes? yes____ no____

4. What two locations or intersections on campus cause the biggest problems for bicyclists?____

5. Is the current six-foot width of marked bicycle paths wide enough? yes no____

6. Have you read the brochure issued by the security office containing bicycle traffic rules? yes____ no____

7. How do you rate the enforcement of bicycle traffic rules by the campus police? too rigid____ not rigid enough____ about right____

8. How do you rate campus bicycle parking facilities? good____ satisfactory____ poor____

9. How do you rate the current bicycle path system? good____ satisfactory____ poor____

10. In your opinion what single change would do most to improve the current bicycle traffic system? ____

Figure 7.2 Sample Question Sheet for Survey Interview

encountered on a college campus, and the purpose of the survey is to gather information for a proposal to improve the system of bicycle paths on campus.

Another survey might be made of pedestrians to get their opinions about the regulation of bicycle traffic on campus.

Telephone Interviews

Conducting a survey by *telephone interviews* has several advantages over face-to-face interviews. The telephone enables a researcher to cover a wider area and a larger number of respondents in an equal amount of time, since the questioner doesn't need to travel. For the same reason it costs less. It also makes the survey more objective since the respondents' answers aren't influenced by the manner or appearance of the questioner. The telephone survey has some disadvantages, however. It may be difficult to locate lists of phone numbers for people in the special groups you may want to survey. An even greater problem is people's reluctance to answer questions over the telephone. Many consider it an invasion of privacy. The interviewer must therefore prepare a tactful and persuasive opening speech to convince the prospective respondent that the cause is worthy and that the ultimate purpose is not to sell something. Once a respondent has agreed to answer your questions, the procedure is the same as for a face-to-face interview.

Questionnaires

A questionnaire is a set of written questions distributed to a group of people in order to gather facts or opinions on a particular subject. Questionnaires vary widely in purpose, length, and format, from the elaborate set of questions sent every ten years to all households by the U.S. Census Bureau to the questions about service that are sometimes found on the back of a restaurant check. They resemble the survey interview in several ways but have a number of advantages over that form. Questionnaires can reach a larger number of people over a wider area in a shorter period of time and at less cost per person than live interviews. They can also include more questions, ask for longer answers, and allow more time for respondents to consider their answers. They are less prone to eliciting biased answers since the respondents are less likely to want to please the questioner and because they are presented to all in exactly the same way. The results are also easier to tabulate.

However, they have some shortcomings: Potential respondents are free to ignore them and often do so in large numbers; if a question is not understood the questioner is not there to explain; and they are less personal and suffer from a general resistance to questionnaires among many people. Finally, since questionnaires are usually sent to a much larger number of people than would be interviewed and since the questions must be formulated with greater care, they are usually more costly both in time and in money.

For these reasons a researcher should consider this method of gathering information carefully before undertaking it. For small projects, however, it may be an excellent tool for the individual researcher.

Preliminary Steps in Designing a Questionnaire

The heart of any questionnaire is obviously the questions themselves, and formulating them is the most difficult part of the task. Before taking up that task, however, you must carry out several planning steps.

Define the Goals of the Questionnaire   Defining the goals will help you decide if you ought to go through with it. Be specific in stating what you want to accomplish. A college department that wants to find out how well it has prepared its graduates for their jobs may simply state its goal in this way: to determine how well prepared our graduates are for their careers. However, a better statement might consist of three parts:

- To determine what positions our graduates currently hold and at what salaries
- To determine how our graduates evaluate their college preparation
- To determine how their superiors evaluate our graduates' college preparation

Select the Target Audience   In light of the goals ask, Who can best supply the needed information? In the previous case, one set of questions would be sent to a group of graduates, another to their superiors.

Do Preliminary Research on the Topic   A survey of the published information on the subject may convince you that a questionnaire isn't needed. If you decide to go ahead with it, however, this information will help you draw up good questions.

Estimate the Costs in Time and Money   Be sure to include the cost of materials, of mailing the questionnaires, of sending out follow-up letters to those that don't respond, of stamped envelopes for return of the questionnaires, and of the hours of work to be spent on the project.

Drawing Up the Questions

After taking care of these preliminary matters, and having committed yourself to the project, you are ready to formulate the questions themselves. They should be

- *Directly related to the goals:* For each question ask yourself, Will the answer help me to complete the project or to evaluate the other

responses? Eliminate those that simply provide information that would
be nice to know.

- *Unambiguous:* Determine if the questions can be interpreted in more
than one way. Murphy's Law applies here: If there is the slightest
chance a question *can* be misinterpreted, it *will* be misinterpreted. Pretesting the questions will help you spot ambiguous ones, but here are
some suggestions for avoiding ambiguity as you make them up.

    Certain words such as *pacifist, liberal,* and *conservative* carry
quite different meanings for different people. A conservative is viewed
by some as a person who conserves the best values from the past, but
for others a conservative is a rigid, self-righteous person who unreal-
istically clings to outdated customs and values. All these terms also
carry fairly strong emotional overtones that get in the way of
objectivity.

    Another group of words, mostly adjectives and adverbs, should be
avoided because of their vagueness; words such as *few, often, most,* and
severe are imprecise and likely to be interpreted differently by different
readers.

    Using a negative word in a true-false or yes-no question is likely
to lead to ambiguity. For example,

    > Should students not be given birth-control information by the Student
    > Health Service?   yes_____ no_____

    Also, avoid questions that are in effect two questions. Here are
some of the commonest kinds:

    > Are you opposed to smoking and drinking?   yes_____ no_____

    Obviously, if people are opposed to one but not the other, there is
no way they can answer truthfully.

    > Is the new city leash law effective and humane?   yes_____ no_____

    The questioner may have intended the two terms to be synony-
mous, but most readers would not interpret them that way.

- *Easy to answer:* The questions should be no longer than two lines,
should require no search through files for an answer, and should require
no more than a phrase or sentence to answer. An exception can be made
for a final question that asks for the respondent's general feeling about
an issue or for comments on any areas not covered by the other questions. Ample space should be provided to write in the answers.

    Multiple-choice questions should provide for all likely answers,
by use of an "other" choice, if necessary. Here is an example:

    > Does your company provide monetary or other support for professional
    > development?
    >
    >   Travel to professional meetings_____
    >
    >   Time off to attend training courses_____
    >
    >   Tuition for college courses_____

Dues for professional societies_____

Other support (please specify)_____

Arrange the questions in a logical order. Group all questions of a similar sort, such as all yes-no questions, together as far as possible. Moving from simple questions to complex ones makes good sense, but often the need to group questions on the same subject or in the same format may take precedence over that arrangement.

- *Worded to Avoid Biased Answers:* Avoid questions that touch on personal pride or biases. If you must know the ages and incomes of respondents, ask them to mark ranges of age and income rather than to provide precise figures. In asking for facts or opinions on religion, sex, politics, race, or minorities, frame the questions in as neutral and objective a way as possible.

  Avoid leading questions that imply by their wording a "right" answer. Here are some wrong and right ways to ask questions on controversial subjects:

  Wrong: Should import duties be raised to keep out unwanted foreign-made autos? yes_____ no_____
  Right: Should import duties on foreign-made autos be raised?
  yes_____ no_____
  Wrong: Should the federal government be taken off the backs of the airlines, leaving them free to set fares and choose routes?
  yes_____ no_____
  Right: Should the Federal Aviation Administration regulate the setting of fares and awarding of routes in the airline industry?
  yes_____ no_____

Designing the Layout

The appearance of a questionnaire often determines whether or not a respondent will fill it out. To make the appearance both professional and inviting, use a good quality of paper and provide wide margins and ample white space within the text as well as sufficient space for the responses. The text should be reproduced by printing, Xerox copying, or mimeograph; ditto usually appears unprofessional.

The first page should contain the title of the study in large type at the top followed by clear instructions for answering the questions, even though some of this information may also be provided in a cover letter. Number the questions and the pages of the questionnaire if it is more than one page long. Use white space or headings or both to indicate divisions between groups of questions, but don't arrange the questions in a way that gives a reader the impression of dealing with a series of unrelated subjects. Arrange the questions in a logical order and provide transitions by repeating key words in the questions. This will help provide continuity.

In designing the layout you will discover exactly how long the questionnaire will be in its final form; you may find that it is too long, given the expected attention span of the average respondent. If so, cut out the least important questions to bring it down to proper size. If the questionnaire turns out to be one or two questions longer than one page, you may want to cut it back to a single page. That would create a psychological incentive to the hesitant respondent, and it would also reduce the cost of the project.

Pretesting the Questionnaire

Once the questionnaire is in finished form, pretest it on people as similar to the target audience as you can find. Pretesting enables you to detect ambiguous or otherwise confusing questions as well as those that may give offense. Analyze the results of the pretest as you would the regular results in order to find out if some questions produce answers that are meaningless or impossible to tabulate. Those with experience in conducting surveys say the pretest usually turns up a few responses of that sort.

Putting on the Finishing Touches

Since questionnaires are usually mailed to a large number of people most of whom you as the researcher don't know and will never see, it is important to introduce them to the questionnaire through a cover letter. If time and your budget allow, a follow-up letter can also be sent a few weeks after the questionnaire itself to those who haven't responded.

Designing the Cover Letter   The two main purposes of the cover letter are to explain why readers are getting the questionnaire and to persuade them to fill it out. It should be prepared with great care for both content and appearance, since the letter is the part first read by the respondents. Use bond paper of high quality and make certain the text is letter perfect. If your sponsoring agency has letterhead stationery, make use of it in printing the cover letter. In the letter do as many of the following things as apply to your questionnaire:

- Explain concisely the purpose of the questionnaire.
- Tell the amount of time it will probably take to complete it.
- Assure respondents about the confidentiality of the information they supply, if any is likely to be sensitive.
- Mention the stamped and addressed envelope that is enclosed for return of the questionnaire.
- Ask that the questionnaire be returned *soon*. Experts seem to agree that a specific deadline does not produce quicker responses or more of them and may, in fact, discourage some as the deadline approaches. If you feel more comfortable setting a deadline, however, do it.

Southern Illinois
University at Carbondale
Carbondale, Illinois 62901

Associate Vice President for
Academic Affairs and Research
and Dean of the Graduate School
(618) 536-7791

November 10, 1983

Dear Faculty Member:

Long-range planning for a number of areas, such as Academic Computing, is a major responsibility of this university. Historically, our faculty have not been directly surveyed for the purpose of providing Academic Computing planning information. The attached instrument is an initial effort to reverse past history and provide you with the opportunity to contribute directly to Academic Computing Long-Range Planning. Your help is needed.

The instrument asks for you to provide information about Academic Computing in the areas of teaching, research, and service that may affect you. Your perception of computing needs will be combined with those of other faculty in order to help predict our collective needs.

It will take approximately ten minutes to complete the survey. Do not include your name. After completing, please fold and staple the survey and return by campus mail. The results of the survey will be made available after compilation.

As we anticipate annual updates in the process of continuing to enhance our computing resources, we would also appreciate receiving any suggestions you have for improvement in this survey instrument, and any ideas for additional items that would be useful in shaping the planning of this university for computing resources.

Thank you for your important involvement in shaping the future of computing at SIUC.

Sincerely,

Barbara C. Hansen

Barbara C. Hansen
Associate Vice President for
Academic Affairs and Research and
Dean of the Graduate School

sb
Enclosure

Figure 7.3   A Cover Letter Using Letterhead Stationery

Reprinted by permission of Barbara C. Hansen

Figures 7.3 and 7.4 are cover letters that accompanied survey questionnaires. Each explains clearly the purpose of the accompanying questionnaire and each attempts to persuade the receiver to respond. They also do most of the other things we have suggested a cover letter should do. Note that one of the letters sets a deadline, though in a tactful way; the other does not set a deadline. Note, also, that one of the letters calls the questionnaire an "instrument"—a clear attempt to overcome the negative attitude many people have toward questionnaires.

Figure 7.5 is a one-page questionnaire sent to recent buyers of Mazda automobiles. The cover letter explains why the senders hope all will respond and provides some instructions on how to return it. The question

1150 W. University, Apt. 236
Tempe, AZ 85281
February 29, 1984

Dear Fellow ABCA Member:

Are university business communications faculty engaging in communications consulting for businesses? If so, how? Your help in answering these questions would be appreciated. I am conducting this research project as partial fulfillment of a graduate course at Arizona State University.

Knowledge of the status of communications consulting being done by university faculty can provide helpful information to those faculty wishing to enter the consulting arena. This knowledge can also be helpful to those faculty wishing to expand their consulting practice.

Would you please take a few minutes to check your answers to the 12 questions on the enclosed questionnaire? The information you provide will be tabulated and used in the research report, but your name will not be used.

If you have not done any consulting in the last five years, please answer the first seven questions and return the questionnaire to me. If you are not a member of the university business communications faculty, please answer the first question on the questionnaire and return it to me.

A stamped and addressed envelope is enclosed for your convenience in returning the questionnaire. I would appreciate your returning the questionnaire by March 31.

Sincerely,

Barbara Elliott

Barbara Elliott
Doctoral Student

Enclosures

Figure 7.4 A Cover Letter for a Questionnaire

Reprinted by permission of Barbara Elliott Hagler. Cover Letter of Survey for Doctoral Research Class, Arizona State University, Tempe, Arizona, February 1984

```
                                                              1BD2219C0608909
                                                              8/205-60129
```

MAZDA CARES ABOUT YOU

1. Do you still own your Mazda?   ☐ YES   ☐ NO

2. If NO, please state the disposition.   ☐ Traded in   ☐ Sold outright   ☐ Other (Please specify) _____

3. How many miles do you currently have on your vehicle?
☐ Under 5,000 miles   ☐ 10,001 — 15,000 miles   ☐ 20,001 — 25,000 miles
☐ 5,000 — 10,000 miles   ☐ 15,001 — 20,000 miles   ☐ Over 25,000 miles

4. Are you the primary driver?   ☐ YES   ☐ NO

5. How would you rate your vehicle on the following characteristics?

	EXC	GOOD	FAIR	POOR			EXC	GOOD	FAIR	POOR
a. Styling	☐	☐	☐	☐	g. Interior Noise Level		☐	☐	☐	☐
b. Handling	☐	☐	☐	☐	h. Front seat roominess		☐	☐	☐	☐
c. Pick up from a standing start	☐	☐	☐	☐	i. Rear seat roominess (if applicable)		☐	☐	☐	☐
d. Acceleration when passing	☐	☐	☐	☐	j. Quality of construction		☐	☐	☐	☐
e. Fuel mileage	☐	☐	☐	☐	k. Overall satisfaction		☐	☐	☐	☐
f. Riding comfort	☐	☐	☐	☐	l. Value for the money		☐	☐	☐	☐

6. What accessories have you added since you purchased your Mazda?   From what source?

ITEM	SELLING DEALER	OTHER MAZDA DLR	AUTO PARTS STORE	MAIL ORDER	DISCOUNT STORE	OTHER (Please specify)
_____	☐	☐	☐	☐	☐	☐ _____
_____	☐	☐	☐	☐	☐	☐ _____
_____	☐	☐	☐	☐	☐	☐ _____
_____	☐	☐	☐	☐	☐	☐ _____

7. What additional accessories would you consider adding to your Mazda?" (Please list even items you feel are of minor importance) _____

8. Have you been contacted by a representative of your selling dealership?
☐ YES   ☐ NO, (Skip to #9)
If YES, who contacted you?   ☐ Sales rep.   ☐ Service rep.   ☐ Other (Please specify) _____
What was the purpose of the contact?
☐ Inquire about your satisfaction with the vehicle.   ☐ Suggest making an appointment for service.
☐ Inquire about satisfaction with service work.   ☐ Other (Please specify) _____

9. Do you follow Mazda's recommended maintenance schedule?
☐ YES   ☐ NO   ☐ Follow it mostly ·   ☐ Do more than recommended

10. Where do you usually have your vehicle serviced?
☐ The Mazda dealer where I purchased my vehicle   ☐ Another Mazda dealer   ☐ Service station
☐ Independent garage   ☐ Car care center   ☐ Service myself ☐ Other (Please specify) _____

11. If currently serviced by a dealer other than the dealer where you purchased your Mazda, then please provide the name.
Name _____ City _____ State _____

[MAZDA USE ONLY]

12. How would you rate your selling/servicing dealer's service department on the following characteristics?

	SELLING DEALER					SERVICING DEALER (Answer only if different from Selling Dealer)				
	EXC	GOOD	FAIR	POOR	DON'T KNOW	EXC	GOOD	FAIR	POOR	DON'T KNOW
a. Courtesy	☐	☐	☐	☐	☐	☐	☐	☐	☐	☐
b. Professionalism	☐	☐	☐	☐	☐	☐	☐	☐	☐	☐
c. Parts availability	☐	☐	☐	☐	☐	☐	☐	☐	☐	☐
d. Hours of operation	☐	☐	☐	☐	☐	☐	☐	☐	☐	☐
e. Service Department appearance	☐	☐	☐	☐	☐	☐	☐	☐	☐	☐
f. Parts Department appearance	☐	☐	☐	☐	☐	☐	☐	☐	☐	☐
g. Ability to service your Mazda	☐	☐	☐	☐	☐	☐	☐	☐	☐	☐

13. Would you recommend Mazda to a friend?   ☐ Definitely   ☐ Probably   ☐ Maybe   ☐ Probably not   ☐ Definitely not

14. Comments: " _____

Please print your name, address, and a telephone number where you can be reached during business hours: (if necessary)
Name _____
Address _____
City _____ State _____ Zip _____
Phone ( ) _____ Today's date _____ Mileage _____

"(Please do not include any ideas which you consider proprietary)   QREV1C6

Figure 7.5   A One-page Questionnaire

Mazda Motors of America (Central), Inc.

sheet itself is self-explanatory in spite of the variety in types of questions. The sheet was obviously designed with a great deal of care. A fair amount of white space remains on the page, and two questions are set off by dark shading. Note the general "comments" question at the end.

Preparing a Follow-Up Letter   Prepare a follow-up letter to be sent to those who have not responded by a certain date. Whether you do this depends on the money available, the need to get a high response rate, and the amount of time remaining before the results must be tabulated.

Letters of Inquiry

A letter of inquiry is especially useful when a few specific facts or opinions are needed and a particular person or organization is known to possess them. In form it is a regular business letter that lists the questions to be answered after an introductory paragraph in which you explain who you are and why you need the information. Try to frame the questions so that you can get what you need without putting the respondent to a great deal of trouble. The questions should be clear and brief and should not require long searches through files.

The letter a student might write to gather information for a class assignment is shown in Figure 7.6.

Additional letters of inquiry and replies to those letters can be found in Chapter 3.

Key Points in the Chapter

1. Field research in sources other than printed ones is a valuable and often essential mode of research for the writer in business and industry.
2. Methods of field research include observation of an object, process, or person; interviews with experts; survey interviews; questionnaires; and letters of inquiry.
3. Field research is sometimes the only means of getting information on subjects that are so current or local that nothing has been written on them.
4. Observation is a useful means of research with subjects such as animals and small children, since they cannot be interviewed or answer questionnaires.
5. Careful note taking at the time of an observation or interview ensures that all the important details will be remembered.
6. Field research often serves as a useful check on information found in printed sources.
7. In most of the field research methods described in this chapter the chances of success are increased by taking care in setting goals, choosing the audience, and framing questions.

Exercises

1. Rearrange and, where you think necessary, rewrite the following questions to make up an effective survey questionnaire on the services offered by a student center at a college.

   a. What three facilities do you use most often? billiard and game room _____ bowling alley _____, TV lounge _____, meeting rooms _____, study lounge _____, cafeteria _____, check cashing and ticket sales _____, other (specify) _____

   b. How would you rate the service offered by student center personnel? Mark more than one, if necessary. efficient _____, friendly _____, satisfactory _____, incompetent _____, other (specify) _____

Room 291, Stevenson Hall
Central State University
Johnson City, IL 62701
August 21, 1986

Mr. John Higginson
Turkey Flats Wildlife Refuge
Elrod, IL 62947

Dear Mr. Higginson:

I am a junior in Wildlife Management at Central State University and am currently preparing for one of my classes a report on lead poisoning of waterfowl at six hunting areas in the southern part of the state. Since your work covers three of those areas—Turkey Flats, Pine Tree Reservoir, and Frenchman's Lake—I hope you will be able to supply the information I need but cannot find in published sources. Here are the questions:

   How long has steel-shot ammunition been required at the three areas listed above?

   How many cases of lead poisoning have been detected among waterfowl in the three areas in the past five years?

   Does the Conservation Department plan any measures, in addition to the steel-shot rule, to combat lead poisoning?

I have heard that a study of the lead poisoning problem was made at Turkey Flats in 1980 but that the results were not published. Do you know if the study was done? If it was, could I see a copy of the report?

I will appreciate any help you can give me in completing my study. If you would like a copy of my completed study, let me know in your reply.

Sincerely,

Edward Wilson

Edward Wilson

Figure 7.6   A Letter of Inquiry

c. Other comments on the service offered by the student center ＿＿＿＿＿＿
＿＿＿＿＿＿＿＿＿＿＿＿＿＿＿＿＿＿＿＿＿＿＿＿＿＿＿＿＿＿＿＿＿＿＿
＿＿＿＿＿＿＿＿＿＿＿＿＿＿＿＿＿＿＿＿＿＿＿＿＿＿＿＿＿＿＿＿＿＿＿
＿＿＿＿＿＿＿＿＿＿＿＿＿＿＿＿＿＿＿＿＿＿＿＿＿＿＿＿＿＿＿＿＿＿＿

d. Do you live on campus?   yes ＿＿no ＿＿
e. Should the center be open longer hours?   yes ＿＿no ＿＿
   If yes, what additional periods would you like covered? ＿＿＿＿＿＿
f. What is your class level? ＿＿＿＿＿＿＿＿＿＿＿＿＿＿＿＿＿＿＿＿＿
g. What student center eating facilities do you use? cafeteria ＿＿, Mohawk
   Restaurant ＿＿, Huddle Lounge ＿＿, vending machines ＿＿,
   none ＿＿
h. How often do you use the student center?   every day ＿＿, two or three
   times a week ＿＿, less than once a week ＿＿, never ＿＿

3. Draw up plans to conduct a set of factual survey interviews on study habits of students who live in your dormitory or students in your field of study (major). Write out the goals of the survey, state where and how you plan to interview the students, and then draw up a set of eight questions.

4. Using the material gathered for question three as a basis, *explain* how you would modify the questions if this task were to be done by means of a *written* questionnaire. You needn't draw up the questions themselves.

5. Write a letter of inquiry asking for information on the availability of tourist accommodations in a vacation spot you would like to visit for two weeks next summer. Find the name of a town near the vacation spot and choose the likely organization or office to receive your letter.

6. Imagine you have been hired as a consultant to a clothing shop near your campus that caters to students. Your task is to conduct a survey of students' preferences in clothing as reflected in what you can observe on campus and in town. The information you supply will be used by the clothing shop's buyer to decide what sort of clothing to stock. Plan a strategy that includes times and places of your observations, conduct the survey, and write up the results in the form of a letter report that includes conclusions and recommendations. You can make it a women's store, men's store, or one that caters to both men and women. Note that you are simply to observe, not interview, the students.

8 Using Graphics

Abstract

Graphics communicate complex information quickly and effectively. You should plan and prepare them by using the same seven-stage process you use for other forms of practical communication, with special attention to choosing the right kinds of graphics for your purpose and audience. Photos, drawings, and diagrams show the reader what something looks like or how it works; tables and graphs present numbers or other data for reference or comparison; and good page and document design make the document more readable and usable. The central guideline in preparing all graphics is simplicity—removing extra lines and data so readers can find the information they need.

Graphics are an important tool in technical and business writing. Photographs, drawings, diagrams, tables, graphs—even the way you arrange text on a page—can help you communicate with your audience. For example, compare the following paragraph to Figure 8.1:

Both hardware and software sales have grown steadily over the past five years. Hardware sales were $1.2 million in 1981, $1.5 million in 1982, $1.9 million in 1983, $2.4 million in 1984, and $3.0 million in 1985. Software sales climbed even faster: from $0.5 million in 1981 to $0.9 million in 1982, $1.6 million in 1983, $2.5 million in 1984, and $3.4 million in 1985.

The text and the figure present the same data, but the figure makes its point more quickly and effectively. When you read the paragraph, did you realize that software sales had surpassed those of hardware? Did you even read that far?

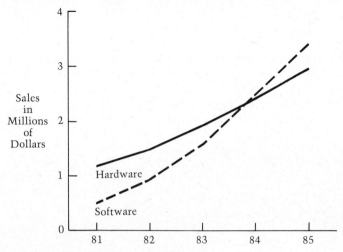

Figure 8.1   Using a Figure to Present Data

In addition, technical material is sometimes so complex that graphics are the only practical form of communication. Figure 8.2, for example, is a fairly simple wiring diagram for the electrical system in a gas stove. You can imagine how many words would be required to describe all the connections, and how much easier it is for an electrician to use the diagram than to scan several pages of text looking for the sentence describing a specific connection.

Finally, graphics can make your document more interesting. They can break up long pages of text, emphasize important ideas, or provide new ways of thinking about the data, holding your audience's attention while you deliver your message. They can make your document look more friendly and inviting, so that the audience is more likely to read and use it than if it were solid, uninviting text. This is not to say that you should throw in graphics at random, just to liven things up, but that you should look for opportunities to use them appropriately.

This chapter provides guidelines for using graphics in practical writing. It outlines general principles for effective graphics, based on the same seven-stage process you use in all practical writing; explains when and how to use illustrations and data displays, how to arrange text and graphics on the page, and how to prepare graphics for oral presentations; and describes a few of the tools available for preparing the graphics you'll use in class assignments or on the job.

Practical Graphics: Using the Seven-Stage Process

Good technical or business graphics have the same characteristics as good technical or business writing: They serve a practical purpose, are directed

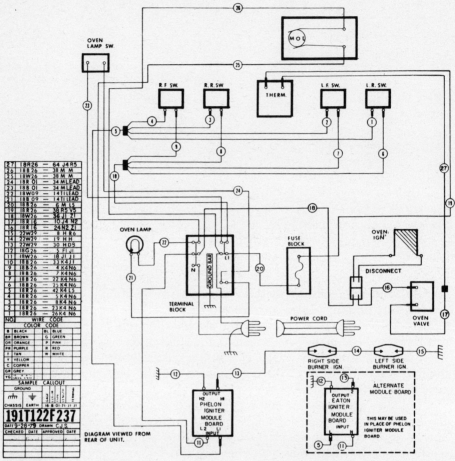

Figure 8.2 Complex Technical Information in Diagram Form

Reprinted with permission of The Tappan Company, Mansfield, Ohio

at a specific audience, convey a single meaning, and can provide an important record. And although graphics are usually only one element of a complete document, each photograph, drawing, table, or graph should be prepared by using the same seven-stage process you use for the document as a whole:

- Defining the problem and purpose
- Determining the audience
- Collecting the data
- Designing the graphic
- Drafting the graphic
- Reviewing and reworking the graphic
- Producing the finished graphic

Defining the Problem and Purpose

Suppose you are in charge of recruiting new engineers for your company. The company was established shortly after World War II, and many of the engineers hired at that time are now approaching retirement age. When they leave, the company will lose many of its best, most experienced engineers, yet next year's budget for hiring new engineers is the same as last year's.

You decide to write a memo requesting a larger budget. One of the problems you face as you plan the memo is how to make a convincing case that the shortage of engineers is real. Simply stating that "quite a few engineers will retire in the next few years" gives no indication of how serious or immediate the shortage is. At the opposite extreme, a list of names and retirement dates is more likely to bore readers than persuade them. A chart or graph offers an effective solution to this problem because it can present supporting data in a format that is dramatic, easy to read, and easy to understand. In this case, the purpose of the graphic is to show convincingly that the current budget is not sufficient to replace all the engineers who are retiring.

Determining the Audience

The budget is controlled by the company's vice president of administration. Like most vice presidents, this one is very busy and has little time to read detailed reports or analyze complex data. And at this time of year, almost every department in the company is insisting that *its* budget must be increased. Your graphic must therefore make its point quickly, clearly, and persuasively.

Collecting the Data

How many engineers are retiring each year? What's the first year the company will face a real shortage, and how long will it last? You can collect the data you need to answer these questions by looking at birthdates in the personnel records or by calling the pension-plan manager.

Year	Number of Engineers Retiring
1981	7
1982	6
1983	4
1984	5
1985	3
1986 (this year)	5
1987	15
1988	21

Year	Number of Engineers Retiring
1989	25
1990	13
1991	5
1992	6
1993	4

In addition to these data, a survey of current salaries for new engineers indicates that the budget you have now will allow you to hire only five engineers each year.

Designing the Graphic

After defining your problem and purpose, determining the audience, and collecting the data, you're ready to decide on the most practical way to present the information. To illustrate the extent of the problem quickly and dramatically, you choose a bar graph showing the number of retirements each year from 1986 (your last "normal" year) to 1991, when retirements return to earlier levels and the problem will no longer exist. (Later sections of this chapter will describe the types of graphics you can choose from, the purposes each is suited for, and how to design them.) This graph will be a central element in your memo, which will also define the consequences of ignoring the problem and say how large a budget increase you need to solve it.

Drafting the Graphic

Your first draft of the graph can be a rough sketch, as in Figure 8.3a. This gives you a chance to see how the graphic looks and how well it achieves its purpose before you invest a lot of time in preparing a finished copy.

Reviewing and Reworking the Graphic

The sketch in Figure 8.3a presents the data accurately, but Figure 8.3b is more effective. Removing the grid lines lets the audience concentrate on the data, shading the bars and moving them closer together makes them easier to see and compare, and simplifying the labels makes them less distracting and easier to read. Figure 8.3c is even better because it concentrates on the original purpose of the graphic: showing that the current budget for hiring new engineers will be inadequate in coming years.

Producing the Final Graphic

Now you're ready to prepare a clean, polished version of the chart. Although a formal presentation might call for a professionally drawn

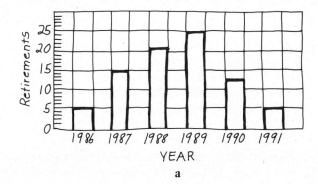

a

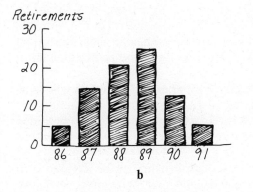

b

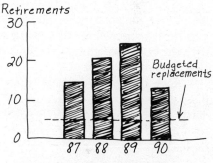

Figure 1. 1987-1990 Engineering
retirements exceed budget for
replacements.

c

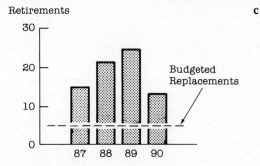

Figure 1. 1987-1990 Engineering
retirements exceed budget for
replacements.

d

Figure 8.3   Several Drafts of a Graphic

graph from the company's art department, such elaborate preparation is inappropriate for a simple memo. In fact, this kind of overkill may give the vice president the impression that you're likely to waste other company resources, including the recruiting budget. In this situation, then, you'll be better off using a ruler to draw the graph yourself, with typed or neatly hand-lettered labels (Figure 8.3d).

Whenever you use graphics, make them an integral part of the text. In your memo to the vice president, for example, you should indicate when to refer to the graph and what to look for ("As Figure 1 shows, more engineers will retire in the next four years than we can replace with our current budget"). Then place the figure where it can be found easily: at the end of the paragraph where you referred to it or, if there's not enough room there, at the top of the following page.

Throughout the process of planning and preparing your graphic, keep your purpose and audience in mind. Keep the figure, graph, or table as simple as possible, removing any unnecessary lines or information so that the audience can easily find, compare, and draw the right conclusion from the data.

One other word of caution: Plagiarizing graphics is just as wrong as plagiarizing text. If you borrow a figure from another document, give credit to your sources (see Figure 8.2 for an example). It's also a good idea to identify the source of data you use to construct your own figures and tables.

The graphics typically used in practical writing can be divided into two major types on the basis of what they depict. *Illustrations* depict physical objects or processes. *Data displays* present numbers or similar data. Each type is discussed in detail in the following paragraphs.

Illustrations

An illustration shows what something looks like or how something works. It could be a photograph of an accident scene in a police report, a drawing of a carburetor assembly in a repair manual, a wiring diagram for a light switch, or a flow chart for a computer program. Illustrations are best for communicating ideas or impressions that are too complex to be easily understood from words alone (like the details of an accident scene or the branches in a computer program) and for helping the audience understand physical relationships (like the arrangement of parts in a carburetor or the correct wiring connections in a light switch).

Photographs

Photographs come as close to the real thing as the flat pages of a document will allow. They are therefore very believable and can be used to provide a record or to prove that something exists. For example, Figure 8.4 could be used in a proposal or sales brochure to demonstrate that your company

Figure 8.4   A Photograph to Convince Readers That Special Equipment Is
Available

Courtesy of McDonnell Douglas Corporation

has the computer equipment needed to do special research work. Photographs can also show your reader exactly what an object looks like or
exactly how to perform an operation (Figure 8.5).

The abundance of detail in photographs can also be their biggest
drawback because too much detail can distract the reader from the point
you're trying to make. You can sometimes solve this problem by covering
or cutting away the background of a photograph, as in Figure 8.5, but a
line drawing (described in the next section) may be a better way to show
only the important features of an object.

Another drawback is that photographs are hard to reproduce on most
photocopiers; details and shades of gray are lost with each "generation"
of copies. If you know that many copies will be needed, plan to use line
drawings. Another option, if you work for a company that has the proper
equipment or budget, is to have your photographs converted to halftones
(a pattern of black dots, as in newspaper photographs) and your document
printed by an offset press. Black-and-white is usually a better choice for
photographs than color. Color is expensive to reproduce, and it is seldom
needed to achieve the purpose of a photograph.

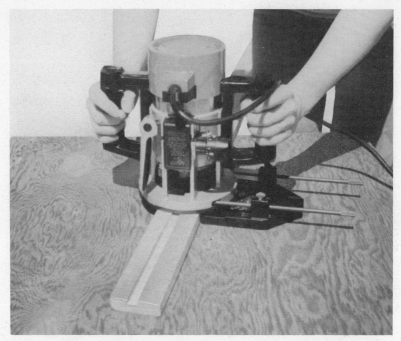

Figure 8.5   A Photograph Showing How to Perform an Operation

To provide a sense of depth in a photograph, position the object at an angle (Figure 8.6). Include something to indicate the size of the object—a ruler, a coin, or a person—and make sure the important details are well lighted. You can add labels when the photograph is incorporated in the document, using dry-transfer letters and arrows (described in the section on aids for preparing graphics).

Drawings

Drawings are not as "real" as photographs, but that means you can do many things with them that you can't do with photographs: leave out unimportant details, depict a hidden interior, or even "explode" an assembly to show how its parts fit together. Drawings can also be prepared quickly, and they maintain their quality when reproduced.

The type of drawing to use and the amount of detail to include depend on your audience and purpose. For someone assembling a ceiling fan, the simple line drawing of Figure 8.7 does an adequate job of showing where to insert a special screw in the fan hub. But the machinists who made the screw and the hub needed several sets of detailed blueprints, with multiple views and exact dimensions of each piece.

When an object's shape or dimensions are important, an **orthographic projection** is the simplest way to present the information. As Figure 8.8a

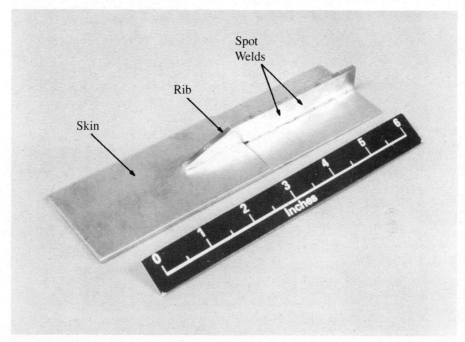

Figure 8.6   A Carefully Planned Technical Photograph

Courtesy of McDonnell Douglas Corporation

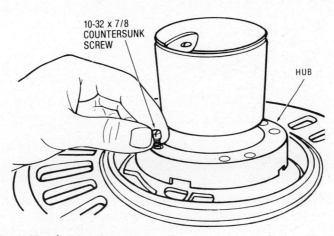

Figure 8.7   A Simple Line Drawing

Emerson Environmental Products

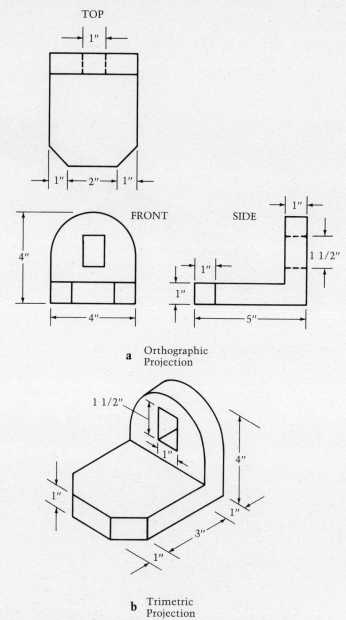

Figure 8.8   Orthographic and Trimetric Projections

shows, this type of drawing presents several two-dimensional views of the same object, as if it were being seen through different sides of a surrounding glass box. A **trimetric projection** (Figure 8.8b) brings those views together in a single image that includes all three dimensions. The trimetric figure is harder to draw but comes closer to the way we actually see the object. It is therefore easier for nontechnical audiences to understand.

Simple **line drawings** like Figure 8.7 are the easiest to "read." Often drawn from photographs, they look much like the actual object and can show the reader exactly how to install a part or what a completed assembly should look like. They are not, however, a reliable source of dimensions because the effects of perspective distort distances.

Two special forms of drawings are **cross-sections** and **exploded views.** A cross-section lets you "saw off" part of an object to show the reader what it looks like on the inside. It's hard to describe the interior shape of a fireplace and chimney, for example, without the aid of a drawing like Figure 8.9. An exploded view, like Figure 8.10, spreads out the parts of an assembly so the reader can identify the pieces and see approximately how they fit together.

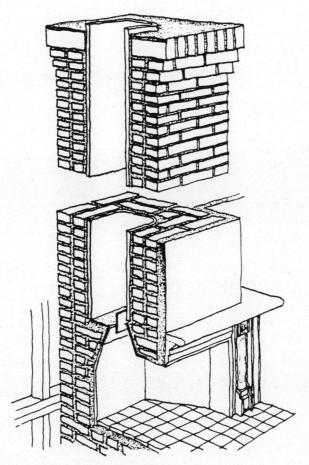

Figure 8.9   A Cross-Sectional Drawing

Drawing by Jonathan Poore, courtesy of The Old-House Journal

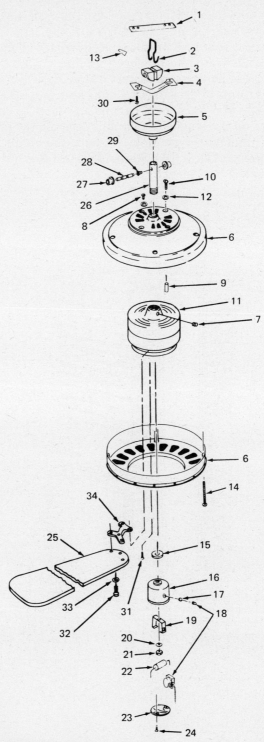

Figure 8.10   An Exploded View

Emerson Environmental Products

Process Illustrations

A number of illustrations—photographs or drawings—can be combined in sequence to illustrate the steps in a process. Figure 8.11 provides a good example. People who need to use a fire extinguisher are probably in too great a hurry to read detailed directions, but they can quickly understand the important steps from these drawings. In more leisurely activities, like assembling model airplanes, process illustrations can be combined with detailed written instructions.

Diagrams

Diagrams, like photographs and drawings, visually represent objects or procedures. They differ from photographs and drawings, however, in that

OPERATING INSTRUCTIONS

Remove from wall hanger or strap/clamp bracket.

Grasp unit and pull red lock pin from lever and handle. Hold unit upright with hand under handle and thumb on top of lever. Unit is designed to discharge the dry chemical agent ONLY IN UP-RIGHT POSITION.

Keep safe distance from fire (at least 6 feet) and near an exit. Aim nozzle at base of fire (not at flames or smoke). Do not get too close as the discharge stream may scatter the fire. If it does, move back. Play it safe. Keep away from the fire's fuel source and avoid breathing vapors, fumes and heated smoke as much as possible.

Press lever downward and spray dry chemical powder (powder stream will shoot over 10 foot distance) at base of flame in quick, side-to-side motion to erase the flames. When the extinguishing agent comes in contact with the fire, the fire will flare and appear to grow larger. Don't Panic. This condition is a normal and temporary reaction before the agent suppresses the fire. Direct all of the discharging dry chemical agent on the fire and make sure the fire is completely extinguished. After fire is out, carefully watch for "flashback".

Figure 8.11   Process Illustrations

Walter Kidde, Division of Kidde, Inc.

they don't actually look like what they illustrate. The diagram in Figure 8.2, for example, bears little resemblance to the bundle of wires and switches it represents. Like most diagrams, it uses symbols rather than pictures of the parts, and it emphasizes the relationship of those parts rather than what they look like.

A **schematic** diagram (Figure 8.12) goes one step farther by using spe-

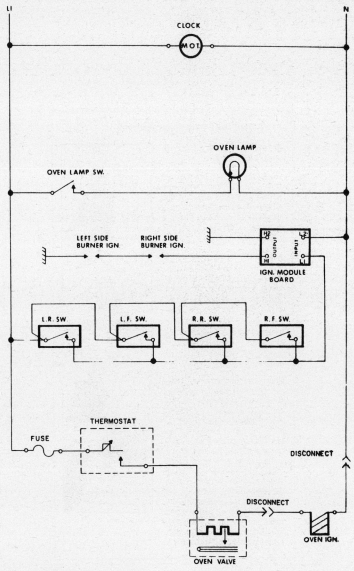

Figure 8.12 A Schematic Diagram.

Reprinted with permission of The Tappan Company, Mansfield, Ohio

cial symbols to show the **function** of each element of the system rather than its physical arrangement. An electrician or electrical engineer, who would be familiar with these symbols, could use this diagram during testing or trouble-shooting to understand what each switch does and how the whole system works. Before including a schematic in a document, make sure your audience needs this type of information and will understand the symbols you use.

A **flow chart** illustrates the chronological flow of activities in a process, especially when the process includes branches or repeated steps (Figure 8.13). Flow charts are often used to describe computer programs, but they can also be useful for defining trouble-shooting routines or the stages of preparing a document (see Figure 2.1). Arrows indicate the direction of the flow (generally from top to bottom and left to right), and each discrete step is enclosed in a rectangle or other shape. In data processing, each type of operation has a specific shape—diamonds for decision points, rhomboids for input or output operations, and so on.

Data Displays

The term *data displays* refers to tables and graphs, which present numbers or other forms of data rather than depicting physical objects or processes. Data displays are very common in the number-conscious worlds of business and technology.

Tables

Tables present a lot of data in a relatively small area, arranged so that a reader can find (or compare) specific pieces of data. The table in Figure 8.14, for example, could be used to look up the 1983 labor costs for the Personnel Department, to compare Personnel's 1983 labor costs to those in 1984, or to compare Personnel's 1983 labor costs to those of the Shipping Department in the same year. More complex comparisons—the changes in Engineering Department labor costs from 1979 to 1985, for example—can be difficult because it is hard to remember the "bigness" of many different numbers when they all look the same size on the page. Graphs do a better job in such situations.

You can do several things to make your tables "user friendly." Label each column clearly and completely, with all type horizontal so readers don't have to turn the page or their heads to read it. On large tables, extra space or a thin line every three to five rows and columns will help readers scan across rows or down columns without losing their place. (Lines between *all* rows and columns can be worse than none at all because they add too much clutter without adding information.) Most people find it easier to compare data side by side (1979 and 1980 in Figure 8.14) rather than above and below (Engineering and Manufacturing), so arrange your

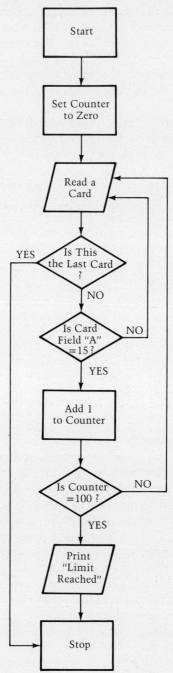

Figure 8.13   A Flow Chart of a Simple Computer Program

TABLE 1   History of Labor Costs

Department	Annual Labor Cost (Thousands of Dollars)								
	1978	1979	1980	1981	1982	1983	1984	1985	1986
Engineering	86	92	102	315	103	365	510	688	820
Manufacturing	705	755	817	852	775	901	926	1015	1312
Personnel	14	15	17	27	19	20	30	33	48
Facilities	77	82	89	98	60	69	90	102	127
Marketing	103	120	125	158	158	170	180	200	250
Administration	219	215	236	243	175	219	227	238	252
Shipping	18	35	37	40	40	47	68	72	90
Maintenance	130	150	157	168	139	155	167	184	188
Public Relations	17	20	23	28	—	—	—	22	23
TOTAL	1369	1484	1603	1929	1469	1946	2198	2554	3110

Figure 8.14   A Table

table to put the data you want compared in adjoining columns rather than adjoining rows.

Tables are usually numbered separately from figures. That means that Table 1 could come between Figure 7 and Figure 8. In addition, table titles are placed at the top, whereas figure titles are at the bottom.

Graphs

Rather than displaying numbers themselves, as in a table, graphs provide a physical representation of how large the numbers are. For example, Figure 8.15 charts the total annual labor costs from the table in Figure 8.14—the higher the costs, the higher the line goes. This makes it easy to spot trends or get the "big picture" that may be hiding in all the numbers on the table. (In looking at the table, did you notice that labor costs had risen steadily every year but 1982?) However, the "big picture" advantage is a disadvantage for those who need precise data: Try reading the exact labor cost for each year from the graph; then compare your answers to the actual numbers in the table.

Line graphs like Figure 8.15 show trends or changes in a single variable,* or they can be used to compare changes in two or more variables, as in Figure 8.16. Line graphs are not the best way to present exact data or to compare how large several different items are. A table is better for presenting exact numbers, a bar graph (described later) for showing the magnitude of different items. Here are some points to keep in mind when you draw line graphs:

- Keep the graph simple. Remove any extra lines (especially the background grids you may have used to draw the graph, but also the unneeded portions of the "frame"). A trend stands out better if it's not competing with other lines for readers' attention.

---

*A *variable* is the item or quantity whose value is shown on the graph.

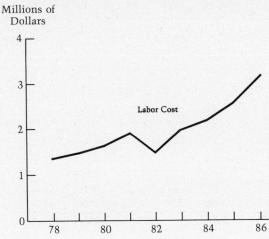

Figure 8.15   A Graph to Help Readers Visualize a Trend

- The line showing the trend is the most important part of the figure, so make it wider than any other line in the graph. You can also use color to make it stand out.
- Label key elements of the graph, but don't overdo it. Identify the units of measurement—dollars, hours, or whatever—on both the horizontal and vertical scales, unless the units are obvious (such as specific months or years). Cut down on clutter by not labeling every mark on the scale and by eliminating extra zeros where you can (as in the vertical scale in Figure 8.16). Put labels for trend lines near the lines themselves rather than in a separate "key" that forces the reader to look away from the data. Add a special label if needed to explain any unusual changes (again, see Figure 8.16). Finally, print all labels horizontally for ease of reading.
- Don't construct a graph that distorts the message of your data. The gradual growth shown in Figure 8.17a looks like a steep climb in Figure 8.17b. There are two problems here. Shortening the horizontal scale and lengthening the vertical one have made any changes seem more sudden, and starting the vertical scale at 1 rather than 0 makes the increase seem proportionately much larger. The first problem can be solved by using your judgment to choose proportions that help the reader see important changes without overdramatizing unimportant ones. The second problem is easier to solve—don't leave off part of your scale unless you make it very clear to the reader that you have done so (see Figure 8.18).

When you want to show your readers the relative size or amount of several items at one point in time, use a **bar graph.** Figure 8.19, for example, demonstrates at a glance that the Engineering and Manufacturing

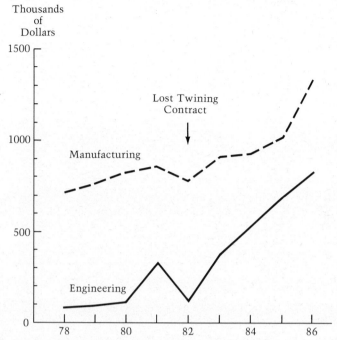

Figure 8.16   A Line Graph Showing Trends in Labor Costs

Departments have higher 1986 labor costs than any other group in the company.

Like line graphs, bar graphs are best for conveying quick impressions, not for presenting exact numbers. If you really need exact data on a bar graph, put the amount just below the top of each bar. Putting it above the bar would make the bar look taller and distort the impression of relative size.

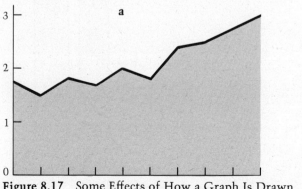
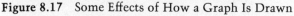

Figure 8.17   Some Effects of How a Graph Is Drawn

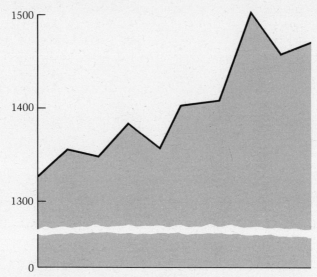

Figure 8.18   A Broken Scale for a Line Graph

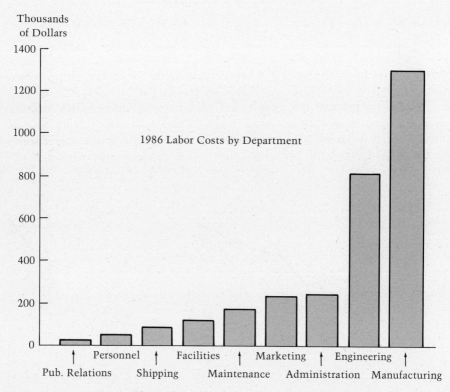

Figure 8.19   A Bar Graph to Show the Relative Size of Different Items

You can also compare more than one set of data within a single bar graph, as in Figure 8.20. However, more than two sets of data can be too much for the reader to juggle mentally, destroying the "quick look" advantage of the chart. Shade the sets of bars differently and supply a key to the shading in an open area of the graph. Shading also lets you compare both the size and the composition of different items (Figure 8.21).

The bars can be either vertical or horizontal (Figure 8.22). You should choose the arrangement that gives the cleanest, clearest impression of the message you're trying to communicate.

Here are a few other tips for making that clean, clear impression:

- As with line graphs, keep things simple by removing extra lines and other clutter. Follow the same rules for labeling the scales and starting them at zero.
- Shade the bars so that they stand out against the background. Making the bars wider than the spaces between them also helps.
- Unless there is a specific order to the items being compared (as there is for test samples A, B, C, and D in Figure 8.21), arrange the bars from smallest to largest or largest to smallest. Such an arrangement makes it easier for the reader to compare similar amounts quickly.

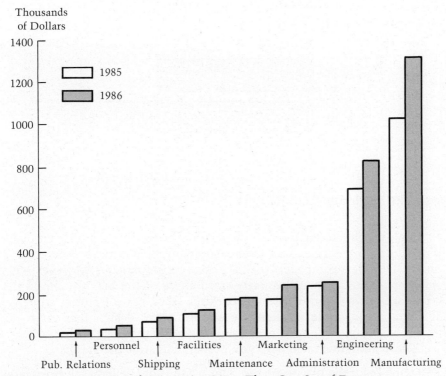

Figure 8.20 A Bar Graph Presenting More Than One Set of Data

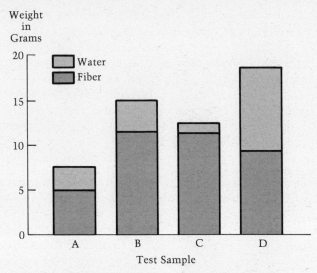

Figure 8.21   Bars Divided to Show Composition of Each Item

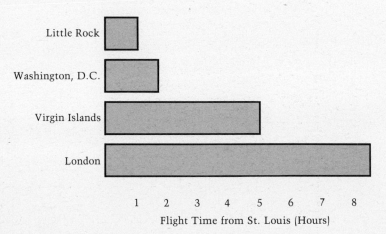

Figure 8.22   A Horizontal Bar Graph

A **pie graph** like Figure 8.23 shows the relative size of parts that make up a whole, in a format that even nontechnical readers can understand quickly. Don't expect readers to make careful comparisons, however—it's very difficult to compare similarly sized slices of the pie. You could list percentages or actual quantities under each label, but the clutter from the additional data would weaken the simple, clean design that gives pie graphs their impact. If your readers need exact data, use a table.

These guidelines will help you prepare effective pie graphs:

- Starting from the top of the pie, arrange the slices clockwise from largest to smallest.

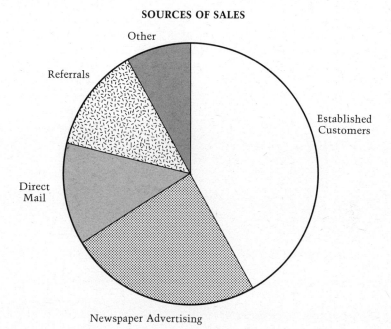

Figure 8.23   A Pie Graph for a Quick Impression of How Parts Make Up a Whole

- Use shadings to make each slice look different from its neighbors. You can also emphasize a single slice by moving it slightly away from the pie (Figure 8.24).
- Avoid many thin slices (those less than 5 percent). They're hard to distinguish from each other, and anything that small probably isn't important, anyway. Put them all together in a larger category labeled "other" or "miscellaneous."
- Put a short, appropriate label near each slice but outside the circle. After all, you want the pie to look like a pie, not a bowl of alphabet soup.

Page and Document Design

The graphic principles discussed so far—clarity, simplicity, ease of use— apply not only to figures and tables but also to the physical appearance of each page and the document as a whole. A page or document that looks inviting and easy to read is likely to *be* read, and that's an important first step in getting your message across. Furthermore, good page and document design can help the reader follow your organization, recognize important points, and understand relationships between ideas.

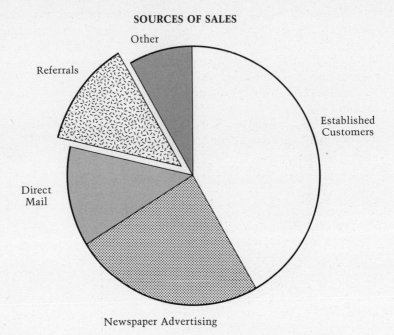

Figure 8.24   Cutting Away a Single Slice of the Pie for Emphasis

The following paragraphs cover some key aspects of page and document design: figure placement, white space, headings and highlighting, type styles and sizes, and document format. One caution: Remember that your goal is efficient communication, not artistic expression. Elaborate designs, "pretty" type styles, and unnecessary graphics can get in the way of your message. For best results, keep it simple.

Figure Placement

Because a figure (or table) helps the audience understand the text, the two should be close together for easy reference. If your document has wide margins, you can put the figure immediately beside the related text. If the margin is too small or the figure too large and you can't change either one, put the figure at the end of the paragraph where it is first mentioned or even at the bottom of the same page. If you don't have room there, put it at the top of the next page. In any event, be sure you introduce the figure *before* it appears.

White Space

White space is a dual-purpose tool. You can use it to make the document more inviting and to emphasize important information.

Pages filled with solid blocks of text intimidate or bore most readers. The denser the type, the less likely it is to be read. You can overcome this intimidation factor by breaking up the blocks of text with white space. For example, you can double-space between paragraphs and triple-space between sections, use wider margins at the top and bottom and left and right, and even use white space around and inside figures. The reader can tackle one small block of text at a time, pause to digest it, then move on to the next. The document may be a few pages longer, but a long document that gets read is more useful than a short one that doesn't.

White space also provides emphasis. In a page or paragraph of otherwise solid text, anything separated by white space stands out

like this.

An important heading should therefore be on a line by itself, where it's sure to be noticed. Headings can also be placed beside the text in a wide margin. Readers looking for a particular section can then scan the margins for the proper heading. Similarly, figures placed in the margins have even greater impact than when surrounded by text.

You can even alter the margins (by indenting) to emphasize paragraphs or longer passages that are different from the rest of the text, such as quotations, special procedures, or lists.

Headings and Highlighting

Headings tell your audience what to expect, providing a framework for the message that follows. Different levels of headings (like the one at the beginning of the chapter, the one at the beginning of Page and Document Design, and the one at the top of this paragraph) help the audience understand the structure of the document and the relative importance of each section. Be sure the differences between levels are clear and consistent. For example, you might use

THIS FOR MAJOR SECTIONS

This for Second-level Sections

And this for subsections. Here the heading is the first part of the paragraph, and an underline provides the appropriate emphasis.

Other graphic symbols can be used to highlight special sections or ideas. Bullets (made by filling in the middle of a lowercase letter o) call attention to individual items in a list, as in the guidelines for preparing pie graphs. A box can be used to set off an important message:

```
┌──────────────────────────────────────────────────┐
│              ┌─────────────────┐                   │
│              {    CAUTION      }                   │
│              └─────────────────┘                   │
│                                                    │
│  Before resetting any of the option switches, TURN OFF THE MAIN │
│  POWER SWITCH AND DISCONNECT THE AC POWER CORD.    │
└──────────────────────────────────────────────────┘
```

<u>Underlining</u>, *italics*, or **bold** type make important words or sentences in the text stand out. You can also emphasize short phrases or heads by typing them in all capital letters LIKE THIS. Long strings of all caps, however, are hard to read. Because all capitals are the same height (*FIGHT* rather than *fight*), readers cannot tell them apart as easily as they can lowercase letters.

If your budget and reproduction method allow, you can even use color to emphasize headings, special messages, or a significant feature on a figure.

Whatever your highlighting techniques, be careful not to go overboard in using them. When too much is highlighted, the really important ideas no longer stand out.

Type Sizes and Styles

You've probably grumbled at one time or another about nasty surprises hidden in the "fine print" of a contract or lease. The size and style of type can make a real difference in how easy and inviting the text is to read. If your document will be typeset, as this book is, you have a broad choice of type sizes and styles. Even if you're limited to a typewriter, you may have some options.

Type size is a key factor. Too small and it can't be read; too large and you can't get it on the page. As Figure 8.25 shows, type sizes are expressed in points. A point is ½ inch; the size of the type is the number of points from the top of a capital letter to the bottom of the tail on a *g, j, p, q,* or *y.* For normal text, the most readable sizes are 8 to 12 points. Most typewriters use 10-point type; this book uses 10 point for the text. If you have access to different sizes of type, you can use larger ones for heads and smaller ones for notes, quotations, or other short passages.

The design of the type itself also affects readability. There are hundreds if not thousands of designs (called *typefaces*) in use today, most of them available in italic, bold, and light versions as well as normal style. Figure 8.26 shows only four basic typefaces plus two common typewriter styles. For most business and technical documents you should stick to common, simple typefaces like these. The fancier styles may be pretty to look at, but they're often hard to read. No one assembling a bicycle at 11:00 P.M. on Christmas Eve cares about the elegance of the type in the

6 Point
7 Point
8 Point
9 Point
10 Point
11 Point
12 Point
14 Point
16 Point
18 Point
21 Point
24 Point

Figure 8.25   Type Sizes in Points

instruction book—the assembler just wants to get sprocket A into slot B by morning.

Of the typefaces in Figure 8.26, Century Schoolbook, Baskerville, and Prestige Elite have *serifs*. Serifs are the small strokes at the ends of the letters. Boston, Geneva and Letter Gothic are *sans-serif* styles (French for "without serifs"). Serif styles seem to be more readable in long passages, possibly because the small horizontal marks pull the reader's eye along the line, but sans-serif styles work well for headings, figure labels, and other applications that are clearly different from the main text. Do not mix

Century Schoolbook

CENTURY SCHOOLBOOK BOLD

Baskerville

BASKERVILLE ITALIC

Boston Medium

BOSTON BOLD

Geneva Light

GENEVA BOLD

Prestige Elite

Letter Gothic

Figure 8.26   A Few of the Hundreds of Typefaces Available

more than two typefaces in a document—the reader will have trouble remembering the significance of each style, and the page will look like a patchwork quilt.

Overall Document Design

The appearance of your final document—its size, shape, binding, and so on—should be one of the first things you consider after analyzing your problem, purpose, and audience. The key question here is *how will it be used?* A handbook of municipal electrical codes must be small enough (and durable enough) for an electrician to carry in a pocket or toolbox. A procedure manual that will be updated frequently can go in a three-ring binder to allow page changes. A status report should be on standard 8½-by-11-inch paper so it can be stored in a filing cabinet with similar reports. Assembly instructions must be large enough to be found in the packing material and bound so they will lie flat while the user has both hands busy. A marketing brochure must look colorful, attractive, and expensive so the customer will think twice before throwing it away. A document designed with the reader in mind stands a better chance of being used—and only if it is used will you achieve your purpose in writing.

Graphics for Oral Presentations

Because oral presentations let you speak directly to your audience instead of through a printed page, they offer special opportunities for the use of graphics—and special problems. The greatest opportunity is the chance to use a variety of communication media: models and samples, films and videotapes, flipcharts, blackboards, 35-mm slides, and overhead projector transparencies. The greatest problem is preparing graphics that can be read by everyone in the room.

Of the media listed, the most commonly used in business and technical meetings is the overhead projector transparency. These transparencies, which are slightly smaller than a sheet of typing paper, can be prepared quickly with a photocopier or by writing on the transparency with a grease pencil or special pen. They are easy to handle and store, and their image can usually be seen without lowering the room lights.

You can prepare graphs or drawings for overhead transparencies by following the guidelines presented earlier in the chapter. Simplicity takes on even greater importance here, though, because small details and clutter become unreadable across a room, and because most transparencies won't be projected long enough for the audience to decipher complex figures or graphs. Photographs can be tricky because photocopiers tend to lose the details of the picture when making it into a transparency. If you have the time and money, a photographic laboratory can prepare a transparency (like an oversize 35-mm slide) large enough to be used on an overhead projector.

A graphic unique to oral presentations is the *word chart*, which uses words or phrases to emphasize a speaker's key points (Figure 8.27). Again, the guiding principle is simplicity. Limit each chart to a single idea (in the sample, a summary of achievements for a specific project). Try to have six or fewer lines on the chart, with each line short enough to be read at a glance (generally, no more than six or seven words). For readability, use at least 16-point type (see Figure 8.25; capital letters on 16-point type are about 4 mm high). A sans-serif typeface like Boston Bold projects well. Some typewriters have special typefaces with oversized letters (like IBM Orator), but the thin lines of the letters are hard to see from a distance. You're probably better off hand-lettering the chart with a broad-tipped pen or using dry-transfer letters (described in the next section).

SUMMARY

- Assembled and tested heat pipe experiment
- Built prototype capillary-pumped evaporator
- Developed program for circuit-board thermal design
- Determined cause of streak heating

Figure 8.27   A Word Chart Summarizing a Speaker's Key Points.
Courtesy of McDonnell Douglas Corporation

For an effective oral presentation, the speaker—not the charts—should do most of the communicating. Use the charts only to highlight important ideas or to present data graphically, and turn off the projector or cover the screen the rest of the time.

Aids for Preparing Graphics

Some companies have special departments to design and prepare graphics, but many do not. Few students, of course, have access to such services, but you can still prepare clear, useful graphics on your own, especially with the help of a few aids.

The **photocopier** is the greatest invention since the pencil. If you want to use a graphic from another source, you don't have to redraw it—simply photocopy the original, cut away the surrounding text on the copy, and use "invisible" transparent tape to tape it into the master copy of your document. Then photocopy the master. The resulting copy will look as if the graphic were drawn directly on your master. (Of course, you must give credit in your document to the source of the graphic, and be careful not to copy any material protected by copyright.) You can use the same "cut and paste" method to rearrange paragraphs in your text without retyping.

A photocopier with a reduction capability can help you "clean up" drawings and charts. Draw them oversize; then reduce them with the copier. Minor flaws will become insignificant.

Blue-line graph paper and a blue pencil make the photocopier an even more powerful tool. Because most photocopiers don't "see" light blue, you can use the blue grid of the graph paper as a guide in drawing charts and graphs, and light blue pencil to mark guidelines for lettering.

Dry-transfer lettering lets you prepare typeset-quality word charts and figure labels with a ruler and a blue pencil. Just draw a light blue horizontal line where you want the base of the letter to fall, position the sheet of dry-transfer letters (available in many sizes and typefaces at office-supply stores) so the letter you want is on the line, and rub over the letter with your pencil until it has been transferred to the paper. Then go on to the next letter.

To center a title or position a label, first put it on a separate sheet of paper. Cut out the title or label with scissors or an X-acto knife and tape it into the desired position (or stick it there with a glue stick or spray adhesive). When all your titles and labels are in place, a trip to the photocopier gives you a finished product that looks professionally typeset.

Dry-transfer shades of gray and dot patterns are also available for filling in bars on bar graphs and slices on pie graphs.

Chart tapes make it simple to draw straight, even lines and to undraw them if you make a mistake or the data change. The tapes come in several widths (1/64-inch, 1/32-inch, and 1/16-inch tapes will give you a good range of choices) and patterns (solid, dashed, dot-dash, etc.). Simply unroll enough tape for your line, stretch it slightly to keep it straight, and press it down where you want the line. Trim off the ends with a razor blade or an X-acto knife. If you want to change the line, just peel it up from either end, move it wherever you want, and press it down again.

Wider plastic tapes can be used the same way to make bars for bar graphs. Positioning the tape and trimming the excess is much easier than drawing a rectangle and shading it in.

Computer graphics can be produced on many personal computers by using software like Lotus 1-2-3. The advantage of these programs is that line graphs, bar graphs, and pie graphs can be created quickly by telling the computer the data values and how you want them arranged. The drawbacks are the mechanical, obviously computer-drawn lines and labels generated by many printers and line plotters and the computer's limited options for solving graphic problems. If your software draws only vertical bar charts, you won't produce many horizontal bar charts—even when you need them. As software and printers improve, however, computers may become the most efficient way to produce many graphics.

Key Points in the Chapter

Graphics are a powerful tool in business and technical communication. To be effective, however, they must be planned and prepared as carefully as any other form of practical communication, using the same seven-stage process. In particular,

1. Use the right type of graphic for your purpose and audience.
2. Simplify the design by removing all unnecessary lines and data.
3. Don't let the design distort the data.
4. Use figures, type, and white space to make your document easy to read and easy to use.
5. Make sure graphics for oral presentations can be read by the entire audience.
6. Take advantage of aids for preparing top-quality graphics.

Exercises

1. Analyze a business or technical graphic from a newspaper or magazine. What is the problem the graphic was designed to solve? What is its purpose, and who is the audience? Did the designer choose the right type of graphic for that purpose and audience? Does the graphic solve the original problem? How would you make it more effective?
2. Design and prepare an illustration or data display to accompany one of the assignments you have already done in this course. Make sure your graphic design is appropriate for the same audience and purpose as the original assignment.
3. Use the following data on second-quarter 1986 expenses to design a graphic that will be used during a presentation to stockholders: cost of products and services, $2,362,600; research and development, $150,000; administration, $393,700; and income taxes, $65,100.
4. Design a graphic display that compares the data in exercise 3 to first-quarter 1986 expenses: cost of products and services, $2,975,700; research and development, $132,400; administration, $356,700; interest on debts, $16,700; and income taxes, $52,500. The comparison will be included in the financial data pages at the back of the company's six-month report to stock analysts.
5. Plan the design and graphics of a simple brochure or instruction sheet to explain your school's class registration system to new students. You might consider flow charts, maps, process illustrations, sample forms, and tables as well as the overall graphic design of the document.

IV

Special Forms

9 Describing a Mechanism

Abstract

A mechanism is anything made up of a system of parts that function together. Many well-established forms of technical writing focus on the description of a mechanism. Descriptions of mechanisms are needed by a variety of people and organizations; the purpose of the description and the readership may vary. To write a description of a mechanism, you may need to consult library reference books to understand the mechanism better and to learn the names of the parts. Before drafting, you must also determine the parts and subparts of the mechanism, choose an order of presentation of parts, select appropriate kinds of description, plan the organization, and choose an appropriate style. After drafting according to your plan, you should again examine the organization of your description, since organization is the key to a successful description of a mechanism. The finished copy may be presented in a number of ways.

A mechanism, to most people, is a machine or mechanical device. However, the term can also be used to refer to a much wider range of objects. A mechanism is anything made up of a system of parts that function together in some way. Understood from this point of view, the term *mechanism* might refer to a resistor, a gun, a spark plug, a stethoscope, a heart, an eye, a volcano, or a thundercloud. The *American Heritage Dictionary*, in defining the word, even speaks of "the mechanism of the universe."

People in many professions must understand, use, and sometimes also write descriptions of mechanisms. Many well-established forms of what is usually referred to as "technical writing" center around the description of a mechanism. An operation manual, for example, usually begins with a description of the mechanism to be operated and concludes with step-by-step instructions for its use. A medical manual designed to teach patients how to operate a piece of equipment at home must include a clear description of the equipment. A brochure introducing a new product includes a description of the item.

In each case, the degree of complexity in the description is determined by the purpose of the description and the needs of the readers. An assembly-disassembly manual provides minute descriptions of every nut and bolt in a device. On the other hand, a brochure describing a newly developed steam iron for prospective customers may describe only major parts and provide a very general description. Whatever the purpose, writing a description of a mechanism will require you to provide concrete information. You will also need to provide *technical*— as opposed to literary—description.

These two kinds of descriptions were contrasted in the writing samples in Chapter 1. Cowper's poem about planting cucumbers is a literary description of planting; it engages a reader by providing vivid impressions and images and by explaining how the writer feels about the task. On the other hand, the directions about how to plant cucumbers provide only factual, objective information. Objective technical description that enables a reader to visualize a product clearly or to duplicate a process are required in much practical and scientific writing.

Writing a description of a mechanism requires a great deal of planning before drafting. You must divide the mechanism into its logical parts and subparts, name the parts, define them, and decide what kinds of description to provide. Producing a description of a mechanism involves consideration of all seven stages of the process of practical writing.

Defining the Problem and Purpose

You will never be asked to describe a mechanism for no particular reason. The need for such a description arises from a problem such as one of the following:

- Customers buying a new microwave oven need a description of it.
- Customers buying a new wallet need a description of the wallet and its special features.
- The U.S. government requests a complete description of a helicopter engine from a company that proposes to build one for a new kind of helicopter the government wants.
- The U.S. Patent Office requests a detailed technical description of a new invention—a solar-powered highway warning light with backup batteries—from an inventor asking for a patent on the device.

- The editors of a children's encyclopedia need a good description of a steam engine for the article on that subject.

Descriptions of mechanisms are needed by many people and organizations for a variety of reasons. The first step in writing such a description is to determine the nature of the problem. In a classroom exercise, your instructor may assign a sample problem, or you may be allowed to invent your own or to use an actual situation. The previous examples cite typical "real-life" problems requiring a description of a mechanism. The problem, however you come to define it, will determine many aspects of your description—such as which parts to describe, what kind of description to provide, and what style to adopt.

Once you have identified the problem, the purpose should not be difficult to determine. If a product brochure is needed, your purpose will be to describe your mechanism in the kind of general terms that customers can understand and to highlight the product's best features. If, on the other hand, your employer needs a technical description of a product as part of a proposal to an important client, you will need to describe it completely and precisely. If a description for a patent application is needed, your purpose will be to describe your mechanism so exactly as to distinguish it from all others of its general type.

Determining the Audience

A description of a mechanism might be written for customers, clients, technicians, mechanics, managers, executives, students, housekeepers, or any combination of such groups. It is critical that you determine your audience and their needs so that your written description will not fail to communicate. Knowing your readership, as well as the specific problem you address, will guide you in deciding what to include and what to leave out.

For example, a description of a small aircraft written for potential customers should focus on the main, visible parts of the plane—such as the wings, propellers, flight compartment, landing gear, tail, and baggage area—because these are the parts with which the customer is most likely to be familiar. However, a description of the same plane written for maintenance personnel would have to meet their very different needs by providing detailed technical information about every part of the aircraft. Entire separate volumes might be written about the engine or the wings. Such complicated technical description would normally be written by teams of engineers and professional technical writers and might take months to complete. As a student, you will not be expected to produce such work, but you should begin to understand the importance of considering the needs of your readers in the same way that you eventually will have to when you write as a professional.

Collecting the Data

To write a good description of a mechanism, you must understand it thoroughly. We suggest that you take it apart if possible. Measure and weigh the separate sections if the mechanism is large. Write down your findings. In addition, you may need to conduct some library research to understand your mechanism better and to learn the conventional names for some of its parts and subparts. A number of reference books can provide assistance. For example, a recently published work, *What's What*, has illustrations of many mechanisms, with major parts and subparts labeled. Mechanisms in a variety of categories—from machines and tools to parts of the earth's surface—are pictured. You can also learn more about a mechanism from discussions with professors, product salespersons, and other knowledgeable people. The amount of research you need depends on the complexity of the mechanism and your familiarity with it.

Designing the Document

Designing a description of a mechanism requires more preliminary work than designing some of the simpler forms of practical writing. To deal with all the variables involved in writing a description of a mechanism you must

1. Analyze the mechanism to determine its separate parts and subparts and name the parts.
2. Choose an order of presentation of the parts and subparts, such as top to bottom or left to right.
3. Select appropriate *kinds* of description to provide throughout the description.
4. Plan the organization of the description, including placement of graphics.
5. Choose an appropriate style, in light of the problem and audience.

Each of these steps is explained fully in the sections that follow.

Analyzing the Mechanism

Analyzing a mechanism refers to dividing it into its main parts and subparts. The divisions are not always apparent, and in some cases there may be a number of logical ways to make them. A good way to represent your analysis is to create an outline exemplifying your divisions. (Read Appendix D on outlining before you begin.)

In creating such an outline, treat each major section of your mechanism as a first-level division. Treat each subpart as a second-level division. Follow outline logic as you divide. That is, never divide a main part into anything less than *two* subparts. If you name only one subpart in a section of your outline, you have not "divided" at all.

It is useful to label any main part that is made up of two or more subparts (or what you may see as a main part with a single attachment) as an *assembly* or *system*. For instance, the *chestpiece assembly* of the stethoscope shown in Figure 9.1 is composed of two subparts: the bell and the diaphragm.

Look also at the C-clamp shown in Figure 9.2. There might be several ways to divide this mechanism into parts and subparts. The illustration, however, indicates that the writer has divided it into just two parts: a frame and an adjusting screw assembly. The adjusting screw assembly has two subparts: a screw body and a handle.

An analysis of the relationship of the main parts to the subparts in this mechanism is shown in the following outline.

    I.   Frame
   II. Adjusting screw assembly
       A.   Screw body
       B.   Handle

On the other hand, the C-clamp could have been divided into three main parts. An outline reflecting that analysis would look like the one that follows.

    I.   Frame
   II. Adjusting screw
  III. Handle

These three divisions reflect the three separate, moving parts of the C-clamp. This may or may not be a better division of the mechanism. The

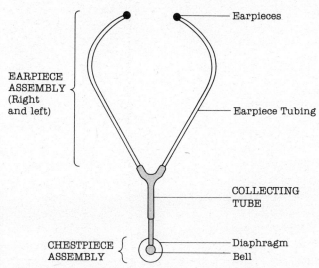

Figure 9.1   A Dynasonic Bowles Stethoscope

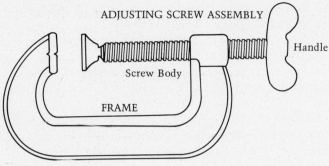

Figure 9.2 C-clamp

advantage of the first analysis is that it more clearly reflects the related function of the parts. The handle and adjusting screw *work together* and are therefore labeled as parts of one assembly; the frame makes up the second part. Both of these analyses are possible ways to "divide" the mechanism.

Figure 9.3 shows a cutaway view of a shotgun shell. It has been divided into two main parts—body and head. Each main part has been divided into a number of subparts. A simple outline of the shell follows.

    I. The head
        A. The brass casing
        B. The gunpowder
        C. The primer
   II. The body
        A. The plastic casing
        B. The shot
        C. The filler wad

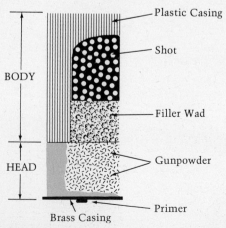

Figure 9.3 Cutaway View of a Shotgun Shell

Since both the head and body are composed of subparts, they might also be labeled *head assembly* and *body assembly*. The terms for these parts are well known, however, so the author omits "assembly" from the labeling.

In deciding how to analyze your mechanism into parts and subparts, consider the following questions:

- Which parts are formed of one continuous substance? Which are not?
- Which parts actually touch or are fastened to each other?
- Which parts work together toward one purpose? Which do not?

After you have identified the separate parts of your mechanism, you will also have to name them. Naming some of the parts and subparts might be easy, but you may find you have identified other parts you cannot name. Reference books in the library, such as *What's What* (already mentioned), may be able to help you. Articles in encyclopedias and special dictionaries may also give you the information you need. Occasionally you may have to make up a name for a part yourself, but you should not turn to that alternative except as a last resort. If you do need to formulate a name yourself, make use of words you already know in order to invent a logical term. You can usually name a part according to its function. For example, if it holds another piece, it is some kind of a *holder*. Combining that term with the name of the material of which the holder is made, you might name the part *plastic holder*.

Choosing an Order of Presentation

Once you have decided on your list of parts and subparts, choose an order of presentation. Random order is not acceptable. As a rule, pick some kind of order by location: List parts in order from top to bottom or bottom to top, left to right or right to left, outside to inside or inside to outside. Occasionally, you may wish to order your list of parts according to their relative importance—most important to least important, as a rule.

You will also need to order subparts within main parts. Follow the same suggestions just given to determine these suborders.

Selecting Appropriate Kinds of Description

The next step in designing your document is to decide the kinds of description to provide for each part and subpart. For some assignments, in industry or in the classroom, your supervisor or teacher may ask you to provide specific kinds of information. In other situations, when the choice is left up to you, make your decision in light of your problem, purpose, and audience. The following list will give you an idea of the kinds of description you might use.

- *Size* (dimension): Measurements should be given for all three dimensions of a part; specify length, width, and depth. If the part is a sphere or cylinder, provide diameter or circumference.

- *Shape:* Shape can be described in various ways: (1) by using geometric terminology—*sphere, cylinder, cube, square, triangle, cone, ellipsoid,* and so on; (2) by comparison to letters of the alphabet—*A-frame, L-shaped, S-curve,* and so on; (3) by comparison to some well-known shape—*egg-shaped, branching, umbrella-shaped, dishlike, heart-shaped,* and so forth.
- *Material* (composition): Try to name the exact substance in describing the composition of a part. Instead of *metal,* specify *aluminum.*
- *Weight:* Weight is usually given for the entire mechanism rather than for each part and subpart, unless the mechanism is large.
- *Color:* If color is important or if the mechanism has a characteristic color range, provide this information. Be as specific as possible. Instead of *blue,* specify *turquoise.*
- *Texture:* Words like *smooth, rough, fuzzy, glazed, hard,* or *soft* describe texture.
- *Location:* Location of a part on the mechanism is explained by noting its placement—such as *near the base, next to the handle, at the top.*
- *Method of attachment:* A part may be attached by glue, by nail, by rivet, by screw, by staple, or by being baked on, welded on, friction fit, injection molded, molecularly bonded, and so on.

You will not ordinarily need to provide *all* these kinds of description in writing the description of a mechanism. For example, the color and texture of some objects may be irrelevant. It is up to you to make the choice of appropriate descriptors. For most mechanical devices, the following list of descriptors will suffice:

1. shape
2. size
3. material
4. location
5. method of attachment

Planning the Organization

The organization of a description of a mechanism can differ according to the problem and purpose involved. A brochure, advertisement, or product description may consist of almost nothing but description, or it may have a separate introduction and conclusion. However, a standard description of a mechanism is often only a part of some larger document, as explained previously, and is followed by instructions for how to operate, repair, assemble, or disassemble—as in a manual—or management and cost sections—as in a proposal. This chapter explains how to write such a standard technical description, which has only two basic parts: an introduction and a body.

The Introduction   The introduction to a description of a mechanism provides an overview of the mechanism as a whole. It includes the exact name of the mechanism, a formal sentence definition of it (for instructions see Appendix C), and an explanation of its purpose, if it can be said to have one. The purpose of a virus, one of the mechanisms described later in this section, would be hard to explain. However, the purpose of most devices—even natural ones such as the human heart or stomach—can be described. In addition, the introduction contains a general description of the mechanism as a whole and a list of the main parts. These introductory elements, along with additional directions, follow.

1. *Name:* Give the exact name (and manufacturing number if appropriate) of the mechanism.
2. *Definition:* Write a formal sentence definition of the mechanism.
3. *Purpose:* Explain the purpose of the mechanism. In determining this, ask yourself what it is used for, why it exists, who uses it, and what its operation produces.
4. *Size:* Give the size of the mechanism as a whole.
5. *Shape:* Describe the shape of the mechanism as a whole.
6. *Weight:* For most mechanisms, especially small ones, specify the weight only in the introduction and only for the entire mechanism; the weight of each part and subpart need not be given.
7. *Material:* If the entire mechanism is made up of one substance, note this only once, in the introduction; there is no need to mention it over and over again with the description of each part and subpart. If the mechanism is made up of *different* substances, do not mention material in the introduction.
8. *Color:* If the entire mechanism is characteristically one color or if it typically appears in a certain range of colors, note this in the introduction. If each part or subpart is a different color, omit color from the introduction.
9. *List of main parts:* In the last sentence of the introduction, provide a list of the parts to be described, in the order in which they will be introduced. Name only main parts, not subparts.
10. *Illustration:* Provide a figure in which you show the entire mechanism, possibly from more than one view, with all main and subparts labeled.

The best way to plan your introduction is to make a brief list of what you want to include: refer to the list of ten introductory elements given in this section. Write out the numbers 1 through 10 on a blank sheet of paper and add the appropriate information after each number. If you decide that some descriptor—such as color—is not necessary or relevant, draw a line after the number. Set this list aside until you are ready to draft the introduction in complete sentence form.

The Body   The best way to plan the body of a description of a mechanism is to formally outline it, because in the body you must provide parallel description of each part and subpart you identify. For example, if you describe the size, shape, and material of part A, you should also describe the size, shape, and material of part B and part C. The easiest way to make sure that you do not accidentally omit part of the description is to create an outline.

You should already have analyzed the mechanism into its separate parts and subparts and named them. In your outline, make each main part a major division and each subpart a second-level division. Writing in complete sentences, begin each first-level division with a definition of the part being described. You may use any kind of definition you think useful; check Appendix C on definitions for an explanation of the different types. After each definition, provide the kinds of description for each part that you decided on previously. Follow a parallel pattern throughout your outline. That is, provide the same *kinds* of description for *each* part.

The following sentence outline of the body of a paper describing a T-2 virus (for which the introduction is shown later) makes clear the parallel description of the main parts. Notice that only two kinds of descriptors— shape and size—are given. These details follow the first-level divisions of the outline, each of which provides an operational definition of a part of the mechanism. The weight and composition of the entire organism have already been described in the introduction. They are not mentioned again in the body because the entire virus is small and is made of only one substance—protein. This avoids needless repetition in the body of the description.

Outline

TITLE: Description of a T-2 virus
THESIS: The T-2 virus is composed of five main parts: head, collar, core, baseplate, and tail fibers.

Definition

I. The head of the virus contains a single strand of DNA, which is used in self-replication.

Shape
Size

A. The head is polyhedronal.
B. It is approximately 6 microns long and 5 microns in diameter.

Definition

II. The collar reinforces and protects the head of the virus.

Shape
Size

A. The collar is doughnut shaped.
B. It has an internal diameter of 1 micron and an external diameter of 2 microns, with a thickness of 1.5 microns.

Definition

III. The core serves as the transport system for the viral DNA moving from the head into the host.

Shape
Size

A. The core is tube shaped.
B. It is 8 microns long, 1 micron in diameter, and hollow.

Definition	IV. The baseplate acts as the site of attachment to the host and contains enzymes that will dissolve a hole in the cell membrane of the host so that viral DNA may be injected into the host cell.
Shape	A. The baseplate has a short, cylindrical shape and is simply an extension of the core.
Size	B. It is 2.5 microns long and has an external diameter of 2 microns.
Definition	V. The tail fibers act to secure the virus to the host prior to the ejection of the viral DNA.
Shape	A. The tail fibers are slender strands of protein.
Size	B. They are 10 to 12 microns long and 850 angstroms in diameter.

The virus described in this outline has been analyzed as having five main parts and no subparts. The outline of a description of a mechanism containing both main and subparts would be further divided. In this case, the practice is to begin by introducing each main part *generally*, by defining it and providing a brief description (of its shape and size, for example) before introducing a list of the subparts of which it is composed. Each subpart is then defined and *thoroughly* described, maintaining the same parallelism of description given for each main part *not* subdivided. The following outline illustrates the typical organization of a description that includes a second main part divided into two subparts.

WITH NO SUBPARTS	I. Definition of part I A. Shape of part I B. Size of part I C. Material of part I D. Location of part I

WITH TWO SUBPARTS	II. Definition of part II
	A. Shape of part II
	B. Size of part II
	C. Subparts of part II: subpart 1 and subpart 2
	   1. Definition of subpart 1
	     a. Shape of subpart 1
	     b. Size of subpart 1
	     c. Material of subpart 1
	     d. Location of subpart 1
	   2. Definition of subpart 2
	     a. Shape of subpart 2
	     b. Size of subpart 2
	     c. Material of subpart 2
	     d. Location of subpart 2

WITH NO SUBPARTS	III. Definition of part III A. Shape of part III B. Size of part III C. Material of part III D. Location of part III

In the next step, when you prepare a draft from your outline, you may combine details from two divisions, such as shape and size, into one sentence. In some cases you may decide to alter the order, reversing the introduction of size and shape, for example, if such a reversal makes the mechanism easier to visualize for your reader. However, if you have taken the time to write an outline and have made sure that all sections are parallel, your draft should include all necessary details and not omit particular points.

Choosing a Style

The style of most technical description is impersonal and objective. Since technical description is often hard to follow, make a special effort to choose clear, understandable terms and to provide plenty of transitions. If you are writing a description for a potential customer, such as in a sales brochure, subjective terms like *easily removable* and *durable* are acceptable. For typical technical description, however, stick to objective language, description that can be verified by another observer. Instead of *high*, explain that it is four feet tall. Instead of *hot*, state that its common temperature is 95°F.

Drafting the Document

Once you have analyzed your mechanism to divide it into parts and subparts, decided on appropriate kinds of description, planned the organization, and given some thought to appropriate style, you will be ready to draft.

Drafting the Introduction

The introduction to a description of a mechanism provides an overview of the entire mechanism. It includes appropriate details taken from the list of ten typical elements described in the previous section. Ordinarily, the entire introduction is written in one paragraph. It should be followed immediately by an illustration of the mechanism with all parts labeled. The word INTRODUCTION, centered and capitalized, may head the section. An example of a complete one-paragraph introduction for a description of a Bowles Dynasonic Stethoscope, along with an illustration of the instrument, appears in Figure 9.4. The description is written for a nonexpert audience, such as a group of students in a licensed practical nursing program.

When a mechanism is more complicated, more detail may be needed to introduce it fully, and the introduction may be longer. Such introductions may be divided, with each division labeled. Three logical divisions are *definition*, *description*, and *list of parts*. The introduction for the

INTRODUCTION

Name
Formal definition

Purpose

General
description

List of main parts

A Bowles Dynasonic stethoscope is a medical instrument used to listen to sounds produced from within the body. Physicians and nurses commonly use it to listen to sounds made by the heart and lungs, but it can also be used to hear sounds made by other internal organs. This enables a medical worker to detect many kinds of disorders. The stethoscope is Y-shaped and approximately 21 inches long from the earpieces to the chestpiece. It weighs approximately three ounces. The main parts of the stethoscope are the earpiece assembly, the collecting tube, and the chestpiece assembly. These parts are shown in Figure 1.

Illustration

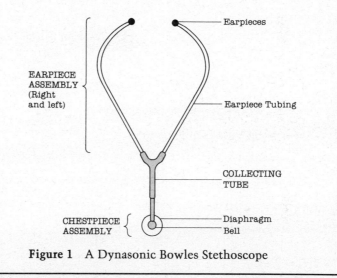

Figure 1   A Dynasonic Bowles Stethoscope

Figure 9.4   One-Paragraph Introduction to a Description of a Mechanism

description of the T-2 virus, for which an outline was previously given, appears in Figure 9.5. This description is addressed to a relatively sophisticated audience, such as the readers of a medical encyclopedia or a basic text in microbiology.

Drafting the Body

When the introduction to a description is labeled separately, as in a typical technical description, the body also begins with a centered, capitalized heading such as DESCRIPTION or PHYSICAL DESCRIPTION. Choose such a heading to begin the body of your paper.

After that, with your outline before you, write one paragraph of description for each main part, including all the kinds of description you previously decided on. Follow a modified procedure when you describe a main part that is composed of subparts. In this case, first write a short paragraph naming and defining the main part. Include a *brief* general description and conclude with a list of the subparts it comprises.

After this, begin a new paragraph for each subpart described, following your outline and providing parallel description of each subpart.

The following complete description of a fixed carbon resistor (see Figure 9.6) shows the relation of the introduction to the body and illustrates how the paragraphs of the body are laid out on a page.

INTRODUCTION

DEFINITION

The T-2 virus (or bacteriophage) is a parasitic infectious vector (an organism that carries a disease-causing agent from one host to another) that will assume control of a host's genetic material and reprogram it to produce viral nucleic acids and proteins. The specific host to this strain of virus is the bacterium Erestericia coli (E. coli). This virus reproduces itself by propagating viral genetic material at the "expense" of the host. The virus will use the host's ribosomes and amino acids to make viral DNA.

GENERAL DESCRIPTION

The T-2 virus is an elongated, arrow-shaped structure with a length of between 12 and 15 microns. The diameter varies along its length. The entire unit is composed of structural proteins of similar atomic weights and Svedberg character. The only nonprotein materials in the virus are the single strand of DNA contained in the head and the hydrolytic membrane enzymes contained in the baseplate. The total dry mass of one T-2 bacteriophage is about 10 micrograms.

MAIN PARTS

The main parts of the T-2 E. coli infecting virus are the head, collar, core baseplate, and tail fibers. (See Figure 1.)

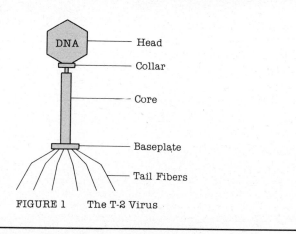

FIGURE 1   The T-2 Virus

Figure 9.5   Introduction to a Description of a Mechanism

INTRODUCTION

A fixed carbon resistor is an electrical component that limits the amount of current and voltage that may flow through a circuit. Fixed carbon resistors come in various shapes and sizes. The unit described here is a cylindrical, two-watt resistor. This device is 4 inches long, including its leads, and ¾ inch long without the leads. The diameter of the resistor is ¼ inch, and the overall weight is ¼ ounce. The main parts of the resistor are the wire leads, the carbon resistance material, and the insulator. These parts are shown in Figure 1.

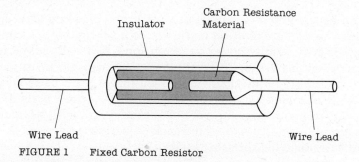

FIGURE 1   Fixed Carbon Resistor

DESCRIPTION

The wire leads of the resistor carry the current and voltage through the carbon resistance material contained inside the insulator. The leads are made of copper wire and extend out from each end of the resistor. The leads are

usually about 1½ inches long, but they are often cut to make them shorter. The

diameter of each lead is about ¹⁄₁₆ inch.

    The carbon resistance material is what actually limits the current and

voltage flow through the circuit. The material is molded in a cylindrical shape

and forms the center of the resistor. In the two-watt resistor it is ½ inch long

and has a diameter of ⅛ inch.

    The insulator keeps the current and voltage from escaping from the carbon

material. The insulator is cylindrical and surrounds the carbon material like a

glove around a finger. The wire leads extend out from within the insulator. The

insulator is made of porcelain and is ¾ inch long. It has a diameter of ¼ inch.

Figure 9.6   Description of a Fixed Carbon Resistor

Writing the Conclusion (Optional)

The conclusion to a description of a mechanism may include various
kinds of information: a summary of the description; comments about
variations in the mechanism—ranges of sizes, for example; comments
about current uses; predictions about future uses. The purpose of the conclusion is to draw the description to a close. If you add a conclusion, introduce it with the word CONCLUSION.

Reviewing and Reworking the Document

After you have completed a draft of your paper, examine it for logic and
usefulness. *Good organization is the key to a successful description of a
mechanism.* It is usually better to group some parts—as subparts of one
main-part assembly—than to treat all parts as separate main parts. It is
easier to understand a mechanism divided into 4 main parts with 3 subparts each than to understand a mechanism with 12 main parts. If you can
see any way to logically group parts of a mechanism with a large number
of parts, do so. In addition, double-check each descriptive section to make
sure you have included the same kinds of description for each part. When
you are dealing with a great number of details, it is easy to accidentally
leave out one kind of description for a particular part or subpart, although
you have provided it for all the rest of the parts.

    When you proofread, pay special attention to spacing, headings, and
the writing of numbers and abbreviations throughout your paper. Check
Appendix B for guidelines on how to write numbers and fractions in a
report. Also, take a final look at your illustration, which should follow

immediately after your introduction. Correct problems of incomplete labeling, crowded labeling, or lack of white space around the drawing. Make sure you have introduced your graphic before it appears.

Producing the Finished Document

If you are writing a technical description of a mechanism for a classroom assignment, retype your draft neatly and incorporate the illustration. Consider adding color to the final version of the graphic. A touch of colored ink, colored pencil, or colored felt-tip pen can make a great deal of difference in the look of an illustration.

If you are writing a variation of a standard description of a mechanism, you may want to consider typing your final draft on a nonstandard size of paper, making the illustration fold out from the page or placing the entire description within the panels of a fold-out brochure sheet. It is not the purpose of this chapter to explain how to handle all these variations, but with your instructor's permission, you may want to experiment with different presentations.

Sample Papers 1 and 2 are examples of finished documents written by students. Evaluate them in the light of guidelines given in this chapter. Remember, though, that you may need to modify your writing on the job to meet the particular problems you are addressing. These guidelines are meant only to familiarize you with the major problems involved in writing a description of a mechanism.

INTRODUCTION

An Autolite PV3 spark plug is an automotive component used to ignite the fuel-air mixture in the cylinder of an internal combustion engine. The spark plug starts the combustion of gas by setting off a small spark at the appropriate time. This particular spark plug is most often used in motorcycles. The spark plug is cylindrical with an overall length of 2½ inches, a maximum diameter of ¾ inch, and a weight of two ounces. The three main parts of the spark plug are the main central conductor, the insulator, and the main body assembly. (See Figure 1.)

DESCRIPTION

The central conductor is an electrical pathway for the positive current flow. It is one piece of metal 2½ inches long and 3⁄16 inch in diameter,

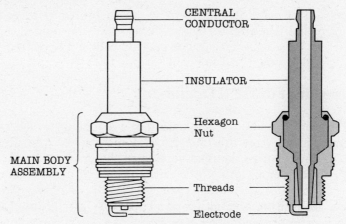

FIGURE 1.   Spark Plug: Outside View and Cross-section

cylindrically shaped with a knob on one end. The central conductor runs down the center of the spark plug.

The insulator is an electrical nonconductor that prevents current flow from the central conductor to the engine block. It is a 2¼-inch porcelain sheath with a maximum diameter of ½ inch. The inside of the insulator is a hollow tube, ½ inch in diameter, through which the central conductor runs. The insulator completely surrounds the central conductor, which it is baked onto, except at the very top and bottom.

The main body assembly is a multipurpose structure that is used as an electrical pathway for negative current flow and for easy installation and anchoring of the spark plug. It has an irregular cylindrical shape with a hollow tube ½ inch in diameter running down its center, onto which the insulator is molded. The main body assembly is made of one piece of metal with a height of 1 inch and a maximum diameter of ¾ inch. The main body assembly is divided into three subparts: the hexagon nut, the threads, and the electrode.

The hexagon nut provides a gripping surface for use in installation and removal of the spark plug. It is located at the uppermost section of the main body. It is a regular, six-sided polygon with a distance of ¾ inch between the opposite flat sections of the polygon. The hexagon nut is constructed of the same metal as the main body and is continuous with

it. The hexagon nut is usually gripped by a wrench when the spark plug
is installed or removed.

The threads of the spark plug form a modified screw shaft to hold the
spark plug in the cylinder head of the engine. They are located at the
base of the main body and have a diameter of ½ inch and a height of
½ inch. The grooves of the threads are cut in a helix around the outside of
the bottom section of the main body.

The electrode provides a pathway for the negative current flow. It is
L-shaped, with a width of ⅛ inch and a length of ¼ inch. The electrode is
located at the base of the threads and is constructed of the same metal as
the rest of the main body. A small gap of about .025 to .030 inch is
maintained between the electrode and the central conductor. When
current is delivered, the electricity will jump this gap, causing a spark
and igniting the fuel-air mixture.

Sample Paper 1: Description of a Spark Plug

INTRODUCTION

DEFINITION AND PURPOSE

A flashlight is a small battery-operated portable electric light. It is most
often used to illuminate a dim or dark place.

OVERALL DESCRIPTION

This Ready-Light flashlight is cylindrical, with one end slightly flared and
the other end slightly rounded. It is 7¾″ long and weighs eight ounces.

MAIN PARTS

The main parts of the flashlight are the ring cap, light assembly, body, and
end cap assembly (Figure 1).

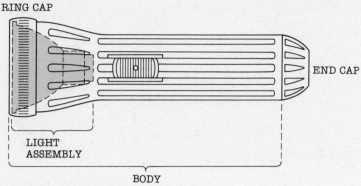

RING CAP

END CAP

LIGHT
ASSEMBLY

BODY

FIGURE 1   Flashlight

DESCRIPTION

RING CAP

The ring cap screws onto the threaded collar at the front of the flashlight body and retains the light assembly. The outside of the ring cap is ribbed to provide a gripping surface. The inside wall of the cap is molded in such a way that the forward part of the cap is the thickest. This part of the ring cap acts as a lip, thereby retaining the light assembly. The inner wall of the ring cap is threaded to allow for attachment to the head of the flashlight. The outside diameter is $2\frac{3}{16}''$ and the inside diameter at the thickest part of the cap is $1\frac{5}{8}''$.

LIGHT ASSEMBLY

The light assembly provides the illumination. It consists of the lens, reflector, light bulb, light bulb socket, and conductor (Figure 2).

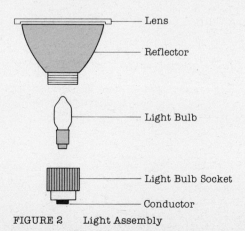

Lens

Reflector

Light Bulb

Light Bulb Socket

Conductor

FIGURE 2   Light Assembly

Lens

A plastic lens protects the light bulb from damage. It is a transparent disc with a diameter of 1⁷⁄₁₆″. A lip, inside which the reflector fits, borders the perimeter of its back surface.

Reflector

The reflector casts the light forward. It is made of copper and shaped like a bowl. Its inside is coated with a chrome finish that reflects the light. It is 1¾″ in diameter and ¾″ high from the lip of the bowl to the bottom of the base. At the bottom of the reflector is a hole that accommodates insertion of the light bulb. The base of the reflector provides a small lip around the hole to hold the light bulb in place. The outside of the base is threaded to allow for attachment of the light bulb socket.

Light Bulb

The light bulb converts electricity into light. The glass part of the bulb is shaped like a teardrop, and the metal base is cylindrical. The bulb measures 1⅛″ from the tip of the base to the top of the glass. There is a small flange bordering the top of the base where the glass and the base are fused together. Upon insertion of the light bulb into the reflector, the flange meets the lip inside the base and aids in retaining the bulb.

Light Bulb Socket

The light bulb socket screws onto the base of the reflector, thereby retaining the light bulb in its place. It is made of molded plastic and resembles the cap of a small bottle. The upper portion of the socket is ribbed to make it easier to attach the socket to the reflector. Its outside diameter at the widest point is ⅞″ and its overall length is ⅞″. The lower portion of the light bulb socket has a slit to provide for the insertion of the conductor.

Conductor

The conductor transmits electricity from the batteries to the light bulb. It is a small strip of conductive metal which slips into the slit in the base of the light bulb socket. Each end of the conductor bends down to hold it in place. It is ¼″ long and ³⁄₁₆″ wide on both the inside and outside of the socket.

BODY

The body of the flashlight houses the light assembly and the batteries. It resembles a cylinder with a "window" cut out near the flared end. It is made from ribbed, molded plastic, which provides a good gripping surface, and it is 6½″ long. The body consists of the casing and the switch assembly (Figure 3).

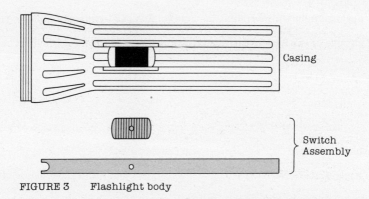

FIGURE 3   Flashlight body

Casing

The casing of the flashlight houses the light assembly and batteries and serves as a handle. A threaded band runs around the perimeter of one end, which is flared. Its diameter at the widest part is 1¾″ and at its narrowest 1¼″. A copper band is pressed to the inside wall of the threaded band. It provides a surface for the lip of the reflector to sit against, so it is kept in position. The threaded band also provides an anchor for the ring cap.

Switch Assembly

The switch assembly completes the electrical circuit between the batteries and the light assembly. It consists of a switch and metal strip.

Switch

The switch is a small, rectangular, plastic plate that fits over the window in the flashlight casing. It is attached by a screw that threads through the switch into a conductive metal strip inside the casing. The back and forth movement of the switch, which also moves the metal strip, turns the flashlight on or off. The switch is 1⅜″ long, ¾″ wide, and ¼″ high. There is a hole in the middle to accommodate a screw and ridges on either end of the switch to make it easier to manipulate.

Metal Strip

The conductive metal strip is made of copper. It is 5⅝″ long and ⅜″ wide. When the switch is on, one end of the metal strip is positioned against a metal band in the lower end of the casing, and the other end rests on the underside of the reflector, thereby completing the circuit. When the switch is off, the circuit is broken.

END CAP ASSEMBLY

The end cap assembly retains the batteries in the flashlight handle and forms a part of the electrical circuit within the flashlight. It consists of the spring, collar, and end cap (Figure 4).

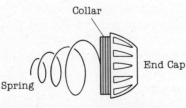

FIGURE 4   End Cap Assembly

Spring

The spring provides a constant pressure against the batteries, which ensures a sound connection with the light bulb. It is made of a conductive metal, is spiral-shaped, and screws onto the copper collar. The spring is $\frac{1}{16}''$ in diameter and 6″ long.

Collar

The collar is a copper band fitted into the end cap. It is threaded to provide for the attachment of the spring. It is $\frac{3}{8}''$ wide above the edge of the end cap and $1\frac{3}{8}''$ in diameter.

End Cap

The end cap secures the batteries inside the flashlight handle. It is bowl shaped and formed of molded plastic. It is $\frac{7}{8}''$ high and $1\frac{3}{8}''$ at its widest diameter. It screws tightly into the handle.

Sample Paper 2: Description of a Flashlight

Key Points in the Chapter

1. A mechanism is an object made up of a system of parts that function together in some way.
2. A description of a mechanism includes definitions as well as descriptions of all parts and subparts.
3. The introduction of a description of a mechanism includes a formal sentence definition, an explanation of purpose, a general description, a list of the main parts, and an illustration.
4. The body of a description of a mechanism is composed of paragraphs of description of each main part and subpart, each section beginning with a *definition*.
5. Whatever *kinds* of description are provided for one part should be provided for every part, as a rule.
6. The description of a mechanism often lacks a conclusion or is simply a part of a longer document.

Exercises

1. Choose one of the following mechanisms and write a description of it for a book to be read by junior high school students.

human eye   plant cell
human ear   pine tree
nerve cell   volcano
amoeba   tulip
animal cell   thundercloud

2. Choose one of the following objects and write a technical description of it to explain what it is to a college freshman who is not a science or technology major.

solar calculator   alcohol torch
voltmeter   electrocardiogram electrode
spirometer   small microscope
disc pack   oscilloscope
Stryker-frame bed   autoclave
cathode ray tube   auto timing light
Bolen gauge   camera tripod
pair of binoculars

3. Write a technical description of one of the following household items for a manual providing a precise description of the item and explaining how to manufacture it. You will write only the *description*, not the manufacturing instructions. Provide a brand name for your item.

claw hammer   handsaw
can opener   adjustable wrench
eggbeater   thermometer
electric blender   basting tube

4. Write a technical description of one of the following musical instruments for a brochure about the instrument. You will write only the *description*, not the entire brochure.

guitar   violin
harmonica   snare drum
wooden recorder   base drum
trumpet   tambourine

5. If you have designed a mechanism as part of your course work in engineering, architecture, or a similar field, provide a detailed description of it.

6. Find out if an instructor at your college could use a description of a mechanism he or she must explain to students. Provide the description in a form that could be handed out to students.

10 Writing Instructions

Abstract

When you become expert in your field, you will be expected to instruct others, sometimes through writing. Instructional documents vary greatly in length, complexity, and appearance, but all are written to meet the needs of particular readers. To write good instructions, you must thoroughly understand the task at hand; you may need to gather information about it or perform the task yourself before drafting. Most instructional documents contain two or more of six standard elements: introduction, tools and materials list, description of a mechanism, theory of operation, operation or performance instructions, and maintenance procedures. The number and order of these sections vary, but in all instructional documents the inclusion of illustrations is important, and clear writing is critical. Once drafted, an instructional document should be "field tested" to ensure its usefulness before it is put into final form.

As a student or novice in your field of study, you are now actively involved in learning the principles and skills that will enable you to function competently as a professional. However, as you become skilled at your profession you will find that the tables will sometimes be turned, and you will be expected to be the teacher. Instructions for simple tasks, especially those that will be done only once, are normally given orally. However, instructions for carrying out procedures that are complicated or that must be repeated are ordinarily put into writing.

An instructional document may be brief or lengthy, simple or complex, written on a typed card or printed in full color with fold-out plates and overlying transparencies. Nevertheless, no matter what the scope, most instructions have certain characteristics in common:

- They are aimed at a particular group of readers.
- They are highly organized and often present instructions in a numbered sequence.
- They make extensive use of graphics to help readers visualize tasks.
- They are written in simple, easy-to-follow language.

This chapter will explain how to write instructional documents that meet all these criteria.

Defining the Problem and Purpose

As with all other forms of practical writing, instructions are written to solve *particular* problems, like these:

- A free-lance computer programmer has just completed a new word-processing program for legal assistants. The programmer believes she can sell the program but knows the legal assistants who need to use it don't understand how to do so and may have little or no experience with word processing.
- A nurse practitioner in a pediatric hospital must explain to parents how to care at home for a child with a tracheostomy (opening surgically cut into the windpipe to allow free breathing). The care required is complex and is critical to the child's recovery.
- An elementary school administrator has worked out a new fire drill procedure for the school. The procedure must be explained to all school staff so they will know how to carry it out correctly and safely.
- A small electronics firm has designed a burglar alarm system for businesses. Before it can be sold, a manual must be written explaining how to install the system, operate it, and trouble-shoot any problems.

Before beginning an instructional document, write out for yourself the problem you face. List the things your readers need to know.

Your purpose when writing instructions is to enable your readers to solve the problem you have described and to do it efficiently, correctly, and (sometimes above all other considerations) *safely*.

Determining the Audience

Before writing instructions, you should determine who your probable readers will be and find out as much as possible about them. Age, educational level, previous work experience, and physical fitness may be important, as these factors can determine what you need to explain, what terms you should define, and what style of language you may use. In determining and defining your audience, write out your answers to the following questions, as they apply to the instructional document you are writing.

1. Who is likely to read your instructions? If you have many readers, describe their different characteristics.
2. What do you anticipate to be the general educational level of your readers?
3. What matters related to your instructions can you reasonably expect them to know? Which matters will they know little about? Consider readers' likely familiarity with equipment, materials, procedures, and safety precautions.
4. What special problems—physical, intellectual, or even emotional— may your readers have in following your directions?

To understand why it is so critical to identify and describe for yourself the readers of an instructional document, imagine you are writing instructions for how to set up and operate a piece of medical diagnostic equipment. Who would be likely to use the instructions? Would your work be read by hospital maintenance personnel, biomedical technicians, the manufacturer's technical representatives, or practicing physicians? These different people have very different backgrounds and informational needs, and your writing would have to take these differences into account.

The time you take to identify your audience can save you a great deal of time later. If you don't understand the needs of your readers, your instructions simply won't work for them.

Collecting the Data

Writing instructions for any procedure, from how to change a tire to how to perform delicate surgery, requires that *you*, the writer, understand the procedure thoroughly. In some instances, you may understand all you need to know already, and you can begin designing your document immediately. If this is not the case, you may need to gather information before you begin. The following suggestions can help.

- Identify any equipment, supplies, or tools needed to perform the task. Be sure you know the correct name for each item and why it is needed.
- Use the library or interview experts to gain a better understanding of the equipment or principles involved in carrying out the procedure. To write an operation manual for a particular piece of equipment, you may need to understand the theoretical principles underlying the operation of the mechanism you are explaining.
- Observe someone else performing the task. Write out what the person does at each step: describe *every* task-related movement the person makes.
- Perform the task yourself; take notes at each step explaining what you are doing.

In gathering information about the task to be performed, be sure you understand *what* should be done, *how* it should be done, and *why* it should be done. Your thorough understanding of the task will make it easier for you to teach others.

Designing the Document

The design of an instructional document—whether brochure, booklet, or manual—varies according to the problem it addresses. Some instructional documents are simple in design, containing little more than an introduction and a set of directions; some are much more complex. Figure 10.1 shows a simple instructional document. The introductory page of this fold-out brochure announces the purpose of the document and features a picture of the product, a telephone. On opening the brochure, a reader sees instructions for how to use the phone, connect it, and adjust the ringing tone. The reverse side shows how to attach a telephone number sticker and how to hold the handset. These easy-to-follow instructions meet the needs of the adults who will purchase the phone.

Designing an instructional document that really works takes time as well as consideration of structure, graphics, and appropriate style.

Choosing a Structure

Many instructional documents are more complex than the simple fold-out brochure just shown. Depending on the problem, you may choose to

Figure 10.1   Brochure: First Panel

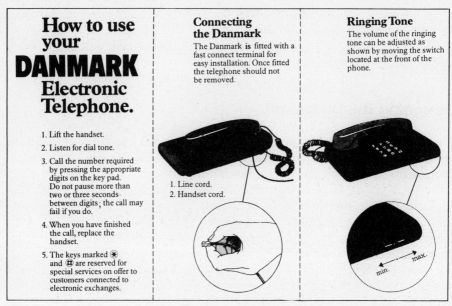

How to use your DANMARK Electronic Telephone.

1. Lift the handset.
2. Listen for dial tone.
3. Call the number required by pressing the appropriate digits on the key pad. Do not pause more than two or three seconds between digits; the call may fail if you do.
4. When you have finished the call, replace the handset.
5. The keys marked ✳ and ⊞ are reserved for special services on offer to customers connected to electronic exchanges.

Connecting the Danmark

The Danmark is fitted with a fast connect terminal for easy installation. Once fitted the telephone should not be removed.

1. Line cord.
2. Handset cord.

Ringing Tone

The volume of the ringing tone can be adjusted as shown by moving the switch located at the front of the phone.

min.   max.

Figure 10.1   Brochure: Second, Third, and Fourth Panels

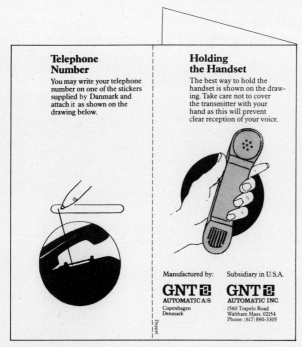

Telephone Number

You may write your telephone number on one of the stickers supplied by Danmark and attach it as shown on the drawing below.

Holding the Handset

The best way to hold the handset is shown on the drawing. Take care not to cover the transmitter with your hand as this will prevent clear reception of your voice.

Manufactured by:

GNT ⊞
AUTOMATIC A/S
Copenhagen
Denmark

Subsidiary in U.S.A.

GNT ⊞
AUTOMATIC INC.
1560 Trapelo Road
Waltham Mass. 02154
Phone: (617) 890-3305

Figure 10.1   Brochure: Fifth and Sixth Panels

include in your work any of the following six elements common to instructional writing:

- Introduction
- List of tools and materials
- Description of a
    mechanism
- Theory of operation
- Operation or performance
    instructions
- Maintenance procedures

Choose the number of these elements you will use and their order of presentation in light of your problem and purpose. Each of these elements is described in the following pages.

Introduction   The introduction to a document containing instructions prepares the reader to follow specific directions. Such introductions typically include many of the following elements:

- The brand name of the device for which operating instructions are provided
- An explanation of the problem to be solved by following the instructions
- An assurance that the reader can successfully handle the job
- A description of what will be explained in the document and, perhaps, of what will *not* be covered
- A statement naming the audience for whom the instructions are intended
- Any vital warnings that apply to the procedures—things readers should know even before beginning

The following introduction, taken from a brochure entitled "How to Reduce Chances for Break-ins in Your Home," contains several of these elements.

> Here are tips and suggestions on how to reduce the chances for break-ins in your home. Read them carefully. The steps are quite simple, but effective. They can provide peace of mind and additional security and perhaps save you from considerable losses through theft.

This introduction informs readers that they can expect to learn ways to prevent break-ins by reading the brochure. The material is obviously addressed to an adult audience. However, because the introduction states that the steps described will be "simple," readers who know little about home improvements should feel confident about proceeding.

Some introductions are longer than this example. Figure 10.2 shows a booklet prepared for parents who must provide home care for children with tracheostomies. It begins with the following page long introduction.

CARDINAL GLENNON MEMORIAL HOSPITAL FOR CHILDREN
St. Louis, Missouri

Tracheostomy Booklet

Introduction

Now that the doctor has decided that your child will be going home with a tracheostomy, preparations will need to be made to care for your child at home. This booklet was written to supplement the instructions the nurses and doctors will give you on how to care for your child's tracheostomy.

We understand that you may be frightened and concerned about your new responsibilities. It is perfectly normal to feel the stresses that this situation brings. However, studies have shown and from our experience we know that properly trained families can manage their child with a tracheostomy well at home.

You and your family will be instructed on how to manage the care of your child with the tracheostomy and how to manage the various pieces of equipment that will be used in your home.

You may have many questions, and we want you to feel free to ask. The doctors, the nurses, and the social worker caring for your child will be your resources for counseling and guidance. You will not be discharged until you are comfortable performing the care. We would like you to spend as much time as possible at the hospital and to have spent at least the twenty-four hours here before discharge to become familiar with the routine.

More than one member of the family should learn how to care for your child. We can assist you with this before discharge. A visiting nurse will be available to give you guidance and assistance at home.

We want to encourage you to treat your child like any other child but to keep certain precautions in mind that will be discussed later in this booklet.

Plans for readmission for reevaluation of the tracheostomy will be outlined by your physician. During these admissions, every effort will be made to put your child in a familiar unit. Please keep in mind that each child is different and the reason for the tracheostomy differs. The length of time your child will need the tracheostomy depends on the particular illness, age, and individual airway response. This booklet is designed to cover as many aspects of care as possible and to be a reference for you now and at home.

Figure 10.2   Introduction to an Instructions Booklet

A final example, taken from a student-written operation manual, contains elements not found in the first two. It names the product for which the instructions are written and describes the readers for whom the instructions are intended.

This manual provides operating instructions for the U.S. Divers No. 7040-95 Buoyancy Compensator. This specialized life jacket is designed for use by experienced scuba divers. It should be used only by or under the supervision of a certified diver.

List of Tools and Materials   To carry out many kinds of instructions, one needs certain tools and supplies. The writer of an instructional document could name the instruments as they are needed, but this might easily cause problems—or anger and frustration. Readers might realize halfway through a procedure that they lack some critical piece of equipment, such as a Phillips screwdriver or 2-inch-wide masking tape.

Therefore, when tools and materials are needed, it is best to follow the introduction with a "Tools and Materials" section, naming whatever is needed to complete the task. Sometimes a description and a picture of each item is also provided. Some equipment lists even suggest where the items can be purchased. Figures 10.3 and 10.4 show different ways a list of the tools and materials might be presented.

> TOOLS AND MATERIALS: a socket wrench and socket to fit drain plug, an oil filter wrench, an oil pan, 3-5 quarts of oil (depending on your car—check your owner's manual), and a new oil filter

Figure 10.3   Tools and Materials for Instructions on How to Change the Oil in a Car.

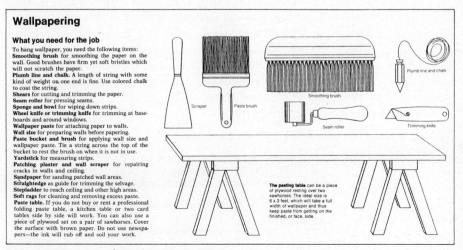

Wallpapering

What you need for the job

To hang wallpaper, you need the following items:
Smoothing brush for smoothing the paper on the wall. Good brushes have firm yet soft bristles which will not scratch the paper.
Plumb line and chalk. A length of string with some kind of weight on one end is fine. Use colored chalk to coat the string.
Shears for cutting and trimming the paper.
Seam roller for pressing seams.
Sponge and bowl for wiping down strips.
Wheel knife or trimming knife for trimming at baseboards and around windows.
Wallpaper paste for attaching paper to walls.
Wall size for preparing walls before papering.
Paste bucket and brush for applying wall size and wallpaper paste. Tie a string across the top of the bucket to rest the brush on when it is not in use.
Yardstick for measuring strips.
Patching plaster and wall scraper for repairing cracks in walls and ceiling.
Sandpaper for sanding patched wall areas.
Straightedge as guide for trimming the selvage.
Stepladder to reach ceiling and other high areas.
Soft rags for cleaning and removing excess paste.
Paste table. If you do not buy or rent a professional folding paste table, a kitchen table or two card tables side by side will work. You can also use a piece of plywood set on a pair of sawhorses. Cover the surface with brown paper. Do not use newspapers—the ink will rub off and soil your work.

Plumb line and chalk

Smoothing brush

Scraper   Paste brush

Seam roller   Trimming knife

The pasting table can be a piece of plywood resting over two sawhorses. The ideal size is 6 x 3 feet, which will take a full width of wallpaper and thus keep paste from getting on the finished, or face, side.

Figure 10.4   List of Tools and Materials

Description of a Mechanism Some instructions are written to explain how to operate a particular piece of equipment, such as a microscope, paint sprayer, or centrifuge. Such instructional documents are referred to as *operation manuals.* In them, the introduction is usually followed by a description of the mechanism involved. (For a review of the principles of writing a description of a mechanism, read Chapter 9.)

A description of the device to be operated, along with a picture of it, is critical in an operation manual. Language simply cannot convey the exact relationship of all the parts of a mechanism to one another, but a picture can. In addition to showing what the mechanism looks like, the picture should contain clear and correct labels of all the important parts. Good labeling helps readers push the right button and turn the right wheel when they are supposed to.

In general, the description of a mechanism appearing within an instructional document need not be as detailed as one appearing in a manual written for someone who will manufacture, assemble, or repair the mechanism—though an operation manual may contain some of this information. To write this section, do three things:

1. Introduce the mechanism first through a general, overall description of the unit and its function. This may be done in a single paragraph.
2. Provide a clear illustration of the mechanism with all important parts labeled clearly and correctly.
3. In a separate paragraph for each part, name it, define it (if is likely to be unfamiliar to the reader), describe the location of the part on the mechanism, and explain the function of the part.

As a rule, an operator of a mechanism needs to know what the part *does* rather than its compostion or dimensions, so you need provide little physical description.

The description of a mechanism shown in Figure 10.5 is taken from the student paper explaining how to operate a buoyancy compensator. The opening paragraph provides an overall description of the device and explains its basic function. This section is followed by an illustration, with each main part of the mechanism *labeled* and *numbered.* The reference number of each part is repeated in the description of each part, which follows the illustration. The use of these numbers again enables a reader to locate the part on the figure easily.

DESCRIPTION OF THE MECHANISM

The buoyancy compensator is a specialized life jacket worn by scuba divers. It is worn around the diver's neck and straps around the back and crotch. It can be filled with air from an oxygen tank or by mouth. Its eight major components are shown in Figure 1.

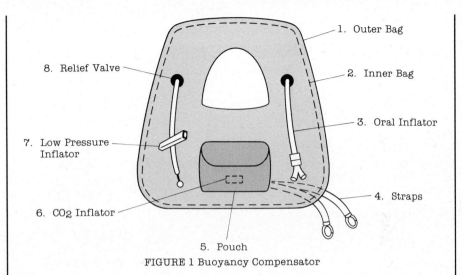

8. Relief Valve
7. Low Pressure Inflator
6. CO2 Inflator
5. Pouch
1. Outer Bag
2. Inner Bag
3. Oral Inflator
4. Straps

FIGURE 1 Buoyancy Compensator

1. Outer Bag

 The outer bag provides a protective covering for the inner bag. It is made of bright yellow, strong, nylon material and provides a base for the attachment of all other parts.

2. Inner Bag

 The inner bag is inflatable and holds the air that keeps the diver afloat. It is contained within the outer bag and made of a tough polyurethane material.

3. Oral Inflator

 The oral inflator is used by the diver to fill the inner bag with air by mouth. It features a contoured mouthpiece and a large air passageway leading to the inner bag. The hose section of the inflator is approximately 8 inches long and very flexible for use at any angle. The inflator is weighted so that it does not float above the diver's head.

4. Straps

 Two 1½-inch-wide straps are attached to the back of the outer bag. They are used to strap the buoyancy compensator around the diver. One strap goes around the waist and the other around the crotch. Each strap adjusts to any desired size and ends with a large snap hook for easy attachment.

5. Pouch

The pouch is a large pocket used to hold a diver's tools and samples that are picked up while diving. It is located on the lower front of the outer bag.

6. CO_2 Inflator

The CO_2 Inflator is a cartridge that can instantly fill the inner bag with carbon dioxide. Located beneath the pouch, the CO_2 inflator provides a safety feature for quick ascent to the surface. By pulling a cord attached to the inflator, a diver can activate the CO_2 cartridge to quickly fill the inner bag.

7. Low Pressure Inflator

The low pressure inflator allows the diver to fill the buoyancy compensator with air from the oxygen tanks. It features a push button that can be used to regulate the amount of air flowing into the inner bag. It also has a valve that keeps the air from escaping from the inner bag.

8. Relief Valve

The relief valve allows rapid release of air from the inner bag when needed. It operates automatically to reduce excess pressure on the inner bag and has a pull cord for deflation and buoyancy control. It is also equipped with a one-way flapper valve to prevent water from entering the inner bag.

Figure 10.5   Description-of-a-Mechanism Section of a Manual

In a description of a more complicated mechanism, a longer general description might be used and the main parts might be divided into subparts, as explained in Chapter 9.

Theory of Operation   Operation manuals often include a section explaining the principles by which a device operates. Understanding *why* something works can help a user handle a piece of equipment more effectively, repair it, or trouble-shoot problems that arise.

However, writing a theory of operation section can present problems. You may need to find additional information about the mechanism and about the principles by which it operates. This may necessitate library research or a talk with an expert. Sometimes principles of chemistry or physics are involved, and you will need to discuss the mechanism's operation with a professor at your college.

The theory of operation section shown in Figure 10.6 explains the principles behind the operation of a microwave oven.

Microwave ovens heat food through the activity of microwaves. Microwaves are very fast, short radio waves; they vibrate back and forth extremely rapidly, approximately two billion times a second. As they pass through food, they cause the food molecules to vibrate also. The friction associated with the movement of the molecules produces heat, and the food is cooked.

Microwaves cause this internal vibration, friction, and heat because of a special characteristic of molecular structure. Many molecules, but especially water and most molecules in food, exhibit a kind of "polarity." The different ends of the molecules have different charges, just as magnets do. When microwaves interact with these molecules, they move them somewhat, just as two magnets affect and slightly move each other.

Some substances, however, have no polarity and are not caused to vibrate by microwaves. Glass, paper, plastic, and most ceramics are very little affected by microwaves. They make ideal containers for food to be cooked in a microwave oven. Microwaves pass right through them.

Metal, however, shields food from microwaves. Aluminum foil wrapping, therefore, slows down the cooking of food. For this reason, some recipes call for placing aluminum foil around the outside edges of a deep dish, to concentrate heat in the center. However, any loop of metal, even a gold edging around the rim of a glass, behaves like an antenna and attracts microwaves, which can deflect from the metal with such force that sparks fly. Metal containers or pans with hooked metal handles are not recommended for use in microwave ovens.

Figure 10.6   Theory of Operation of a Microwave Oven

Operation or Performance Instructions   The heart of any instructional document is the list of commands directing the reader to perform a task or operate a mechanism. This section often appears under a heading such as "Operating Instructions" or "Steps To Follow." The directions provided in this section are usually presented in strict chronological (time) order and are often numbered.

Readers will often follow instructions without first reading through a document completely. Therefore you should not bury critical information toward the end of your instructions. For example, if instructions on how to hang wallpaper explain how to cut, trim, paste, and hang wallpaper *before* mentioning that it is best to remove cover plates on outlet boxes and switches before beginning, this good advice may be lost. Such information should be placed *early* in the sequence of instructions.

In addition, it may be necessary to place headings such as CAUTION, WARNING, or even DANGER throughout a document to alert readers to any step that could result in danger to them or damage to equipment. Warnings are often printed in such a way as to stand out on the page. They may be printed in capital letters or bold type and may be underlined. It's also useful to explain *why* the danger exists and what will happen if care isn't taken.

Proper placement of these warning labels is critical. In nearly all cases, warnings should be placed *before* the step to which they apply. This prevents the reader from beginning a step without realizing the possible problems involved. Nevertheless, when the step is simple enough to be explained in a line or two and is relatively harmless, the warning label is sometimes placed immediately after a step rather than before it because a reader may find it easier to understand there.

However, a caution label should *never* appear on a separate page from the step it explains, and it must *always* precede directions that could involve danger to readers.

When the steps in a procedure can be performed in any sequence, the instructions need not appear in chronological order and need not be numbered. In such cases, the steps are often preceded by dots, bullets, daggers, boxes, or some other graphic device intended to draw attention to the separate directions. To precede nonsequential instructions with numbers implies that they must be performed in a specific sequence and may therefore be misleading.

For example, assume you are writing directions for motorists to tell them what to do if stranded in a blizzard. You might explain a number of things, such as how to conserve body heat, when and how to run the car's engine and heater, how to avoid the dangers of carbon monoxide poisoning, whether or not to go for help, and so on. These things need not be approached in a particular chronological order.

Maintenance Procedures   Instructional documents, especially those explaining how to operate a mechanism, often contain sections of tips on how to clean, maintain, or even repair equipment. Some manuals also include an explanation of how users may diagnose and correct common problems; this is usually referred to as the "trouble-shooting" section. Sometimes these elements are all included in one section labeled "Maintenance Procedures." Sometimes each one is labeled as a major section itself.

In writing maintenance procedures, follow the same general guidelines as for writing operating procedures. As a rule, present directions in chronological order and number them. Insert CAUTION and WARNING labels where appropriate. The following two figures are taken from instructional brochures. Figure 10.7 is from a brochure explaining how to use a Root-Lowell Polyethylene Sprayer. Figure 10.8 contains a section from the *Touchmatic Amana Radarange Use and Care Manual.*

After reviewing the elements commonly featured in instructional documents, choose the combination that seems most appropriate for the document you are writing. Consider including additional kinds of sections if necessary, keeping in mind the needs of your readers. Decide also on the order of presentation of the elements. Many combinations are

MAINTENANCE SUGGESTIONS

1. Keep it clean. Clean it after every spraying. Flush thoroughly with clear water to remove all spray materials. Remove pump and hang up separately. Hang tank upside down. Hold lever open until hose drains.

2. Pump works easier and pumps faster if you apply petroleum jelly to the plunger cup occasionally.

ALWAYS USE THE FOLLOWING PROCEDURE TO RELEASE TANK PRESSURE

If you should have any problems, please call our toll free number as listed on the front cover.

1. Turn tank upside down and hold shut-off valve open until all air pressure is gone from tank.

2. Stand sprayer up and tilt it so top is pointed away from you. Slowly turn handle counter-clockwise until pump assembly is loose and can be removed.

BE SAFE!
If you interrupt spraying, follow the procedure described above and release pressure to prevent build-up.

TROUBLE SHOOTING

If it becomes necessary to remove the plunger assembly from the cylinder on the 1996 or 1997, be sure that the metal striking plate is properly placed in cylinder grooves. Then securely tighten cap until there is only a small crack between the cap and the flange on cylinder.

Always remove liquid and clean sprayer before testing. Refer to service parts diagram for replacement part numbers.

IF YOU CANNOT BUILD UP PRESSURE:

Remove pump. Hold rubber check valve on end of pump closed and operate the pump. If little or no resistance is felt on downstroke, the plunger cup or its check valve are probably at fault. Pull out plunger assembly and inspect cup for scoring, cracking, or dirt under cup check valve. Apply petroleum jelly to side of poly plunger cup. To replace plunger cup, unscrew old cup and screw new cup on until top of cup just touches bumps on side of rod. Check that rod has not entered cup so far that it is pushing check valve out of cup. Inspect pump cylinder gasket and check valve for damage or dirt. Carefully insert plunger assembly into cylinder and test pump operation.

SHUT-OFF VALVE

If the valve fails to shut off, remove body and check for dirt around "O" Ring 805-305. If liquid is leaking back or coming out around lever, then the V-Gasket, part number 151-403 should be replaced.

Figure 10.7   Maintenance and Trouble-shooting

Maintenance Tips/ Cleaning the Unit

To Clean The Oven Interior
The inside walls and floor are made of stainless steel. If they should become splattered, all you do is wipe them with a paper towel or clean with a mild detergent in warm water using a soft sponge or cloth. If desired, a cup of water can be boiled in the oven to loosen soil before cleaning.

Do not use an abrasive to clean the inside. It might damage the stainless steel. Never pour water into the bottom of the oven.

To Clean The Glass Tray, lift up the tray and remove. Wash in warm water and detergent or in a dishwasher. Replace with drip tray pattern up. Do not operate the oven without tray in position.

Always Keep The Touchmatic Plate Clean.
If it is not clean, it may not register the instructions you touch. To clean the Touchmatic plate merely wipe with a **damp** soft cloth or sponge. If the time of day display is accidentally erased from the Touchmatic

Control, merely touch RESET , then set the correct time of day.

To Clean The Temperature Probe wash the metal probe in hot soapy water. Do not immerse the probe plug or wires in water. Do not wash probe in dishwasher.

To Clean The Discharge Air Vents
There will be a slight build-up of cooking vapors in the discharge vent located in the upper right hand corner, above the control panel. This vent should be cleaned occasionally. Do not attempt to remove the front of the Touchmatic Control module; it is an integral part of the oven. Clean the air vent with a damp cloth.

To Clean The Splatter Shield Inside Oven
The splatter shield keeps the top of the oven and antenna from getting dirty. Normally, a damp cloth will remove any splatter from the shield.

However, if you want to clean it more thoroughly, remove the splatter shield. **Be careful not to bend the antenna when removing the splatter shield.** The shield is secured by four screws in recessed wells in the front underside of the shield and four tabs which fit into slots in the back oven wall. Remove the four screws. Then carefully lower the shield and, clearing the antenna, pull the shield forward out of the back wall slots and out of the oven.

Wash the shield in hot, soapy water. **Do not** wash in a dishwasher. **Do not** use harsh or abrasive cleansers.

When replacing, again be careful not to bend the antenna. Also be sure the splatter shield tabs fit snugly into the slots in the back of the oven before replacing the screws.

Figure 10.8   Maintenance Tips and Cleaning the Unit

used, but here are four common designs. Your instructor may assign you to write an instructional document in one of these patterns.

1. Introduction
   Performance Instructions
2. Introduction
   List of Tools and Materials
   Performance Instructions
3. Introduction
   Description of a Mechanism
   Operation Instructions
   Maintenance Procedures
4. Introduction
   Description of a Mechanism
   Theory of Operation
   Operation Instructions

When you have worked out the number and order of sections, you will have created a basic outline of your document. Before drafting, however, you will probably want to further divide and organize the data within these first-level divisions. Outlining to at least the second level throughout will make drafting easier. See Appendix D for advice on outlining.

This is also a good time to ask other people to review your work. Before beginning a first draft, technical writers typically discuss their outlines of major manuals with engineers, managers, and marketing personnel to ensure that all necessary information is scheduled for inclusion. You would do well to ask for similar feedback from instructors, fellow students, or anyone knowledgeable about the procedure you are explaining.

Using Graphics in Instructions

Illustrations are often necessary in instructions. Words can convey only so much of how to perform a complicated procedure, especially if it involves special equipment. Once you have chosen the sections for your instructional document, identify areas where graphics would be useful.

The visuals appearing most commonly in instructional documents are drawings and photographs. Chapter 8 describes various kinds of illustrations and their use. Review that chapter before you decide what kinds of graphics to include and where to place them.

Remember also that a drawing or photograph *must* accompany the description of a mechanism section of an operation manual. Additional illustrations, such as blowups or exploded drawings, may also be helpful. Process drawings, illustrating exactly what to do in carrying out step-by-step instructions, are also commonly included.

Spend time developing and selecting graphics for your instructional document. In many instances, illustrations are essential.

Choosing a Style

A special feature of instructional writing is the use of the imperative (command) mood. When you write in the imperative mood, you command your reader directly. This textbook is written mainly in the imperative mood. It commands you to plan, write, and revise.

Writing in the imperative mood requires you to *direct* rather than to describe and explain. Write sentences such as "Adjust the tension" and "Thread the needle" rather than "The tension should be adjusted" or "The seamstress then threads the needle." This imperative mood may be used in any section of the instructional document, but it is used most often in the operating or maintenance instructions.

The other sections may be written from the third-person point of view. Sentences such as "This manual provides operating instructions for the Dominion No. 10999 Steam Iron" describe, rather than direct, and are appropriate for the introduction, general description of a mechanism, and theory of operation sections.

Throughout your document, keep in mind the needs of your readers. Make your work easy to read. As a rule, use simple declarative sentences and avoid complex sentence structure. Remember that when you write instructions you are *always* writing to a person who knows less than you do. It is better to explain too much than too little, and better to be overly careful in defining terms and providing examples than to leave your readers puzzled.

Drafting the Document

A brief instructional document can be drafted in a single sitting if you have collected enough information and worked out the organization. If you are drafting a longer document, you may find it easier to begin by drafting the section you feel most prepared to write—whether or not it is the introduction. It may also be better to draft the various sections at different sittings rather than to proceed through the entire piece of writing.

However you proceed, don't be a slave to your organizational plan. If you realize that additional sections or details are needed, make the necessary changes in your outline and your draft; you may well discover a number of things you should add or alter. You may also notice additional places where a graphic would provide clarification. Sketch in drawings of what you want as you draft and contine writing. Don't stop at this point to create finished illustrations.

Remember also to pay close attention to the proper sequence of directions when you write the performance or operation instructions. This is probably the most important part of the document and may take the most time to draft.

Finally, if your instructional document is longer than a page or two, consider numbering the *sections.* You may use Arabic or Roman numerals. Many manuals make use of a decimal numbering system. In such a manual, the introduction would be labeled 1.0; the tools and materials, 2.0; the description of the mechanism, 3.0; and so on. Divisions of a section would be introduced with the numbers 3.1, 3.2, 3.3, and so on. Be careful with this technique, however; more than two or three levels of digits can become confusing.

Try not to become discouraged as you draft this sometimes complicated form of practical writing. You will have the opportunity to test and revise your work later, so simply do the best work you can at this point. The purpose in drafting is not to write a perfect document but to produce a work you can later revise and edit until you feel it is satisfactory.

Reviewing and Reworking the Document

Instructional documents often need extensive revision. The best way to evaluate a draft is to observe someone trying to perform a task according to your directions. This can make abundantly clear any problems in basic explanation, sequence of instructions, or clarity of writing.

For your "field test," choose someone typical of the group you believe will use your document. Before the test begins, ask him or her to read through your instructions. Then ask your subject to carry out your instructions. Watch and take notes. Don't interfere or add any additional explanation or help. Note steps with which your subject has trouble. Write down any comments your subject makes. After the test run, ask for additional reaction to the instructions.

Once you have discovered problem areas in your work, revise the document and test again. Repeat the procedure, preferably with a new subject each time, until your subject can perform the task correctly. Once you are certain your instructions work, proofread your draft for errors in spelling, grammar, punctuation, and mechanics. Be sure all the graphics are correctly introduced and labeled.

Producing the Finished Document

An instructional document must be functional. It should be easy to use in the situation for which it is written. For this reason, you may choose to produce your instructional document in some form other than a booklet of 8½-by-11-inch pages. In choosing a final form, ask yourself these questions:

• Where will the reader be when using these instructions?
• Will the reader need to carry the instructions around?
• Where will the instructions typically be kept? In a file cabinet? In a desk drawer? In a pocket? In a purse? In the medicine cabinet?

Depending on your answers to these questions, you may choose to produce your instructions in any of a variety of forms: a booklet typed on sheets half standard size; a fold-out brochure; a full-size booklet; or a single sheet to be taped up in some area, such as next to a copying machine. These are only some of the possibilities.

For your final copy, consider adding color to the graphics. You may also add an illustration to the title page. This part of an operation manual often features a picture of the mechanism.

Also, be sure to *date* your document. Dates commonly appear on the cover sheet or at the conclusion of a document. In some manuals, dates may appear on each page, so that as sections are updated, the dates of the revisions are indicated.

In addition, in a long manual (one of five or more pages), a table of contents should be added. The title of each major section (in the same typeface in which it appears in the manual) and the page number on which it appears should be listed. If the major sections are numbered, these numbers should be included. Illustrations, grouped separately under the subheadings "Tables" and "Figures," should be listed also.

Two sample tables of contents follow. The first, Figure 10.9, is taken from "Parent Booklet: Care of Your Child with a Tracheostomy." The table of contents shown in Figure 10.10 is taken from a student-written manual on how to use a steam iron.

Table of Contents

List of Illustrations

Figure 10.9   Table of Contents from a Booklet, "Care of Your Child with a Tracheostomy"

If you are writing an unusually long instructional manual—one of 25 or more pages—include a complete index to enable a reader to turn immediately to the page dealing with some particular bit of information. Professional technical writers spend considerable time producing detailed indexes for their documents, since an index offers a much more specific guide to details within a work than does a table of contents. Most student work, however, will not require an index.

Finally, to complete your instructional document, consider concluding with a few blank pages labeled NOTES or NOTES AND QUESTIONS, especially if the document is to be presented to a group of people in an educational setting. You might also consider adding a "what to do if you're stumped" section—with the name of a person to contact for additional information, as well as an address and telephone number if appropriate. These elements are optional.

TABLE OF CONTENTS

LIST OF ILLUSTRATIONS

Figure 10.10 Table of Contents from an Operation Manual

The following instructional documents (Figures 10.11 through 10.13), one written by a student and the others by professionals, illustrate the principles explained in this chapter. Read and analyze them for organization, sequence of instructions, use of graphics, and clarity of language. Determine the audience for whom each one is intended.

CARDINAL GLENNON MEMORIAL HOSPITAL FOR CHILDREN
DIRECT PATIENT SERVICES
St. Louis, Missouri

Lumbar Puncture

Purpose: To obtain cerebral spinal fluid for examination, for measurement of the cerebral spinal fluid pressure, or for placement of medication.

Equipment: Spinal Tap tray and Central Venous Pressure manometer from Central Service
Betadine solution
Sterile gloves

Procedural Steps	Additional Information
1. Obtain consent for procedure from parent. 2. Assemble equipment. 3. Explain procedure to patient and parent. 4. Assist the patient to rest on his or her side with both knees and head acutely flexed. 5. Assist the physician while prepping the area and performing the puncture. (You may need another nurse to do this.) 6. Label all tubes with the patient's full name, room number, and date and time, and number the tubes in the exact sequence they were obtained. 7. Send specimens with appropriate requisitions to the lab immediately. 8. Instruct the patient to remain flat in bed 1-2 hours or as ordered. 9. Document procedure, specimens sent to lab, and observations of the patient in the patient's record.	Include that it may be uncomfortable and that patient needs to stay immobilized during the procedure. Place one hand behind the patient's knees and the other on the shoulder. Keep the "up" shoulder from falling forward to prevent rotation of the spine Be prepared to pour Betadine into receptacle on L.P. tray in a sterile manner. Specimens usually sent for: (a) Culture & Sensitivities - Tube 1 (b) CSF sugar and protein - Tube 2 (c) Cell Count - Tube 3 Dianne Cruvant, M.S.N. Formulated: January 1980 Reviewed: January 1981 Revised: March, 1982

Figure 10.11   Instructions for Lumbar Puncture

Blackboard

This double-sided blackboard can keep two children happy at the same time. Blocks under the hinges minimize the chance of legs closing and pinching small fingers, and carpet tape stops the legs from opening too far.

A fold-away blackboard made from hardboard and 1 x 2s.

CONSTRUCTION

If you have a table saw, set it for ½-inch depth to cut the grooves in inside edges of legs (2) to accept hardboard panels (1). Glue panels in grooves, flush at top. If you have no table saw, cut the panels 26 inches wide with a rip saw and screw them to the wide surfaces of the legs. Glue hinge blocks (3) to tops of legs and hinge the two assembled panels together. Use medium-grade sandpaper to round off tops of the tape blocks (4) to protect tapes. Position tape blocks on inside of panels, centered ½ inch above bottom edges. Fasten each tape (5) between panel and tape block with two ¾-inch No. 8 flathead screws. Countersink screws and fill holes with wood putty so that panels will be smooth. Tape should limit angle between legs to about 30 degrees.

Use blackboard paint on the panels or a colored flat latex paint for use with contrasting chalk. Allow either type to harden thoroughly before use. Varnish the legs with clear varnish.

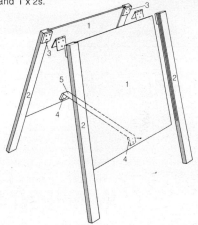

Fig. 2. The hinged boards are kept from opening too far by carpet tape.

PARTS LIST

No.	Name	Quantity	Nominal Size	Length	Width	Material
1	Panels	2		25″	24″	⅛″ hardboard
2	Legs	4	1 x 2	36″		pine
3	Hinge blocks	4	2″ x ½″	2″		pine
4	Tape blocks	2	2″ x ½″	2″		pine
5	Tape	1		18″	1½″	carpet binding tape

Hardware: Two 1½″ galvanized butt hinges with screws. Four ¾″ No. 8 flathead steel screws; 16 screws if panels are screwed to legs.

567

Figure 10.12   How to Build a Blackboard

HAMILTON BEACH MINI DRIP COFFEE - TEA MAKER
Household Appliance

INTRODUCTION

It is a known fact that the best coffee made is by the drip filter method. With your Mini Coffee/Tea Maker, you can brew coffee or tea quickly and deliciously.

The basket cover is designed to distribute water evenly over coffee or tea grounds, extracting only the most desirable flavor and aroma. And the paper filter catches even the smallest particles to insure a clean, delicious, cup of coffee or tea.

So enjoy!

IMPORTANT SAFEGUARDS

When using electrical appliances, basic safety precautions should always be followed including the following:

1. Read all instructions.
2. Do not touch hot surfaces. Use handles.
3. To protect against fire, electric shock and personal injury, do not immerse cord, plugs, or base in water or other liquid.
4. Close supervision is necessary when used by or near children.
5. Unplug cord from outlet when not in use and before cleaning. Allow to cool before putting on or taking off parts and before cleaning the appliance.
6. Do not operate any appliance with a damaged cord or plug or after the appliance malfunctions or is dropped or damaged in any manner. Return appliance to the nearest authorized service facility for examination,

electrical repair, mechanical repair or adjustment.

7. The use of accessory attachments not recommended or sold by the appliance manufacturer may cause fire, electric shock or injury.
8. Do not use outdoors.
9. Do not let cord hang over edge of table or counter, or touch hot surfaces.
10. Do not place appliance or any parts on or near a hot gas or electric burner, in a heated oven, or in a microwave oven.
11. Be sure switch is off, then plug cord into wall outlet. To disconnect, turn any control to "Off," then remove plug from wall outlet, being sure to grip plug firmly. Never yank on the cord.
12. Scalding may occur if the coffee basket or carafe and cover are removed during the brewing cycle.
13. Do not use appliance for other than intended use.
14. Do not remove glass carafe from warmer plate until hot coffee has completely drained from basket.
15. Keep lid on carafe during brewing operation and while pouring coffee.
16. Do not operate in the presence of explosive and/or flammable fumes.
17. Do not use glass carafe if damaged in any manner. A chip or crack could result in unseen glass particles in the beverage which could be harmful if swallowed.
18. Do not allow all liquid to evaporate from carafe.
19. Do not pour liquids other than water and cleaning solutions specified in this manual into the water tank. (See section "How to Clean Coffee Maker.")
20. Do not lift and/or move entire unit when carafe contains hot liquid.

SAVE THESE INSTRUCTIONS

3

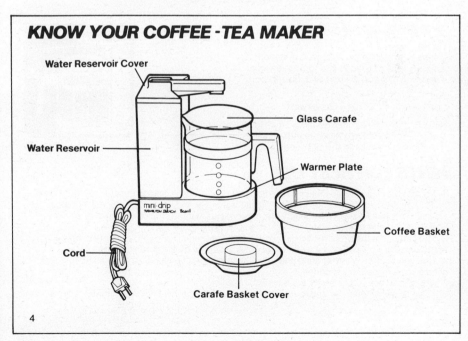

Figure 10.13   How to Use a Coffee–Tea Maker

HOW TO USE

COFFEE
1. The Coffee Tea Maker brews 2 to 4 cups
2. Before using first time, operate unit once with clean water only to assure a clean system.
3. Remove coffee basket and place a 3½ inch flat filter in basket.
4. Measure coffee (drip or regular grind) or tea into basket. Spread evenly.
5. Fill the carafe with fresh cold water to the level you wish (4 cup level is to bottom edge of band).
6. Pour the water into reservoir on top of unit (Do not overfill). Replace cover.
7. Place filled basket in carafe, cover and place on warmer plate. ALWAYS MAKE SURE CARAFE IS IN PLACE BEFORE PLUGGING IN.
8. Plug unit into any 120 volt wall outlet.
9. As soon as the brew cycle is complete and the coffee or tea stops dripping out of basket remove basket and grounds. Replace cover.
10. The brew is now ready to pour. It will stay warm if not all is used immediately. The warmer plate will not, however, reheat cold coffee.
11. Unplug when carafe is empty.

5

AMOUNTS OF COFFEE AND TEA

Coffee
2 cups – 1 to 2 scoops or 2 to 4 tablespoons
3 cups – 1½ to 3 scoops or 3 to 6 tablespoons
4 cups – 2 to 4 scoops or 4 to 8 tablespoons

Tea
Use 1 teaspoon for each cup of water.

NOTES: A standard coffee scoop is equal to two level tablespoons. Taste for coffee and tea differ for individuals. You may wish to vary the amounts mentioned to suit your own taste.

HINTS FOR BEST USE

1. Start with a clean coffee maker, since oil and sediment which cling to the pot may impair flavor.
2. To keep any excess grounds from falling into water, you may wish to dampen filter before placing in basket. This can be done by first dampening filter and placing in basket or placing dry filter in basket and running water through it, emptying excess.
3. The amount of the brew will be slightly less than the amount of water you started with. Approximately ½ ounce of the water (per cup) is absorbed by the ground coffee.
4. Drip grind coffee is a finer grind and allows greater extraction for a full body taste. Regular grind gives a milder cup of coffee.
5. Never pour brewed coffee or tea back into reservoir.
6. Once brewed, never dry and reuse coffee grounds. Not only will flavor be impaired, but a

6

potential safety problem could occur since the temperature and moisture levels involved are ideal for mold growth.

7. If desired, you may use your coffee/tea maker to heat water for use in preparing instant soups, broths, hot chocolate, gelatin, etc. Simply pour water from carafe into reservoir and let it pump through system back into carafe.

Extension cords may be used if care is exercised in their use.
  A. A short power-supply cord is provided to reduce the hazards resulting from becoming entangled in or tripping over a longer cord.
  B. Longer cord sets or extension cords are available and may be used if care is exercised in their use.
  C. If a longer cord set or extension cord is used,
    (1) The marked electrical rating of the cord set or extension cord should be at least as great as the electrical rating of the appliance.
    (2) The longer cord should be arranged so that it will not drape over the countertop or tabletop where it can be pulled on by children or tripped over accidentally.
Do not plug in appliance before adding water, and do not add water to hot coffeemaker.

HOW TO CLEAN COFFEE-TEA MAKER

1. After unplugging, cool down. DO NOT IMMERSE BASE IN WATER. Wipe with a damp cloth and dry.
2. Wash carafe, lid, basket assembly in sudsy water, rinse and dry. Do not use abrasive materials.
3. All piped water contains minerals which eventually will build up as scale on any water heating appliance. This build-up can affect the taste of good coffee and should be removed periodically. To do this, operate unit with 2 ounces white vinegar and 4 cups water twice a year in soft water areas and four times a year in harder water areas. Then to rinse out possible vinegar taste, operate at least twice with clean water.

7

THE CARE AND USE OF GLASS CARAFES

Avoid Abrasion - Do not use abrasive cleaners, brushes with metal parts, steel wool, etc. to clean the container. Rinsing with water or mild detergent and a cloth or boiling a solution of baking soda and water for cleaning is recommended. Also, avoid placing metal utensils, finger rings (i.e. diamonds) etc. into the glass item. Internal abrasion greatly reduces the strength of the glass.

Glass containers should not be used directly upon electrical elements, an intermediary metal screen or pad is required.

Avoid Impact - Glass will break under a severe enough impact.

The container must not be boiled dry as this may induce a permanent stress in the glass. If this happens, the glass should be discarded.

Gas flames or direct electrical burner heat can melt the hardware or break the carafe. Do not use glass carafe on a burner.

Hamilton Beach Division
Scovill
Washington, North Carolina 27889
PRINTED IN U.S.A.

P.N. 3-230-784-0000 R 3-83

How to Use a Coffee–Tea Maker *(cont.)*

Sample Paper

HOW TO OPERATE A

POWER-PAK PORTABLE FIRE EXTINGUISHER

Marilyn Williams
Report Writing 103
Mr. Rabushka
January 22, 1985

TABLE OF CONTENTS

1.0 INTRODUCTION   1

2.0 GENERAL DESCRIPTION   2

3.0 DETAILED DESCRIPTION   2

    3.1 TANK   2

    3.2 HANDLE   2

    3.3 SAFETY PIN   2

    3.4 LEVER   2

    3.5 HEAD   2

    3.6 NOZZLE   2

    3.7 PRESSURE GAUGE   2

4.0 THEORY OF OPERATION   4

    4.1 PROPULSION   4

    4.2 DEOXIDATION   4

5.0 OPERATION   4

    5.1 TO USE   4

    5.2 TO RECHARGE FIRE EXTINGUISHER   4

1.0 INTRODUCTION

This manual provides operating instructions for the Power-Pak, Model 5 ABC portable fire extinguisher. This extinguisher can be used to put out small class A, B, and C fires (paper, wood, gasoline, oil, and electrical). It should be used only by adults or by children under supervision.

2.0 GENERAL DESCRIPTION

The Power-Pak extinguisher contains chemicals packed under pressure. These chemicals can be discharged from the nozzle to put out small fires. The extinguisher works like an aerosol spray can. When pressure is released, dry chemicals pass through the nozzle and onto the fire, extinguishing it. The main components of the fire extinguisher are shown in Figure 1.

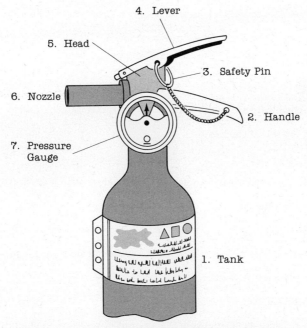

FIGURE 1 Power-Pak Portable Fire Extinguisher

3.0 DETAILED DESCRIPTION

3.1 TANK

The tank (1) contains dry chemicals packed under pressure. It stores the chemicals until they are needed. The tank is light weight for easy handling.

3.2 HANDLE

The handle (2) serves as a gripping surface for a user. It can be used to lift the extinguisher and to direct the flow of the dry chemicals. It is located on the top of the tank.

3.3 SAFETY PIN

The safety pin (3) is a protective device, consisting of a metal ring that passes through small holes in the lever and head. It keeps the extinguisher from being accidently discharged. The safety pin is located at the base of the lever just above the handle, to which it is attached by a short chain. The extinguisher cannot be used unless the safety pin is removed.

3.4 LEVER

The lever (4) operates the fire extinguisher. When pressure is applied to the lever, dry chemicals are released from the tank through the nozzle. The lever is located on the top of the head.

3.5 HEAD

The head (5) is the top of the fire extinguisher, to which the handle, lever, and nozzle are attached.

3.6 NOZZLE

The nozzle (6) directs the discharge of dry chemicals from the tank. It is located on the head of the fire extinguisher.

3.7 PRESSURE GAUGE

The pressure gauge (7) displays the amount of pressure in the tank. The gauge is located at the top of the tank. It contains two color fields and an indicator arrow.

3.7.1 RED COLOR FIELD

The red color field extends to the left and right of the blue color field. The position of the indicator arrow in the red color field indicates that the pressure is either too low or too high, and the extinguisher should not be used. If pressure is too low, the extinguisher must be recharged. (See 5.2.) If the pressure is too high, pressure can be reduced by inverting the extinguisher and pressing the lever slowly, then releasing it.

3.7.2 BLUE COLOR FIELD

The blue color field is at the top center of the gauge. If the indicator is in the blue color field, the extinguisher is ready to use.

3.7.3 INDICATOR ARROW

The indicator arrow moves freely from left to right, displaying the level of pressure within the tank. It pivots from a pin at the center of the pressure gauge. The indicator arrow and both color fields are shown in Figure 2.

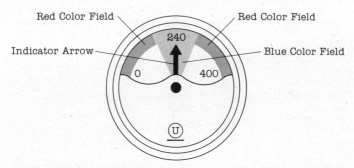

FIGURE 2 Pressure Gauge

4.0 THEORY OF OPERATION

4.1 PROPULSION

Pressure maintained inside the tank forces the dry chemicals within to be quickly expelled through the nozzle when the nozzle is opened via the lever. Adequate pressure within the tank must be maintained for the fire extinguisher to function.

4.2 DEOXIDATION

Fires need oxygen to burn. When the dry chemicals within the tank are sprayed over a fire, they cover it, cutting off its oxygen supply. The fire then dies out. The dry chemicals within the Power-Pak portable fire extinguisher will cover gasoline and electrical fires, unlike the liquids within some fire extinguishers.

5.0 OPERATION

5.1 TO USE

1. Hold upright.
2. Pull safety pin (3).
3. Squeeze lever (4).
4. Direct the discharge of dry chemicals to the base of the flames, using a side-to-side motion. Continue until fire is extinguished.

5.2 TO RECHARGE FIRE EXTINGUISHER

1. Invert extinguisher and press lever slowly to release all pressure inside tank.
2. Remove gauge (7).
3. Clean gauge ring and threads (located behind pressure gauge) with a clean, dry cloth.
4. Lubricate the gauge ring with light household appliance oil.
5. Fill the tank with 5 pounds of Power-Pak triple class ABC powder. WARNING! Do NOT use other types of dry chemicals in this extinguisher.
6. Screw pressure gauge back in place.
7. Remove and clean nozzle (6) with cloth or brush
8. Screw in place behind nozzle an MT-3 moisture trap.
9. Press lever (4) and pressurize to 240 psi.
10. Remove moisture trap.
11. Replace nozzle.
12. Insert safety pin again.

Key Points in the Chapter

1. Before drafting instructions, determine who your probable readers will be. Age, educational level, previous work experience, and physical fitness may all be important.
2. You must thoroughly understand the task you are going to explain; gaining this understanding may require library and field research or performing the task yourself
3. The design of an instructional document may be simple or complex, and the document may contain any number of sections. However, six common elements are introduction, list of tools and materials, description of a mechanism, theory of operation, operation or performance instructions, and maintenance tips. The number of elements and their order of presentation may vary.
4. Operation or performance instructions are usually numbered and presented in chronological order.
5. Instructional documents usually include graphics, especially if special equipment is involved.
6. Instructional writing must be easy to read. Many parts of an instructional document are written in the imperative (command) mood because directions are easier to follow than descriptions.
7. As you draft an instructional document, don't be a slave to your organizational plan. If you realize additional sections would improve the document, add them.
8. All instructional documents should be "field tested" if possible before being put into final form.
9. The final form of an instructional document may take many shapes. In choosing a form for production, a writer should take into account how the document will be used, carried, and stored.

Exercises

1. Rewrite the following selection. Create an easy-to-follow format. Add anything you think might help a reader and omit what you feel is not needed. Assume your reader to be a person training to be a licensed practical nurse.

    Taking a blood sample is an important procedure because blood can be analyzed by a laboratory technician for any type of disease or disorder that could, in some cases, be fatal. Although it is a fairly easy task, you should have some knowledge of the needle and syringe and its use. Before taking a sample, you need a tourniquet (usually a small rubber hose), some alcohol-soaked cotton balls, and a needle and syringe. In taking a blood sample, you have two major steps: First, prepare the patient, and, second, draw the blood.
    First, place the tourniquet on the patient's arm approximately three inches above his elbow. With his arm straightened out and extended, have the patient clench his fist. If the patient has long nails, give him a small object

such as a wadded tissue or a bath cloth to grasp to prevent his nails from digging into the palm of his hand. Next locate the vein with your forefinger. The vein is usually protruding because of the pressure from the tourniquet and clenched fist. If the vein is not protruding, you must "feel" it with your forefinger. Then, after finding the vein, cleanse the area with a cotton ball soaked in alcohol.

Now you are ready to draw the blood. Inject the needle into the vein. Be sure not to inject the needle completely through the vein. It is very important to be cautious here! Pull back on the plunger with your thumb until the required amount of blood is in the syringe. After drawing the blood and after also loosening the tourniquet with your free hand, place an alcohol-soaked ball of cotton over the needle and vein and pull the needle from the vein. Have the patient bend his elbow up tightly to prevent unnecessary bleeding.

After taking the sample, you usually put the blood in a test tube with the donor's name on the label and take the tube to a laboratory where the prescribed tests are made.

2. Assume your company has just developed a new model of one of the following items. Write an operation manual or fold-out brochure of at least four panels for the product.

Simple calculator	Stapler
Timing light	Pencil sharpener
Movie camera	Garden shears
Blender	Curling iron

3. Assume the organization where you work has just purchased one of the following pieces of equipment but that many staff members are not familiar with its use. Write a one-page instruction sheet to be posted next to the equipment.

Microfilm reader	Photocopying machine
Mimeograph machine	Movie projector
Autoclave	IV (intravenous) fluid pump
Drafting table and machine	

4. Assume you are a technical writer. You are asked to write an instructional document explaining how to complete any of the following procedures. Write the document.

How to give an injection
How to sterilize equipment
How to use a .22 caliber rifle safely and properly
How to use a simple computer program
How to attach an electrical plug to a cord
How to grow roses
How to clean, flush, and refill an automobile radiator
How to strip and refinish furniture with particular products
How to plan a sales, training, or skill-enhancing conference
How to introduce new buyers to a newly developed product
How to tune up a 10-speed bicycle
How to give a haircut
How to install a wall light switch
How to stage a successful political fundraising event

How to develop an advertising campaign
How to suction the nose and mouth of a baby properly

5. Create a problem of your own and produce the necessary instructional document to solve it. Before proceeding, submit a memo to your instructor explaining these things:
   a. The problem
   b. The organizational context of the writing
   c. The type of document—brochure, manual, and so on—needed
   d. The tentative title of the document
   e. Your probable audience (name the group and describe it in 25 to 50 words)

11 Writing an Abstract

Abstract

An abstract summarizes the important points of an extended piece of writing. Abstracts are now used more than ever before because they help busy people keep up with professional and on-the-job reading. There are two kinds of abstracts: descriptive and informative. Composing an abstract requires consideration of all stages in the writing process except collecting the data, since the work to be abstracted is available when you write. Abstracts appear along with articles and reports but are also collected and published separately in journals.

An abstract is a careful summary of an extended piece of writing such as an article or report. The terms *abstract, introductory summary, executive summary*, and *synopsis* are often used interchangeably. This chapter will use the term *abstract* to refer to any of these forms of condensed writing. The summaries appearing at the beginning of this and every chapter provide examples of the form.

Abstracts are now used more frequently than ever before because they help busy people keep up with on-the-job and professional reading. Reading the abstract of a report instead of the complete work saves time, and when it is possible, a manager will do just that. This is particularly true for executives in any field and for professionals in rapidly expanding fields like microcomputer engineering and data processing, where new developments and procedures make continual professional reading mandatory. In addition, even when the complete work must be read, abstracts are helpful because readers who have scanned a well-written abstract can read the complete work more efficiently, having already learned its main points.

Two Forms of Abstracts

There are two kinds of abstracts: descriptive and informative. The organization of each type is different, and they also have different uses. Before you begin writing an abstract, you will need to understand these two common designs so you will know which form to choose.

Descriptive Abstracts

A descriptive abstract sets forth the subject of an article but does not state its main points. A typical descriptive abstract is one sentence long and reads like the sample in Figure 11.1. Note that in this descriptive abstract the "alternative methods" mentioned are not listed. The abstract lets the reader know what subject is addressed but provides little information about it.

"Recruiting Women Engineering Students in Colleges"—This article describes alternative methods for recruiting and retaining women engineering students in traditionally male-dominated engineering programs.

Figure 11.1   Sample Descriptive Abstract

Because descriptive abstracts say so little, they are probably the least-used kind. However, they are useful as subtitles to articles or chapters because they can help to engage the reader's interest; and some reference books, which describe many works, use only descriptive abstracts in order to save space.

Informative Abstracts

In contrast, informative abstracts convey considerable information and are, therefore, preferred by most readers and editors. An informative abstract is actually a miniature, or "scale model," of the original—something like an outline or table of contents of the complete work written in paragraph form. It conveys all the important points of the original work, usually in the original order. Informative abstracts commonly precede both business reports and articles appearing in professional journals.

The abstract of a formal report is *always* an informative abstract. It precedes the report, on a separate page, and outlines the *purpose* and all the *important points* of the work, generally in the same order as in the original, as well as any *recommendations*.

A sample informative abstract from the "Final Environmental Impact Report for the California Energy Commission Solar Program and Wind Program," an environmental impact study written in 1981, is shown in Figure 11.2.

The first sentence of this abstract informs the reader of the subject and scope of the report, and the sentences that follow summarize each major section. A study of this abstract will reveal that it has three major sections: The first explains why the solar program "is not expected to have any significant environmental effects"; later, the abstract explains that the solar program "will have socioeconomic effects"; finally, the report concludes, the California Wind Program may have significant environmental impact. The additional details in this informative abstract explain the nature of the various effects. The complete report, of course, is quite lengthy—203 pages, in fact.

Abstracts of published articles are also commonly informative rather than descriptive. The abstract of "The Retarded Offender: A Problem Without a Program" (*Corrections Magazine*, 1980) is shown in Figure 11.3.

This Final Environmental Impact Report (FEIR) analyzes the California Energy Commission's (CEC) Solar Program and Wind Program. The Solar Program is not expected to have any significant environmental effects. The assembly of solar systems will require the manufacture of certain component materials such as steel, aluminum, glass, copper, fiberglass insulation, and polyurethane insulation. With the exception of copper and aluminum, all the materials can be manufactured in California. The air quality impacts associated with the production of these materials are insignificant and, in most cases, are more than offset by reduced emissions from decreased electrical generation and natural gas consumption. It is also indicated that there are no expected water quality impacts associated with the production of the materials; however, the operation and maintenance of closed type solar systems can introduce certain toxic substances into public waterways. The Solar Program will also have socioeconomic effects, since the purchase price of some new housing will increase as a result of installing solar systems. However, solar energy systems, in certain circumstances, can be shown to be more cost-effective than conventional electric and natural gas systems. The California Wind Program was directed to locate and verify sites for wind farms, establish a wind information center, and test a medium-scale wind turbine generator as a demonstration of the feasibility and reliability of wind energy. Construction impacts from turbine pad leveling, access roads, and transmission corridors could be considerable. Conflicts with existing and future land use may also occur. Operational effects include minor changes in microclimate, bird collisions with the turbine blades, noise, increased off-road vehicle use, aesthetics, and radio and television wave interference.

Figure 11.2   Sample Informative Abstract

At least five percent of the inmates in America's jails and prisons are mentally retarded. Experts on retardation are convinced that many retarded offenders could be prevented from committing crimes, or rehabilitated once they do commit offenses, if the courts and correctional agencies would only make the effort. Diversion programs designed for retarded offenders are rare. In general, the retarded in prison are a problem without a program. The Washington State correctional system is making a special effort to protect retarded inmates, and the Virginia system is currently operating programs for retarded inmates. North Carolina has the most sophisticated approach to identifying and helping retarded juvenile offenders.

Figure 11.3   Informative Abstract of an Article

The main point, or thesis, appears in the second sentence: "Experts on retardation are convinced that many retarded offenders could be prevented from committing crimes or rehabilitated once they do commit offenses, if the courts and correctional agencies would only make the effort." The final two sentences name the agencies that are making the effort. If this abstract were "laid out" as an outline, it would look like the following analysis.

Outline

Title: "The Retarded Offender: A Problem Without a Program"

Thesis: Experts on retardation are convinced that many retarded offenders could be prevented from committing crimes or rehabilitated once they do commit offences, if the courts and correctional agencies would only make the effort.

  I. Diversion programs designed for retarded offenders are rare.
 II. In general, the retarded in prison are a problem without a program.
III. Three states are attempting to address the problem.
   A. The Washington State correctional system is making a special effort to protect the retarded inmates.
   B. The Virginia system is currently operating programs for retarded inmates.
   C. North Carolina has the most sophisticated approach to identifying and helping retarded juvenile offenders.

As a professional, you will be likely to both read and write abstracts, so it is important to understand this form of practical writing. Composing a complete and readable abstract is a critical skill and requires consideration of all stages in the process of practical writing except for collecting

<u>the data.</u> The data needed to write an abstract—that is, a complete report or article—will normally be available when you need to write.

Defining the Problem and Purpose

When might you need to write an abstract? Why might someone ask you to write one? Consider the following situations:

- The President of the United States needs to be informed of thc developments reported each morning by the major newspapers in the country but cannot possibly read through all the newspapers.
- An instructor wishes to give students a list of major reference works for a particular subject but knows that the students won't know by the titles alone what each book emphasizes.
- A busy director of marketing has not yet responded to a 40-page committee report, with no introductory summary, which has lain on the director's desk for a week.
- Before inviting speakers to present papers at a professional convention, the organizer of the conference needs to know what the people who wish to speak would like to discuss.

There are many situations in which a problem exists because someone needs a concise summary of information but cannot or does not want to read through pages of writing. These problems can be solved by providing an abstract. Sometimes the need for an abstract may be very evident— but sometimes not. The instructor just described may not be aware of how useful descriptive abstracts of works cited on a bibliography might be, or how much students might need them. However, the President of the United States will certainly be aware of the need for summaries of events, and someone will be assigned to write them. Likewise, a director of marketing who is too busy to read through a 40-page report will probably send it back to the committee that submitted it with a request for an abstract and a stern reminder never to submit reports without abstracts again.

As a rule, when an abstract is required to solve some problem, the situation will be clear: You will have written an article or report and will know that you must include an abstract of the work in order to submit it for publication or in order to submit it to a superior, such as the director of marketing.

Your purpose will also be clear: You must aim to produce a readable summary of all the important points of an extended piece of writing for a reader or readers who need the information in an easily accessible form.

Determining the Audience

Although identifying the problem and purpose involved in writing an abstract should be little trouble, defining your readership may take a little more thought than might at first seem evident.

The task of defining your audience is especially important when you are writing the abstract of a formal report. As explained in Chapter 12, an abstract is now a standard element of such reports and is, in fact, the most frequently read section. For this reason, many of the people who read the abstract of a formal report are likely to have little or no expertise in the particular technical area on which the report may focus. A manager reading the abstract of a proposal from the data processing department for the purchase of a new piece of equipment may not be an expert in data processing or computer science. However, he or she should be able to read at least the abstract of the report with complete understanding. It is your responsibility as a writer to make the abstract understandable to such readers.

You will also be writing for an audience of generalists—rather than of experts—when you write an abstract of an article for publication. An abstract of an article appearing in a journal should be readable by any professional working in the field the journal addresses. Very few people are expert in every aspect of their profession, but they should be able to read the abstracts of articles dealing with any aspect of their work. And of course, the abstract of an article appearing in a popular magazine should be clear to someone in the general public who might read it.

In short, before you begin to design or draft an abstract, identify clearly the audience for whom you are writing and write to meet their needs.

Designing the Document

The first decision you face now is the choice of whether to write an informative or a descriptive abstract. If you can solve the problem you identified in stage 1 by explaining the main idea of a work and omitting coverage of supporting points, a brief descriptive abstract will do. In this case, there is little need to design, since the abstract will be no longer than a sentence or two and will include few details. If, however, you decide that an informative abstract is best, more preparation will be necessary. We suggest the following three steps: (1) read the article; (2) determine how long your abstract may be; (3) outline the work you are abstracting.

After you have worked out the organization, through outlining, you need to give some thought to appropriate style before you actually draft the abstract. You will not, however, need to give any attention to graphics in designing an abstract; they are not a part of the form.

Determine How Long Your Abstract May Be

The generally recommended length for an informative abstract is from 5 to 10 percent of the length of the complete work. Sometimes a specific length—such as 150 to 300 words—is dictated by the editor of a publication in which an article or abstract might appear. As a rule, however, the longer the original work, the longer the informative abstract. Nevertheless, no matter how long the original, the general practice is to limit an abstract to no more than a page and to confine it if possible to one well-developed paragraph. Abstracts of a page or more are used only to summarize extremely long reports.

To determine how long an abstract may be, you need to know the approximate length of the original. If the work is long, simply count the pages. Your final abstract may be no longer than 10 percent of the complete work. If a report is 15 pages long, your abstract of it may be up to a page and a half in length, although a page or less might be more useful.

If you are writing an abstract of a brief work, such as an article, determine the approximate number or words in the piece. You don't have to count each word; here's one simple way you can do it:

- Begin by marking off the first 10 lines. Count the number of words in this 10-line block and write down the number.
- Next, mark off every 10 lines of the article, adjusting for incomplete lines of type as best you can. Count the total number of these 10-line sets and write down the number.
- Multiply the first number (words per 10-line set) by the second number (number of 10-line sets). This will give you the approximate number of words in the article.

Let's say that the first 10-line set of type contained 89 words and that you counted 11 10-line sets with 5 lines left over. Multiplying 89 by 11.5 (the .5 represents the 5 lines remaining) will give you the approximate number of words in the article, 1023.5. Rounded off to the nearest 10, the approximate number of words is 1,020.

When you know the approximate number of words in the article, multiply by .10 and round off the figure for the approximate maximum length of your abstract. Thus, the abstract of a 1,020-word article should be 102.0 (or about 100) words or less.

Outline the Work You Are Abstracting

When you have determined how long your abstract may be, outline your article or report. An article often has an introductory section, or "lead," which may be one or more paragraphs long. It usually contains the thesis sentence for the entire article, though it may not be directly stated. Underline or write out what you think is the thesis statement. If you are abstracting a report, begin by examining the introduction. The purpose or scope statement or a combination of both will provide the main idea of the work.

Once you have determined the thesis or main idea, look for topic sentences throughout the work. These sentences will introduce sections of more specific detail. Underline or mark these topic sentences. Also, *pay close attention to section headings*, since they highlight main points. The better organized a report or article is, the easier it is to separate main and supporting points. Experience in outlining your own essays and reports will help you see the organization in other writing more easily.

When you have read through the work and marked what you think are the main points or major divisions of the work, go over it again and reconsider your analysis. Eliminate any points you now consider to be less than major divisions and add any you may have omitted.

In the following article, "Space Trash" by Linda Garvey, the main points have been underlined and supporting detail sections have been checked.

Space Trash

On a clear night you can sometimes see a starlike object winking its way across the sky. If you look up with binoculars just after sunset, you might see four or five of these twinkling specks of light passing every hour. A few of them are artificial satellites, evidence of man's increasingly productive use of space. But most of them are garbage.

"There are only about 235 operational payloads now in orbit," explains Donald J. Kessler, an astrophysicist at the Johnson Space Center in Houston.

Thesis
The rest of the estimated 10,000 to 15,000 bodies circling the Earth are pieces of useless junk, which according to Kessler could soon pose a greater hazard to spacecraft than meteoroids.

I.
Space junk ranges from nonfunctioning satellites and spent rockets to tiny fragments left over from collisions and explosions of spacecraft. "There have been about 50 explosions in space that we know about," Kessler explains, "and those have generated about 60 percent of the total tracked population of junk."

Many of the accidental explosions involved American Delta rockets that blew up as long as three years after launching, says Kessler. By burning off residual fuel and opening vents to relieve the pressure in combustion chambers, U.S. space officials hope to prevent future Delta explosions. There have also been intentional detonations in space. The Soviet Union has tested killer satellites on eight occasions, each time blasting dummy targets into millions of pieces too small to track but still perilous to space vehicles. Because of their high impact velocities, even fragments as tiny as one-sixteenth of an inch across can penetrate and damage most spacecraft.

II.
The debris is thickest and collisions are most likely in the regions from 100 to 1,200 miles above the ground, the area of greatest unmanned activity to date. Kessler says the most probable accident is

the ramming of two inactive objects such as an old
rocket body and an explosion fragment. That collision would unleash a rain of millions of new pieces,
which in turn could hit other spacecraft. Such collisions, rather than explosions, will probably create
most of the space junk of the future.

III.   Scientists are also worried about the growing
amount of debris in higher orbits, particularly the
22,000-mile-high geosynchronous orbit. Because satellites there remain fixed over one spot on the Earth
as it rotates, the geosynchronous orbit is vital for
communications. Some experts have suggested protecting it from litter by establishing a "garbage
dump" at a slightly higher altitude. "Satellites could
carry just enough fuel to remove them from geosynchronous orbit once they have lost their usefulness,"
says Kessler.

Other proposed solutions include orbiting trash
cans, or scavenger satellites. Marshall Kaplan, a
Pennsylvania State University aerospace engineer, is
working on preliminary designs for a scavenger 20
to 30 feet across. Its mechanical, trash-collecting
arms would be controlled by technicians on Earth.
"The trash can would be released by the space shuttle," says Kaplan. "It could float around for weeks or
months doing its mission and then be picked up on a
later shuttle and brought back to Earth for
emptying."

The Ground-based Electro-Optical Deep Space Surveillance system, soon to be put into operation by
the Air Force, could also aid in protecting valuable
orbits. Operating from five sites around the world,
the system could greatly increase the current catalog
of 4,600 useless items that Earth-based sensors now
keep tabs on.

IV.   For all the mess up there, the risk of collision for
any particular craft is low. If the space shuttle were
in orbit for a full year, for example, there would be
less than one chance in 10,000 of its being struck by
a known piece of junk. Still, the number of stray
items is growing by 11 percent a year, and scientists
expect that something will crash into at least one
hapless spacecraft within the next decade.

As is typical of magazine articles, this article from the December 2
Science 81 contains a "lead" of several sentences. The purpose of the lead
is to draw the reader into the body of the article. The thesis sentence of
the piece does not appear until the last sentence of the second paragraph.

The next *two* paragraphs explain the source of space junk—"nonfunctioning satellites and spent rockets" and "fragments left over from

collisions and explosions of spacecraft." These two paragraphs form the first division of the body of the article. The next paragraph describes the area of thickest debris and constitutes the second major division. Following this is a description of the area of debris that most worries scientists and for which three methods of protection are proposed. This section comprises the third major division.

The concluding paragraph of the article brings up a final major point—that "the risk of collision for any particular craft is low"—and forms the last major division. Although a typical college essay would not introduce a new major point in the conclusion, one often sees it in journalistic writing.

Once you have finished your analysis of the major divisions and supporting points, construct a sentence outline of the work. Follow conventional outline form. (See Appendix D for instructions on outlining.) Include first-, second-, and possibly some third-level divisions.

Work carefully. *Outlining will probably take more time than any other step in the process of writing an abstract, but it is the most important step.* Your abstract can be no better or no more complete than your analysis of the writing, as shown in your outline. Outline for *meaning*, not particular wording. You may occasionally need to compose a general statement (for a first- or second-level division) to introduce sections of detail. Sometimes an article will present sections of grouped detail without such an introductory statement.

An outline of "Space Trash" follows. Compare the divisions and wording of the outline with the marked divisions and wording of the original article. You will notice that some of the sentences have been simplified and condensed. Rewording an article as you outline is a good technique, but never reword unless you are sure you understand the meaning of the original and can translate it accurately.

Outline

Title: "Space Trash"

Thesis: Space junk could soon pose a greater hazard to spacecraft than meteoroids.

I. Space junk includes nonfunctioning satellites, spent rockets, and tiny fragments left over from collisions and explosions of spacecraft.
  A. Many of the accidental explosions involved American Delta rockets.
  B. There have also been intentional detonations by the Soviets.
    1. The Soviet Union has tested killer satellites eight times, each time blasting dummy targets into millions of small pieces.
    2. Because of their high impact, even fragments as tiny as one-sixteenth of an inch across can penetrate and damage spacecraft.

II. The debris is thickest and collisions are most likely to occur in the region from 100 to 1,200 miles above the ground, the area of greatest unmanned activity to date.
  A. The most probable accident is the ramming of two inactive objects, which would produce more fragments.

    B. Such collisions, rather than explosions, will probably create most of the space junk of the future.

III. Scientists are also worried about protecting satellites in the 22,000-mile-high geosynchronous orbit, where satellites remain fixed over one spot, since this orbit is vital for communications.
    A. Some experts suggest protecting it from litter by establishing a "garbage dump" at a slightly higher altitude, where satellites with just enough extra fuel to maneuver could be carried once they had lost their usefulness.
    B. Orbiting trash cans, or scavenger satellites, have also been proposed.
        1. These could be released by the space shuttle.
        2. After doing their mission, they could be picked up by a later shuttle and brought to Earth for emptying.
    C. The Ground-based Electro-Optical Deep Space Surveillance system, soon to be operating, could aid by greatly increasing the current catalog of useless items the Earth-based sensors now keep tabs on.

IV. For all the mess up there, the risk of collision for any particular craft is low.
    A. A space shuttle in orbit for a year would stand a 1 in 10,000 chance of being struck.
    B. Still, the number of stray items is growing by 11 percent a year, and scientists expect some spacecraft to be struck within the next decade.

Although there might be slightly different ways to outline this article, a complete outline would have to point out the four major divisions shown. The extent of subdividing necessary to outline a piece before abstracting it depends on its length. The preceding outline divides the article to the third level in some sections in order to show subordination of detail.

You should now be nearly ready to turn the outline into an abstract, choosing points from the outline and rewriting them, in the outline's order, in paragraph form. Before you begin, however, remember to write in a style that will be clear. Because the audience for any abstract is likely to be composed of generalists, it follows that you should choose your words carefully and simplify technical language as you work. Remember, also, that an abstract is not a review in any sense, so don't evaluate or criticize what you abstract. Finally, since an abstract is a summary and not a narrative, use the third person point of view and avoid the pronoun *I* or any reference to yourself.

Drafting the Document

Referring to both your marked original and to your outline, draft the abstract. Begin the abstract with the thesis statement (if you are abstracting an article) or the purpose/scope statement (if you are abstracting a formal report). Occasionally a sentence of background information begins an abstract, but that is rare. Continue your draft, adding the gist of every first-level division entry, if not the exact words. Add whatever second- and third-level information you think necessary to convey key points and make the abstract intelligible. Remember that a reader should be able to understand the abstract *without* referring to the original work. As you draft, keep the information in your abstract in the same order as it appeared in your outline. When you have completed your first draft, count the number of words to determine how close you are to the maximum length.

The following is the first draft of an abstract of "Space Trash." It contains the thesis sentence, all first-level division sentences, and some second-level division information.

Space junk could soon pose a greater hazard to spacecraft than meteoroids. Space junk includes spent satellites and rockets and tiny fragments left over from collisions and explosions of spacecraft. The debris is thickest and collisions are most likely to occur in the region of 100 to 1,200 miles above ground, where the most unmanned activity takes place. Scientists are also worried about protecting valuable communications satellites in the 22,000-mile-high geosynchronous orbit. Suggestions include establishing a "garbage dump" at a slightly higher level by giving satellites just enough extra fuel to move out of orbit after losing usefulness, creating orbiting scavenger satellites to pick up the trash, and increasing surveillance through the Ground-based Electro-Optical Deep Space Surveillance system. Luckily, even with all the debris, the chance for collision for any particular spacecraft is low—about 1 in 10,000.

"Space Trash" contains approximately 710 words, so an abstract of it should contain no more than 10 percent of this number, or 71 words. This first draft, with 137 words, is far too long. It will need to be shortened.

Reviewing and Reworking the Document

The first draft of an abstract can always be improved. Commonly it is too long and its sentences too choppy. Rework your draft by eliminating any unnecessary information. Learning to judge what must remain and what may be deleted will take practice, but if your outline is well done, it will guide you. You will also need to consider the needs and technical expertise of your probable readers in deciding what explanatory details must remain so that the abstract will make sense.

After rejecting unnecessary data, revise your sentences. Omit all needless words, especially jargon, awkward constructions, and redundancies. (Check Appendix A for guidance on style.) Work for the simplest, clearest style possible, but use only complete sentences. Look at the verbs and change the passive voice to active voice whenever possible. Finally see if you have used enough transitions to achieve a smooth style. Without enough transitions, an abstract can be difficult to follow.

When you have finished revising, count the words again. If the abstract is still over 10 percent of the original, revise it again. When the length is satisfactory, edit your draft for errors in grammar, mechanics, and spelling.

The following is the second draft of the abstract of "Space Trash." Notice what changes have been made.

Space junk—spent satellites and rockets and tiny fragments from collisions and explosions of spacecraft—could soon pose a greater hazard to spacecraft than meteoroids. The thickest debris occurs 100 to 1,200 miles above ground, where most unmanned activity takes place. Scientists also worry about protecting communications satellites in their 22,000-mile-high stationary orbits. If satellites were given just enough extra fuel to move out of orbit after losing usefulness, a "garbage dump" orbit could be established. Scavenger satellites to pick up the trash and better ground-based surveillance have also been suggested. Luckily, the chance for collision for any particular spacecraft is still very low.

This draft contains 104 words, which is closer to the goal but still beyond it. A third draft follows.

Space junk—spent satellites and rockets and fragments from collisions and explosions of spacecraft—may pose a hazard to spacecraft. Although the thickest debris occurs at the 100- to 1,200-mile level, scientists worry about protecting communications satellites in their 22,000-mile-high stationary orbits. Suggestions include establishing a "garbage dump" orbit, creating scavenger satellites, and improving ground-based surveillance. The chance for collision for any particular spacecraft is still low.

The third draft contains 71 words; it is about 10 percent of the length of the original, so its length is acceptable.

The abstract could be shortened even further. At some point, however, it would cease to be informative and become a descriptive abstract, like the following example.

This article describes space junk and explains three ways scientists propose to eliminate the problem of space junk colliding with spacecraft.

This abstract, of only 21 words, describes the article but does not summarize it in the way that an informative abstract would. It clearly states the topic but gives little other information.

Producing the Finished Document

The look of the final copy of an abstract depends on what has been abstracted and whether or not the original work also appears.

Abstracts Appearing with the Work

When an abstract is printed along with its article in a journal or magazine, it usually appears between the author's name and the first paragraph of the article, often in a smaller typeface, as shown in Figure 11.4.

An abstract appearing along with a formal report is always on a sep-

J. TECHNICAL WRITING AND COMMUNICATION, VOL. 8(2), 1978

IT IS EASY TO COMMUNICATE ELECTRONICALLY; IT IS HARD TO COMMUNICATE ELECTRONICS

THOMAS M. SAWYER
College of Engineering
The University of Michigan

ABSTRACT

Electronic systems are difficult to describe and explain because: 1) electronic systems involve an unusual layering of several different languages, 2) electricity itself is invisible, and may be indefinable, 3) developments in electronics are occurring so rapidly that few people understand its history, and 4) electricity or electronics is impossible to dramatize and make human.

It is sometimes hard for us living in the United States to appreciate how easy it has become to communicate electronically. We have become accustomed to it. I am no longer surprised at the simplicity of making a telephone call to England or France. But I can recall the hand-crank telephone in my grandfather's house

Figure 11.4   Abstract Appearing with an Article

arate page. The word ABSTRACT is typed in capital letters and centered about 1½ inches from the top of the page. The abstract is typed two or three lines beneath this heading, double-spaced. (See Figure 11.5.) This abstract page appears between the table of contents or list of illustrations page and the introduction of the report.

Abstracts Appearing Apart from the Work

Abstracts sometimes appear apart from the original works. Abstracts of articles from magazines and journals, of reports, and of other documents

ABSTRACT

Problem and purpose

A hearing aid service is being considered as an extension of the Vision Center Division of Medicare-Glaser Corporation. This report investigates the operational requirements for the service. There are both federal and state regulations concerning the sale of hearing aids and the

Important points

licensing of sellers. The FDA has set strict conditions for the sale of these devices. The instrumentation necessary for detection of hearing loss and for the fitting of the hearing aid consists of an audiometer, a hearing aid analyzer, and various small hand tools. Three professionals—a physician, an audiologist, and a hearing aid dispenser—will be needed.

Recommendations

The office requirements, however, are minimal. Further study of market area and product line are recommended.

Figure 11.5   Abstract Appearing with a Formal Report

pertaining to a particular discipline are gathered together and republished in periodicals such as *Biological Abstracts, Computer and Control Abstracts, Agricultural and Horticultural Abstracts, Engineering Abstracts,* and *Sociological Abstracts.* There are many others. Such published collections of current abstracts are very useful to professionals trying to keep up to date and to anyone researching a topic. Indexes in each journal enable you to find abstracts about particular subjects.

Journals of abstracts accompany each reprinted abstract with enough bibliographic data to enable you to obtain a copy of the complete work. The first few pages of each abstracting journal explain the particular citation form used by that journal. The forms differ. In addition to standard bibliographic information, these citations may provide additional information, such as contract number, report number, or availability. Figure 11.6 shows how abstracts may appear with citations in a journal of abstracts.

When you turn in an abstract of a published report or article to an instructor, precede it with a bibliographic citation. Use whatever citation form the instructor assigns. A sample student-written abstract preceded by a citation is shown in Figure 11.7. Since some instructors will want to know the number of words in the original and the number of words in the abstract, this information is added also.

ABSTRACTS IN *ENERGY RESEARCH ABSTRACTS*

The principal elements of abstract entries for a typical research and development report and a typical technical journal article are illustrated below.

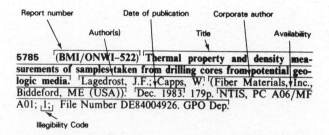

Density, steady-state conductivity, enthalpy, specific heat, heat capacity, thermal diffusivity and linear thermal expansion were measured on 59 materials from core drill samples of several geologic media, including rock salt, basalt, and other associated rocks from 7 potential sites for nuclear waste isolation. The measurements were conducted from or near to room temperature up to 500°C, or to lower temperatures if limited by specimen cracking or fracturing. Ample documentation establishes the reliability of the property measurement methods and the accuracy of the results.

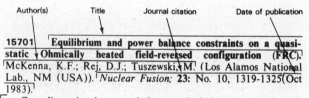

Zero-dimensional power balance calculations are performed for a quasi-static, purely Ohmically heated field-reversed configuration. Without compression, the constraint imposed by radial pressure balance limits the power input. Estimates of the energy loss from impurity line radiation as well as from classical and anomalous transport are given. Effects of cold puff gas injection are also investigated.

Figure 11.6   Abstracts Appearing in *Energy Research Abstracts*

Key Points in the Chapter

1. An abstract is a careful summary of the contents of an extended piece of writing.
2. There are two kinds of abstracts: descriptive and informative.
3. Informative abstracts are probably the most used.

ABSTRACT

Garvey, Linda. "Space Trash." Science 81 2 December 1981: 84.

   Space junk—spent satellites and rockets, and fragments from collisions and

explosions of spacecraft—may pose a hazard to spacecraft. Although the

thickest debris occurs at the 100- to 1,200-mile level, scientists worry about

protecting communications satellites in their 22,000-mile-high stationary

orbits. Suggestions include establishing a "garbage dump" orbit, creating

scavenger satellites, and improving ground-based surveillance. The chance for

collision for any particular spacecraft is still low.

   Number of words in article: ~~approximately~~ 710

   Number of words in abstract: 71

   Percentage: 10%

Figure 11.7   Student's Abstract and Citation

4. An abstract should be no longer than 10 percent of the length of the complete work and almost never longer than two pages, no matter how long the original work.
5. The order of details in an abstract usually matches the order of details in the complete work.
6. The language of an abstract should be clear enough so that a generalist can read and understand it.
7. An abstract appearing separately from the work should include a bibliographic citation of the complete work.

Exercises

1. Read the following article or one your instructor assigns. Outline it to the second level or further and write an informative abstract of it. Turn in the *outline* and your *abstract*. Beneath the abstract, note (1) the number of words in the article and (2) the number of words in your abstract.
2. Make a clear photocopy of an article of approximately 1,500 words from a journal in your field of study. Outline the article and write an informative abstract of it. Turn in the photocopy, the outline, and the abstract.
3. Select a chapter of a textbook you are now using for a class. Outline the chapter and write an informative abstract of it. Submit the outline and your abstract.

Hideaways for Nuclear Waste
Frederick Golden
Time, 16 March 81: 86

They are great underground mountains of salt, some of them six miles deep and three miles across. They were formed tens of millions of years ago— some even before the age of the dinosaurs—by the evaporation of ancient saline seas. Layer upon layer of sediment piled atop the dried-up ocean beds. Gradually, columns of the lighter salt were forced upward by the pressure, like putty squeezed through the fingers of a slowly clenching fist. In the U.S. alone, there are more than 500 such salt domes, all of them in or around the Gulf of Mexico.

For centuries the domes have served as a source of cheap table salt. In Louisiana, salt miners have carved out huge underground caverns. The domes act as traps for oil and natural gas, which collect in neighboring rock in cracks and fissures created by the upthrust of the salt. In 1901, drilling around a dome near Beaumont, Texas, produced a gusher of unprecedented size. It was called Spindletop and gave birth to the modern petroleum industry. Since then, salt domes in the Gulf States have helped point the way to more than six billion bbl of oil.

Today those riches have dwindled, but salt domes may again be pressed into service, this time as a solution to one of the country's hottest energy problems: getting rid of nuclear wastes, which can stay dangerously radioactive for 10,000 years. Some scientists suggest storing this debris deep inside salt domes.

The proposal is highly controversial, and residents of dome areas are already up in arms. In Louisiana, a group calling itself Citizens Against Radioactive Storage has been formed. During the last session of Congress, Louisiana Senator J. Bennett Johnston introduced a bill that would have blocked the use of salt domes by calling for storage in shallow beds, where, in the case of leakage, the material would be more easily retrievable. Vows Louisiana Governor David Treen: "Unless it could be demonstrated that storing nuclear waste in salt domes is absolutely safe, I would oppose it."

Lately, popular fears have been stirred by a rash of mishaps involving salt domes. Last June methane gas exploded at a salt mine in Belle Island, LA, killing 3 miners and injuring 17 others. In November an oil-drilling rig accidently punctured a salt-mine shaft under Jefferson Island, LA, sending much of the 1.5 sq. mile lake gurgling down into the dome. The most frightening accidents have involved still another use of salt domes: as cheap convenient storage tanks for crude-oil and natural-gas products. Last fall hundreds of people had to flee Mont Belvieu, Texas (pop. 2,700), which sits atop the largest such hydrocarbon reserve in the U.S., after gases began leaking from it.

These accidents have not altered scientific interest in the domes as nuclear-age crypts. Scientists point out that domes appear geologically stable. They do not have ground water circulating through them to carry off radioactive material. (If such water were present, the soluble salt would long ago have been washed away.) Even if the salt were cracked by heat from radioactive materials, the rupture would tend to close itself, a self-healing characteristic of salt not found in, say, granitic or volcanic rock masses, which are also being investigated as radioactive refuse sites. Says Physicist Neal Carter of the Battelle Memorial Institute in Columbus, Ohio, which is studying the problem of nuclear-waste disposal. "We've concluded that salt domes are fully capable of containing radioactivity."

IV Containment is certainly needed. Nuclear wastes have been piling up from years of military, medical, and powerplant operations. At present, most of it is temporarily —and perhaps dangerously—stored in huge steel-and-concrete tanks. No decision has yet been made on any of the various types of geological storage dumps under study. Carter explains that unlike the oil or gases kept in the ground under pressure at places like Mont Belvieu, solid nuclear wastes could not trickle through salt. In fact, he and his colleagues already have some preliminary ideas about how the debris should be buried. Vertical shafts, he explains, would be sunk in solid salt to a depth of about 2,000 ft. Horizontal tunnels would fan out from the bottom of the shafts. The wastes, packaged in corrosion-resistant containers, would be buried beneath the tunnel floors. Then the entire mine would be refilled with salt and sealed.

VI The chief danger: long after all record of radioactive crypts has vanished, someone may accidentally intrude into the dome.

Report Forms

12 Writing a Formal Investigative Report

Abstract

A formal investigative report deals with an important subject of long-term interest. It is written in a formal style and uses a structure consisting of several parts. Because a formal report is large and complex, a writer should plan carefully, using all seven stages in the writing process. Adequate time must be set aside for the collection of data, which is usually the most time-consuming stage. Of all the parts, the body of the report should be designed, drafted, and revised first, since all other parts are dependent on it. In revising, the writer must pay attention to the coordination of the parts as well as the quality of each. Careful editing and proofreading and the use of a well-planned layout will ensure a professional appearance.

What is called a formal report in business and government is a fairly well-defined type of document. It is formal not only in its language and point of view but also in its format, which is set by long-standing tradition. It differs from the informal report, covered in Chapter 4, in a number of obvious ways. Most of these differences stem from the fact that the subjects are generally larger and more complex and the purposes of the writing are more important:

- The structure is more elaborate, consisting of a number of distinct parts.
- The parts are intended for readers at several levels of expertise or familiarity with the subject, and hence the report can be used in parts rather than read straight through.

- The style is often, though not always, more impersonal and formal.
- The audience is larger and more diverse, and part of the audience usually includes those in positions of authority.
- The report is longer.
- It deals with subjects of long-term interest and hence is often kept on file longer.

Formal reports are not formal in style and elaborate in structure for no particular reason; these qualities have definite, practical functions, as the descriptions later in the chapter will make clear.

A formal report may contain some, though usually not all, of the following parts, generally in this order:

Letter of transmittal
Title page
Table of contents   } Front matter
List of illustrations
Abstract

Introduction
Body   } Main text
Conclusions and recommendations

Bibliography or list of references } End matter
Appendixes, if needed

A formal report can treat almost any subject that is important and needs to be dealt with in some depth. Thus many of the subjects that might be treated in an informal report can also be treated in a formal report. A proposal can be presented as a brief, informal memo or as a formal report, as described in Chapter 13. A feasibility study to determine if a company should expand its operations overseas would almost certainly be written as a formal report, as would a detailed progress report on a project that extends over a long period of time. Thus, although the formal report is a clearly recognizable kind because it is made up of a set of conventional parts, it can deal with almost any subject, provided the subject is important enough to the writer or the readers. The form is prescribed; the subject is not. Since a formal report is a large undertaking, all seven stages in the writing process come into play.

Defining the Problem and Purpose

Like all practical writing, the formal report deals with problems, but they are usually bigger and more complex than those in informal reports. Hence it is much more important that the problem be carefully defined and a clear purpose be framed.

Analyzing the Problem

Here are some problems that might be dealt with in a formal report:

- Researchers in a chemical products company have been working on a new adhesive to seal joints in pipes underwater. Although some problems remain in the product they have come up with, they feel they need to report the results of their work to supervisors and others higher in the company. They are uncertain about what form to use.
- The lake where your city gets its water supply has been found to contain small amounts of PCBs, and the citizens have become worried about the safety of their water. You, as city engineer, have been asked to study the feasibility of using another lake in the area as a water supply.
- Fellow students in your undergraduate engineering organization, especially the seniors, want a clear idea of the career outlook in your field— chemical engineering. The president of the group appoints an ad hoc committee to research the question and report to the members.
- The president of a small, family-owned underground coal mine has had problems with roof cave-ins. By good luck, none of them has caused deaths or serious injuries, but the president has asked you to find the most economical and effective method of avoiding them.

Although these problems differ in a number of obvious ways, they have several things in common. All deal with complex subjects that are important to the company or the groups of people they touch—the citizens of a town or all students in a particular field. The situations are also of continuing concern to those people. These characteristics seem to make the situations good subjects for formal reports, but the decision to use that form should come only after the problems and potential audiences have been analyzed and the purposes of the reports identified.

In the first two cases the problems have already been analyzed up to a point. The chemical researchers have developed a better adhesive. The problem is now to find the best method of conveying the results of their work. The water supply problem is even broader and more complex, and its potential audience of concerned people more diverse. The city's problem is the apparent need for a new source of water or for cleaning up the old one. The problem faced by the city engineer, who has been directed to make a study of an alternate source, is to cover all the details important to a decision. After finding out the advantages and disadvantages of using the new source and weighing them against staying with the current source, the engineer must make a recommendation to shift or not to shift.

The problem faced by students in chemical engineering is the need to find a job after graduation. The ad hoc committee's research should help them decide where to begin looking and what salary to ask for. It should also tell them how much competition they can expect from other graduates in the field, what duties they can expect on their first job, and what sort of career path they are likely to follow. These are the elements or issues in their problem; the committee's report should help them find the sort of job they want.

The coal-mine problem seems at first to be fairly simple and straight-forward: A method of preventing roof cave-ins is needed. Actually it is fairly complex since finding the best method involves an inspection of the geological characteristics of the area and then finding, through research, the method of roof control that best fits those characteristics. Since the company is small, it probably can't afford large outlays for new equipment or new personnel to carry out the solution. It needs to know if the current floor-to-roof supports will work if properly maintained or if a new system of support is needed. Careful research both on the site and in the literature on the subject will be necessary. The stages in the remainder of the chapter show how a writer planned and carried out the task of reporting on the research. The finished coal-mine report appears at the end of the chapter.

Analyzing the Audience

The audience for a formal report is different from that for most other kinds of practical writing in several ways: It is generally large and includes people at several levels of authority and of expertise, most of whom may be unknown to the writer. The audience is almost never a single person. These general characteristics of the audience have helped to shape the formal report. To fit a large and diverse audience, the report is objective, formal, and impersonal, and it contains parts that are intended for different levels of readers. For example, the abstract, the most-often-read part, must fit the widest possible range of readers, from experts to laypeople. Appendixes, on the other hand, often contain highly technical information that may be comprehensible only to the expert, and only a few of the experts may be interested in reading them. Others among the readers may pick out, by scanning the headings in the table of contents, those portions of the body of the report that apply to them: Accountants may read the budget section, technicians may concentrate on the methods section, and some engineers may be interested only in background theory.

The coal-mine cave-in problem was assigned by the president of the mining company and therefore the report is addressed to this person. The president is the primary reader but by no means the only one. In making a decision about what method of roof control to adopt, the president will consult with a number of others in the company and ask them to look at the report. First are the members of the company board, who, like the president, know something about coal mining but are not experts in mine roof control or any other highly technical aspects of mining. Second are the company mining engineers, of which there may be only one or two, since it is a small company. Yet they are important because the president and board will rely heavily on their advice. Finally, there are the supervisors and workers who are responsible for maintaining the roof supports in the mine.

The first two groups will very likely make the decision, but the third, the supervisors and some workers, will no doubt be consulted about it. Thus three groups with differing levels of technical knowledge will read the report. Since the letter of transmittal, abstract, introduction, and conclusions will probably be read by the first group, these parts should be kept free of highly technical concepts and language but should, at the same time, contain all the important points. The body of the report should be accessible to both engineers and supervisors, though the latter may not be as interested in background theory as the engineers.

As it turns out, no parts of the report are so technical that they cannot be read by reasonably knowledgeable readers. The few terms that may be unfamiliar to lay readers, such as *immediate roof, overburden,* and *abutments,* are defined in the text rather than in a glossary. Drawings and a graph help to clarify ideas that would be difficult to understand if put only in words. All these things help to adapt the report to the readers.

Collecting the Data

In preparing a formal report, you will find this stage the most time-consuming of all, since these reports are longer than most and very little of the data will come from your memory. Chapters 6 and 7 on library and field research are directed mainly to the task of collecting material for this kind of report. These chapters deal with the two main sources of information for a research paper: printed sources—mainly from the library— and empirical research, that is, research requiring you to experiment with or observe the things you are writing about. It also includes interviewing people who are experts in the subject and conducting surveys.

Since this stage is time-consuming, you need to plan it carefully. First, make a preliminary outline based on brief research in sources that give an overview of the subject. Your definition of problem and purpose and your analysis of the audience will also provide ideas for main points or categories for note taking. Second, set a time limit for your preliminary research to avoid running short of time for designing and drafting the report. Making a preliminary outline early on will enable you to narrow your research quickly and hence save time and effort. Too many writers of long reports spend too much time collecting information, and the reason is that they make too many false starts and take too many notes they never use. Defining the problem and purpose and analyzing the audience will enable you to draw up a good preliminary outline after only a small amount of research.

Setting a time limit for the collection of data does not mean you can't go back to that stage if, during the design or drafting stages, you see the need for more material. In fact, most writers find it useful to go back and forth often between the collection and design stages. The more information you have, the better design you can draw up, but a good design enables you to carry out the research more efficiently. These two stages are closely related, and you should plan to alternate between them.

A preliminary outline for the report on the career outlook in chemical engineering, simply using ideas from memory, might look like this:

Starting salaries over the past x years
Number of graduates in chemical engineering over the past x years
Number of openings in the past x years
Predictions of number of graduates and openings for this year
Geographical distribution of openings
Duties of beginning engineers who will fill these openings

Note that this is nothing more than a list of topics, but it does provide direction for the research. The research itself will no doubt turn up other topics. As to places where information can be found, inquiry among faculty members in the department might turn up these possibilities: the college of engineering placement office, the university placement office, the university library, and firms that employ chemical engineers (to be contacted by letter).

Getting started with the research on the mine roof will probably be more difficult since the number of potential sources is much greater. In a report of this sort, where most of the information will come from printed sources in company or research libraries, one of two methods might be used. One is to make a *systematic search* of the literature on the subject, using reference works such as bibliographies, periodical indexes, and computer search programs. The result is a list of printed sources that the researcher hopes will include all the important books and articles on the subject. The next step is to pick out the most promising sources and begin reading or skimming them.

The other method is to find one good recent book or article on the subject (articles are likely to be more recent than books) and to use the references in it to move on to other good sources. You might find this one good source by inquiry among fellow workers or by scanning a periodical index or recent issues of a likely journal. This method might be called *research by association*, in contrast to systematic search, since you move from source to source by following a chain of references. If you find a good recent source, chances are excellent that the writer of it will have done a systematic search and will present, in the list of references, the best of what he or she has found. Those articles and books will in turn lead you to other good sources.

In working on the mine roof problem, the researcher used the second method. He found the 1979 article on cable bolting—item 10 in the bibliography—by scanning recent issues of *Mining Engineering,* a journal he knew might carry articles on the subject. That article eventually led to all the others in the bibliography. The name of the mining engineer who was interviewed came from the DuPont publication, item 11.

The two methods aren't completely different, and much research is conducted by using a combination of the two. Thus a certain amount of systematic searching will turn up a few promising articles; once they have been found, the search can proceed by association.

The advantage of research by association is that one gets to the most promising sources quickly and hence saves time. Its main disadvantage is that the best articles might be missed and the validity of the findings thereby reduced. The advantage of the systematic search is that the best sources will very likely be found. The disadvantage is that the method is time-consuming in itself and may tempt the researcher to read and take notes on far more sources than are needed.

Whichever method you choose, remember not to linger too long in this stage; move on to the design stage when you feel you have enough information to draw up a reasonably good, but not perfect, outline.

In taking notes be sure to get all the information you will need as you read or conduct interviews, since it is time-consuming to go back to verify a page number or the wording of a quotation. How to use notecards and bibliography cards, what to include and what to leave out, and how to prepare for accurate documentation are all described in Chapter 6.

Designing the Formal Report

The elaborate structure of formal reports grows logically from the fact that they usually deal with large and complex subjects. Having a fixed form to pour the material into makes it easier for both the writer and the readers. Yet appearances can be deceiving, as they are here. Although there is a conventional set of parts making up the front and end matter of a formal report, there is no conventional format for the main elements—introduction, body, and conclusion. Some definite things can be said about the introduction and the concluding section; much less can be said about the organization of the body, except in the kinds that are most common, such as reports on the results of experiments.

Since no single organizational pattern works for the main text of all formal reports, the rest of this chapter will show how the organization of the sample report on coal-mine cave-ins was arrived at. As we describe that process, we will also make some generalizations that may be applied to other subjects and other kinds of reports. For the organization of one special kind of formal report, the proposal, see Chapter 13.

Designing the Main Text

The main text is the first part to be designed since all the other parts depend more or less on its contents and organization. Here is a list of the parts of a formal report in the order they can most efficiently be designed and drafted:

Main text
  Introduction ⎤ The order in which you prepare
  Body   ⎬   these two parts can be reversed,
  Ending   ⎦ for reasons discussed later.

(It is best to design, draft, *and* revise the main text before moving on to the next parts; editing and proofreading can wait until later.)

Bibliography and documentation
Glossary
Appendixes
Abstract
Table of contents and list of illustrations
Title page
Transmittal correspondence

Getting Started   The preliminary outline used as a guide in collecting data can be used as the starting point in drawing up a design for the body. What you should come up with is a fairly detailed outline to be used as a guide in drafting. Appendix D contains a thorough discussion of the mechanics of outlining. If when you have finished collecting data you know what your main points are going to be, you can begin by working out a design for the introduction; if not, it is best to begin designing the body, since the contents of the introduction depend on the contents of the body.

The researcher who wrote the coal-mine report had a good notion of what his main points would be after collecting most of the data. His notes were arranged under these headings:

Geological Background to the Problem
Point-Anchor Bolting System
Resin Bolting System
Cable Bolting System

In looking over his notes he discovered that he had material on two functions (not methods) of roof bolting that needed to go into the report but that didn't fit under any of the headings first used. He therefore added another main point, called "Functions of the Roof Bolt," after "Geological Background." With this basic outline for the body worked out, he was ready to design the introduction.

Designing the Introduction   A number of parts might be included in the introduction. How many you include depends on the purpose, subject, and audience for the report. Keep in mind that some readers will not want to read the whole report but will limit their reading to the table of contents, abstract, and introduction. These parts should therefore include all the essential points. Here are the parts that *could* be included in the introduction, though only rarely are all of them there:

Statement of the problem
Background to the problem
Purpose of the report
Limitations—used when things that might be expected are left out
Procedure or method
Theory—for example, in a report on aircraft design, a section on the theory of aircraft flight
Glossary—a list of definitions of unfamiliar terms used in the report
Scope of the report
Summary of conclusions and recommendations

If any of these parts needs to be more than a paragraph long, it should be shifted to the body. If that is done, a brief comment on the part might also be included in the introduction.

In the coal-mine report only three of these parts are included in the introduction: statement of the problem, purpose, and scope. The final version of the introduction appears on page 307. The whole of the first paragraph helps to explain the *problem*, but one sentence sums it up well: "A more effective and less expensive method of roof support is needed to replace the outdated floor-to-roof supports currently being used in the Saline Flats Mine." The *purpose* of the report is clearly set forth in the second paragraph. Since the discussion of the geological *background to the problem* is long and important, it has been included as the first main point in the body under the heading "Background to the Problem of Mine Roof Failures." The only *limitation* on the report—the lack of test results under wet conditions—has been mentioned in the letter of transmittal and also in the recommendation. No *procedures* or *theories* are involved, so these sections have been omitted. The function of a *glossary* is served by definitions within the text of unfamiliar terms like *immediate roof*. If there are many of these terms, say four or more, it would have been better to put them in a glossary and place it either in the introduction or in an appendix. The last paragraph of the introduction to the coal-mine report is a *scope* statement, which reflects the organization of the body and leads into it.

Designing the Body   No universally accepted format is available or feasible for the body of formal reports, given the variety of their subjects, purposes, and audiences. Yet a few suggestions can be made. As noted earlier, if any of the parts that might be included in the introduction are extensive, they should be placed in the body. In a report on an experiment, for example, the procedure or method section would be placed there.

In general, the body contains the facts or results that emerge from research, whether they are obtained from printed sources, observations, interviews, surveys, or experiments. They form the basis for the conclusions that come after the body. Thus in a report of a survey of opinions on a new product, the body might contain these parts:

Survey Method
  Population
  Questionnaire
  Method of Circulation
Results
  Number Responding
  Analysis of Results
Conclusions

In the coal-mine report the design finally settled upon is similar to the preliminary plan worked out as data were collected. The only changes were these: A section was added on the functions of roof bolts, containing two subpoints, suspension and beam binding. Also, the section on cable bolting was made an additional subpoint under resin bolting instead of remaining as a separate method. These additions and refinements yielded a workable design for the body:

I. Background knowledge of the geological structure surrounding a coal seam is essential to understanding the problem of mine roof failures.
  A. The immediate roof is the greatest potential hazard.
  B. Cave-ins of the immediate roof cause 50 percent of all mine-related fatalities.
  C. Removal of coal leaves a layer of shale, clay, or slate exposed and subject to falling.
    1. Five distressed areas are created in the vicinity of the excavation.
    2. The overburden is supported by leaving columns of coal as support.

II. Roof bolts can serve two functions in supporting the immediate roof.
  A. Roof bolts can suspend sagging layers from solid layers above.
  B. Roof bolts can bind or laminate sagging layers together, forming a thicker, firmer layer.

III. Two methods of roof bolting have predominated since 1947.
  A. The point-anchor system uses an expanding shell to grip surrounding rock.
  B. The resin bolting system uses a larger bonding area to increase its holding power over that of point-anchor bolts.
    1. Resin bolting has several additional advantages.
    2. Use of cable bolts with the resin bolting system increases its efficiency and lowers its cost.

Designing the Ending   The parts of the ending are generally few and simple. There are two kinds of endings: (1) a summary statement or (2) a statement of conclusions and recommendations. If the main purpose of the report is to convey information, all that may be needed is a *summary* of the main ideas, since the report doesn't call directly for a decision or other action. However, if the report is expected to serve as the basis for action, as the coal-mine report does, conclusions and recommendations are called for. *Conclusions* can be stated in paragraph form, as in the coal-mine report, or placed in a list. If more than one *recommendation* is made, they should always be listed so that each stands out clearly. Here are the conclusions and recommendations in list form taken from a report on research to find a better substance for filling teeth:

> Epoxy Electrodeposition Filling (EEF) shows great promise as a substance to be used as tooth filling by dentists.
>
> - Our research shows that EEF is relatively simple to fabricate.
> - Used with a new drilling technique, EEF is more durable than currently used substances.
> - More research is needed to test EEF under extreme temperatures and with hard and soft substances.
> - More research is needed on the effects of mouth and stomach acids on EEF.
>
> Recommendations: The following additional tests are recommended before we attempt to market EEF.
>
> - Test EEF under extremely hot and cold conditions, using hard and soft materials.
> - Test the effects of body acids on EEF in a variety of temperatures.

Graphic Aids

If you have clearly in mind the number and kind of graphic aids you plan to use in the main text, make notes in the outline where they will appear. However, ideas for graphic aids may not occur to you until you are well into the drafting stage. The important point is to be aware, from this point on, of the possibility of their use. The five drawings used in the coal-mine report were all taken from sources listed in the bibliography. To fit graphic aids to the purposes of your report, you may find it better to create some of your own rather than copying them from books or articles. See Chapter 8 for a full discussion of graphic aids.

Drafting the Formal Report

The Main Text

Because the text of a formal report is so large, the task of drafting it can be intimidating. Some precautions are necessary. Don't attempt to produce a complete first draft at one sitting as you do with letters and might do with informal reports. Break the task into several sessions, but within each session attempt to complete a clearly defined section of the report.

Since writing goes more easily after a page or more is finished, it makes good sense to stay at the task as long as you can. Avoid working on it in fits and starts.

A second precaution has to do with the starting point. You needn't start at the beginning of the introduction since beginnings are usually difficult. Therefore, pick the section of the report where you feel most confident and comfortable. That may be the third or fourth point in the body. Once you have done a good job with that part, you will have confidence to attack more difficult sections.

Use of Notecards in Drafting   Although notecards may seem to some students to be an invention of the devil to make their lives miserable, they *can* make life more bearable, if not completely happy. They are especially useful in drafting. If you have been careful to limit notes on each card to one subject, and you have written the name of the subject at the top of each card, as suggested in Chapter 6, you can easily put all the notes for one section in a pile. After deciding where you will begin, take in hand all the notes covering that section and review them. This will refresh your memory and store it with the material you will need to call up as you draft. Of course, you can always refer directly to the notes as you write, but it is good to have in mind the main ideas of each paragraph, as well as some of the details, before you begin. Most of the report will be in your own words, not in quotations, and the wording of your draft will probably be different even from the paraphrase or summary you may have put on the notecards. Thus it generally doesn't work well to copy directly from the notecards. They contain the facts you need, but the wording in the draft must fit in with parts that come before and after. If you simply copy from your notecards, whether in paraphrase or quotation, your draft will sound like a collection of bits and pieces, not a smoothly integrated discussion.

Yet *quotation* is sometimes useful and on rare occasions necessary. Use direct quotations under these conditions:

- When the author has summarized well an important point that you find fits into your own discussion.
- When the author has made a point that sounds incredible but yet is true. Putting it in the author's words tells the reader that this is indeed what the author has written.
- When the phrasing of a point is especially apt or interesting stylistically.

Most ordinary factual statements should be paraphrased or summarized when put into your report. *Paraphrase* is a point-by-point rendition of the original source but in your own words. It is usually about as long as the original. If all the details of the original aren't needed, you should *summarize* the passage when including it in your report.

As you gain experience in drafting, you will discover that it is sometimes best to paraphrase or summarize ideas that were quoted on your notecards and to summarize passages that have been paraphrased. In taking notes you probably quoted or paraphrased more than you actually needed—just to be on the safe side. Yet if you have taken notes efficiently, this won't happen often. The clearer your idea of the shape and content of the final report as you collect information, the more efficiently you can take notes. That is why we suggested drawing up a preliminary outline as early in the research stage as possible.

Analysis and Generalizations in the Body of the Report   The notecards will supply most of the facts you will put into your report, in addition to some opinions or conclusions of the authors you have read. That material will make up the majority of an investigative report based on printed sources. Yet part of the report must be your own if it is to fit the audience and fulfill the purpose. The main things you will supply are analyses of the facts and generalizations based on the facts and analyses. If a report simply repeats the facts and the conclusions found in other printed sources, it probably isn't of much use to anyone. Readers can simply go to your sources directly to get what they need. Your work should be creative in the sense that you *integrate* facts and ideas from a variety of sources and draw your own conclusions from those integrated elements. Most of these generalizations will have come to you as you organized the report and should thus appear in the outline. Others may occur to you as you write the first draft. Your analyses and generalizations are usually the most valuable parts of your report.

In the coal-mine report, for example, the writer concluded that resin bolting with cable bolts was the best method for the Saline Flats Mine. He reached this conclusion before beginning the design stage and thus was able to include it in his outline.

Other Points to Consider While Drafting   Several additional things should be kept in mind as you draft the main text. *Documentation* should be provided for, though not completed, by noting in the text the author and page number of each source that you make use of as you draft. Thus in the coal-mine report, the one sentence that eventually appears near the bottom of page 11 in the final draft looked like this in the first draft: "The Australian mines reduced their direct mining costs per ton by 16 percent by using cable bolting (Schmuck 1680)." If you are using the Modern Language Association system of documentation, the elements in the parentheses will remain the same in the final draft. If you are using the number system common in technical publications, you would substitute a number for the author's name, as in the final version of the sample report. You must make this change because at the time of drafting you won't know what number the Schmuck article will have in your list of references. The final shape of the list of references won't be determined until after the main text of the report is finished, since you may add new material late in the writing process. Appendix E contains more detailed information on documentation.

As you write, keep in mind that some readers may be laypeople or executives who are unacquainted with technical aspects of the subject. You should therefore make a note of the terms you use that may be unfamiliar to any of your potential readers. If they eventually add up to four or more, put them in a glossary. If fewer than four, go back and add short definitions at the point where you first use them.

You may discover a need for more information as you draft some parts of the report. Don't get upset. If your drafting is going well in other respects, make a note of the kind of information needed and skip on to parts for which your notes are sufficient. Later you can go back to stage three and collect more information to fill the gaps you have noted. If the drafting gets hopelessly bogged down, you must, of course, go back to the collection phase immediately.

The same sort of strategy can be used if you find that the organization you have devised doesn't work. You can either skip to a part you feel confident about or stop immediately and revise the organization. Since the revision stage that follows drafting is included to handle problems in design, you should try to finish a draft in spite of design faults, knowing that you can fix the problem later. Sometimes it is simply a matter of rearranging drafted sections that in themselves are satisfactory. It is generally better to push through to the end of a draft and let it incubate for a day or so before changing the organization. The wait may provide you with better ideas than you might have at the moment.

The End and Front Matter

Once the main text is completed, you have at hand the material needed to finish most of the other parts. Because the end matter is a kind of extension of the text, it makes sense to do it next, in this order: bibliography (or list of references), glossary, and appendixes.

Bibliography   This part consists of the sources used in researching the report, listed in alphabetical order by authors' last names. Interviews, filmstrips, and other nonprint sources are also listed. The details of bibliographical form are explained in Appendix E.

The bibliography is sometimes given other names, such as References, List of References, and Works Consulted. Giving it the name Bibliography or Works Consulted allows you to include items not actually referred to in the text. Whatever name it may have, it serves several purposes: Along with the reference numbers in the text, it serves to document the sources used by the researcher. It also serves as a resource to those who might want to read more on the subject.

Glossary   This is an alphabetized list of definitions of highly technical or otherwise unfamiliar terms used in a document. The definitions can be written either in complete sentences or in phrases. The important thing is to make the form consistent. Here is part of a glossary from a report on photo developing, with the definitions made up of noun phrases.

Accelerator—the ingredient in a developer that speeds up development, usually sodium carbonate or a milder alkaline.

Acid fixer—a fixing bath containing acetic acid.

Alum—short for potassium aluminum sulfate, the hardening ingredient in most fixers.

Bromide paper—fast, cold-toned photographic paper made with silver bromide as the chief ingredient.

Color-blind film—a common term for a black-and-white film sensitive only to blue light.

Diffused light—nondirectional or all-directional light, like that on a cloudy or foggy day.

Appendixes   For a number of reasons, anything important enough to go into a report, yet not appropriate for the main text, should go into an appendix. First, the material might be highly technical data, supporting ideas in the main text but comprehensible only to a small portion of the readers. Among other things it might include tables of statistics or theoretical explanations of an aspect of the subject. Second, the material might be easily understood but of interest to only a few people, such as a thorough explanation of brainstorming in a book on advertising. A third reason is that the material might not fit into the organizational plan of the main text yet is relatively important to many readers. This reason prompted us to place discussions of style, grammar and mechanics, definitions, outlining, and documentation in appendixes. The same reason prompts some writers to make the glossary an appendix.

Appendixes often consist of material written by someone other than the author of the report, and they may consist of brochures, texts of speeches, or portions of books such as tables of statistics, graphs, or even separate chapters. There is no limit to the kind of material that can be included in an appendix. Most are only a few pages long, but they can be much longer.

Appendixes are placed directly after the bibliography and are labeled sequentially with capital letters, as in this text. If you are wondering about the spelling of the plural, note that *appendix* is a Latin borrowing and the Latin plural is spelled *appendices*, whereas the anglicized spelling is *appendixes*. Either is acceptable, but be consistent.

Table of Contents   Since a report has no index, the table of contents is the only place readers can locate specific parts or subjects. This makes the report more accessible to a variety of readers, many of whom will not be interested in reading the whole thing. It resembles an outline but has fewer subdivisions and is in phrases rather than in complete sentences. Just as an outline provides the writer with a plan for writing, the table of contents enables a reader to read more efficiently.

In order for it to carry out these two functions—as a finding device and as an overview of the content—a table of contents should be prepared carefully. It should reflect the headings in the text exactly down to the second or third level, the depth of the coverage depending on the total number of headings. The items in the table should imitate the headings in typeface—upper- and lowercase—as well as in indentation and wording. In short, they should appear in the table just as they do in the text. In making up headings, avoid making all of them generic terms, as in the following example:

Abstract
Introduction
  Problem
  Purpose
  Scope
Procedure
Results
Conclusions
Recommendations

It is best to combine generic terms with a majority of headings that name specific subjects. Here is a table of contents for a report on forecasting earthquakes along the San Andreas fault.

List of Illustrations   If you have more than two or three tables and figures, it helps readers locate them if they are listed after the table of contents, either just below it on the same page or on the next page. The rules about form given for the table of contents apply. Use the same typeface and wording as the titles in the text. If the illustrations are all figures, call it List of Figures; if all tables, call it List of Tables. Here is the list from the paper on earthquakes:

Abstract   An informative abstract precedes most formal reports. Since it is the part of a report most often read, its absence would be sorely missed. It should convey the purpose as well as the substance of the main points and the conclusions and recommendations. Keep it free of unfamiliar language, since it is likely to be read by many who are not experts. It should also make no references to other parts or contain any documentation; it should stand by itself. See Chapter 11 for directions on writing an abstract. The coal-mine report at the end of the chapter contains an example.

Title Page   This page serves as a formal announcement of the title of the report. It should impress by its formality, its uncluttered design, and the care with which elements are balanced on the page. In addition to giving the title, it should also name the person or organization the report was prepared for, the name and title of the author, and the date it was issued. It *may* contain several other elements from the following list but never all of them, since to include all would make the page far too crowded.

- Title (see the following comments on formulating a title)
- Name of the person or organization the report was prepared for
- Name of the person or group that prepared the report
- Date of submission
- Authorization—including contract number and organization
- List of collaborators (others who contributed to the report)

Your company may specify other elements to be included on the title page. Check your company's report-writing manual or look at the format of reports in company files.

The title is the only part that may be hard to make up. A title should be brief, direct, and informative. Don't attempt to be clever by making it allusive or otherwise indirect. Since titles are often used in computer search programs, they should contain several key words that reflect important ideas in the report. Here are some sample titles:

The Parents' Role in Cleft Palate Habilitation
Forecasting of Earthquakes Along the San Andreas Fault
The Effect of Grain Exports on U.S. Grain Prices
Choosing a College Program for a Career in Hospitality Management

All of these are specific without being too long. Shortening any of them would reduce their effectiveness as titles, as you will discover if you try to do so. The use of a subtitle after a colon enables you to be specific without sounding awkward. The sample report at the end of the chapter uses a subtitle, making it possible to include two somewhat separate elements easily—"Mine Roof Control: Background and a Comparison of Two Methods." The same form can be used with some of those listed earlier: "Cleft Palate Habilitation: The Parents' Role."

The elements are arranged on a title page in the following order, though more spread out to fit a full page:

FORECASTING OF EARTHQUAKES
ALONG THE SAN ANDREAS FAULT

Prepared for
Dr. Anders Johanson
Professor of Geology
South Dakota State University
Brookings, South Dakota

by
Joseph Richman
Research Assistant

April 26, 1984

Transmittal Correspondence   The main purpose of transmittal correspondence is to present the report to the person to whom it is addressed. It may take the form of a memo (for in-house reports) or a letter. If it is a business letter, it follows letter format in all details—except that instead of being mailed separately, it is usually attached to the report, either placed on top or bound in after the title page. Since it brings good news, you should use the direct approach in writing it. The first sentence should transmit the report, giving the title and telling why it is being sent to the person addressed. That usually means telling when and by whom it was authorized and for what purpose. These items normally make up the first paragraph.

In the second paragraph, writers usually draw attention to one or two highlights of the report or to especially interesting or striking discoveries. Since an informative summary can be found just after the title page, there is no need to summarize the report in this letter. You can, however, note any limitations on the coverage or things purposely excluded.

The report itself is highly formal, as its name implies, but the transmittal correspondence gives you the opportunity to be more personal. In a third paragraph you can acknowledge help received in preparing the report and can mention any difficulties encountered. Feel free to use personal pronouns, as in any business correspondence, and take care to convey a positive, friendly tone. Close with a personal comment—a hope that the report fulfills its purpose or an offer of additional help. In a few cases, however, as when the persons addressed are high officials in government, the tone should be quite formal.

In writing this correspondence follow the stages for writing business letters and memos given in Chapter 3 and Chapter 4. The letter in the coal-mine report at the end of this chapter contains most of the elements discussed here and provides a good model.

Reviewing and Reworking the Document

In revising the main text, divide the task into two parts: First revise the organization and content; then edit and correct mechanical elements such as spelling and punctuation. The second part of this job can wait until all the other parts are drafted.

Organization and accuracy of content are the two aspects to look at most closely as you revise. The reasons are simple: First, the text of a formal report is long and complex, unlike that of a letter or memo. You have many more opportunities to make errors in organization, while at the same time the readers need good organization to help them comprehend the report.

Second, the investigative report depends for its success on the accuracy of the facts recorded. In reading over your draft, look up in the notes any facts that you suspect might have been transcribed inaccurately. Have a fellow worker read your draft with an eye to the credibility of the facts, and double-check those he or she questions.

Producing the Finished Report

Of all the kinds of practical writing you will do on the job, the formal report is most like a book in its content, especially in the front and end matter. Just as publishers make certain their books are as close to letter perfect as they can make them, you should see to it that your formal report is accurately typed, contains lots of white space in its layout, and is correctly assembled. It annoys a reader to find a page missing or out of place, especially if the report is bound. Most formal reports are double-spaced in the main text. See the sample coal-mine report for the format of all the parts.

If the report is relatively short, say 10 to 12 pages, and you are submitting it in a college course, you can use a paper clip or staple to hold the pages together. If it is longer, you should consider using a cover and binding. A variety of styles can be found in office supply stores and college bookstores. If you use a cover, attach a gummed label containing title, author, date, and if the report is for a course, the course number. Here is a cover label for the coal-mine report:

Mine Roof Control:
Background and a Comparison of Two Methods

by David L. Dare, Missouri Mining

November 9, 1985

The length and importance of a formal report force you to put a great deal of effort into the task. Don't spoil its chances for success by letting it go out looking less than professional. Give it one final proofreading and check the order of pages after it has been put into its cover.

The coal-mine report is given here in its final form.

MISSOURI MINES
1824 West Dakota Avenue
Joplin, Missouri 65241
November 9, 1985

Mr. Rinehold Callies, President
Saline Flats Mining Company
1614 Crab Orchard Drive
Harrisburg, Illinois 62791

Dear Mr. Callies:

Here is the report on methods of roof control in underground mines that you
asked me to prepare in your letter of August 11, 1985. The report focuses on a
comparison of the two leading methods of preventing mine roof cave-ins—the
point-anchor bolt method and the resin bolt method. Evidence points to the
superiority of the resin bolt method on a number of grounds, all of which are
discussed in this report.

In preparing the report I made a thorough search of the literature on roof
control in mines and have used a number of recent articles to describe the
characteristics of the two methods. A brief description of the very latest
method in roof bolting, called cable bolting, is also given. I am grateful to
William R. Mallicoat, mining engineer with the Island Creek Coal Company, for
sharing his test results on roof bolting made for the DuPont Company. Please
note that I found no information on the performance of either kind of bolt
under wet conditions, such as occur in some southern mines.

I hope the information in the report will enable you to solve the roof cave-in
problems you have been having in your mine recently. If you have any
questions after reading the report, please feel free to call or write me.

Sincerely,

David L. Dare

David L. Dare
Research Associate

DLD/jr

MINE ROOF CONTROL:

BACKGROUND AND

A COMPARISON OF TWO METHODS

Prepared for

Rinehold Callies, President

Saline Flats Mining Company

By

David L. Dare, Research Associate

Missouri Mining

November 9, 1985

Table of Contents

List of Figures

Abstract

The mining of a vein of coal removes support for other layers of rock in the vicinity, particularly the immediate roof, which consists of the layers just above the excavated area. The resulting threat of roof failure is now usually controlled by use of a roof bolting system. Immediate roof layers are suspended either by bolts attached to stronger layers or by being clamped together to form a single thicker unit. Bolts are of two kinds: Point-anchor bolts are the commonest and are held in place by use of an expanding shell; resin bolts employ a new method of gluing to hold the bolts in place. The resin bolt, used in combination with cable bolts, offers a four-times stronger hold, greater resistance to shearing, and lower cost of installation than point-anchor bolts. Resin bolting is recommended for the Saline Flats Mine.

-1-

INTRODUCTION

Roof failures, or cave-ins, account for about 50 percent of all mining-related deaths in the United States (1:72). The Saline Flats Mining Company has been fortunate in escaping both fatalities and serious injuries despite several roof cave-ins during the past two years. A mining company cannot trust its luck to hold indefinitely. A more effective and less expensive method of roof support is needed to replace the outdated floor-to-roof supports currently being used in the Saline Flats Mine. The supports are rapidly deteriorating and will need to be replaced in any case, and less expensive but more effective methods are now available.

The purpose of this report is to recommend a method of roof control for the Saline Flats Mine that meets current Bureau of Mines standards, is easy to install and maintain, and is less expensive than the floor-to-roof supports now in use.

This report consists of a detailed geological description of the nature and causes of roof cave-ins by way of background, an account of the functions of roof bolting systems, a comparison of the two leading methods of roof bolting, and a brief description of a new variation in one of those methods, called cable bolting. Conclusions and a recommendation complete the report.

BACKGROUND TO THE PROBLEM OF MINE ROOF FAILURES

When workers go underground to mine natural resources such as coal, they enter an environment entirely different from that in any other form of business. In a limited space and with limited lighting, they must contend with hazards such as explosive gases, a limited supply of oxygen, the dangers

-2-

associated with working with explosives, and the threat of roof cave-ins. The company these people work for has an obligation to make the underground mine as safe an environment as possible. Engineering aspects of this safety problem involve controlling the earth's internal forces that affect the seam of coal itself and the rock strata both above and below the coal.

Immediate Roof as a Potential Hazard

Roof control is a problem that begins as soon as coal is removed from the entrance to a mine. As a rectangular opening is made in a coal seam, the coal that once supported the strata above it is removed. The rock—shale, clay, or slate—located just above the coal seam, which is referred to as immediate roof, extends upward until reaching a stratum of self-supporting rock, such as limestone or sandstone. Immediate roof may be anywhere from a few inches to several feet thick, its width varying extensively throughout a single mine. The immediate roof should not be confused with the main overburden consisting of several hundred feet of rock that lies above it. Large blocks of coal are left to support the overburden (2:79–80).

Stress Zones Created by Excavation

As coal is removed, two events occur simultaneously: First, the immediate roof gradually sags into the opening; second, the load originally supported by the coal that is now excavated is transferred to both sides (ribs) of the opening. The ribs serve as abutments—areas in which pressures are now much greater than average. As a result, five zones of influence are formed around this newly created rectangular opening (2:83). Figure 1 illustrates these five zones and the forces working upon them.

Zones 1 and 2 are distressed areas shaped like an arch. If the lowest layer in Zone 1 is thin or weak, it tends to sag more and separate from the overlying

-3-

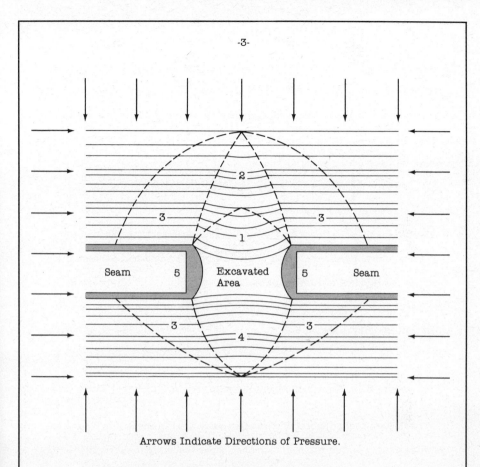

Arrows Indicate Directions of Pressure.

Zone 1—Bed separation is due to differential sag or buckling.

Zone 2—Layers sag but without separation.

Zone 3—Horizontal and vertical pressures build up to their undisturbed

values.

Zone 4—Floor heave (uplift) occurs without bed separation.

Zone 5—Seam expands toward excavation because of the release of horizontal

stress at the ribs.

FIGURE 1   Disturbance Produced Around Coal Seam by Excavation (From R. D. Caudle, Mine Roof Stability: In Ground Control Aspects of Coal Mine Design, U.S. Bureau of Mines, Report No. IC 8630, 1977, p. 80.)

-4-

layers. The separation is greatest between the two lowest layers. It gradually reduces in width near the sides until the separation no longer occurs. The height of the arch above the opening depends on the composition of the layers that compose it, the uniformity of its density, and the magnitude of the horizontal pressures created by the main roof overburden. Zone 1 comes to a point at the top because of the clamping action of abutment pressure and frictional resistance between the layers (2:83–84).

Failure of the immediate roof (Zone 1) to support itself, in addition to accounting for approximately half of all mining-related deaths, causes untold expenses for removal of rubble, for damaged equipment, and for delays in production. Until the late 1940s conventional floor-to-roof supports, such as wood timbers, steel I-beams, and concrete, were used exclusively to prevent these cave-ins.

CONDITION OF SALINE FLATS ROOF SUPPORTS AND MINE ROOFS

The floor-to-roof supports of wood currently used in the Saline Flats Mine are increasingly difficult to maintain the deeper the shafts become. Inspection of these supports shows that fully one-third are in need of replacement and about one-sixth are in dangerous condition. The two serious roof falls and several minor ones that have occurred in the past two years are a direct result of the failure to maintain the roof supports properly.

Inspection of the mine roof in the Saline Flats Mine reveals that one of several systems of roof bolting would probably be an economically feasible method of supporting the immediate roof. To carry out the inspection, bore samples were taken from the tunnel roof in 17 sites throughout the mine. The immediate roof (the layers prone to sag or fall when coal is removed) varies in depth from 6 inches to 27 inches, with an average of 11 inches. The rock above the immediate roof consists entirely of limestone, as expected, and would

-5-

provide a good base for securing supporting roof bolts. Given the thin average width of the immediate roof, the bolts should be relatively inexpensive to install and maintain. The leading methods of roof bolting are described in the next sections of the report.

INTRODUCTION OF THE ROOF BOLT

In 1947 the Consolidation Coal Company of Illinois introduced the roof bolt to the mining industry (4:35). Roof control through roof bolting is possible because of two principles: suspension and binding, or lamination.

Suspension

The sag and separation of the immediate roof are reduced or eliminated when roof bolts are placed in a strong, self-supporting section of the main roof and tightened, holding up Zone 1. (See Figure 2.) The same principle

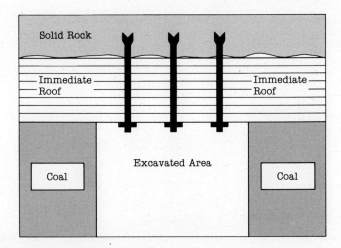

FIGURE 2   Roof Bolts Used for Suspension (From L. Obert and W. I. DuVall, Rock Mechanics and the Design of Structures in Rock, p. 626. Copyright 1967, John Wiley & Sons, Inc., New York. Material reproduced by permission.)

-6-

is used in house construction in putting up a suspended panel ceiling. The effectiveness depends on the strength of the steel bolt and the ability of the anchor to keep a strong grip in the self-supporting stratum and thus hold the added weight in suspension (4:39).

Beam Binding, or Lamination

Zone 1 might extend too high to make it possible for bolts to reach a strong rock layer. In that situation bolts are used to clamp or hold several weak layers together to produce a thicker, and thus stronger, layer. This reduces the bending strain on any single layer. The method is illustrated in Figure 3. In a similar fashion and for the same reason, layers of wood are glued together to form plywood. As in the suspension method, the effectiveness depends on the ability of the anchor to secure a firm grip before sagging begins (8:626).

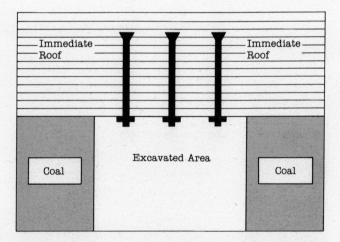

FIGURE 3   Roof Bolts Used for Beam Binding, or Lamination (From L. Obert and W. I. Duvall, Rock Mechanics and the Design of Structures in Rock, p. 626. Copyright 1967, John Wiley & Sons, Inc., New York. Material reproduced by permission.)

-7-

METHODS OF ROOF BOLTING

The two commonest methods of securing mine roofs are the point-anchor and the resin bolting methods.

Point-Anchor Bolting

Most mines now use the point-anchor system to secure the bolts that support mine roofs. To install the bolts, holes are drilled in the roof at intervals that vary with the estimated need for support. The length, or depth, of the holes is dependent on the distance to a solid stratum and the length of the bolts being used. With the point-anchor system, an expansion shell, which is a wedge-shaped nut on the end of the roof bolt, is screwed down into a set of inverted serrated wedges that dig into the sides of the hole drilled into the roof, as illustrated in Figure 4. The anchor is held in place by tension created

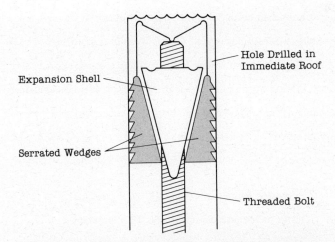

FIGURE 4   Expansion Shell for Point-Anchor Bolt (From D. W. Mitchell and W. J. Debevec, "A New Look at Roof Bolts," Coal Mining and Processing, February 1970, p. 35. Copyright 1970, Maclean Hunter Publishing Company. Material reproduced by permission.)

-8-

by several hundred foot-pounds of torque. The pressure, or force, is transferred into the rock in both horizontal and vertical directions. Unfortunately, these high concentrations of force tend to break the rock in the vicinity of the serrated wedges and cause anchors to slip. Eventually, the roof bolts fail and the rock of Zone 1 comes down. Once started, a chain-reaction roof fall results. The average fall is 13.5 feet long, 9.5 feet wide, and less than 1 foot thick. It weighs from 7 to 9 tons (3:77).

Resin Bolting

Roof layers can also be supported by filling the gap between the bolt and the wall of the drilled hole with a groutlike material such as a resin. The result is full-length bonding between the bolt and the hole wall (7:34). This process, generally known as resin bolting, is relatively new. It works on the principle that a resin bolt maintains complete contact between the resin and the entire surface of the hole wall. This increases the holding capacity to several times that of point-anchored bolts. The resin bolt's superiority is borne out by the results of tests, wherein both types of bolt were literally weighted down until they ripped loose from their holes. Results of the test are shown in Figure 5.

The components of the resins used differ among various manufacturers. In addition, using different percentages of components results in different strengths, gel times, and resistance to the elements of given environments. Key components of a resin bolt might typically be as follows (4:12):

Resin {
Polyester Resin   28.5% + catalyst
Filler (crushed limstone) 66.0% + catalyst
Accelerator   0.5% + catalyst
}

The bolt itself is made of the same material as the serrated steel bars used in reinforcing concrete. The catalyst and resin must be kept separated until they

-9-

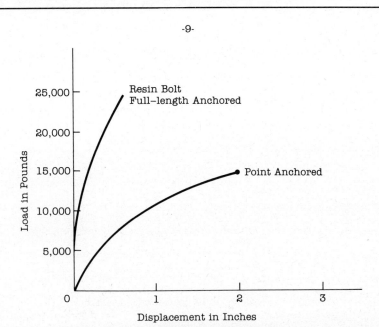

FIGURE 5   Pullout Test of Two Types of Roof Bolt in Hard Rock (From William R. Mallicoat, personal notes on tests of roof bolts, 1980.)

are in place in the hole. Common practice is to pack them in the form of sausage cartridges, as shown in Figure 6. In this form the proper number of cartridges can be inserted into the hole before being ruptured and mixed by insertion of the bolt. Another method would be to seal the bottom of the hole

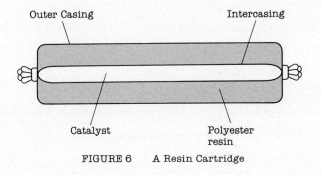

FIGURE 6   A Resin Cartridge

-10-

around the bolt and pump premixed resin up into the hole. Both methods offer the same physical characteristics (5):

Compressive strength	12,000–16,000 psi
Tensile strength	2,500– 3,200 psi
Shear strength	5,000– 7,500 psi

Additional Advantages of Resin Bolting.   In practice, resin bolts work not only by suspension but also by friction and reinforcement to prevent sliding between layers. The resin bolt reinforces the layers by developing shear resistance as layer slippage occurs. With regular point-anchor bolts, the amount of resistance to displacement depends on the intimacy of the contact between the bolt and the rock. A slight gap between the hole and bolt anchor would very seriously reduce the effectiveness of the bolt. By contrast, the resin between the bolt and the hole wall provides a firm fit the entire length of the hole. As with the point-anchor bolt, an important factor determining the effectiveness of the resin bolt is the ability of the workers mining the coal to install the bolts soon after the immediate roof is exposed—before sagging begins.

The stress distributions on the resin bolts are quite irregular; they do not follow any fixed pattern. On the other hand, with the point-anchor system a torque wrench may be used to check periodically the load each bolt is holding (9:164). With resin bolting, dependability is based on the quality of the materials used and the ability of the operators who install the bolts. These factors are not easily measured.

Cable Bolting with the Resin System.   Resin bolting is still in its infancy, and the possibilities for variations in its use are numerous. In Australia, mines are experimenting with the use of cables as bolts in place of steel rods. The

-11-

cable is the type used on heavy construction equipment. Mines are able to buy

coils of bulk cable, and crews cut each length individually as it is installed. The

cost per hole is less than for prefabricated bolts, and there is a big reduction in

waste. Instead of drilling a hole to the depth required for a particular bolt,

lengths of cable are cut to match holes of optimum length. With the use of

resin bolting and cable bolts, capital expenditures would be at a minimum,

since a conventional rock drill for point-anchor roof bolting could double the

cost of drilling. The only extra expense for resin bolting would be the pump for

resin. This could mean reducing the cost to much less than the current $5 per

bolt for point-anchor bolting. The average is estimated at $3 per bolt. The

Australian mines reduced their direct mining costs per ton by 16 percent by

using cable bolting (10:1680).

CONCLUSIONS

Mining companies have a responsibility to provide the safest possible

working conditions, since potential hazards in mines are numerous. Since

roof cave-ins account for about half of all fatalities in mining-related

accidents, it is essential that the best method of roof control be used. The resin

bolting system, using cable bolts, is superior to the conventional point-anchor

bolting system in a number of ways. Because the resin bolt adheres to the hole

wall over its entire length, its holding capacity is about four times that of the

point-anchor bolt. Costs per hole are about $3 per hole for resin bolting in

contrast to $5 per hold for point-anchored. Resin bolts also provide greater

protection by increasing friction, and hence they prevent sliding between

layers. However, point-anchor bolts have one advantage: It is possible to

measure the load they are bearing by use of a torque wrench, whereas it is

impossible to measure the load borne by resin bolts. Nevertheless, resin bolts

are superior to point-anchor bolts in most respects.

-12-

RECOMMENDATION

It is recommended that the Saline Flats Mine use resin bolting with cable bolts as the primary means of roof control. If the mine is extended into areas where heavy moisture is common in the immediate roof, however, tests should be made to determine the holding ability of the resin bolt under those conditions. None of the areas currently mined by the company has excessive moisture in the immediate roof.

-13-

LIST OF REFERENCES

1. Cassidy, Samuel M. Elements of Practical Coal Mining. Baltimore: Maryland Port City Press, 1973.

2. Caudle, R. D. Mine Roof Stability: In Ground Control Aspects of Coal Mine Design. U.S. Bureau of Mines, Report No. IC 8630, 1974.

3. Daugherty, J. J. A Study of Fatal Roof Fall Accidents in Bituminous Coal Mines. Morgantown: West Virginia University Press, 1971.

4. Illinois Coal Facts. Springfield: Illinois Coal Association, 1979.

5. Karabin, G. J., and W. J. Debevec. Comparative Evaluation of Conventional and Resin Bolting Systems. U.S. Mine Safety and Health Administration, Report No. IR 1033, 1976.

6. Mallicoat, William R., Mining Engineer, Island Creek Coal Company. Interview on testing of resin bolts, Marion, Illinois, October 23, 1985.

7. Mitchell, D. W., and W. J. Debevec. "A New Look at Roof Bolts." Coal Mining and Processing, February 1970: 34–36.

8. Obert, L., and W. I. Duvall. Rock Mechanics and the Design of Structures in Rock. New York: John Wiley & Sons, 1967.

9. Peng, Syd S. Coal Mine Ground Control. New York: John Wiley & Sons, 1978.

10. Schmuck, Carl H. "Cable Bolting at the Homestake Gold Mine." Mining Engineering, December 1979: 1677–81.

11. Tolstoi, Bertrand. Fasloc Resin Anchored Bolt System. E. I. DuPont Company, June 1974.

Key Points in the Chapter

1. A formal report differs from an informal report in a number of ways: Its structure is more elaborate, its length is greater, its parts are intended for a larger and more diverse audience, the subject is more important and complex, and the style is more impersonal and formal.
2. Since the formal report is a large undertaking, all seven stages in the writing process are essential.
3. The framing of a clear statement of problem and purpose will help the writer design the report effectively, and the inclusion of an explicit statement of problem and purpose will help the readers.
4. Because the report itself is long, the data-collection stage will be time-consuming; it should therefore be carefully planned to avoid wasted effort.
5. Although prescribed formats are available for many of the parts, there is no set form for the body, which is usually the longest and most important section of the report.
6. The body of the report should be designed, drafted, and revised first, since all other parts in the report depend on its structure and content.
7. Revision and editing of a formal report should be directed to making certain that all parts fit together as well as to making sure that each part is well written.
8. Because of the importance of their subjects and the breadth of their audiences, formal reports should be finished in a way that makes their appearance impressive and professional.

Exercises

1. Make a list of the likely sources of information for a formal investigative report on each of the following topics:
   a. Travel and study abroad by students at your college in a report directed to the dean of students
   b. An evaluation of services offered and prices charged in all veterinary clinics in a five-county area where you live (Direct it to a county extension agent.)
   c. A report on job opportunities for graduates in your field of study (Topics might include salaries in the last five years, number of graduates and number of openings in the past five years, geographic location of openings, and kinds of work done by recent graduates in your field.) (Direct it to the president of the honorary fraternity in your field.)
   d. A report on intercity transportation available from the city where you live or from a nearby larger city (Direct it to the chamber of commerce of the city you have chosen.)
2. Make up appropriate formal report titles for each of the topics named in the first exercise.
3. Describe a search strategy that would enable you to collect data most efficiently

for one of the topics listed in the first exercise or the topic you have chosen for a formal investigative report.

4. Rewrite the letter of transmittal of the sample report on coal mines printed in this chapter so that the report could be sent to a mine equipment supply company that has asked for a copy.

13

Writing a Proposal

Abstract

A proposal is a form of practical writing that addresses a problem with a plan for its solution. Proposals that have been requested are referred to as *solicited*. Proposals not written in response to requests are referred to as *unsolicited*. Writing a proposal requires attention to all seven stages in the process of practical writing, with special emphasis on defining the problem. Without a problem there is no need for a proposal. The bodies of most proposals contain three parts: a technical section, which describes the proposed solution; a management section, which describes how the work will be managed; and a cost section, which provides a detailed description of the cost of carrying out the solution.

A proposal is a form of practical writing that addresses a problem with a plan for its solution. Proposals are written by both organizations and individuals for a variety of reasons.

A business concern, for example, ordinarily writes a proposal to secure a job contract; the company most often proposes a solution to a problem expressed by another organization. An employee, however, might write a proposal to an individual, such as a supervisor, in order to gain approval for a special project or for the purchase of a new piece of equipment. An artist might write a proposal to a funding agency, such as the National Endowment for the Humanities, to obtain money in support of an arts project. A scientist or college professor might write a proposal to the directors of a private endowment fund or to a government agency to obtain funding for research.

Nearly all proposals include a description of the problem to be remedied. Sometimes the problem is identified by one organization in a Request for a Proposal (commonly referred to as an RFP) made to other organizations that might be able to provide a solution. An RFP commonly includes a description of the problem to be solved, a required proposal format, and a proposal deadline.

State and federal government agencies issue many RFPs. For example, after years of working with rockets that could be used for only one mission, the National Aeronautics and Space Administration (NASA) wanted a new kind of spacecraft capable of flying numerous missions and bringing malfunctioning satellites back to earth with it for repair. NASA then issued RFPs to aerospace companies capable of designing and manufacturing such a conveyance. Many responded with proposals, and NASA selected the one it felt best solved the problem. The result was the development of the space shuttle by Rockwell International.

A company receiving a contract to complete work for the government may in turn issue its own RFPs to organizations that will produce some of the parts or handle any specialized work involved in the project. The problems that must be solved by all those receiving this second round of RFPs will be spelled out in detail by the company receiving the first contract.

Many proposals, however, are written by people or organizations to address problems that may not yet have been identified by others and for which no proposal has been requested. For example, a supervisor at a plant manufacturing cardboard cartons may be aware of a developing problem: an increase in the number of defective cartons produced. To address this problem, the supervisor writes a proposal to a plant manager, outlining a plan for the institution of a plant-wide quality-control system. In this case, the supervisor must first convince the manager that a serious problem indeed exists and then that the proposed quality-control program will eliminate it. The task of convincing others that a problem exists is a difficulty facing anyone writing an unsolicited proposal.

These two kinds of proposals, those written in response to requests for proposals and those that have not been requested, are commonly referred to as *solicited* and *unsolicited* proposals. Although the two types contain many similar elements, they differ in the emphasis given to various sections because they are written for different kinds of readers.

Solicited Proposals

Writing a solicited proposal can be simpler than writing an unsolicited one in the sense that the problem has already been defined, sometimes in great detail, by the originator of the RFP. There is no question about a problem existing, and the proposal writer need not convince the reader that it does. Solicited proposals written by small companies addressing minor problems, such as a homeowner's need for new plumbing or repairs to a roof, may be very brief—perhaps a single page. However, solicited proposals written by large corporations such as McDonnell Douglas or General Electric are typically very long and complex, often running to two or three bound volumes of several hundred pages each.

Writing or helping to write solicited proposals for large organizations is one of the major activities of professional technical writers. Solicited proposals are often written under tremendous pressure, against difficult-to-meet deadlines, and at considerable cost. The entire process of writing must often be compressed more than the writers would wish. In fact, because of time constraints, these proposals often cannot be written completely "from scratch." Commonly included sections are sometimes produced ahead of time, for rapid inclusion in company proposals. These standardized, prewritten sections of a company's solicited proposal are referred to as *boilerplate*, and they are generally available to technical writers and editors working for large organizations. Even short proposals, however, may include standardized sections, such as a guarantee on parts and labor.

Though preparing a good solicited proposal is difficult, the rewards gained make the job worth the effort. After all, companies that do not produce successful proposals can find themselves with no work at all.

Unsolicited Proposals

Unsolicited proposals are often written by people applying for funding or for permission to pursue special projects. These proposals tend to be shorter and less complex than proposals produced by organizations bidding for contracts. Nevertheless, writers of unsolicited proposals face a special challenge: the need to convince their readers that a problem exists. The major distinction between the two types of proposals is this need to demonstrate the presence of a problem.

Writing a successful unsolicited proposal and doing a good job of describing a problem that others have not yet seen can bring many rewards. It can even help to create or advance careers. Two clerical workers at a large medical center in St. Louis created new positions for themselves through a proposal. After working at the complex for several years, they had come to realize that a problem existed: No staff development programs were available for clerical staff interested in improving their job skills.

To further investigate and define the problem, they developed a list of possible topics for staff development and surveyed 500 other clerical workers to assess their needs and determine the areas of highest interest. The two then wrote a proposal to establish a training program that they felt would meet staff needs. Hospital administrators were impressed with the proposal and approved the establishment of a year-long, twice-monthly series of workshops. The two proposal writers were chosen by management to direct the new program.

Writing both solicited and unsolicited proposals requires attention to all seven stages in the process of practical writing. However, as you go through the stages, you will find that the complexity of proposal writing may require you to begin collecting information for the project almost immediately, as you define your problem, purpose, and audience. This is one form of practical writing for which collection of information cannot be isolated in a single stage, as it can be for simpler forms.

Defining the Problem and Purpose

Anyone writing a proposal must clearly identify the problem being addressed. Without a problem, there is no need for the proposal.

The following problems might all be addressed in a proposal. The list will give you some idea of the variety of situations that might lead to proposal writing.

- The Intensive Care Unit in a hospital is small and overcrowded; more space is needed in each room so staff working with patients can move freely without interfering with one another's work. A biomedical technician considering the situation believes that replacing the present bulky patient-monitoring system with newer and smaller monitors would provide the needed space.
- A large, four-story motel provides too few soft drink vending machines for its guests. The motel manager has discussed the problem with the representative of a soft drink vending machine distribution company. The manager asks the distributing company for a proposal that will provide more convenient vending of soft drinks for guests.
- The Animal Control Division of a county health department has been expanding its services and hiring new staff. Because the staff is new and inexperienced, efficiency is low and confusion has developed. One of the experienced staff members realizes that a new and complete procedures manual should be developed to help train the new staff.
- A state college with an open admissions policy has admitted many students who spell very poorly. Few effective ways to upgrade the spelling of college-age students have been developed and little research has been done in this area. Teachers need advice about how best to cope with the problem. A graduate student proposes a research study to teach three spelling strategies to one section of General Studies English; to teach the traditional syllabus (with no spelling instruction) to another section; and to compare the results, report on the findings, and offer a workshop for other instructors to discuss the findings.

Before designing a proposal, define the problem you will address as clearly as possible. Review the techniques for identifying problems described in Defining the Problem and Purpose, Chapter 2. You may have to begin collecting data now, using library research or employing some of the methods described in Chapter 7 to survey students, employees, or other groups about the problem you perceive. Don't assume *immediately* that you already understand the problem at hand. Take time to give the situation some thought.

Even when responding to an RFP, you must be extremely careful to show that you understand the problem that has been identified for you. A solicited proposal normally contains the proposer's restatement of the problem, in terms that show comprehension of the situation; a simple rewording of the RFP is not usually considered sufficient evidence to demonstrate the required understanding. In fact, many RFPs warn that it isn't.

Once you have defined the problem, determine the purpose of your proposal. In general your purpose is to propose a solution to a problem—and to do so convincingly. However, it may be easier to think of the purpose as threefold: (1) to demonstrate your grasp of a stated problem or to demonstrate that one exists, (2) to describe the best imaginable solution to the problem as stated (and in competitive situations to prove it is better than any alternative solutions), and (3) to convince the readership that you or your company can carry out the proposed solution efficiently and at a reasonable cost.

Determining the Audience

As a proposal writer, you must persuade your readers that your proposal is sound. It will be easier for you to be convincing if you know something about the people who probably will read your work. This is not always possible, but usually you can find at least general information about whatever company, agency, organization, or individual will be reading your work. The more you know, the more you can gear your proposal to your readers' needs and interests.

During this stage, as in defining your problem, you may need to collect information through library or field research. Search for specific details about your readers' interests and preferences and about the kind of proposals they tend to approve. When writing a proposal for a business or organization, use the sources of information for researching an employer that are described in Chapter 5.

If you are writing an unsolicited proposal, try to find out what your probable readers already know about the problem you have identified. If they disagree with you about the need you perceive, a major part of your proposal must be written to convince them that a problem exists. It is often possible to discuss a problem with a supervisor or manager before submitting a proposal; a person who has already been consulted about a problem and whose views have been taken into account in the writing of a proposal will generally be more favorably inclined toward it.

Also, you can sometimes obtain samples of successful proposals from government, educational, or private funding agencies. If there is any way for you to obtain copies, do so. By analyzing such samples, you may be able to determine what kinds of details you must include to obtain approval of your proposal from your audience.

Collecting the Data

In many kinds of practical writing, a design of a document arises out of the data collected. There is sometimes no way to work out the organization of the document before the facts themselves are available to be grouped and introduced. However, proposals contain certain kinds of information that a reader needs in order to make a decision about the proposal. There is no need for you to discover or develop these required sections on your own, as they are matters of convention. You will need enough information to write three major divisions:

- *The technical section:* The solution to the problem you have defined
- *The management section:* The kinds and number of people to be involved in carrying out the solution and how their efforts will be coordinated to get the job done on time (and within budget)
- *The cost section:* The price of carrying out the solution, including equipment, salaries, and any other related costs.

You may have to make telephone calls or visit suppliers of equipment to find out costs of any items needed to carry out your proposal. If extra personnel are required, you will need to determine appropriate salaries. For some proposals, you may suggest payment in terms of released time from other duties. Sometimes you can propose securing volunteer workers, or sometimes proposed work can be handled at no cost by in-house staff. It is up to you to figure out exactly what you want to do, who will do it, and how much the project will cost.

As you prepare your proposal, you will probably find yourself moving back and forth between stages three and four, collecting information and designing your document, before you can proceed to stage five, actually composing the first draft.

Designing the Document

As explained earlier, a proposal can be very brief if the problem addressed is simple. However, this chapter will discuss a proposal that addresses a problem large enough to require writing a full formal report. As Chapter 12 explains, a formal report contains a number of set elements. A proposal is one kind of formal report. The various kinds of formal reports differ mainly in the kinds of sections that make up their main text, or body.

The body of almost any proposal, whether solicited or unsolicited, includes the three sections just described: (1) the technical section, (2) the management section, and (3) the cost section. Each of the sections may contain a number of subsections. In addition, a fourth section—background to the problem—may precede the technical section or be the first part of it.

The elements of a full proposal are shown in the following list in the order in which they should appear. All elements of a full formal report are included, except a recommendations section because the entire proposal *is* a recommendation. You will not draft the elements in the order shown, however, because some of them—such as the table of contents and the abstract—cannot be drafted until the body of the proposal is complete, and because others require so much research and work that you must start on them earlier.

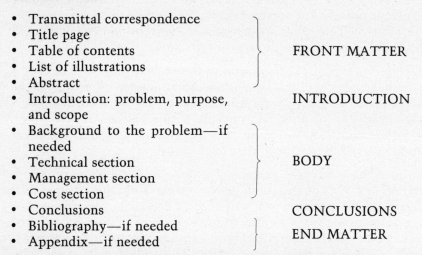

- Transmittal correspondence
- Title page
- Table of contents   } FRONT MATTER
- List of illustrations
- Abstract
- Introduction: problem, purpose,   INTRODUCTION
  and scope
- Background to the problem—if
  needed
- Technical section   } BODY
- Management section
- Cost section
- Conclusions   CONCLUSIONS
- Bibliography—if needed   END MATTER
- Appendix—if needed   }

The main problem to be faced in designing a proposal is the choice and order of subsections that make up the body of the proposal. Also, because a proposal may include a statement of the problem in either the introduction alone or also in a background section, the depth of detail in the introduction must also be planned.

Introduction

Like the introduction to any formal report, the introduction to a proposal includes a statement of the problem being addressed, the purpose of the proposal, and the scope. The statement of the problem may be more detailed than in other kinds of formal reports because it is especially important that a proposal's writer and its readers agree completely about it. However, since a proposal may also include a separate background section, the problem section within the introduction may be brief. In designing a proposal, you must make a decision about how best to present your analysis of the problem.

Figure 13.1 shows the introduction to a proposal addressing a relatively simple problem: a lack of adequate soft drink vending machines at

---

INTRODUCTION

PROBLEM

The vending machines now provided at the St. Louis Inn are too small and too few to meet the needs of the guests at the motel. They also present a safety hazard as they vend only bottled drinks, even in the pool area.

PURPOSE

The purpose of this proposal is to recommend a system of vending soft drinks that will be convenient and pleasing to all guests of the motel and that will return a profit to St. Louis Inn.

SCOPE

This proposal recommends a vending system for soft drinks. It also includes a description of the vendors to be used and a list of suggested soft drink products. It proposes a system of management for the system and describes costs and potential cost recovery.

Figure 13.1   Introduction to a Proposal

the St. Louis Inn. This proposal includes a separate background section, so the problem description within the introduction is brief.

Background to the Problem

A background section is optional in many proposals. However, you may sometimes feel that your readers need additional information about a problem to be convinced that it exists. Also, since you must convince your readers to approve your proposal, you want them to believe that you thoroughly understand the problem yourself.

The length of this section may vary a great deal. However, if you do choose to include it, make good use of it. Think in terms of the needs and interests of your audience, not your own desire to get the proposal approved. Possible problems for any organization or group include loss of income or loss of opportunity to make income; possibly unsafe or unhealthy conditions; poor products or services; poor public image; unhappy employees; or lack of some service, department, piece of equipment, or staff position possibly critical to the success of the organization.

Figure 13.2 shows the background section of the proposal to the St. Louis Inn. The writer has carefully investigated the situation at the motel and has written a description of the problem that lets the manager know the writer clearly understands why the present vending system is inadequate.

BACKGROUND TO THE PROBLEM

The only sources of soft drinks now available to guests at the motel was two small bottle vendors with a vending capacity of 56 bottles each. One of the vendors is located at the entrance to the indoor swimming pool. This vending machine presents both an inconvenience and a hazard. It is too small to accommodate a 250-room motel such as the St. Louis Inn, and in addition, the vending of bottled soft drinks poses a safety threat to guests using the pool. Breakage could easily occur, and people could be injured by broken glass. Such injuries could lead to lawsuits against St. Louis Inn.

The second vending machine is located in the lobby of the motel. There are no vending machines on the first, second, third, or fourth floors of the building. Guests on these floors must take the elevator to the ground floor to use the vending machines in the lobby or in the swimming pool area, both at a considerable distance from the motel rooms on the second floor or higher. Having to travel so far for soft drinks could cause guests to simply do without them, and St. Louis Inn would lose income that could be made from the sale of the beverages.

Figure 13.2   Background Section

Technical Section

The section or sections following the introduction or background to the problem compose the technical section of a proposal. The purpose of this part is to describe in detail the technical solution to the problem—that is, what you wish to do as opposed to how you will carry it out or how much it will cost.

Sometimes the technical section is written as a single unit; sometimes it comprises several sections. Headings such as Proposed System, Proposed Reorganization, Proposed Purchases, or Proposed Research Program are used to introduce these divisions. The technical section of a research proposal may contain a Review of Pertinent Literature.

The technical section of the proposal to the St. Louis Inn includes three subsections. Together, they explain the proposed placement of the vendors, the equipment to be used, and the recommended soft drinks to be sold in the vending machines. The technical section is shown in Figure 13.3.

PROPOSED SYSTEM

This proposal recommends the removal of the two existing bottled soft drink vendors located in the lobby and in the indoor swimming pool area. These bottle vendors should be replaced with can vendors offering 7-Up, I.B.C. Root Beer, and a variety of Taylor Made flavors. The use of can vendors will eliminate the danger of breakage, and at the same time, can vendors will ease the existing storage problem at the motel because cans take up much less space than bottles.

In addition to the vendor in the lobby and the vendor in the indoor pool area, this proposal recommends that can vendors be placed by the elevator on each floor of the motel adjacent to the existing ice-making machines. Many motel guests enjoy having mixed drinks in the privacy of their motel rooms, and the placement of a 7-Up vendor next to the ice machine provides a convenience that motel guests will appreciate. Furthermore, the strategic placement of a can vendor on each floor of the motel eliminates the need for guests to leave their floor in search of soft drinks.

PROPOSED EQUIPMENT

There are many fine can vendors available for motel use. Virgil Scott Distributing recommends placing a 7-Up Vendalator Model VFC 384-8 on each of the four floors of the motel. We also propose replacing the existing bottle

---

vendors in the lobby of the motel and in the indoor swimming pool area with additional can vendors of this model.

The Model VFC 384-8 is recommended because it has a capacity for vending 384 12-ounce cans, including 124 that are precooled, and can dispense eight different flavored soft drinks. The coldest cans are vended first. The machine is a heavy-duty, hermetically sealed unit with forced air circulation.

The 7-Up Vendalator Model VFC 384-8 is also a visually attractive soft drink vendor, 38" wide, 22 13/16" deep, and 79" high. Figure 1 provides an illustration of the model.

FIGURE 1   Vendor Model VFC 384-8

RECOMMENDED SOFT DRINK SELECTION

We recommend that the soft drinks shown in Table 1 be offered in each Vendalator VFC 384-8.

All these soft drink flavors are popular in the St. Louis metropolitan area. 7-Up (both regular and sugar free) is the nationwide no. 1 seller in the lemon-lime flavored soft drink market. It is an excellent mixer as well as a refreshing, clean-tasting soft drink.

I.B.C. Root Beer is the best selling root beer in the St. Louis metropolitan area. It was developed in St. Louis and has long been the favorite soft drink at Busch Stadium.

TABLE 1   FLAVOR SELECTION

Selection Favored	Flavor	Capacity for Vending 12-oz. Cans
1st	7-Up	68
2nd	7-Up Sugar Free	68
3rd	I.B.C. Root Beer	68
4th	I.B.C. Root Beer Sugar Free	68
5th	Taylor Made Cola	34
6th	Taylor Made Orange	34
7th	Taylor Made Grape	30
8th	Taylor Made Creme	30

The Taylor Made soft drinks are also produced locally and offer many flavors that are popular with adults and children alike. The order of choices of Taylor Made soft drinks given in Table 1 is based on the distributor's percentage of sales in the year 1983–1984.

Figure 13.3   Technical Section

Management Section

The management section of a proposal, like the technical section, may be composed of a number of subsections or may be a single unit. The purpose of this section is to explain to the readers exactly how the writer proposes to carry out the proposal. Included could be such subsections as the following:

• *Personnel available:* A flow chart showing the chain of command to be used for the project may be provided; sometimes one-page résumés of all staff involved may be included in the appendix and referred to in the management section.
• *Equipment:* Available equipment to complete the proposed project may be listed.
• *Schedule:* If the project will take more than a day to complete, a day-by-day or weekly summary of work to be done, in narrative or chart form, may be provided.
• *Past successful jobs:* A narrative of successful jobs completed by a company submitting a proposal may be added.

The management section of the St. Louis Inn proposal is written as a single unit of several paragraphs. It is shown in Figure 13.4.

MANAGEMENT OF THE VENDING SYSTEM

A Virgil Scott Distributing Company field representative can call on the motel purchasing agent within the next few days. At this time, a delivery date for the six Vendalator VFC 384-8 vendors can be set up, and at the same time our representative can set up a delivery schedule for the soft drink products. It is suggested that the soft drinks be delivered weekly to keep the vendors operating at full capacity.

If all arrangements are satisfactory with St. Louis Inn, a designated driver-salesperson will deliver the soft drinks needed each week at a time convenient to the motel's receiver.

In addition, we will dispatch factory-trained maintenance personnel at any time, day or night, if a mechanical or refrigeration problem develops in any of the six vending machines.

Finally, the vending machines will be inspected monthly by factory representatives to ensure that they are in good working order.

We suggest that the motel manager appoint one of the motel's staff members to fill the soft drink vending machines and collect the coins from the coin mechanism at least once a day. The motel manager and the individual selected to fill the machines and collect the coins will have the only available keys to the coin mechanism of each vending machine.

Figure 13.4   Management Section of a Proposal

Cost Section

The cost section is normally the last section in a proposal. In this section you must account for the cost of every item that is introduced in your proposal, including the costs of equipment, supplies, salaries, special fees, or any other items. You may name the costs within the cost section of the body or simply summarize them in the body and provide detailed price lists in an appendix.

Sometimes proposal writers also include an explanation of how the reader may be able to recover any money invested in the proposed purchase or activity. In solicited proposals prepared by large organizations, these *cost recovery* sections, as they are called, can be lengthy and complex, requiring considerable background in business and accounting to prepare. However, you need not be an accountant to write a cost recovery section if your proposal is fairly simple.

A cost recovery explanation has three parts: an account of how much the proposed project will cost, how much money will be earned, and finally what profit may be expected after subtracting the cost of the project from the projected revenue.

Figure 13.5 shows the cost and cost recovery section of the proposal to the St. Louis Inn. These two subsections together make up the cost section of the proposal.

COST

We recommend that the St. Louis Inn lease six 7-Up Vendalator Model VCF 384-8 vending units. Delivery, installation, and all maintenance and service calls required to operate these vendors will be provided to the motel without charge. The cost to lease the six vendors is $3.00 per unit per week, or $18.00 per week total.

The cost of the recommended soft drinks to be sold in the vendors is shown in Table 2.

TABLE 2   SOFT DRINK COST BREAKDOWN

Selected Flavor (24 12-oz. cans/case)	Cost per Case
7-Up	$9.84
7-Up Sugar Free	9.84
I.B.C. Root Beer	9.84
I.B.C. Root Beer Sugar Free	9.84
Taylor Made Cola	8.40
Taylor Made Orange	8.40
Taylor Made Grape	8.40
Taylor Made Creme	8.40

COST RECOVERY

This proposal recommends that motel management set up the coin mechanism of each of the six vending units to dispense soft drinks at $.50 per can. The cost recovery and profit margin of soft drinks sold through this proposed vending system are expressed in Table 3.

TABLE 3   COST RECOVERY

Choice of Soft Drink	Cost Per Can	Selling Price Per Can	Profit Per Can	Percent Markup
7-Up	$.41	$.50	$.09	21.9
I.B.C.	$.41	$.50	$.09	21.9
Taylor Made (all flavors)	$.35	$.50	$.15	42.9

The investment of $18.00 per week to rent the six vending units can quickly be made up by the profit to be made on the soda sold in the vendors. Selling 90 cans of 7-Up and 70 cans of any of the Taylor Made drinks (a total of 160 cans) would return a profit of $18.60. This would return the investment of $18.00 paid to rent the Vendalators for one week. Beyond this all sales would return clear profit to the St. Louis Inn.

According to the information provided us, St. Louis Inn normally accommodates 350 people a day, approximately 70 percent of your capacity of 500 a day, two to a room. This means that you provide accommodations for approximately 2,450 people a week (counting separately for each night those guests stay more than one night). After about the 160th can, each beverage consumed by these guests will return money to St. Louis Inn.

If only one-quarter of the guests (or 612) purchase soda, St. Louis Inn will take in $69.78. This assumes that 60 percent of the purchases are 7-Up or I.B.C. and 40 percent are of Taylor Made drinks. Subtracting the Vendalator leasing cost of $18.00 leaves a profit of $51.78 a week, or $222.65 a month (4.3 weeks).

Figure 13.5   Cost Section of a Proposal

Now that you know the divisions of a proposal, design your document. Write a list of the elements you plan to include, from the transmittal correspondence through the appendix. List the subsections you plan to write *within* the technical, management, and cost sections of your proposal. You may, of course, alter your design as you draft, revise, and collect additional information, but draft an initial outline now.

In planning the design, consider also where graphics could be used effectively and indicate on your outline where you plan to place them. One logical place for a graphic is in the cost section, where a table is often helpful.

Finally, before you begin writing, consider style. Remember that all proposals must be *persuasive* since a proposal is normally submitted in a competitive situation. It must convince management, a client, or the originators of an RFP that you understand a problem better than anyone else and can be trusted to provide the best solution. The tone of a proposal, then, must be confident and positive—without being suspiciously grandiose. Never promise more than you can deliver, but don't be afraid to "sell" your idea through good descriptive writing and attention to detail.

Drafting the Document

With your design in hand and after sufficient research to gather the facts you need, begin to draft. We suggest you start by writing the introduction, background to the problem (if included), technical section, management section, and cost section. After these are completed, it makes sense to draft the conclusion, the end matter, and then the abstract. After that you can prepare a draft of the title page, table of contents, list of illustrations, and finally the transmittal correspondence.

We have already described the introduction and three main sections of the body of a proposal and provided examples of each division. We'll now provide advice about how to draft the rest of the elements.

Conclusions

The conclusions section of a proposal provides an opportunity to remind the reader of the strengths of the proposal. In paragraph or in list form, it highlights the potential positive impact of the proposed project or plan. It may include a brief restatement of why the proposed measures are needed and what they will accomplish. Figure 13.6 provides an example of a conclusions section in list form.

Bibliography

A bibliography is seldom needed in a proposal because the details included seldom come from research of printed, copyrighted material. Unless you

CONCLUSIONS

1. A soft drink vending system is needed to provide guests at the St. Louis Inn with a safe and convenient source of soft drinks.

2. A vending system of six Vendalator Model VFC 384-8 units dispensing 384 cans of assorted sodas each would provide a safe and convenient source of soft drinks for all motel guests.

3. Virgil Scott Distributing Company, Inc., would provide for virtually all maintenance needs, leaving motel personnel free to perform other tasks.

4. As Table 3 of this proposal shows, the proposed vending system will provide the motel with a good return on its investment.

Figure 13.6   Conclusion of a Proposal

quoted information obtained from periodicals or books, you can omit this element. If you did make use of information from such sources, list each source in a bibliography on a separate page, after your conclusion.

No bibliography was needed for the proposal to St. Louis Inn. For a sample bibliography, see Chapter 12 on the formal investigative report and Appendix E on documentation.

Appendix

An appendix to a proposal may include any highly technical or detailed information that may be of interest to technical experts reading your proposal or that may be too specific to bear inclusion in the body of your report.

An appendix may include detailed price lists, schematic diagrams of equipment you propose to purchase, or other such technical information. One-page résumés of key company personnel may also be included.

Abstract

After completing a draft of the text of your proposal, draft the abstract. Provide an overview of the entire report: introduction, body, and conclusions. Chapter 11 provides detailed instructions on how to produce this element. The abstract of the proposal to the St. Louis Inn is shown in Figure 13.7.

ABSTRACT

The soft drink vendors now in use at the St. Louis Inn are too small and too few to satisfy customers' needs and present a possible safety hazard. Replacing the two existing bottle vendors with six modern can vendors, model VFC 384-8, each with a vending capacity of 384 cans, would solve the problem. The distributor can provide weekly delivery of the soft drinks to be vended. The vendors can be installed immediately and leased to the motel at a minimal cost of $3.00 per unit per week. There will be no charge for installing, maintaining, or servicing the vendors. The cost recovery from the sale of recommended soft drinks will provide a profit for St. Louis Inn.

Figure 13.7   Abstract of a Proposal

Table of Contents and List of Illustrations

To draft the table of contents, use the list of elements you wrote in planning the design of your proposal, adding any sections you later decided to include. Indent the subheadings for divisions of major sections (such as the problem, purpose, and scope subdivisions of the introduction) three spaces to the right. Use the same typeface for each heading within the table of contents as you used in the body of the proposal.

When the list of section headings is brief, the list of illustrations may also appear on the table of contents page. Otherwise, place it on a separate page.

Figure 13.8 shows the table of contents of the proposal to St. Louis Inn. Page numbers have been added to this example, but you may not be able to add accurate page numbers until you have typed the final copy of the body of your report.

Title Page

As for any formal report, the title page of a proposal includes (1) the title of the proposal, (2) the name and title of the recipient, (3) the name and title of the writer, and (4) the date. The title page of the sample proposal to the St. Louis Inn is shown in Figure 13.9.

TABLE OF CONTENTS

LIST OF ILLUSTRATIONS

-i-

Figure 13.8   Table of Contents/List of Illustrations

Transmittal Correspondence

The purpose of the transmittal correspondence is to introduce your proposal to its readers. Until you have completed a draft of your proposal, you have nothing to introduce, so draft the transmittal correspondence last.

    If you are writing to someone outside your organization, write the transmittal correspondence in letter form. If you address someone within

```
┌─────────────────────────────────────────────────────────────┐
│                                                               │
│                      PROPOSAL FOR                             │
│               A SOFT DRINK VENDING SYSTEM                     │
│                                                               │
│                                                               │
│                                                               │
│                     Prepared for                             │
│                                                               │
│                David Anderson, Manager                        │
│                     St. Louis Inn                             │
│                                                               │
│                                                               │
│                                                               │
│                          By                                   │
│                                                               │
│                Faye L. Scott, Secretary                       │
│              Virgil Scott Distributing Co., Inc.              │
│                 Your 7-Up/I.B.C. Distributor                  │
│                                                               │
│                   December 11, 1984                           │
│                                                               │
└─────────────────────────────────────────────────────────────┘
```

Figure 13.9   Title Page of a Proposal

your organization, make it a memo. Include at least brief reference to the following matters:

- The date of the request for the proposal, if it was solicited
- The problem, if it was unsolicited
- The title of the proposal
- The purpose of the proposal
- A recognition of the help of anyone who might have been instrumental in assisting with the preparation of the proposal, especially for in-house unsolicited proposals

Figure 13.10 shows the letter of transmittal written to introduce the proposal to the St. Louis Inn.

Reviewing and Reworking the Document

A full proposal is often a lengthy document. After completing all the work just described, you will need to gain some distance from your proposal to evaluate and revise it objectively. We recommend that you put it aside for at least a day before you begin revision.

When you reread your draft, try to determine whether or not your writing is convincing, since above all else a proposal must be persuasive. In revising your work to make it more persuasive, ask yourself the following questions.

- Has the problem been described in sufficient detail to convince a reader that a problem exists and that you understand it clearly?

VIRGIL SCOTT DISTRIBUTING COMPANY, INC.
185 CAPRI DRIVE
FLORISSANT, MO 63033   (314) 837-8784

December 11, 1984

Mr. David Anderson, Manager
St. Louis Inn
15002 Southland Road
St. Louis, MO 63141

Dear Mr. Anderson:

I am submitting for your consideration the "Proposal for a Soft Drink Vending
System" that you requested during our telephone conversation of November
26, 1978.

I believe this proposal will demonstrate that you can provide a convenient
source of soft drinks for guests at the motel and at the same time realize a
reasonable return on your investment.

If you have any questions about any phase of the proposal, please do not
hesitate to call me. I will be glad to answer any inquiries you might have.

Sincerely,

Faye Scott

Faye L. Scott, Secretary
VIRGIL SCOTT DISTRIBUTING CO.
Your 7-Up/I.B.C. Distributor

FLS:dr
Enclosure

Figure 13.10   Letter of Transmittal for a Proposal

- Is the wording of the technical section clear? Can a nonexpert follow the description of what you propose?
- Will your audience be convinced that what you propose is the best solution to the problem?
- Are all potential questions about how the proposal can be carried out explained fully in the management section?
- Are the cost figures complete and accurate?

As in revising any document, ask another person to read your proposal and to note any sections that appear unclear or incomplete. Ask your reader how convincing the work is and what might make it more so. Finally, read it through yourself and mark any words or sentences you feel might be ungrammatical; use your dictionary and handbook to help you correct errors. Then ask for a final reading by another person to spot any errors you may have overlooked.

Producing the Finished Document

As we have emphasized throughout this chapter, a proposal is a persuasive document, so make the final product look good. Type all pages and provide a binder for the text of the proposal. Attach the transmittal correspondence to the front of the binder with a paper clip.

In addition, proposals written as class assignments should have an additional cover sheet, addressed to the instructor. Place this cover sheet over the transmittal correspondence. It can be attached with the same paper clip.

Examine the following sample proposal, which addresses the need for a quality-control system in a factory. It is presented in its entirety.

ACME BOX COMPANY
MEMORANDUM

TO: Gerald R. Cizadlo, Plant Manager

FROM: Kevin McClain

DATE: May 16, 1984

SUBJECT: Proposal for a Quality-Control System at the Plant

The attached report, entitled "Proposal for Quality-Control System," is an unsolicited proposal that I would like you to consider.

The report proposes a quality-control program for our plant, beginning with the establishment of a separate quality-control department. It also discusses the makeup of the department, its management, and the costs that would be involved.

In assembling the report, I requested help and suggestions from many of my co-workers; they contributed greatly to this proposal.

PROPOSAL FOR
A QUALITY-CONTROL SYSTEM

Prepared for

Gerald R. Cizadlo
Plant Manager
Acme Box Company

By

Kevin McClain
Machine Operator

May 16, 1984

TABLE OF CONTENTS

LIST OF ILLUSTRATIONS

ABSTRACT

A new quality-control system is needed in our plant. A separate department for quality control could be located in an unused office, which would provide a base of operation. Quality would be monitored at each step along the production process by both management and hourly employees. Most of the facilities and equipment needed to implement the new system are already available, but some new people would be needed. The system would be phased into one department at a time to minimize problems. The money saved by the new system should more than offset the costs.

INTRODUCTION

PROBLEM

Too many defective cartons are going all the way through our plant and getting out to our customers. At present, cartons are checked only at the very end of the production process. Since hundreds of thousands of cartons are produced in any given day in our plant, only a random selection can be checked. This present method is inadequate to control quality effectively.

PURPOSE

The purpose of this report is to propose the establishment of a plant-wide quality-control system to stop the production of substandard products.

SCOPE

In this report a description of a department for monitoring quality is presented, followed by sections concerning facilities available, equipment needed, personnel needed, costs, cost recovery, and finally, conclusions.

PROPOSED SYSTEM

Our present system of quality control is inadequate. Cartons are checked only at the very end of the production process, thus making it possible to check only a random selection of cartons. Because products are not checked anywhere along the production process, subquality material can be "passed along" through the entire plant. This is a waste of time and money. The purpose of this proposal is to stop subquality material before it can go any further.

The report proposes the creation of a separate department called "Quality Control." Under the proposed system, a quality-control person would be put in each department on each shift. In the printing department, sheets would be checked immediately as they come off the presses. In the cutting department,

-1-

sheets would be checked as they come out of the cutting presses. Cartons would be checked as they are stripped, and the stripping operation would be monitored. In the finishing department, cartons would be checked as they come out of the finishing machines. Also, in the finishing department, cartons would be checked again before they are sealed in cases for shipment.

Quality-control people would have the authority to shut down a machine at any one of these stages if it were producing substandard material. This authority is very important, for without it, the quality-control department would carry no weight. It is proposed that the lead person in quality control on each shift be from management. The rest of the quality-control people would be hourly employees with the authority designated above. Should any problems or arguments arise, the management person could step in.

In conjunction with this, it is important that all employees be made aware of just how important quality control is. The best way to do this is by letting everyone know how costly it is when subquality material must be sent back to us for reworking. They should be made aware that our very jobs depend on the quality of our work. This, it is believed, would create beforehand an atmosphere of cooperation. Also, suggestions should be encouraged from all employees. Management should solicit suggestions often and show a genuine interest in them. In this way, everybody gets involved.

The quality-control managers, in conjunction with the plant management, would set minimum standards on each new job. Thus the quality-control managers would not only implement these standards but have a hand in the setting of them as well. This would be beneficial as it would give the quality-control managers a clear understanding of what is and is not acceptable.

FACILITIES AVAILABLE

The quality-control department would be made up of management and hourly employees and would occupy a definite area of the plant. At present, quality control has no base of operation. This should be the first thing established. Employees would then have a place to take problems related to quality control. There is, at present, an unused office in our plant, room 230. This should be the base of operation.

EQUIPMENT REQUIRED

It would be necessary to purchase basic office equipment and some color and board testers. Also, four of our counters and two scales should be replaced. However, a few office supplies and some quality testing materials are available now.

PERSONNEL AVAILABLE

Some of the proposed quality-control jobs could be filled by present employees. The people in our present quality-control system could be used, and our present supervisors could act as quality-control managers. However, it would be necessary to hire at least six new people to implement the system fully. I believe that these new hirees would eventually pay for themselves.

SCHEDULE

The new quality-control system should be phased in gradually. One department, such as printing, should be chosen to be first to receive around-the-clock quality control. Problems in implementation in this one area could be dealt with as they arise without having to deal with other departments' quality problems at the same time. When the system is well established in one department, it would be expanded to all the other departments one at a time. Obviously, problems will arise and we'll need to learn as we go, but problems should be minimal.

COSTS

With the use of as many present employees as possible and with an office and some materials already available, the annual cost of the proposed system would be affordable. The biggest cost would be new hirees—six at $20,000/yr. Initial cost of establishing the office (signs, moving supplies, etc.) would be approximately $320. Materials and facilities (office materials, lighting and heating the office, etc.) would cost around $3,000. Also, some overtime wages must be be paid for the implementation phase in each department—approximately 25 hours at $12/hr. The total first-year cost would be $123,620 (see Table 1).

TABLE 1   COST ESTIMATES

6 Employees @ $20,000/yr.	$120,000
Initial cost of establishing office	320
Materials and facilities	3,000
Overtime necessary for implementation	300
Total	$123,620

COST RECOVERY

An effective quality-control system in our plant could more than pay for itself. The costs of poor quality are great. For example, our company must pay freight costs of rejected stock sent back to us by our customers for rework, and our people must work off the line on reworking the rejected stock. This is valuable time lost. Overtime is often involved in reworking, multiplying the cost. Most importantly, we have lost customers because we've sent them substandard cartons. In the past year we lost the accounts of P&D Inc. and Mead Folders solely because of our inability to meet their basic quality standards. These two accounts were worth over $130,000 annually. When other costs are added, the amount we pay for poor quality is much greater than the cost of the proposed system (see Table 2).

-4-

TABLE 2   COSTS VS. COSTS SAVED

1983

Lost customer business	$130,000
Freight costs	12,000
Labor (including overtime on rework)	2,000
Total	$144,000
Cost of the proposed system	$123,620
Difference	$ 20,380

Also at stake is something we cannot place a dollar value on: our reputation in the industry. A good reputation is our best ticket to future business.

CONCLUSIONS

1. The present method of quality control in our plant is inadequate. Only a random selection of cartons are checked and only at the end of the production process. Too much subquality stock is getting out to our customers.

2. The proposed system provides an effective method of monitoring quality. It provides for the setting up of a separate department for quality control and the checking of quality at each step along the production process.

3. Poor monitoring of quality has been very costly to us. The new system is necessary to ensure no further losses in business.

Key Points in the Chapter

1. A proposal is a form of practical writing that addresses a problem and provides a plan for its solution.
2. Solicited proposals are those that have been requested by someone inside or outside an organization.
3. Unsolicited proposals are those that have not been requested.
4. Be especially careful to define the problem addressed in a proposal; without a clear problem, there is no need for a proposal.
5. Writing a proposal may require you to collect data during all writing stages that precede drafting; you may need to research the nature of the problem and the needs and interests of your readers before you begin to collect the information you need to describe your solution.
6. A proposal is often written as a formal report and includes all conventional elements of a formal report except a recommendations section; the entire proposal is a recommendation.
7. The technical section of a proposal conveys the proposed solution and may include a detailed statement of the problem.
8. The management section of a proposal describes the kind and number of people to be involved in carrying out the proposal as well as how management will ensure that the job gets done.
9. The cost section of a proposal conveys the price of carrying out the proposed solution.

Exercises

1. Select a problem you perceive at your college or dormitory. Interview at least 10 other students to determine more fully the nature of the problem. Determine who has the authority to approve a solution. Then write a proposal to that person, describing the problem and your proposed solution to it.
2. Define a problem at your job. Determine who has the authority to approve a solution. Write a proposal to that person, defining the problem and describing your proposed solution.
3. Consider a problem that may exist in your neighborhood, local government, place of worship, or any other organization in which you are interested. Research the problem by talking with other people who may be affected by it. Determine who may have the authority to approve a solution. Write a proposal in which you describe the problem and your proposed solution to it.
4. Identify some problem in your family or home. Perhaps your heating bills have been high and you would like to install a solar heating system or new storm windows. Pretend you are the sales manager of a fictitious company selling or providing the kind of product or service you need. As the sales manager, address a proposal to yourself, proposing a solution to your problem.

14 Giving an Oral Presentation of a Report

Abstract

Information is not always communicated through writing; often verbal explanation is necessary. The most common kind of oral presentation of information in business and industry today is the extemporaneous address. It does not involve simply reading a report or manuscript aloud. Instead selected highlights of a report, problem, program, or idea are presented, and the address is designed with the needs of the listeners in mind. Most oral presentations should be rehearsed several times before delivery, but too much rehearsal will damage spontaneity.

Communication on the job is not always handled through writing. You will sometimes be called on to *speak* to a group of people rather than to write to them. Speaking to a group is necessary in many situations:

- Criteria for promotion in a bank have just been changed. The bank manager must explain the new procedures to the staff at a department meeting.
- An engineer is involved in a research project requiring several months to complete; a vice president within the organization requests a brief verbal update of the progress.
- The director of a large public library has prepared an annual report describing major accomplishments of the library during the preceding year. The director is asked to present the report to members of the Board of Trustees.
- A nurse working in an acute care hospital has developed an original solution to a patient care problem. The work is so noteworthy that the

355

nurse has been asked to explain the new techniques at a meeting of the American Nursing Association.

All these situations require information to be communicated orally—sometimes instead of writing and sometimes in addition to writing. Relaying information verbally, whether to large or small groups or in formal or informal situations, is referred to as giving an *oral presentation*.

The previous chapters of this book have explained how to produce a variety of forms of practical writing, such as the memo, letter, and report. These different forms have evolved because they most efficiently solve different writing problems. Different forms of oral communication have also evolved to handle various situations requiring speaking instead of writing.

In general, oral presentations can be divided into four categories: the impromptu talk, the memorized presentation, the manuscript reading, and the extemporaneous address. Each form will be described briefly. However, since the extemporaneous address is the form of oral presentation most commonly used in business today, only it will be described in detail, and only this form of oral presentation will be assigned in this chapter.

The Impromptu Talk

An impromptu talk is, by definition, a talk given without preparation. It is appropriate only for extremely informal situations. When you are asked by your supervisor during a staff meeting to describe briefly some departmental problem, you will probably respond with an impromptu talk. However, most business and technical presentations are given in more formal situations and involve complex material, so an impromptu talk is not advisable.

Memorized Presentation

A memorized presentation is one you have committed to memory, word for word. However, business and technical presentations are seldom delivered as memorized speeches. Only experienced actors and speakers do this well, and few people in a business or professional audience will expect you to recite from memory.

Manuscript Reading

Reading aloud word for word from a previously prepared script or report is referred to as giving a *manuscript reading*. You may someday be asked to read an article you have written or report you have prepared at the meeting of a local professional society or at a convention. Afterward, the paper you read may be published in a proceedings journal. However, reading aloud is not usually the best way to communicate with a group, especially during informal meetings. Reading aloud can bore listeners and waste their time. After all, most people can read a report for themselves and get more out of it that way. Therefore, manuscript readings are generally given only in extremely formal, even ceremonial, situations.

Extemporaneous Address

The most common form of oral presentation given in business and industry is the extemporaneous address. During such an address, the speaker is expected to talk naturally and conversationally from brief notes or from an outline prepared beforehand. An extemporaneous address is given for many reasons, such as to summarize or introduce a report to a group of listeners or to explain several aspects of a company problem, program, or development.

As you will see, preparing an extemporaneous address involves many of the same seven stages that we have suggested for preparing written communication. Attention must be given to problem, purpose, and audience. In addition, the report is designed and rehearsed (which is very like drafting a paper) before it is finally presented (which is comparable to producing a finished product).

Throughout this chapter, advice is given about how to respond to one particular communication problem requiring an extemporaneous address: the need to summarize the key points of a formal report for a small listening audience. Since this is a textbook mainly about writing, not speaking, we feel students will be best served by learning how to give one kind of presentation well. However, nearly all the guidelines provided also apply to giving any kind of extemporaneous presentation.

Though you may feel especially nervous about this assignment—many and perhaps even most students do—you may find the ability to give an effective extemporaneous address to be one of the most useful skills you acquire in college.

Preparing an Extemporaneous Presentation

Preparing the extemporaneous presentation of a report you have written involves considering again the same matters you had to clarify for yourself before you wrote.

- What problem are you addressing? Why are you speaking?
- What is the purpose of your presentation?
- Who is your audience?

The problem—the reason you wrote the report—remains much the same; however, the purpose changes. Your new purpose is to communicate clearly the main points of your work to a different kind of group—listeners. Listeners have different needs from readers; consequently, you will have to make a number of changes in your material to prepare it for oral presentation.

A business or technical report is commonly presented to a small group, often a committee or a board. Some members of an audience will read through the report after hearing its presentation; some will skim it or read selected sections; others may gather *all* the information they will learn from the speech alone.

Written work (especially formal reports) can be lengthy and complex. Of course, the reader of a report can sit down and go through a report entirely, reading again anything too complicated to be understood at a glance; someone needing specific information can turn to the appropriate section. However, a listener is in a different situation.

To begin with, it is difficult for members of an audience to concentrate on and remember information presented orally. Unlike readers, they cannot go back and reread complex material, and if too many points are presented, even knowledgeable listeners will get lost. In addition, listeners must normally sit through an entire presentation. There is no way they can turn to a particular page half-way through to find the information they need.

Before selecting the points you want to feature, try to find out who will hear your presentation. If only managers will attend, present the points relevant to them. If your listeners will be mainly technicians, communicate the information they need. If the audience is to be mixed, try especially to highlight points relevant to all groups.

Designing for Listeners

After determining your problem, purpose, and audience, you will be ready to design your speech. First, select the three to five central points you wish to make. If you try to communicate much more than that, your listeners will not be able to remember everything. Order your points logically; you will probably follow the order of their presentation in your report.

After you have selected your central points, design the presentation. Like a written composition, an oral presentation consists of three parts: introduction, body, and conclusion. An explanation of what you should include in each of these sections follows.

Introduction   If you are to be introduced by a presiding person, you will begin by thanking that person. You may want to prepare what you will say.

The presentation of a report need not begin with the kind of humorous story or anecdote often used in less businesslike situations. Instead, you can introduce your presentation by explaining the *problem* that resulted in the need for your report and the *purpose* of your presentation.

The introduction should conclude with an announcement of the three or four main points you will cover. It will help your listeners tremendously if they know what to listen *for* in your speech.

Body   The body of an oral presentation is organized around main points, in the same way that an essay is organized around points supporting a thesis. Prepare the body of your speech by writing out the points you wish to make; if subpoints are involved, use outline form. Try to write everything on one or two sheets of paper. Include any specific facts or figures you must present. If the points can be simply expressed, you can write them all on one notecard.

It is usually better to write phrases than full sentences, as this will keep you from trying to memorize the presentation word for word. Your notes should tell you what *ideas* to cover, not how to express them. Figure 14.1 shows sample notes for an extemporaneous address on one of the proposals in Chapter 13, "Proposal for a Soft Drink Vending System."

PROBLEM: Vending machines at the St. Louis Inn are too few and too small; the vendors at the pool entrance present a safety hazard.

PURPOSE: To propose a soft drink vending system that will be convenient for guests and return a profit for St. Louis Inn.

LIST OF POINTS: (1) Proposed system, (2) proposed equipment, (3) proposed drink selection, (4) management proposal, and (5) profit to be made.

I. Proposed system will solve current problems.

   A. Replacement system vendors on each floor and in lobby will make drinks much more accessible to guests
   B. Can vendor at pool will eliminate safety hazard

II. Proposed equipment (7-Up Vendalator Model VFC 384-8) is excellent.

   A. Vends 384 12-ounce cans and precools 124 cans
   B. Dispenses 8 different flavors
   C. Attractive   SHOW PICTURE
   D. Heavy-duty, hermetically-sealed unit with forced air circulation; coldest cans are vended first

III. Proposed selection of soft drinks meets customers' needs.   SHOW TABLE I

   A. 7-Up: nationwide no. 1 seller in lemon-lime market
   B. I.B.C. Root Beer: best-selling root beer in St. Louis
   C. Taylor Made soft drinks: popular with children
   D. Percentage of flavors recommended reflect last year's sales

IV. Proposed system requires little management.

    A. Delivery schedule to be set at your convenience
    B. Driver-salesperson will deliver drinks weekly
    C. Factory-trained maintenance personnel will be dispatched day or night
       to correct problems
    D. Machines will be inspected monthly
    E. St. Louis Inn need have only two responsibilities: filling machines with
       soda and collecting coins

V. Replacing current vendors with ours will create profit.

    A. Cost to lease the six vendors: $3/unit, or $18/week
    B. Cost of soft drinks: from $8.40–$9.84/case   <u>SHOW TABLE 2</u>
    C. Selling drinks at 50 cents/can will return profit of 21.9–42.9% per can
                                                           <u>SHOW TABLE 3</u>

CONCLUSIONS

    1. Proposed soft drink vending system is convenient and safe.
    2. Equipment is virtually maintenance free.
    3. Vendors will return a reasonable profit.

Figure 14.1   Outline for an Extemporaneous Presentation

Using full-sized pages of notes will work well only if you are to speak from in front of a podium that will hold your notes. If you have no podium or want to be free to move around in front of or among members of your audience, writing your notes on 3-by-5-inch cards will be more useful. Small notecards are much easier to work with than sheets of paper.

A good system might be to write your problem, purpose, and list of main points on the first card; each division of notes on a separate card; and your concluding points on the final card. A sample notecard for an extemporaneous address is shown in Figure 14.2.

II. Proposed equipment is best available.

    A. Vends 384 1-ounce cans

    B. Precools 124 cans

    C. Dispenses 8 flavors

    D. Attractive   SHOW PICTURE

    E. Heavy-duty, hermetically-sealed, forced-air circulation; coldest cans

       vended first

Figure 14.2   Notecard for Section of Extemporaneous Address

Conclusion At the end of your prepared talk, let the audience know that you are ending by including a cue such as "Finally, then . . . " or "In conclusion. . . . "

Include a final summary of the main points of your presentation. Since your listeners must rely entirely on memory to grasp the essentials of your talk, a recapitulation is extremely helpful.

Comment again on the purpose and significance of your work. Let your audience know why the presentation is important.

Know definitely how you will end your presentation and end it definitely. When you finish, you might close by thanking the audience and sitting down.

Visual Aids Prepare and use visual aids to help your audience follow your speech. Listeners appreciate visual reinforcement of key concepts; even a simple list of main points can help.

However, a graphic aid doesn't help if it can't be easily seen, so take time to prepare good visuals. Make sure the letters of any charts you use are large enough to be seen by your group; as a rule, make any lettering at least 1½ inches high. If you plan to use a transparency, arrange if possible to type the copy in extra-large lettering. If you present information on posterboard, be sure the sheets are strong enough to stand erect without bending. You may also need to secure some kind of stand or holder to support your charts; don't count on the availability of a stand unless you have already checked the room in which you will speak. When you have finished with a visual aid, remove it from view so it will not distract your audience's attention from your next point.

Additional advice about how to prepare visual aids is given in Chapter 8.

Rehearsing Your Presentation

Once you have worked out the design of your presentation, rehearse. This stage can be compared to writing and revising a first draft after preparing an outline. In this case, the notecards with main points constitute your outline. You need to practice adding details to the outline *as you speak*, instead of writing them out as you did for your report. Rehearse only until you feel comfortable speaking extemporaneously about the points you have selected; three to four times is usually sufficient. Follow these additional guidelines as you prepare your presentation.

1. Rehearse with your cards once or twice. Then rehearse without your cards another time or two. Work until you can avoid long pauses between sections as you try to think of what to say, but don't rehearse more than five times. If you overrehearse, you will lose spontaneity in your final address and may actually hurt your presentation.

2. Although you begin by rehearsing with your outline or cards in front of you, plan simply to carry your notes in your pocket when you give your oral presentation. Bring them out to help you keep on track only if you get flustered. For many people, just knowing that notes are at hand is enough to make them feel comfortable, and a presentation proceeds smoothly. If you find during rehearsal that you must use your notes, prepare a clean, readable copy for yourself.

3. Keep the pace lively. Make your speech as engaging as possible by using natural, conversational language and appropriate humor. Don't be afraid to use first person pronouns (*I*, *we*, and *me*) even though your report may be written strictly from the third person point of view. As you speak, use language such as "I have discovered that . . . " or "We had to conclude. . . . "

4. Add as many examples and analogies as you can think of, whether or not they appeared in your report. For example, if you were about to explain to a group how word processing can be used for writing, you might say that learning to use a microcomputer to write is something like learning to drive a car with a clutch. A new user of word processing, like a new driver, has to think through every step at first, but soon the steps become automatic and the writer, like the driver, can proceed without thinking very much about it. Comparing an unfamiliar situation such as this to an old and familiar one can help the audience understand new concepts.

5. Consider using rhetorical questions. Rhetorical questions are questions you answer yourself as soon as you ask them. For example, you might lead to a new section of your presentation by using a rhetorical question and answer combination such as "Is this new system state-of-the-art? You bet it is!" The technique helps to keep an audience alert. People listening to a talk need stimulation to keep them interested.

6. Time yourself. Often you will be asked to speak for a specified length of time, such as 15 minutes. If you are to be part of a program, it is important that you give a presentation not much longer than the time allotted, nor much shorter.

7. Present your points in the same order as you announced them and *introduce* each point by referring to it again. Don't worry about repeating; listeners need to hear things several times to remember them. Remember also that your listeners have no text in front of them, so you must, in effect, announce the "headings" that would appear in a written report.

8. Consider practicing at least once in front of a mirror or, if possible, using videotape or audiotape equipment to play back a tape of your rehearsal. Seeing yourself can help you notice and correct bad habits such as slouching, fiddling with a watchband or collar, or looking at the ceiling instead of the audience. Making an audiotape of your rehearsal and listening to it can help you spot troublesome habits

such as clearing your throat too often or inserting too many *uh*s or *and*s while you think of what to say. You can also listen for problems of poor or sloppy diction. This does not mean that you should attempt to sound like a television announcer; using your own regional dialect with your own speech inflection is usually perfectly acceptable. However, you may find on listening to your voice that you are not speaking as clearly as you think you are, and you may need to work on that.

9. Speak slowly and evenly as you rehearse. Try to keep your speech from "racing." Because they are nervous, many people speak too rapidly when they give a talk. Work against this tendency by consciously slowing the pace. If you find when you time yourself that you are one of the few people who speak too slowly, work to correct that problem.

10. Speak loudly enough to project your voice to the audience. You may have to raise your normal tone of voice considerably. Women, especially, sometimes speak too softly to be easily heard and must project forcefully.

11. Move! If you stand stiffly with your arms at your side, you will put people to sleep. Attempt to convey the *transitions* of your speech through movement or language. Use your body and hands. Lean slightly toward the audience as you speak. Consider stating something like "My second point is that . . . " when you begin a new section. You might even hold up two fingers as you say it, to convey the idea visually as well.

12. Plan your attire. You should dress for your audience and look as professional as possible.

Giving Your Presentation

When you are about to deliver your presentation, consider the following suggestions.

1. If you can, choose to speak in front of a bare wall or space. If you are speaking in front of a blackboard, erase it before you begin. Ideally, no writing, artwork, or other visual stimuli should distract your listeners' attention from you.

2. If you can, make sure the chairs are facing so that the door is to the rear of the room in which you are speaking. This ensures that latecomers can enter quietly, without passing in front of you as you speak.

3. Maintain eye contact with your listeners. If you feel nervous about looking people in the eye, stare at the ends of their noses or between their eyes; it will appear as if you are looking straight at them. Look around the room at various people. If you see a particularly sympathetic face, return to that face as your "home base" each time you scan the room.

4. After your talk, ask for questions from the audience; repeat each question for your audience before you answer it. Paraphrase the question if the wording is awkward or if the query needs to be clarified so all members of the audience will understand it. Often, listeners cannot hear a question being asked and therefore do not understand the answer when it is given. If you *cannot* answer a question, say so. If you think you can find the answer and get back to the questioner later, also say so.
5. If you have any material to distribute, such as typed copies of your report, pass it out after you have answered questions. If you distribute it earlier, people looking through it will be distracted from your speech.
6. Try to look as if you are enjoying yourself!

Major Sections of an Extemporaneous Address

In summary, the presentation of your report can be divided into three major parts. Each section, with its subdivisions and approximate length, is shown in outline form.

    I. INTRODUCTION (2 to 3 minutes)
      A. Acknowledge your introduction by presiding person.
      B. Explain the problem you are addressing and the purpose of your presentation.
      C. Provide an overview of the three or four points you will make in your presentation. Consider using a visual aid.
   II. BODY (5 to 10 minutes)
      A. Introduce and explain a main point; consider using a visual aid.
      B. Repeat the preceding for each main point of your presentation.
  III. CONCLUSION (2 to 3 minutes, without questions)
      A. Repeat the list of main points.
      B. Comment on the purpose and significance of the presentation.
      C. Ask for questions from the audience.
      D. Distribute any materials.
      E. End the presentation.

The key to a successful oral presentation is organization, along with the use of natural, conversational language and sufficient—but not too much—rehearsal. After a few successful presentations, you'll feel much more comfortable with this aspect of practical communication.

Key Points in the Chapter

1. Make no more than three to five central points in an extemporaneous address.

2. Select the points you will make with the needs and interests of your listeners in mind.
3. Write out the points to be presented in outline form or on notecards; carry your notes with you when you give your presentation, but try to give the presentation without them.
4. Rehearse until you are comfortable giving the speech and then stop; don't overrehearse.
5. Make your organization "crystal clear" to your audience by announcing the points you will cover, repeating each point as you come to it, and recapping the points again during the conclusion.
6. Speak in a natural, conversational style.
7. Speak clearly and slowly during your presentation.
8. Move during your talk; use your body and hands to communicate transitions and main points.
9. Use good visuals to reinforce the central concepts of your presentation.
10. Distribute materials or copies of your speech after, not before, your presentation.

Exercises

1. Assume your classmates are the audience for whom you wrote your formal report or proposal. Present the report to them orally, adapting content as necessary. Also adapt one of your illustrations for presentation to the group.
2. Choose a subject that some particular group would find interesting or important. Write a memo to your instructor naming the group, its reason for wanting to know about your subject, and your subject. Give an oral presentation of the subject, including at least one visual aid.

APPENDIXES

A Style

When applied to writing, the term *style* brings quite different ideas to different people. Some may think of it as ornament added to the plain, unvarnished truth; others, as the quality that sets the writing of one person apart from that of another—a writer's fingerprint, so to speak—and still others may think of it as something that distinguishes business from academic writing or scientific from creative. These descriptions all have something to do with style in certain kinds of writing, but we will here speak of it simply as the selection and arrangement of words in sentences and paragraphs. Thus all writing, even the plainest, has a style, and it can be judged, according to our reasons for reading, as good or bad, effective or ineffective.

Good practical writing also has a style, but when the writing is most effective the style is not noticed; the reader is undistracted by the manner of the writing and can concentrate fully on the ideas being conveyed. Writing that does its job in this way is characterized by clarity, conciseness, and simplicity.

Clarity enables writing to convey ideas, with a minimum of distortion, from the mind of the writer to the mind of the reader. Conciseness enables it to convey the ideas economically, in the fewest words, without sacrificing meaning or the attitudes and feelings that are often important in forms like the business letter. Simplicity enables a piece of writing to appeal to a broad audience and yet say what needs to be said.

All three qualities are relative, depending as they do on the readers. What is clear, concise, and simple to one set of readers—experts in physics, for example—may be unclear, too brief, and too complicated to chemists. Here are two pasages on the flight of birds, the first from a high school biology textbook, the second from a scientific journal. The audience for

369

the first is high school sophomores, for the second well-educated laypeople or possibly ornithologists, who study birds professionally.

> Although some birds such as penguins and ostriches do not fly, most birds are well adapted for flight. The forelimbs are modified as wings, the shape of which is important to flight.

> The range of speeds at which the gull flew most economically in the tunnel (19 mph for endurance, 28 mph for distance) was about the same as the usual range of airspeeds for freeflying gulls. Laughing gulls have been tracked at 29 mph by a double-theodolite system.

Each passage is clear, concise, and simple for the audience to which it is directed, but a high school student would find the second difficult, largely because of the term *double-theodolite system.* Ornithologists may find the first clear and simple, but irrelevant, since as experts they have moved far beyond that level.

The content of the documents from which these passages are taken is also different, in keeping with the differing purposes of the two. In fact, all writing differs in meaning if it differs in style. In other words content and style cannot be separated. Consider these two ways of wording a sentence in a letter of request:

> I would appreciate your sending me brochure A129 on floor-cleaning solutions.

> Send me brochure A129 on floor-cleaning solutions.

The first is clear, concise, and simple; the second may be simple, but to the extent that its tactlessness gets in the way of the reader's carrying out the request, it is not clear. As to conciseness, it is *too* concise, and thus it fails on that score, also. The second version might work in a memo to a co-worker whom you know well. It won't work if sent to someone in a distant company.

It is therefore important to adjust your style to fit your reader and purpose. This adjustment depends on the words you choose and the way you put them together in sentences and paragraphs. These three elements, words, sentences, and paragraphs, will form the basis of the discussion of style in this appendix.

Choosing Words in Practical Writing

It is easier to explain how *not* to select proper words in practical writing than to explain how to do it. As writers all of us have a store of words, and of patterns for those words, that we have acquired over the years. When we write we must depend on that gradually accumulated store, along with the new words and ideas acquired in research, to carry us through the first draft. True, we can decide to write for one audience rather than another as we plan the first draft, and that decision will make a difference. Yet an important part of the adjustment to audience and purpose will come as we revise and edit. There are a number of kinds of language you should consider as you write and revise. Of these some apply to many kinds of writing; all apply to practical writing. These kinds of language are jargon, technical terms, pompous language, clichés, figurative language and analogy, and discriminatory language.

Jargon

Jargon is the language of speech and informal writing that originates in one trade or activity—terms such as *bloop single* and *high hopper* in baseball, and *hardware* and *memory dump* in the computer trade. Jargon is good to the extent that it provides variety and color in what might otherwise be an extremely dull activity, such as play-by-play broadcasts of baseball games on radio or TV. It is also one of the most fruitful sources of the new terms that are constantly coming into the language. Without the additions from special fields, language would lose much of its vitality and ability to adapt. Jargon also serves a useful social function, especially in speech, by distinguishing those who belong to a special group from those who don't. Many workers, such as long-haul truck drivers, take great pride in the language of their group.

However, jargon is bad to the extent that it isn't understood by some readers or distracts by drawing attention to itself or by annoying some readers. Many words, such as the computer term *input*, are objected to when used in fields unrelated to computers, even though that use is now widespread.

Abbreviations and acronyms are one kind of jargon that is frequently not understood by readers outside the fields in which the terms originated. *Form 1040* and *W-2* may be known to all taxpayers, but *ETA* (estimated time of arrival) and *EKG* (electrocardiograph) may not be. Appendix B gives advice on the use of abbreviations and acronyms.

The narrower the group, the more acceptable jargon may be, especially in informal writing. Yet remember the advice given earlier to aim your writing at a broader group than specifically addressed, since others will often be required to read it. This should be kept in mind particularly when writing formal reports or letters and memos on important subjects.

Technical Terms

It is hard to draw a line between jargon and technical terms, which make up the special language used in various technical fields, without a trace of slang or colloquialism. Technical terms are the *correct* names; jargon is an alternative, often shorter, name for the same thing. For instance, the official name of a small waterfowl common in North America is *pied-billed grebe.* A jargon name common among duck hunters is *hell-diver.* Some, however, would lump jargon and technical terms together as language peculiar to a special field. Whereas jargon may not always be acceptable, even among those in the field where it originated, technical terms are, as long as they are understood by the reader. In fact, most technical terms are essential to communication in those fields. Terms like *accelerated depreciation* in accounting, *leverage* in finance, and *mytosis* in biology cannot be dispensed with since they express an idea so much more precisely and efficiently than any substitute. As the audience widens, however, a writer must use them less freely, and when the backgrounds of some in the audience are unknown, writers should use terms as common as possible while still conveying the message with precision. Technical terms are useful, and often essential, because they say precisely, often in one word, what it might take many words to say in laypeople's terms.

The question you must ask is this: Will the readers I address, and others likely to read the document, be able to understand the technical terms used? When no substitute can be found for an unfamiliar term, you should provide a definition to help readers out. See Appendix C for ways of forming definitions.

Clichés

Clichés are a lazy person's way of saying something, since they are simply a set of expressions that others have created and used over decades—or centuries. To write "That figure is in the ball park" or "If we don't get the contract we will be up the creek without a paddle" is bad, not because these expressions are easy to write but because they are vague and strike most readers as too familiar to be attended to. Clichés warn us that the writer has switched off at least half the brain, and therefore we can't fully trust what is written. The best rule is to avoid comparisons and figures of speech that you have read before. To be effective they need to be fresh and original.

Figurative Language and Analogy

Clichés illustrate the wrong way to use comparisons and other figures of speech. Because some writers use worn-out comparisons, however, does not mean all figurative language should be avoided in practical writing. In fact, both figures of speech and analogies (extended comparisons) can be an excellent means of putting across difficult ideas and at the same time enlivening the writing style. Chapter 9 suggests ways of using comparisons to describe the shape, arrangement of parts, and operation of mechanisms. They can be equally useful in describing more complex structures, from the organization of a company to the structure of the universe.

In practical writing all figurative language works by comparing what is fairly well known (the thing used to illustrate) with the less well known (the subject of the writing). Consider this sentence from an article on the flight of birds:

> If ordinary birds are sailplanes with feathered propellers at their wingtips, then hummingbirds are helicopters.

The first part of the sentence makes the point that birds can both glide like a sailplane and power themselves, as with a propeller. The second part says that hummingbirds can fly in any direction—up, down, to either side, and backward—and can hover as well.

The world is full of parallels that can be put to use to make difficult ideas easier to grasp. Division of labor in a factory can be compared to the functioning of a beehive, the nervous system to an electronic communication system, and a submarine to an underwater mammal. Often a general comparison is sufficient. When pushed too far, parallels can become ridiculous and might lead readers astray rather than enlighten them.

Pompous Language

Imitation of bad models probably accounts for as much ineffective writing as does lack of experience. Writers who have not read widely in a field may have weaknesses as writers, but generally they don't write pompously. It takes a certain amount of practice to use *implement* for *carry out, utilize* for *use* and *selective discontinuance* for *cuts* or *firings*. Whether writers will admit it or not, they usually use expressions such as these to impress. Few readers fall for it. Since these words draw attention to themselves and may be misunderstood, the effect is more likely to be annoyance and confusion. Resist the temptation to impress; use simple words whenever they permit you to say what needs to be said. Here is a passage containing a number of pompous phrases followed by a translation into plain English.

> But the challenge now rests with the individual academic institution to assess recent experience and to design its own integrated, multifaceted program for enhanced relations with the industrial sector.

The passage can be translated into plain English by removing most of the long, pompous, and in some cases vague words and replacing them with shorter, more familiar ones.

> But it is now up to each university to learn from recent experience and design its own program for improving its relations with industry.

The number of words has been reduced from 29 to 24, but the effect is greater than those numbers indicate because the new passage has replaced pompous words with simple ones.

Discriminatory Language

In the past 20 years writers have become increasingly conscious of the need to avoid discrimination against any group in society, whether racial, sexual, or ethnic. Discrimination in writing often occurs without writers' being aware of it when they use words like *he* and *man* to refer to people in general, not just males:

> The operator should take a complete shower after he leaves the contaminated area.

> Man's achievements in the exploration of outer space have come in a remarkably short period of time.

Discrimination also appears when writers use words like *policemen* or *firemen* to refer to all those in a police or fire department even though some are now women. The rapid entry of women into the work force in the past few decades has helped to bring this issue forward.

It is sometimes difficult to avoid all potentially discriminatory expressions, but it is essential to make the effort. In some kinds of practical writing, such as job descriptions and contracts, discriminatory language is forbidden by law; using it in other situations is simply insensitive and impolite. Experienced writers have worked out a number of ways of avoiding this kind of language, and you can handle most situations by following their example. Ways of avoiding masculine pronouns, except when referring to males, will be given first:

- Shift to the plural and use a form of *they*

  > A lathe operator is responsible for keeping all his equipment in working order.

  > Lathe operators are responsible for keeping their equipment in working order.

- Shift to the passive voice and omit the doer of an action when it isn't important to know who it is.

  > The researcher added a dilute alkaline solution to the mixture he had prepared a day earlier.

  > A dilute alkaline solution was added to the mixture prepared a day earlier.

- Use *a* or *the* in place of masculine pronouns.

  > The recreation director should send his monthly report directly to the park supervisor.

  > The recreation director should send the monthly report directly to the park supervisor.

- Use second person (a form of *you*) when addressing a person or group directly, as in letters, memos, and instructions.

The operator places the strips of colored tape across his left arm.

Place the strips of colored tape across your left arm.

- When the third person pronoun can't be avoided, use *he or she*, but use it sparingly. When used often, it becomes annoying and interferes with clear communication. Avoid the even more awkward expressions such as *he/she* and *s/he*. The following sentence from an actual set of instructions shows how awkward these forms can be.

  The student should be expected to intelligently discuss whatever information he/she has collected for his/her research report and be prepared to answer relevant questions.

Here the problem can be easily avoided by shifting to the plural.

Discriminatory expressions are not limited to the use of the masculine pronoun. Here are some examples of other situations along with suggested substitutes that illustrate how the problems can be avoided.

The masculine endings to many names of occupations and positions should be avoided unless a specific person is being referred to and that person is male. These are forms of sexual stereotyping that arose long before women began entering those fields. Instead of *policeman* and *fireman* use *police officer* and *firefighter*. For *businessman* substitute *executive, personnel director, proprietor, financial officer*, or some other name that more precisely describes a person's position, if it is known.

The term *chairman* presents special problems since many women prefer it, and suitable substitutes are difficult to find. Terms that might be used are *chairperson, chair*, and *presiding officer*. If you are writing about a specific woman and you know she prefers *chairman*, use it. The same applies to the use of the titles *Ms., Miss*, and *Mrs.* If you know a woman prefers one of them, you should comply with her wishes whatever your own feelings on the matter may be. In all other cases use *Ms.*

Finally, avoid old-fashioned expressions such as *proprietress, stewardess, woman doctor*, and *male secretary*, all of which imply sexual stereotyping. Instead use *proprietor, steward* or *flight attendant, doctor*, and *secretary*.

In this textbook we have attempted to avoid, as inconspicuously as possible, the use of discriminatory language. If you examine any extended passage carefully, you will see how this has been done.

Choosing the Right Words

Most of the preceding sections on words and phrases tell you what to avoid; this much briefer section will give some advice on the kinds of words to choose. In addition to preferring words that are short and familiar to those that are long and unfamiliar, you should also try to pick words that are as specific and concrete as the context requires. The most specific terms are often the most concrete as well, as is made clear by the following list. It moves from general to specific at the same time as it moves from abstract to concrete.

abstract and general $\longrightarrow$ **concrete and specific**
transportation → vehicle → aircraft → passenger jet → Boeing 727

However, specific terms are not necessarily concrete, as the next list illustrates.

general $\longrightarrow$ **specific**
area of activity → applied science → engineering → civil engineering → bridge building

Bridge building is still an abstraction, since it names an activity, but it is much more specific than *area of activity*.

Sometimes it is useful to be more general than specific, since you may want to include more activities or things than a specific word can carry. The terms *service station* and *gas station* mean the same thing to most people, but *service station* clearly implies that more than gas is offered to customers. When writers move beyond *service station* to something like *auto maintenance facility*, they become not only wordier but more pompous and less clear as well. Pomposity and vagueness are two of the dangers in using general and abstract language.

Here are some sentences that contain general and abstract words that do not convey ideas as effectively as the revised sentences that follow.

1. The director indicated her disapproval of several aspects of the project.

   The director, Clarice Whiteside, outlined her objections to the way scheduling and cost control were handled for the Sikeston project.

2. The animals were confined for an extended period in an unsuitable place.

   The sheep were kept in a 20-by-40-foot loading pen for two weeks.

3. The officials did not arrive on the scene until long after the principals had fled.

   The state police did not arrive in Tombsboro until two hours after the three bank robbers had fled.

Writing Effective Sentences

In practical writing, sentences, like the style in general, should be clear, concise, and simple. That means they should, on the average, be relatively short and simple in structure, and they should contain strong verbs. The heart of any sentence is made up of its verbs and nouns. The section on words and phrases gave advice on the choice of nouns and supporting words like adjectives and pronouns. Since verbs are equally important to effective sentences, we will consider them from several points of view.

Voice in Sentences

There are two voices in English sentences: active and passive. In active sentences the subject is the agent or doer of the action. If the thing acted upon is named, it becomes the object of the verb:

> The engine produced an unusual sound in the first minutes of operation.

In a passive sentence the subject receives the action of the verb, and the agent, if named, usually appears in a prepositional phrase:

> The engine was overhauled by a team from Onan Company.

You may have been told by writing teachers to avoid the passive voice—period. Some may make some concessions, but most disapprove of it because, they say, it produces weak, vague, and evasive sentences. In practical writing, however, the passive voice can serve many useful functions and is sometimes more effective than the active voice. For that reason good practical writing occasionally contains more passive sentences than active, and as Don Bush makes clear in an excellent article on the subject, the reasons for this preference for the passive can be pinpointed (*Technical Communication*, 1st Quarter 1981).

First, because the passive needs no agent, that part can be omitted when it is unimportant.

> The carburetor was removed for repair and cleaning.

> Apples are harvested in early September.

As in these cases, it frequently happens that the identity of the agent, in addition to being unimportant, may not be known. To think up an agent is a waste of time. Furthermore, if a series of actions are performed by the same person, it becomes repetitious to name the agent again and again, as in a description of an experiment.

The passive voice also enables a writer to put important elements in a sentence in emphatic positions. In the sentence about apples, the important elements are the apples and the time they are harvested. Apples are the subject of the article, and the time of harvest is the new piece of information in the sentence. To make the sentence active by writing "Pickers harvest the apples in early September" puts the emphasis on an unimportant element, the pickers. The original version put the two important parts in the two emphatic positions—the beginning and the end.

It is true that the passive is sometimes used to evade responsibility: "It was recommended that . . . " or "You are asked to refrain from. . . . " Use the active voice when it is appropriate, and that may be a majority of the time, but don't overlook the advantages of the passive in some situations.

Strong Verbs

Both active and passive sentences can, and should, contain strong verbs. The sentence "Apples are harvested in early September" would be weakened and made longer if it were written "The harvesting of apples takes place in September." The verb *are harvested* is turned into a verbal noun, *harvesting*, and a colorless and weak verb, *takes place*, becomes the main verb. This revised version illustrates one of the biggest reasons for the ineffectiveness of much practical writing: Verbs are converted into nouns, a process called *nominalization*, and they are replaced by weak verbs, often a form of *to be* such as *is* or *was*. Here is an extreme example of this sort of sentence.

> The commission's attempt at an inquiry into the company's handling of travel costs was met by its denial of a request for an examination of its financial records.

Note how many of the nouns are derived from verbs, while the main verb, *was met*, is weak and insignificant. All the action is hidden in the nominalized verbs *attempt, inquiry, handling, denial, request,* and *examination.* The sentence is technically a simple sentence; it begins with a long noun phrase as subject, and the single verb is followed by a series of prepositional phrases. So-called simple sentences are often not simple.

To make an effective sentence, we must convert some of the nouns back into verbs and put agents and objects in their normal positions.

> The commission attempted to investigate how the company handled its travel costs, but the company refused to turn over its financial records.

Instead of a simple sentence we now have a compound-complex sentence containing two independent clauses and one subordinate clause. Strangely enough, this more complex sentence is actually simpler and easier to read because of the strong verbs in the three clauses. As a result, the sentence is shorter, clearer, and more forceful.

Here are some other sentences containing nominalizations and weak verbs. Notice that most contain more words than necessary and that important ideas and actions are buried in a flood of prepositional phrases. Try converting them into clear and forceful sentences. This exercise will give you practice in writing concisely as well as in using strong verbs.

> The reaction of the supervisors to the announcement of the new regulations by the vice president was predictable.

> Building a spirit of cooperation among workers is a task requiring the expenditure of much time and effort by managers.

> The discovery of the cause of the breakdown was the result of an investigation by the standby crew.

> To handle the annual preparation of tax returns by turning the task over to part-time workers is a poor way of attempting to reduce the cost of preparation.

Sentence Length

Long sentences, if well written, can be easy to read, and short sentences, if badly written, can be difficult. Generally, however, it is easier to read short sentences than long ones. Experts agree that for most kinds of practical writing, sentences with an average length of 15 to 20 words are easiest to read. Note that this is an *average;* don't make all sentences fit that range since it is also important to vary the length of sentences to make the document as a whole readable. Also, don't count the words in your sentences each time you write a draft. A spot check once in a while will give you a good idea of your average, since you probably are fairly consistent. Average sentence length should be chosen with at least three things in mind, in addition to purpose: the educational level of the readers, their knowledge of the subject, and their motivation. The higher the level of these three characteristics, the longer and more sophisticated the sentences can be.

As the section on using strong verbs made clear, the question of sentence length is not a simple one. A well-made sentence containing three or four clauses and 30 or more words may be easy to read because the clauses form clear units with clear relationships to one another. Consider the following two sentences:

> When a book arrives at the library, it is cataloged, marked with call numbers, and shelved, and several cards are added to the card catalog so that the book can be found by searching for author, title, or subject.

> A door, after being hung properly, for many years is unlikely to cause problems.

The first is far longer than the second, yet because it consists of three clauses containing strong verbs, it is relatively easy to read. The second contains only 14 words, but since they are poorly arranged, the sentence is hard to read. Nevertheless, a short average length for sentences produces more readable writing.

Very short sentences serve to emphasize important points, especially at the beginning or end of a paragraph. If they are to be effective for this purpose, however, they should be used sparingly. Brevity commands attention.

Arrangement of Words and Phrases

How words are arranged in sentences has much to do with readability. The best strategy is to stick to what is called *normal sentence order:* subject-verb-object or subject-verb-complement. The short sentence shown in the last section is hard to read mainly because the elements are poorly arranged:

> A door, after being hung properly, for many years is unlikely to cause problems.

It illustrates several problems in arrangement. Two phrases are awkwardly inserted between the subject and verb, and the time indicator, "for many years," is out of its normal position immediately after the idea it modifies. In addition, one of the ideas is stated negatively when it could better be stated positively. Here is a better version:

> After being hung properly, a door is unlikely to cause problems for many years.

The subject is now placed next to the verb and the time indicator is in the right place, but the main idea is still stated negatively. To put it positively requires changing some of the words:

> A properly mounted door will give trouble-free service for many years.

Poorly arranged sentences often contain poorly chosen words and phrases. Don't hesitate to change the words as well as their arrangement as you revise and edit.

One particularly troublesome habit among practical writers is using a long string of adjectives to modify one noun. The problem is made worse when the words in those strings appear to be nouns but function as adjectives, as in the following sentence:

> The research overhead cost computation problem remains unresolved.

Here all four of the words in adjective positions are nouns, and partly for that reason it is hard to tell how the phrase should be interpreted. The writer has attempted to write more concisely but has only made the sentence confusing and difficult to read. Spreading the words out solves the problem.

> The problem of how to compute the overhead costs of research remains unresolved.

Here is another example and a suggested revision.

> Assessing the validity of the earth's magnetic field navigation hypothesis as it relates to birds has been difficult for scientists.

> Scientists have found it difficult to assess the validity of the hypothesis that birds navigate by using the earth's magnetic field.

Among technical writers the jargon term for these constructions is *freight train*, an apt name.

Writing Paragraphs

Paragraphs can be viewed in two ways: as units of meaning and as graphic devices for making a document more readable. The first is the most common way of looking at them, but in some kinds of writing the second clearly predominates.

Paragraph Length

In newspapers, where columns are long and narrow, paragraph breaks are made after every two or three sentences, regardless of the content. The more writers are intent on making the writing easy to grasp, the more they resort to short paragraphs, as in advertising copy. On the other hand, the "small print" in contracts and warranties is often written in long paragraphs to save space and perhaps to discourage close reading.

The more mature and well educated the audience and the more formal the writing, the more freedom writers have to make a paragraph a unit of thought. Yet even in formal reports the paragraphs should be kept to a reasonable length. If an idea requires more than 200 words for its development, it is best to find some way of breaking it into two or more parts. In letters and memos, paragraphs should not exceed 8 or 10 lines, and very short paragraphs, such as a line or two, are acceptable. Look at the letter and memo chapters for examples of short paragraphs.

Other Qualities of Paragraphs

When developed as units of meaning, as in formal reports, paragraphs should be

- Unified by a single idea, which should usually appear in a topic sentence.
- Ordered logically by chronology, spatial arrangement, order of importance, or some other rational method.
- Sufficiently developed to fulfill the writer's purpose, by use of specific and concrete details that support the generalizations.
- Made coherent by means of connections within and between paragraphs.

Here is a four-paragraph section of an article on tarantula spiders and digger wasps ("The Spider and the Wasp," *Scientific American*, August 1952), by the zoologist Alexander Petrunkevitch, that illustrates these qualities.

But provides a transition from the preceding paragraph where two *weak* senses were described. The first two sentences introduce the four-paragraph section, which describes the spider's three kinds of touch. The phrase "Pressure against the body" introduces the first kind.

But all spiders, and especially hairy ones, have an extremely delicate sense of touch. Laboratory experiments prove that tarantulas can distinguish three types of touch: pressure against the body wall, stroking of the body hair and riffling of certain very fine hairs on the legs call trichobothria. Pressure against the body, by a finger or the end of a pencil, causes the tarantula to move off slowly for a short distance. The touch excites no defensive response unless the approach is from above where the spider can see the motion, in which case it rises on its hind legs, lifts its front legs, opens its fangs and holds this threatening posture as long as the object continues to move. When the motion stops, the spider drops back to the ground, remains quiet for a few seconds and then moves slowly away.

The first two sentences of this paragraph introduce its subject, but the third functions best as a topic sentence since it introduces the two ideas developed in the paragraph.

The entire body of a tarantula, especially its legs, is thickly clothed with hair. Some of it is short and woolly, some long and stiff. Touching this body hair produces one of two distinct reactions. When the spider is hungry, it responds with an immediate and swift attack. At the touch of a cricket's antennae the tarantula seizes the insect so swiftly that a motion picture taken at 64 frames per second shows only the result and not the process of capture. But when the spider is not hungry, the stimulation of its hairs merely causes it to shake the touched limb. An insect can walk under its hairy belly unharmed.

In this paragraph, also, the first sentence introduces the subject; the second makes an important new assertion about it.

The trichobothria, very fine hairs growing from dislike membranes on the legs, were once thought to be the spider's hearing organs, but we now know that they have nothing to do with sound. They are sensitive only to air movement. A light breeze makes them vibrate slowly without disturbing the common hair. When one blows gently on the trichobothria, the tarantula reacts with a quick jerk of its four front legs. If the front and hind legs are stimulated at the same time, the spider makes a sudden jump. This reaction is quite independent of the state of its appetite.

This paragraph summarizes the preceding three and then makes a new point by way of introducing the subject of the rest of the article, the digger wasp. It is thus a transitional paragraph.

These three tactile responses—to pressure on the body wall, to moving of the common hair and to flexing of the trichobothria—are so different from one another that there is no possibility of confusing them. They serve the tarantula adequately for most of its needs and enable it to avoid most annoyances and dangers. But they fail the spider completely when it meets its deadly enemy, the digger wasp Pepsis.

This passage, in addition to illustrating careful use of topic sentences and transitions, contains paragraphs that are coherent and unified. The organization of the passage provides the basis for that unity. Each paragraph is also developed by the use of concrete and specific detail, and it is done in a way that makes it easy for a lay reader to grasp. All the words are familiar except *trichobothria*, which is carefully defined. The sentences are relatively short but are varied in structure and length, and most of the verbs are strong action words. You might check this by underlining all the verbs.

These four paragraphs might have been developed as one since they are introduced as one and are closely related in idea. But the first is 141 words long, and adding the next three would make a paragraph of more than 400 words. The author apparently decided that graphically the section works better when broken into four parts, and it does. Each paragraph treats a subtopic of the main one, so the division is logically sound.

Each of the first three paragraphs is clearly organized by describing the process of eliciting responses from the spider—if this is done, this will happen; if that is done, that will happen; and so on. Petrunkevitch shows how an interesting subject can be made even more attractive by careful organization, excellent choice of detail, and a simple but forceful style.

On Using Readability Formulas

Readability formulas are widely used in industry and government to predict the reading difficulty of a piece of writing. The two most popular are

Rudolph Flesch's Reading Ease Formula and Robert Gunning's Fog Index. Like a number of similar formulas, these attempt to measure two characteristics of a text: word difficulty, measured in number of syllables; and sentence difficulty, measured in words per sentence. Since the formulas yield a readability measure that corresponds to level of education, and do it by means of a mathematical formula, they have an air of scientific precision about them. The Fog Index, for example, works like this:

1. In a 100-word sample, find the average number of words per sentence.
2. Find the number of "difficult" words in the same 100-word sample, "difficult" meaning words of three syllables or more. Omit proper names; words formed by joining two or more simple words, such as *housemother* and *trendsetter;* or verb forms made into three syllables by adding *-ed* or *-es.*
3. Add the numbers—average sentence length and number of hard words.
4. Multiply the result by 0.4:

    Number of "difficult" words   10

    Average number of words per sentence   15.6

    $$\overline{25.6} \times 0.4 = 10.24$$

The passage should fit the reading ability of the average tenth-grade student.

One of the leading authorities on readability, George R. Klare, concluded in 1977 that "a readability formula can provide a quick and useful prediction of the reading difficulty of a text—but *no more than that* should be asked"[*] He warned against using the formulas to tinker with word length and sentence length in an attempt to increase the readability of a passage. "Instead," he said, "more basic changes must be made in producing readable writing." Many of these basic changes, such as use of concrete details, familiar words, and strong verbs, have been recommended in other sections of this appendix.

More recently, other experts have voiced strong doubts about the value of the formulas even in *predicting* readability. As you might expect, they also agree with Klare that the formulas should not be used to help *produce* readable writing. Although the formulas give the appearance of scientific accuracy in predicting readability, the actual situation is much more complex. Some kinds of short sentences can be harder to read than well-constructed long ones; some short words are more difficult than many long ones; and many factors not taken into account, such as the motivation of the reader and number of examples in the writing, can strongly affect readability.

It is probably better to read your draft aloud with your potential reader in mind, or get others whose judgment you trust to give you their

---

[*]"Readable Technical Writing: Some Observations," *Technical Communication,* 1977.

opinion. If you combine these techniques with the practice of reading good technical prose by recognized writers, you will have a better sense of the readability of your own writing than the formulas can provide. Since they are still widely used, however, you should know what they are and how they are applied.

B Common Problems with Grammar and Mechanics

Grammar, punctuation, and other "mechanical" aspects of writing do for readers what road signs do for drivers: They indicate conditions or signal changes in direction. Used improperly, they can be just as confusing as a misplaced detour sign that sends motorists down the wrong road.

This appendix, with the entries arranged in alphabetical order, covers just a few of the more common pitfalls of grammar and mechanics. You should supplement it with a good handbook or stylebook and a dictionary. If the company you work for has its own "house style," that's the one to use. Bear in mind, also, that "rules" can and often do change to reflect common usage.

Abbreviations and Symbols

Abbreviations and symbols save space and time, but they can be a headache for a reader who isn't familiar with the ones you're using. Use abbreviations and symbols only when all three of these conditions are met:

- The full word is so long and used so often that it becomes distracting or cumbersome: *Pounds per square inch* is fine if you use it only two or three times; *psi* or *lb/in²* is more efficient if you need to use the expression repeatedly.
- Everyone in your audience will understand the abbreviation or symbol, either because it is common (check a dictionary to make sure) or because you have defined it the first time you use it.
- There's no chance of a misreading; for example, *60″* can look a lot like *6′0″*, but *60 in.* looks different from *6 ft 0 in.*, and *60 inches* looks very little like *six feet.*

Abbreviations are written in lowercase letters unless the dictionary indicates otherwise. Besides postal service abbreviations for states, the exceptions are generally for units named after a person (like *Watts*, named for the eighteenth-century inventor James Watt).

In most cases, modern style omits the period after an abbreviation unless the abbreviation could be misread as a word, as in *in.* for inches. Also, abbreviations for units of measure have no plural form—*1 ft* and *100 ft* are both just *ft.*

Here are a few common abbreviations and symbols.

in.	inch	W	watt
ft	foot	kW	kilowatt
ft-lb	foot-pounds	F	Fahrenheit
in^2	square inch	C	Celsius
ft^3	cubic foot	amp	amperes
mi	mile	dc	direct current
nmi	nautical mile	ac	alternating current
lb	pound	rpm	revolutions per minute
deg	degree	V	volt
qt	quart	atm	atmospheres
gal	gallon	hr	hour
yd	yard	min	minute
m	meter	sec	second
cm	centimeter	min	minute
mm	millimeter	°	degree
km	kilometer	'	foot
g	gram	"	inch
mg	milligram	%	percent
kg	kilogram	Ω	ohm
l	liter	Å	angstrom
ml	milliliter	>	greater than
Hz	hertz	<	less than

Acronyms and Initialisms

Acronyms are a special form of abbreviation, made up of the initial letters of several words in a long title but pronounced as a single word: *NASA* for *National Aeronautics and Space Administration, BART* for *Bay Area Rapid Transit.* Initialisms are formed the same way but are not pronounced as a word: *CPR* for *cardiopulmonary resuscitation, EPA* for *Environmental Protection Agency, I/O* for *input/output.*

Acronyms and initialisms provide a handy verbal shorthand when we write or speak to others who understand the code. They can be very confusing and annoying, however, to anyone who doesn't know their meaning or who doesn't know which of several meanings you have in mind.

Does *ECR* mean *Engineering Change Record* or *Experimental Coherent Radar?*

The best way to avoid problems is to use acronyms and initialisms as little as possible. After you spell out the title the first time, you can use a shortened form for later references. For example, *Experimental Coherent Radar* could become simply *the radar.*

If you must use acronyms and initialisms, follow these guidelines:

- Use all capital letters, unless the acronym has become a commonly accepted word (like *radar* for *radio detection and ranging,* or *scuba* for *self-contained underwater breathing apparatus*).
- Do not use periods between the letters.
- Form the plural simply by adding *-s* (*ECRs*).
- Spell out the full name the first time, with the acronym or initialism in parentheses immediately following, like this: *independent research and development (IRAD).* If you don't use the short form for several pages, repeat the process when the term is needed again—just in case the reader forgot.
- If you use more than half a dozen acronyms and initialisms, define them all in a list near the beginning of the document.

Agreement

If the subject of a sentence or clause is singular, the corresponding verb must be singular. If the subject is plural, the verb must be plural. The same is true for a pronoun and its antecedent (the noun it refers to).

> Cheryl usually **lends** me *her* lab notes.

> Most good writers **revise** what *they* have written.

Some terms—called **collective nouns**—can be either singular or plural depending on how they are used. A *band,* for example, can refer to the group as a unit or as individuals.

> The band **plays** concerts whenever *its* schedule permits.

> The band paid for *their* own uniforms.

Other collective nouns include *audience, committee, majority, number,* and *series.*

Anyone, anybody, someone, somebody, each, every, everyone, everybody, no one, nobody, either, and *neither* are singular and require a singular pronoun.

> Anyone who **drives** that car **is** risking *his* life.*

> Each of the instruments **was** stored in *its* own case.

> Neither candidate **accepts** *her* opponent's arguments.

*For guidelines on using gender-specific pronouns, see Appendix A.

Two subjects or antecedents connected by *and* require a plural verb or pronoun (My MOTHER and FATHER **built** *their* first store in Missoula), but two singular terms joined by *or* or *nor* require a singular verb or pronoun (Neither ACKERMAN nor MENDOZA **is** expected to finish *his* project in time). When a singular term and a plural term are connected by *or* or *nor*, the verb or pronoun agrees with the term closest to it (Neither the captain nor the SAILORS **are** willing to admit *they* were lost.)

Exercises   Choose the correct verbs and pronouns.

1. Each of the actors (wants, want) to play the lead.
2. Neither the employees nor the boss (knows, know) about the contract.
3. No one in the courtroom wanted (his, their) picture taken.
4. Mixing ammonia and bleach (is, are) dangerous.
5. The faculty committee submitted (its, their) report to Dean Birkby two weeks late.

Apostrophes

Apostrophes are used to form contractions, plurals, and possessives.

In a **contraction,** use an apostrophe to mark the place where letters have been omitted. Thus *do not* becomes *don't* (not *do'nt*), *they are* becomes *they're*, *I am* becomes *I'm*, and *it is* becomes *it's*.

Use an apostrophe and *s* to form the **plural** of single letters (*P's* and *Q's*) and of any abbreviations that include periods (Ph.D.'s). No apostrophe is needed to form the plural of acronyms or initialisms (*ECRs*) or of numbers (*7s* and *3s*, the *1980s*).

Use an apostrophe (and sometimes *s*) to form **possessives** as follows.

- For a singular noun, add '*s* (*the dog's collar, Ms. Smith's briefcase, Colorado's highway system, James's desk*).
- For a plural noun that does not end in *s*, add '*s* (*children's toys, men's clothing, sheep's wool*).
- For a plural noun that already ends in *s*, add only the apostrophe (*the dogs' collars, the Smiths' house*).

Do *not* use an apostrophe with possessive pronouns (*his, hers, ours, yours, theirs*). Note especially that the possessive form of *it* is *its*—not *it's*, which is the contraction for *it is*.

Exercises   Add apostrophes where needed.

1. Ampox Corporations new vice president is Windedales leading attorney.
2. He wasnt able to accept Sears offer.
3. The zs on Good Times Pizzerias neon sign are burned out.
4. Workers in the womens garment industrys biggest union have decided to strike their employers.
5. Its not known whether IBMs plans include new models this year.

Capitalization

Capital letters signal importance or uniqueness. Used too often—for every part name in a repair procedure, for example—they lose their punch and become merely distracting. The following uses, however, are required.

• The first letter of any sentence, including a quoted sentence within another sentence

> When Dr. Zavala asked, "Where does it hurt?" the patient replied, "Mostly in bed."

• The names of persons or specific members of a class (proper nouns) but not generic labels for any member of the class (common nouns)

> Cathy Whipple is Copymaster Company's service representative for Xerox brand photocopiers.

> That woman, a contract analyst for a large Chicago-based corporation, is taking a new job in a much smaller city.

> The Department of Engineering and Physics handles academic counseling for all engineering majors.

• Titles when used as part of a person's name rather than as a description of a position or profession

> Vice President Peter Chin is expected to be the company's new president.

> I believe Dr. O'Rourke has been a doctor for more than 35 years.

• The names of specific regions but not words used to give general directions

> The Midwest is east of the Rockies but northwest of the Old South.

> The new branch office will be located in the Northeast.

> Drive north until you reach Highway 100.

• Days of the week and months of the year but not seasons

> This year fall begins on Saturday, September 22.

Exercises Add capital letters where required.

1. professor moore has served as chairman since the department of foreign languages was reorganized in march.
2. this summer deltasoft incorporated will move into its new headquarters south of dallas.
3. popular programs like wordstar and lotus 1-2-3 run on most personal computers.

4. snow fell last night in western kansas and rain in the oklahoma panhandle.
5. ms. ford bought a new mercedes with her profits from investing in ibm stock.

Commas

Commas serve many purposes and therefore provide many opportunities for error. The following guidelines cover the most common uses.

• Use commas to separate elements in a series.

> The alloy includes nickel, manganese, and tungsten.

Although some style guides do not require the last comma (before the *and*), including it helps avoid confusion in cases like this:

> The wires were color-coded blue, violet, green and white and black.

Were some wires green and white and other wires black? Or were some green and others white and black? A comma before one of the *ands* would prevent any misunderstanding.

• Use commas to separate adjectives that describe the same noun.

> High-strength, lightweight, low-cost composite materials make up much of the aircraft's skin.

Be careful, however, not to use a comma between an adjective and a group of words (including other adjectives) that it modifies.

> Composite materials can provide high tensile strength and a low unit production cost.

• Use commas to separate independent clauses* connected by the conjunctions *and, or, for, nor, yet, but,* and *so.*

> The test succeeded, *but* the part was damaged.

Do not use a comma between two parts of a compound subject or compound verb unless they are elements in a series.

> The part *showed signs of strain* but *did not break.*

• Use commas to set off interrupting elements that are not part of the main idea in a sentence. A comma comes *after* an interrupter that starts

---

*An independent clause has both a subject and a predicate and can stand alone as a complete sentence. *The actors rehearsed the play* and *Roy took notes carefully in longhand* are independent clauses. *Rehearsed the play* and *carefully in longhand* are not—the first has no subject; the second cannot stand alone as a complete thought. See the entry on **sentence faults.**

the sentence, *before* an interrupter that ends the sentence, and both *before and after* an interrupter that falls in the middle of a sentence. This rule covers a number of situations.

1. Long introductory phrases or clauses

   After the meeting broke up, everyone went back to work.

   You can omit the comma for very short phrases.

   After lunch we went back to work.

2. Transitional words and phrases that show the relationship between ideas: *however, therefore, furthermore, consequently, otherwise, for example,* and *on the other hand*

   The test did not achieve all objectives; however, we were able to collect some valuable data.

   For example, we now know the maximum load the part will bear before breaking.

   All the planning and preparation, therefore, were not wasted.

3. Embedded modifying clauses or phrases that are not essential to the meaning of the sentence

   Our newest computer, a Berg-Wampler Model C, will cut processing time 50 percent.

   The test instrument, which malfunctions often, is being repaired.

   But do not use commas if the modifying clause is necessary to say which instrument is being repaired.

   The test instrument that malfunctions often is being repaired.

   Note that *which* is used to introduce nonessential clauses (those that use commas), *that* to introduce essential clauses (without commas).

4. Direct address to your audience

   The problem, Professor Fitzpatrick, is now beyond our control.

5. Elements of addresses or dates

   Our office at 1700 Glenstone, Springfield, Missouri, will be closed from Friday, December 28, 1986, through Wednesday, January 3, 1987.

   The commas after *Missouri* and *1986* must be included to mark the end of the interrupting phrases. The military style for writing dates requires no commas at all:

   18 January 1986.

6. Quotations

   "I need another clamp," he said.

His assistant replied, "We don't have any more. We used the last one half an hour ago."

"In that case," he instructed, "hold this."

Note that the comma always comes before the quotation mark.

The comma is not needed if the quotation ends with a question mark or an exclamation point.

"Hold this!" he shouted.

Commas are also unnecessary for a partial quotation that cannot stand alone.

What he called "the biggest project in the company's history" ended as a disaster.

For more information on punctuating quotations, see the entry for **quotation marks.**

Exercises   Add commas as necessary.

1. Until I read this report I thought the project was going smoothly.
2. Now however I realize we have only until April 21 1989 to finish construction perform all structural tests and prepare the building for occupancy.
3. The mail has arrived Ms. Mordaunt but the check was not in it.
4. The word processor which we bought last year is already technically obsolete.
5. Tired hungry laborers filed out of the plant and headed home for dinner.

Colons and Semicolons

The colon (:) and semicolon (;) look alike but differ in function. The colon points to something that follows; the semicolon separates parts of a sentence or list.

Use a colon at the end of an independent clause that points to a list or a separate idea.

We assembled all the materials we needed: rope, pulleys, a tripod, and plenty of baling wire.

The supervisor had forgotten one thing: No one knew how to operate the machine.

Use a semicolon to separate independent clauses not joined by a comma and coordinating conjunction (*and, or, but, for, so, nor,* or *yet*).

The lecture ended an hour ago; everyone has gone home by now.

Postmodern architecture is certainly eye-catching; however, it is not to everyone's taste.

Also use a semicolon to separate items in a series whenever one or more of the items includes a comma.

The travel department makes airline, hotel, and rental car reservations; writes out itineraries and tickets for travelers; and audits travel expenses.

Exercises Add colons or semicolons as necessary.

1. Please go to the stockroom and bring me the following items a 250-ml Erlenmeyer flask, a 100-ml graduated cylinder, and a 10-ml test tube.
2. Titles of short articles are placed in quotation marks titles of books are underlined or italicized.
3. The customer gave us a choice get back on schedule or lose the contract.
4. We had higher expenses in materials, research and development, and administrative, secretarial, and support services.
5. I don't care how you did it I just don't want you to do it again.

Hyphens

A hyphen can link parts of a word that is divided at the end of a line, or it can link whole words that together describe a single concept (like an *aluminum-recycling* plant). There are many sets of "rules" for using hyphens. Some of them are contradictory, most are very complex, and all are subject to change as the language changes. For example, a missile *nose tip* first became *nose-tip* and then *nosetip*.

Your best bet in settling questions of hyphenation is therefore a recent dictionary. But although dictionaries show how to divide almost any word into syllables, they cannot include all possible combinations of whole words to show whether a hyphen is needed. The following guidelines will help you decide on your own whether to keep the two words separate, link them with a hyphen, or combine them in a single word.

• If there's no question that the two words belong together, you don't need to link them or combine them. An "automotive repair technician" is clearly a technician who does automotive repair work and not a repair technician who is automotive, so there's no need to clutter up your page with hyphens or to create a monstrosity like *automotiverepair.*
• If there is some possibility of confusion about which word is paired with which, use a hyphen to link words that act together as a single adjective. For example, does a "high cost awareness level" mean a high level of awareness about any cost or an unspecified level of awareness about high costs only? A hyphen can answer the question by making the phrase either "high cost-awareness level" or "high-cost awareness level."

When one of the words in a pair is an adverb ending in *-ly*, no hyphen is needed.

> Newly released documents prove there was a conspiracy.

- Prefixes (such as *pre-*, *re- post-*, *non-*, *over-*, and *ultra-*) are usually attached directly to the root word without a hyphen *(prewar, reattach, postoperative, ultralight)* unless that creates a particularly hard-to-read word like *preemployment* or *reexamine*. (Some such words, like *reentry*, are becoming standard forms, so check the dictionary or several recent publications in your field.)
- Numbers and units of measurement are hyphenated when they serve as adjectives *(a 30-ft shaft; two 10-pound bags)* but not as nouns *(the shaft went down 30 ft; each bag weighed 10 pounds)*.

Exercises Clarify the following sentences by adding or deleting hyphens or by dividing or combining words. Check your work against a dictionary.

1. Our under powered car can't even reach the 55 mph speed limit.
2. The new home furnishings business always booms in the spring.
3. Her pre-adolescent attitudes are disturbingly abnormal in a 19 year old college student.
4. Spiralling aircraft maintenance costs mean less frequent major overhauls.
5. The 100 meter free style race begins in 10 minutes.

Misplaced Modifiers

Modifiers describe or characterize or otherwise modify the reader's perception of another part of the sentence. They range from simple adjectives and adverbs (the *red* car accelerated *rapidly*) to long phrases and clauses (*heavily damaged by the explosion*, the generating station will be unable to supply power to the city for several days).

Readers assume that a modifier describes the nearest eligible word. In the second example, we assume that what was damaged was the generating station, not the city. You should therefore place a modifier close to the word it describes and keep it away from any other words to which it might be applied. Here's what happens if you don't.

> Gyrating rapidly, we watched as the vibration table reached the maximum stress level.

> The cat John was holding nervously hissed at the veterinarian.

> I've just received the report from the Denver office that I wanted.

A little rearranging clears up the confusion.

> We watched as the vibration table, gyrating rapidly, reached the maximum stress level.

The cat John was holding hissed nervously at the veterinarian.

I've just received the report that I wanted from the Denver office.

Be particularly careful with sentences written in passive voice (see Appendix A for an explanation of active and passive voice). Because passive-voice sentences sometimes omit the subject of the action, modifiers intended to describe that omitted subject can be left dangling.

Having failed to read the instructions, the fuel pump was installed improperly.

What does "Having failed to read the instructions" modify? The nearest eligible noun phrase is "fuel pump," and the intended object of the modifier—whoever did the installing—has disappeared completely. Putting the sentence back in active voice solves the problem.

Having failed to read the instructions, the mechanic installed the fuel pump improperly.

Exercises Correct any misplaced modifiers in the following sentences.

1. Rolling down the hill, I saw the driverless car hit at least three others before coming to a stop against a tree.
2. By measuring the conductivity of the two metals, copper was selected.
3. The trailer Greg and Lois were towing slowly broke loose from the hitch.
4. The children only trusted their parents.
5. When announced, the administration expects the policy to be welcomed.

Numbers

Business and technical people rely heavily on numbers, whether to represent last month's sales or the thrust needed to launch a satellite. Numbers therefore appear often in practical writing. The most common problem writers have with numbers is deciding whether to write them as a word *(seven)* or a numeral (7).

Generally, you should write out one-digit numbers and fractions less than one and use numerals for everything else.

We've lost eight potential recruits in the last 15 months.

Only one third of the students attended.

Nearly 4,000 society members attended the 2½-day convention.

The car traveled 41.3 miles on one gallon of gas.

Do not, however, start a sentence with a numeral. Either spell out the number or rewrite the sentence.

One hundred forty miles separate the two cities.

The two cities are 140 miles apart.

When listing several numbers to refer to identical elements or objects within a paragraph or other short passage, make the numbers easier to compare by using numerals for all if at least one is a two-digit number.

The company opened 3 stores last year and 5 this year. Business is now growing so rapidly that we plan 15 openings in the next three months.

Use numerals with abbreviations or symbols.

Everyone on the team is at least 6'7".

Numbers in the millions, billions, and trillions can be written as a combination of numerals and words.

The lottery prize reached $40 million this week.

The world population is now 3.6 billion.

Exercises   Change numerals to words and words to numerals as appropriate.

1. The temperature reached one hundred five degrees on July eighteenth.
2. The boss pointed out that five million three hundred thousand dollars is a lot of money to lose in less than three years.
3. Each of the 4,500 employees received an 8-page pamphlet on business ethics.
4. The charity race included three separate runs: two km, six km, and 15 km.
5. 1985 was the best sales year we've ever had.

Parallel Structure

Elements of a sentence (or paragraph or document) that are alike in function should be alike in form or structure.

Not parallel: Gabriella put away the chemicals, I washed the glassware, and the floor was swept by Roger.

Parallel: Gabriella put away the chemicals, I washed the glassware, and Roger swept the floor.

Each of the three clauses serves the same function—to describe one of a series of events. In the first example, however, the third clause uses a different structure from the other two: The name of the person doing the work comes at the end instead of the beginning. The difference in structure implies a difference in purpose or content, just as a switch from regular type to **bold** implies there's something different about the bold words.

If there is no real difference, readers are likely to be confused by their inability to find one.

Parallel structure is especially important with compound subjects or predicates. All elements in the compound part of the sentence must be parallel so that each makes sense when paired with the other part of the sentence. Thus "The thieves broke into the office, stole four typewriters, and ransacked the files" can be understood as

The thieves broke into the office.

The thieves stole four typewriters.

The thieves ransacked the files.

Exercises   Rewrite these sentences to make them parallel.

1. The guards led in the prisoner, everyone was told by the bailiff to rise, and the judge entered the courtroom.
2. We couldn't decide whether we should ignore the directive or to obey it.
3. To prepare the apparatus, performing the experiment, and analyzing the results could take all day.
4. We are either late or the clock is fast.
5. Representatives hold office for two years, the president for four years, and senators serve six years.

Pronoun Reference

A pronoun *refers* to an antecedent (the noun it replaces). When the reference is not clear, readers must waste time looking for the proper antecedent. Four common problems of this type are ambiguous references, distant references, broad references, and implied references.

An **ambiguous reference** gives the reader too many choices of antecedent.

The supervisor told the machinist that *he* was being transferred.

Who was being transferred—the supervisor or the machinist? To clear up the ambiguity, you can replace the pronoun with the correct noun.

The supervisor told the machinist that *the machinist* was being transferred.

Or you can rewrite the sentence.

The machinist learned of his transfer from the supervisor.

A **distant reference** occurs when a pronoun is used so far from its antecedent that the reader may have trouble remembering which noun it refers to.

Building a house, whether you hire someone else to do the work or pound in every nail yourself, is the one sure way to become aware of everything wrong with *it*.

You should generally try to put the pronoun close to its antecedent.

Whether you hire someone else to do the work or pound in every nail yourself, building a *house* is the one sure way to become aware of everything wrong with *it*.

Similarly, the same pronoun should not be used repeatedly without occasionally substituting the original noun, just to refresh the reader's memory.

In **broad references** the pronoun (often *this*, *that*, *which*, or *it*) refers to an entire sentence or idea rather than a specific noun.

We finished the report two weeks early; *that* should please Mr. Jefferson.

The dean was reluctant to fire Professor Campbell. *It* would almost certainly lead to a lawsuit.

Broad references like these are common in speech and informal writing, but formal writing calls for more precision. You can rewrite the sentence to avoid the problem or make the broad reference more specific by answering the question "*That* what?" or "What is *it*?"

Our finishing the report two weeks early should please Mr. Jefferson.

We finished the report two weeks early; that achievement should please Mr. Jefferson.

Fearing a lawsuit, the dean was reluctant to fire Professor Campbell.

The dean was reluctant to fire Professor Campbell. The dismissal would almost certainly lead to a lawsuit.

Implied references are to antecedents that are not explicitly stated.

We went to the Indianapolis 500 to watch *them* race.

The new voting rights bill ensures that *they* cannot be taken from us.

In the first sentence the writer assumes everyone knows who or what *them* is. In the second sentence the only noun for *they* to refer to is *bill* ("voting rights" is an adjectival phrase here). In both cases the easiest solution is to substitute an explicit noun for the pronoun.

We went to the Indianapolis 500 to watch the top drivers race.

The voting rights bill ensures that these rights cannot be taken from us.

Exercises   Rewrite the sentences for better pronoun reference.

1. When the rope came loose from the scaffold, it fell 18 stories to the ground.

2. At the post office they told me I had to seal the package with strapping tape before mailing it.
3. When Nancy won the lottery, she gave her sister half of it.
4. Although the researcher had originally planned to submit a paper on his work to several journals simultaneously, he decided that wasn't ethical.
5. The students threatened to occupy the faculty's offices if the administration did not meet their demands.

Quotation Marks

The primary purpose of quotation marks (" ") is to mark the beginning and end of someone's exact words (a direct quotation), clearly separating those words from the rest of the text.

> Mr. Armbruster said, "The auditors will be here tomorrow."

> "I don't think," the accountant replied, "that they'll find anything amiss."

> Her assistant added, "We checked all accounts last week. Everything balanced."

Note that

- A comma, as well as the quotation marks, separates the quotation from the rest of the sentence.*
- The first letter of the quoted sentence is capitalized, even when it's in the middle of the main sentence.
- Commas and periods always come *before* the quotation marks. Question marks, exclamation points, colons, and semicolons go inside the quotation marks if they are part of the quoted material, outside if they are not.

> Who said, "Give me liberty, or give me death"?

> "What did you say?" she asked incredulously.

If you quote a passage that itself includes a quotation, use single quotation marks (typed with the apostrophe key) for the inner quotation and regular double quotation marks for the surrounding quotation.

> The teacher told the students, "The dean said, 'No more incomplete grades will be accepted.' "

Words omitted from a quotation are replaced by an ellipsis, which is typed as three periods (. . .). Thus the full quotation

> "The movie, which I enjoyed very much, starred Humphrey Bogart and Lauren Bacall in their first appearance together."

*See the entry on **commas** for exceptions to this rule.

would be written as

"The movie . . . starred Humphrey Bogart and Lauren Bacall in their first appearance together."

If the ellipsis comes at the end of the sentence, use a fourth period as well.

"The movie, which I enjoyed very much, starred Humphrey Bogart and Lauren Bacall. . . . "

Quotation marks are also used to indicate the titles of short documents, such as articles in journals, magazines, and newspapers; chapters in books; and short reports. Titles of longer works, such as books or lengthy reports, should be underlined or italicized instead.

Exercises Insert quotation marks and related punctuation as needed.

1. Just breathe into this straw instructed the officer.
2. Where were you asked the judge on the night of March 17, 1979?
3. The new equipment has arrived in the laboratory reported the technician. Shall I unpack it?
4. I expect you to read the chapter titled The Future of Electro-Optics by tomorrow said Dr. Andujar.
5. The mayor added Next year, of course, we'll have to raise taxes.

Sentence Faults

Three common sentence faults are fragments, fused sentences, and comma splices. To avoid these errors, you first need to understand what a sentence is.

A sentence contains both a *subject* (a noun phrase identifying somebody or something) and a *predicate* (a verb phrase that says something about the subject—what it is or what it does). When you put a subject and a predicate together, you get a complete thought, also called an *independent clause* because it can stand alone as a sentence.

Subject (noun phrase)	Predicate (verb phrase)
Ulsh	retired.
The renowned Dr. Vance Ulsh	retired early last year.

Without both a subject and a predicate, you do not have a complete sentence. The exception comes in direct commands, such as "Fasten the restraining strap," where the subject is understood to be "you."

Not all sentences are this simple. Some have other phrases or clauses*

---

*A clause has both a subject and a verb; a phrase does not.

that modify the independent clause. In the following sentences the modifying phrases and clauses are italicized.

> *Early last year,* Dr. Ulsh retired.

> Dr. Ulsh retired, *which left us shorthanded.*

> *Although the project had just started,* Dr. Ulsh retired.

These *dependent* phrases and clauses cannot stand alone as complete sentences.

Sentence Fragments   A fragment can be a subject without a predicate, a predicate without a subject, or a dependent phrase or clause with no independent clause to modify.

> *Subject only:* the expensive new oscilloscope

> *Predicate only:* shattered when dropped from the top shelf

> *Dependent phrase:* after careful analysis of the results

> *Dependent clause:* although the ingredients were mixed properly

Each of these can be turned into a sentence by completing the thought.

> The expensive new oscilloscope has been used only twice in the last month.

> The beaker shattered when dropped from the top shelf.

> We did not consider the test successful until after careful analysis of the results.

> Although the ingredients were mixed properly, nothing happened.

Fragments are common in spoken language and used occasionally in informal writing, but they are usually out of place in technical and business writing. If you suspect you've written a fragment, make sure you have both a subject and a predicate. Then read the words aloud to see if they sound like a complete thought. A trick that may help you spot fragments is to look for words like *as, since, because, when, which, who,* and *that,* which often mark the beginning of dependent clauses. If you find one, make sure there is also an independent clause in the sentence.

Fused Sentences   A **fused** (or run-on) **sentence** occurs when two or more independent clauses are run together without punctuation.

> The supplies have arrived we can start the experiment.

There are four ways to correct a fused sentence.

1. Split it into two sentences by putting a period at the end of the first independent clause and capitalizing the first letter of the second.

> The supplies have arrived. We can start the experiment.

2. Use a semicolon to divide the two clauses.

   The supplies have arrived; we can start the experiment.

3. Insert a comma followed by a conjunction *(and, or, for, nor, so, yet, but)* between the clauses.

   The supplies have arrived, so we can start the experiment.

4. Make one of the clauses dependent on the other.

   Since the supplies have arrived, we can start the experiment.

Comma Splice   Just as two independent clauses cannot be fused together without punctuation, they cannot be spliced together with only a comma. **Comma splices** can be corrected by using the four options described for correcting fused sentences.

   Wrong: Tungsten carbide is strong, it is also very expensive.

   Right: Tungsten carbide is strong. It is also very expensive.

   Tungsten carbide is strong; it is also very expensive.

   Tungsten carbide is strong, but it is also very expensive.

   Although tungsten carbide is strong, it is also very expensive.

Exercises   Correct any sentence fragments by adding words or phrases. Correct comma splices or fused sentences as shown in the preceding paragraphs.

1. Mrs. Gleason arrived yesterday we expect her husband tomorrow.
2. The disk drive that they sent out for repairs.
3. Your tickets and itinerary are enclosed enjoy your trip.
4. Although the company and the union have not yet agreed on a contract.
5. The mail room is understaffed they seldom lose a package.

Writing Definitions

Definitions are an important part of practical writing. Such writing relies on precise communication, so special or technical terms often must be defined for readers. In addition, many typical forms of practical writing (such as the description of a mechanism, a proposal for the manufacture of a piece of equipment, or an instructions manual) include sections of definition. A few forms, such as an entry in a handbook, may consist of one extended definition.

This appendix reviews the three kinds of definitions commonly used in practical writing: the formal sentence definition, the informal definition, and the extended definition. You may need to refer to this section as you work on a number of the chapters within the textbook.

The Formal Sentence Definition

The most precise kind of definition is the formal sentence definition. This is a classical form that has been used for hundreds of years. A good formal sentence definition has three parts:

- The *term* being defined
- The *class* of things to which what is being defined belongs
- A *differentiation* between what is being defined and everything else in its class

The Term Being Defined

Naming an item precisely is the first step in defining the term precisely. Sometimes when you begin to define a term you will need only to name it and to spell it correctly. At other times, however, you may need to add additional information to better *identify* what you are trying to define. For example, when naming a tool, you may need to provide its brand name and model number. If you are defining a biological term, such as an *eye*, you may need to specify that you are defining a *human eye;* the eye of some other organism could be very different.

The Class

Classifying something requires you to think of the class, or *larger group*, to which it might belong. There is no single correct classification for most terms or items. The problem in classification is to name a class that is accurate, familiar to the reader (since the term being defined may not be), and neither too large nor too narrow.

If you name a class that is too large, you will be faced with the problem of separating your term or item from everything else in its class when you write the differentiation section of your formal sentence definition. For example, classifying the word *watch* as a "device" would leave you with the task of explaining how a watch is different from all other devices, including toasters, voltmeters, lawnmowers, and so on. That would require too much detail to make a useful definition. Narrowing the class to "time-keeping device" would make writing the rest of the definition much easier. You would have only to explain how a watch is different from other time-keeping devices such as sundials, hour glasses, and wall clocks.

Generally speaking, the narrower the class, the better the formal definition. However, you must be careful to name a class your readers will recognize. For example, classifying a **paramecium** as a *microorganism* would probably work for most educated lay readers, but terming it a *protozoan* or a *ciliated protozoan* might not. For a young audience you might have to call it *a kind of very small animal* or *a microscopic animal.* It is also possible to write a false classification in an attempt to narrow the class too much. For example, classifying a watch as an electrical time-keeping device would illogically exclude mechanical watches.

The Differentiation

The final section of a formal sentence definition is the differentiation, often also referred to as the *differentiae,* the Latin term for this section. The differentiation is usually the most difficult section to write because you must complete the definition in such a way as to separate your term or item from all others in its class. If the differentiating characteristics are explained precisely and well, the final formal sentence definition will apply *only* to what is being defined, and not to anything else. Sometimes you will need to write several sentences of differentiation to complete the job, but you should aim to write a formal sentence definition in one sentence.

Consider again the term *watch*. If you classify it as a time-keeping device, in the differentiation you must consider what makes it different from all other time-keeping devices in the differentiation. A major difference between watches and all other time-keeping devices is that a watch, in contrast to an alarm clock, grandfather clock, or hourglass, is *worn* in some way. A complete formal sentence definition of a watch, then, might be the following:

| *Word* | *Class* | *Differentiation* |

A watch is a time-keeping device that is worn on the person.

Here are a number of other possible formal sentence definitions. The three parts of each definition are separated by slash marks.

A cardinal *(Richmondena cardinalis)* / is a medium-sized American songbird / having a short, wide bill; crested head; and bright red feathers in the male.

A generator / is a machine / that converts mechanical energy into electrical energy.

A compass / is a direction-finding device / usually consisting of a magnetic needle suspended so that it is free to move into alignment with the earth's magnetic field.

Informal Definitions

The formal sentence definition is the most precise kind of definition, but there are a number of other useful ways to define words. Short informal definitions are used when a high level of precision is not needed. In a description of a mechanism, for example, a formal sentence definition is often used to define the mechanism as a whole, whereas informal definitions are used to define main parts and subparts. Three common kinds of informal definitions are the operational definition, the synonym, and the negative definition.

Operational Definitions

Webster's New World Dictionary defines *operational* as "of, having to do with, or derived from the operation of a device, system, process, etc." An operational definition is one that explains how a mechanism works—in other words, what it does or what it is used for. An operational definition does not require you to classify the term being defined. The following sentences are operational definitions.

A watch measures time.

A heart pumps blood through the circulatory system.

A hammer is used primarily for pounding nails or shaping metals.

Synonyms

The synonym of a word is another term that means the same thing. When you must use a term that not everyone can be expected to understand, such as *effluent,* following it with a synonym such as *wastewater* will clarify the term. Often the synonym is placed in parentheses after the original word. Since the purpose of adding a synonym is to provide a more commonly known term for a little-known one, never use as a synonym a word that is just as difficult or technical as the original. Writing that a *phosphate* is an *ester of phosphoric acid* won't help many people.

Negative Definitions

Occasionally, telling what something is *not* helps to define what it *is.* This kind of definition is referred to as a *negative definition.* Such definitions are useful when people are commonly confused about the meaning of a word or are likely to confuse it with others in its class.

For example, one might define the term *secretary* by explaining that a secretary is not a host or hostess or a department chauffeur and shopper. After the negative definition, a positive one should follow to complete the identification. A complete negative definition of *secretary* might be the following:

> A secretary is not a host or hostess, chauffeur, or purchasing agent responsible for shopping for department parties or birthday presents for the boss's spouse. A secretary is an office worker, often specially trained, whose main job is to help an organization run smoothly by handling filing, typing, correspondence, and other paperwork.

Expanded Definitions

Sometimes practical writing requires longer definitions than those just discussed. A full paragraph or several paragraphs may be needed to define a word. In writing expanded definitions, you may use any or all of the techniques already described, in addition to these other methods of definition:

- *Analogy:* Comparing the word being defined to some other more familiar item or process. You could, for example, compare the brain and nervous system to an infinitely complex telephone switchboard and network. The space shuttle is said by some to open the frontiers to space in the same way that the railroad opened the frontier to the American West.
- *Causation:* Explaining what causes a phenomenon. For example, the Aurora Borealis may be partially defined by explaining that this beautiful display of lights in the northern sky is caused by an occasional stream of electrons shot from the surface of the sun into space and the Earth's upper atmosphere, where these electrons cause the molecules of the atmosphere to glow.

- *Division:* Separating a term into its various branches or sections. You might divide *natural science* into two branches, *life science* and *physical science.*
- *Effect:* Naming some of the effects of what is being defined. For example, *air pollution* might be partially defined by listing its effects: breathing problems such as pneumonia and emphysema; damage to crops and livestock; and damage to metal, concrete, rubber, and other surfaces in homes and businesses.
- *Etymology:* Describing the historical development of a term, from the original (or "root") meaning, perhaps in another language. For example, the word *galaxy* might be defined in part by explaining that it comes from the Greek word *galaxias,* which comes from their word for milk, *gala.* Like us, they thought our galaxy, the Milky Way, looked like a stream of milk across the sky.
- *Exemplification:* Naming examples of what is being defined. For example, the term *derived demand* (a demand for a product created by the demand for some other product) may be clarified with examples, such as the demand for quality computer software, modems, appropriate furniture, and other accessories created by the demand for personal computers.
- *History of development:* Explaining the historical development of what is being defined. For example, *computer* might be partially defined by describing its development from the first massive units of the 1940s to the miniature models developed in the 1980s.
- *Narrative:* Telling a story to define a word partially. The term *radar* might be made clearer by telling the story of its development by the British during World War II as a means of using radio waves to detect German planes en route to bombing London. With their new device, the British engineers were able to tell the British pilots and navigators what direction to fly to intercept the planes and how far to go (the "range"). The device was known as "*ra*dio *de*tection *a*nd *r*anging" and later came to be known as *radar.*
- *Physical description:* To picture in words the physical characteristics of an object being defined. For example, an animal or plant may be best defined by explaining what it looks like. The cardinal defined earlier is differentiated from other songbirds by its physical appearance; it is a bird with a short, wide bill; crested head; and bright red feathers in the male.
- *Uses:* Listing various uses of a product. For example, the word *petrolatum* may be defined in part by listing its uses: as a lubricant in baking, as a base in cosmetics, as a rust preventive, and as a waterproofing product.

In writing expanded definitions, as in all practical writing, the writer must keep in mind the *needs of the audience.* Examine the following expanded definitions. Each one makes use of several of the techniques just described, but word choice and differences in sentence complexity make them appropriate for different kinds of readers.

HIDDEN INFLATION: A reduction in the real value of goods sold, by changing the quantity and the quality of the goods supplied and without or with small dollar price increases. Examples are machines that are less well made, reflecting far poorer material and less labor than the same goods in prior years, and packaged foods that come in smaller quantities but larger packages and are adulterated with less expensive and usually far less nutritious ingredients. These very real price increases do not show up in the Cost of Living Index, yet are quite normal features of the American economic landscape. [David Brownstone, Irene Franck, and Gorton Garruth, eds., *The VNR Dictionary of Business and Finance* (New York: Van Nostrand Reinhold Co., 1980.)]

PORCELAIN: A high-grade ceramic ware characterized by high strength, a white color (under the glaze), very low absorption, good translucency, and a hard glaze. Equivalent terms are European porcelain, hard porcelain, true porcelain, and hard paste porcelain.

Porcelain is distinguished from other fine ceramic ware, such as china, by the fact that the firing of the unglazed ware (the bisque firing) is done at a lower temperature (1000–1200°C) than the final or glass firing, which may be as high as 1500°C. In other words, the ware reaches its final stage of maturity at the maturing temperature of the glaze.

The white color is obtained by using very pure white-firing kaolin or china clay and other pure materials, the low absorption results from the high firing temperature, and the translucency results from the glass phase.

The term porcelain has been applied to such items as electrical insulators and bathroom fixtures. Very often these are made in a one-fire process, the glaze being applied to the green or unfired ware; where this is the case and high-grade materials are used in compounding the body, the term porcelain may be correctly applied. However, the pieces have no translucency because of their great thickness. On the other hand, the term porcelain is often applied to quite different ware. For example, zircon porcelain is used to describe a material made largely of zircon (ZrO_2SiO_2), with small amounts of fluxes to yield a low absorption. [J. F. Mc Mahon, *McGraw-Hill Encyclopedia of Science* 5th ed., 1982.]

ION: In electrolysis, parts of a molecule seem to travel to one electrode and parts to the other. The water molecule, for instance, breaks up into hydrogen and oxygen, the hydrogen appearing about the negative electrode, or cathode, and the oxygen appearing about the positive electrode or anode.

The traveling parts of the molecules were given the name *ion* in 1830 or thereabouts by the British physicist Michael Faraday, from a Greek word "ienai" meaning "to go." The Greek word "ion" means "going." After all, they were going to one electrode or the other. The ions that traveled to the cathode were *cations*; those that traveled to the anode were *anions* (both words are pronounced in three syllables). Exactly what ions were, however, remained a mystery for about fifty years.

Then, in 1884, a 25-year-old Swedish physical chemist, Svante August Arrhenius, presented a dissertation at the University of Uppsala, with which he hoped to earn the degree of Doctor of Philosophy. He suggested that under the influence of the electric current, molecules broke up to form atoms or groups of atoms that carried electric charges. Those with a negative charge were anions, attracted to the positive electrode, while those with a positive charge were cations, attracted to the negative electrode.

Since chemists had, at that time, never heard of atoms carrying an electric charge, his theory was considered quite ridiculous and he got his degree with a minimum passing grade. However, in 1903, Arrhenius received the Nobel Prize in chemistry for that same dissertation.

Between 1884 and 1903, you see, the negatively charged electron had been definitely shown to exist and to form a part of all atoms. It was recognized that an atom or group of atoms might lose one or more electrons to become positively charged, or gain one or more to become negatively charged. In the former case, a cation resulted; in the latter, an anion. [Isaac Asimov, *Words of Science* (Boston: Houghton Mifflin, 1959.)]

D Outlining

Why should you outline an article or report before writing it? If you are an experienced writer, you may be able to compose a short piece of organized writing, such as a letter or memo, after jotting down a list of points or simply taking thought. However, before writing anything much longer than a page, you will need to organize your ideas more carefully.

Outlining is one of the best ways to organize information. It can save you from the tedious task of completely rewriting a document, sometimes over and over, to work out its structure. Through outlining, you can experiment with different organizational patterns *before* drafting. Outlining is part of what some authors refer to as *prewriting:* all the thinking, talking, listing, and possibly "free writing" that may be necessary to determine the organization of a composition.

There are several ways to go about outlining. The most efficient way is probably to outline before doing *any* drafting; however, some writers will try a "discovery" draft first, in which they begin writing just to get some ideas going, knowing all the while that the draft will be disorganized. After this they create a first outline and draft a second time according to the outline structure.

To outline is simply to represent thinking graphically. An outline is a tool, a *means* to an end: your composition. A writer outlining a composition can be compared to an architect preparing the blueprint of a house. Both writer and architect have in mind an end product, and both engage in a creative process of planning and revising before creating the final *design.* After that, the document is written or the house built.

The Eight Steps of Outlining

Producing a good outline takes time, but you will find that the results are worth the effort. Although different writers engage in somewhat different processes to produce their outlines, the basic steps are the same.

1. The first step in outlining is to clarify for yourself the central idea of your composition—at least tentatively. Selecting your subject and deciding what point you wish to make about it may require considerable thought or research. The main point of a composition is often referred to as a **thesis sentence.** This statement is composed of two parts: a subject and an assertion.

    A **subject** can be a noun or noun phrase: Possible subjects include subliminal advertising, electronic engineering, local hospice care, or the role of women in state politics. Most essay writers begin thinking about a general subject and then narrow it to a particular subject within the general field. Report writers are often simply assigned the subjects on which they must report.

    An **assertion** is the point you wish to make about your subject. For any one subject, an endless list of assertions is possible. If X is the subject, you might write that "X is needed," "X should be reevaluated," "X is dangerous," "X can be accomplished in four steps," and so on. Most assertions express a *point of view* about the subject, but some objectively state what aspects of the subject will be discussed or analyzed in a composition.

    Four sample thesis sentences follow. The subject of each one is italicized; the assertion of each is bracketed.

    My first day at work [was very hectic.]

    Subliminal advertising [is ineffective.]

    Preparing antivenin for snakebite [involves three separate stages.]

    A career in electronic engineering [is lucrative today because there are many job opportunities, the salaries are good, and there are many special benefits associated with the field.]

2. With your assertion in mind, create the first-level divisions of your outline, labeling each division with a Roman numeral. These divisions should name major areas of support or development of your thesis.

    As you create these divisions, focus on your *assertion*, not your subject. Suppose your thesis sentence is "Microprocessing will change society in many ways." You must address the changes to come, not the general field of microprocessing, its development, its complexity, or any other matter not explaining the "ways" in which microprocessing will change society.

A first-level outline of this statement follows:

>   **Title:** Microprocessing and the Future
> **Thesis:** Microprocessing will change society in many ways.

>   I. Microprocessing will affect business communications.
> II. It will also change education and training.
> III. Microprocessing will alter the labor force.

Notice that the topic (microprocessing) or a synonym for it is in the *subject position* in each sentence of the outline. The predicate of each sentence names a way in which microprocessing will create changes. Writing in this pattern will help you divide a section logically.

This outline is written in complete sentences. Outlines are conventionally written either in complete sentences throughout or in phrases throughout. The first kind of outline is called a **sentence outline;** the second is referred to as a **topic outline.** Beginning outliners usually should work with sentence outlines since it is easier to check sentences for logic and consistency than it is to analyze phrases. However, topic outlines may be simpler and just as useful for reports that mainly classify information.

3. Check the logic of your first-level divisions before going further. Each first-level division must clearly develop the thesis of a report that argues a point. If a division is irrelevant or badly stated, it must be discarded or reworded. Examine the following outline. Does each first-level division clearly support the thesis?

>   **Title:** Why Take English?
> **Thesis:** English composition courses teach critical skills.

>   I. English courses provide instruction in the basics of our writing system, how we represent speech on paper.
> II. English courses are often exciting.
> III. English can be a demanding class.
> IV. Writing courses teach students to clarify their ideas and to think logically.
>   V. Many English courses provide instruction in both academic and on-the-job writing.

You should see that divisions II and III do not belong in this outline because they do not give examples of critical skills. Related ideas such as these can sometimes be worked into the introduction or conclusion of a piece of writing but do not belong in the body.

Finally, before moving on, consider the *order* of your first-level divisions. Is the order really effective? Do you want to rearrange to keep strict chronological order? Should you rearrange to build up to your strongest division for a "dramatic" finish? Should you do the reverse?

4. Work out additional divisions of your outline after you have written the first-level divisions. An outline written to first level is better than no outline at all, but it does not provide a guide to organization within each major section. Sometimes outlining to the second level is sufficient, but long compositions must often be outlined to the third level or further.

You can begin working on whichever division you know the most about, whether or not it comes first on your outline. Beginning with the section you are most prepared to write may give you more confidence when you begin subdividing the more difficult sections.

When you divide, move from general statements to more specific ones, from abstract terms to concrete examples. An outline may be thought of as a kind of "abstraction ladder." The first divisions of the outline cite the most abstract or general points to be made, and the furthest divisions list the most specific details, facts, and figures to be used to demonstrate those general points. Suppose you were writing a report about the effects of littering, not usually considered a major problem. However, your research shows the problem to be severe. How would you create an outline for the thesis statement: "Litter is dangerous"? What does "dangerous" (an abstraction) mean in this instance? You might begin to define this abstraction by dividing it into several specific examples of what constitutes the danger: harm to plants, harm to wildlife, and harm to people.

These ideas are still very abstract, however; how does litter harm people? The division "Litter harms people" might be subdivided to "Litter provides a breeding ground for disease-bearing agents" and "Litter can cause physical injury." Divisions of each of these second-level entries might name the specific damage done.

Written in outline form the discussion might look like the following example. Only division III, the section under discussion, has been divided to the third level. In a full outline of the thesis statement, *nearly all sections would be divided in the same way.*

    Title: The Effects of Litter
   Thesis: Litter is dangerous.

    I. Litter is harmful to plant life.

    II. Litter is harmful to wildlife.

    III. Litter is harmful to people.

  A. Litter provides a breeding ground for disease.

    1. Garbage and trash can carry bacteria and other agents of disease.

    2. Litter attracts insects and rodents that spread diseases.

  B. Litter can cause physical injury.

    1. Broken bottles and jagged cans can cause serious cuts and lacerations.

    2. Trash and debris can cause people to fall and injure themselves.

In forming levels of division, introduce second-level divisions with *capital letters*, third-level divisions with *Arabic numerals*, and fourth-level divisions with *small letters.* Use Arabic numerals in parentheses for fifth level, and small letters in parentheses for sixth level. Follow each symbol with a period. The preceding example demonstrates several characteristics of outlines.

• Two spaces follow the period after each division label.
• Each entry is single-spaced, but two lines of space are usually left between each entry, especially in student work.
• Each new *level* is indented farther to the right.
• Various divisions of a level line up *vertically* down the page. For example, B's, C's, and D's are all directly beneath the A's in a column.
• All divisions need not be subdivided, but when they are, logic requires at least *two* divisions. In other words, an A must be followed by a B, a 1 must be followed by a 2, and so on.

Figure D.1 shows one section of an outline for a research paper investigating the answer to the question "Was the sinking of the *Titanic* due to human error or impossible sailing conditions?" Examine the section for logic and layout.

5. Check the logic of your outline, making sure that your divisions make sense in terms of the abstraction being divided.

First, divide according to some principle. Consider the thesis "Alcoholism creates many problems." This concept should be divided

TITLE: The Tragedy of the Titanic
THESIS: The loss of many lives in the disasterous sinking of the superliner <u>Titanic</u> was the result of human error.

I. Before the <u>Titanic</u> even left harbor in Southhampton, England, it was in unnecessary danger.

   A. The liner was not built as strong as people believed.

     1. The structural strength was not proportionate to the liner's size.

     2. The <u>Titantic</u> was not fully divided by watertight compartments, as it should have been, but only partly divided.

   B. The ship lacked proper safety equipment.

     1. Even after numerous requests, the lookouts in the crow's nest were not supplied with binoculars.

     2. There was an inadequate supply of lifeboats.

   C. The crew mistakenly believed the ship could not sink.

     1. One deckhand told a passenger, "God Himself could not sink this ship!"

     2. E. J. Smith, the captain, remarked, "I cannot conceive of any vital disaster happening to this vessel; modern shipbuilding has gone beyond that."

Figure D.1   Section of an Outline for a Research Paper

according to the *effects* of alcoholism, that is, the "problems": damage to the alcoholic's body, stress at home, and loss of a job. Therefore, a statement such as "People often begin drinking because they want to forget upsetting things" does not belong in this division. It is a *cause*, not an effect.

Second, remember that when you divide you must form at least two parts. The following examples show **illogical** divisions of topics. Each example is followed by an explanation.

  I. When you test drive a motorcycle, listen for unusual noises.
    A. Listen for knocking.
 II. Also, look for signs of neglect.

Analysis   The division of section I is illogical. If one should listen for only *one* sound—knocking—then there are no unusual *noises* to note. Sentence I should be rewritten to read "When you test drive a motorcycle, listen for knocking noises." No further division of the section should be made unless the knocking noises are to be described.

   II. Litter harms wildlife.
      A. Containers thrown in rivers, streams, and lakes trap small fish and cause their death.
  III. Litter harms people.

Analysis   The division of section II is illogical. If containers are the only kind of litter that harms wildlife, sentence II should be rewritten to "Discarded containers can harm small fish." If other kinds of litter cause additional harm, or if containers cause other kinds of harm, additional divisions of sentence II should be added.

6. As a rule, word all subdivisions of a particular section in a parallel fashion. This helps clarify your point. Look at the following problem taken from a student's outline. The wording is not parallel.

   II. Hypertension can be treated in a number of ways.
      A. Does smoking affect hypertension?
      B. Some foods seem to increase hypertension.
      C. Exercise seems to influence hypertension.

   Written in parallel form, the division might look like this:

   II. Hypertension can be treated in a number of ways.
      A. Eliminating all smoking can reduce hypertension dramatically.
      B. Reducing intake of certain foods from the diet can help.
      C. Exercising regularly can greatly reduce hypertension.

7. Read over your outline, looking for "gaps." When you check an outline, you can tell immediately which sections have little development. If you have divided most sections to third level but have no third level divisions for a particular section, consider adding more details there, if developing that section is consistent with your purpose. The way to write a good (and often longer) composition or report is usually to *add more subdivisions and detail*, not more major divisions.

8. Don't outline your introduction or conclusion. They are not organized in the same way as the body of a composition and are not included in an outline. If you wish, write the word *Introduction* before your first division and the word *Conclusion* after your last.

Using Your Outline

Remember that an outline is only a blueprint. What you write from your outline should nearly always include more detail than the outline shows.

As you add details to "flesh out" the outline, place them in the appropriate places; your outline should provide a clear *guide to the arrangement of detail* within your composition.

Paragraph according to your outline. Normally, each first-level division with all its subdivisions forms a single paragraph, with the main entry of the division serving as the topic sentence. In a long composition or report, however, you may need to paragraph according to second-level divisions.

Also, you will need to add *transitions* to your work when you draft. Consider adding transitions whenever you move from one division or subdivision to another.

Finally, if you submit an outline along with a paper or report, place it immediately after the cover sheet, before the composition.

The following outline was written for a report investigating the future of electronic engineering technology for the 1980s. The report was written to provide information for the head of a department of electronic engineering technology in a Missouri community college. The department head needed the report to give accurate information to students and to have data for long-range department planning.

TITLE: Report on the Future of Electronic Engineering Technology in the 1980s

THESIS: The future of the field of electronic engineering technology looks good, though there are some drawbacks.

I. Job opportunities in this field are numerous.

A. The current rate of job growth is extraordinary.

1. Recruiters have gone from local to nationwide searches in an attempt to find technicians to fill vacant positions.

2. The most rapidly growing market for technicians with 2-year degrees is on the West Coast.

B. It is expected that the rapid growth of this field will continue throughout the 1980s.

1. The American Electronics Association estimates that the industry will need some 160,000 technical paraprofessionals by 1987.

2. A growth in demand of from 7 to 14.9 percent is expected for Electronic Engineering technicians in Missouri by the end of the decade.

C. As electronics technology is applied to more and more areas of business, commerce, industry, and the consumer marketplace, the demand for electronic engineering technicians is expected to escalate.

II. Salary rates for those in the field of electronics engineering technology are good.

   A. The average starting salary of an electronic engineering technician this year (1983) is $16,500.

   B. The average starting salary varies according to three factors.

      1. Salaries are different in different areas of the country.

      2. The product area affects salary levels.

      3. The level of responsibility a particular position entails affects starting salary.

   C. Because of the increasing demand for people with electronics skills, pay levels can be expected to rise even further.

III. Advancement potential in the field of electronics engineering technology is good.

   A. Technology is always expanding and providing "new frontiers" for people who are flexible and creative.

   B. Advancement is more rapid for those technicians willing to further their education; some technicians eventually complete bachelor's degrees in engineering or engineering technology.

   C. Some technicians have gone on to form their own companies.

IV. The field does have some drawbacks.

   A. Technicians must keep up on advances in this rapidly developing field so their skills will not become obsolete.

   B. The electronics industry is sensitive to changes in the economy.

 Crediting Sources

Articles and reports written for college classes and for publication, as well as for business purposes, are often developed with information gathered from a variety of sources such as books, periodicals, and personal interviews. For each quotation, paraphrase, or summary included in a document, credit must be given to the author or expert providing the data. Not to do so would be not only unprofessional but also illegal.

There are a number of ways to credit sources. Until recently, the system most commonly used by college students was probably that recommended by the Modern Language Association and described in the *MLA Handbook for Writers of Research Papers, Theses, and Dissertations,* 1977 ed. However, the MLA Committee on Documentation Style recently revised its recommendations. Although it formerly required the inclusion of both footnotes and a bibliography, it now recommends the use of in-text, parenthetical citations of sources and a list of works cited at the end of a document, a system that eliminates the need for footnotes. This new system is the main one described in this appendix.

However, various professional organizations, such as the American Psychological Association, publish their own documentation style guides. An instructor may ask you to document your sources according to one of these systems. Some commonly assigned style guides are these:

American Medical Association. *Style Book: Editorial Manual,* 6th ed. Acton, Massachusetts: Publishing Sciences Group, Inc., 1976.

Publication Manual of the American Psychological Association, 2nd ed. Washington, D.C.: American Psychological Association, 1979.

Author's Guide to the Publications of ASCE. New York: American Society of Civil Engineers, 1975.

Council of Biology Editors Style Manual, 4th ed. Arlington, Virginia: Council of Biology Editors Committee on Form, 1978.

Chicago Manual of Style, 13th ed. Chicago: University of Chicago Press, 1982.
U.S. Government Printing Office. *Style Manual.* Washington D.C.: Government Printing Office, 1973.

When to Cite a Source

You do not need to credit the source of short dictionary definitions or of commonly known facts, such as that water boils at 212° F. However, when you include in your writing short quotations, paraphrases, or summaries, you must acknowledge the source of the information. Even if you have rewritten the material in your own words, you must acknowledge the source of the *idea,* if not the exact language.

Provide acknowledgment through in-text citations. Each citation includes a reference to a particular work and page number. The citation usually takes one of two forms:

1. *When an author is named:* Provide the name of the author of the work quoted from and the number of the page from which information was taken.
2. *When no author is named:* Provide the title of the work quoted (in a shortened form if the title is long) and the number of the page from which information was taken.

This author and page citation is placed within the text of a paper, usually immediately after quoted or summarized material. A List of Works Cited page at the end of the paper provides a full bibliographic citation for each source.

Incorporating Short Quotations and Paraphrases

For paraphrases of material or for direct quotations of fewer than four typed lines, use one of the following methods of incorporating the citation.

1. Provide the name of the author within the text of your writing and cite the page number within parentheses, either at the end of the sentence or immediately after the author's name.

   Examples

   Francis O'Donnell asserts that economic arguments of the industrial establishment against air pollution control have been shown to be illogical and invalid when the facts are examined (30).

   According to Francis O'Donnell (30), the economic argument the industrial establishment makes against air pollution control has been largely discredited by the facts.

2. If you do not cite the author's name within the text of your writing, cite it and the page number within parentheses at the end of the quoted or paraphrased material.

   Example

   Another biologist explained, "A good case can be made for our nonexistence as entities. We are not made up, as we had always supposed, of successively enriched packets of our own parts. We are shared, rented, occupied" (Lewis 2).

   If you are citing part of a multivolume work, include the volume number in the citation: (Whitner 3: 33-34). In this example, 3 is the volume number.

3. If you cite *one of several works by one author* on your list of works cited, you must identify which work you are referring to. In the sciences, this is usually accomplished by adding the date of the work to the name: (Lewis 1980: 2). In the humanities, the preferred form is to add the title or a shortened version of it: (Yeats, *Collected Poems:* 87).

4. If your work includes *information from more than one work written by an author in a single year*, the in-text citation must indicate which work is referred to. You can do this by adding the title or a shortened form of it after the author's name, especially for works in the humanities. In the sciences, the common practice is to assign a different *letter* to each separate work; the letter is added to the date in the in-text citation as well as to the citation in the list of works cited. Thus two different works by Isaac Asimov, both written in 1978, might appear as (Asimov 1978a: 20) and (Asimov 1978b: 67).

5. If you quote from *a book that includes a reference to another work*, use the following citation form.

   As Samuel Taylor Coleridge wrote, "Pedantry consists in the use of words unsuitable to the time, place, and company" (qtd. in Williams 125).

   This would indicate that the Coleridge quotation was read in Joseph E. Williams's book *Style: Ten Lessons in Clarity & Grace.*

Extended Direct Quotations

Quotations that exceed four typed lines are handled in a special way. Before presenting the quotation, introduce the passage by naming the author, and then use special spacing to set the quotation apart on the page. Follow these guidelines:

- Double-space the quotation.
- Do *not* enclose the quotation in quotation marks.
- Indent the quoted matter 10 spaces from the margin.
- If the quoted matter begins with the opening of a paragraph, indent the

first line of the quotation five additional spaces. If the quoted matter is from within a paragraph, do not indent farther.

• Place the page number in parentheses immediately after the last word and final punctuation of the quote. You need cite only the page number.

See Figure E.1 for an example.

Isaac Asimov explains how the two poles of a battery came to be called the "anode" and the "cathode."

> The electrode connected to the positive pole of the battery is the positive electrode; the other, the negative electrode. The British physicist Michael Faraday first suggested (in 1834) that the positive electrode be called the "anode," the negative the "cathode," from the Greek prefixes "ana-," meaning "up" and "kata-," meaning "down." At that time, it was believed the electric current traveled from the battery's positive pole to its negative pole, just as water current travels from a hilltop to a valley; hence the choice of prefixes. As a matter of fact, just the reverse is true; electricity, or at least electrons, travel from negative pole to positive. (83)

Like so many words of science, these two words derive from terms used by the Romans or the Greeks.

Figure E.1 Extended Quotation

The "List of Works Cited" Page

At the end of your document, provide a list of all sources cited. Entitle the page "List of Works Cited." In this list, include bibliographic citations for all works actually quoted, paraphrased, or summarized in your work. Follow these guidelines in writing citations.

General Rules

• Reverse each author's name so you can alphabetize by last names. If no author is given, alphabetize by the title instead, but do not alphabetize by *A, AN,* or *THE* if these words appear first in the title; in these cases, alphabetize by the second word.
• Do not list page numbers for books listed as sources.
• Do list *inclusive* page numbers for articles taken from periodical sources or for cited chapters within books. That is, cite the range of pages for the entire article or section, indicating how long it runs.
• Use "hanging indentation" for the citations. Begin the first line at the

---

LIST OF WORKS CITED

Bagley, Sharon, et al. "Gene Splicing on the Farm." <u>Newsweek,</u> 10 August 1981:
74–76.

Bertrand, Anson, R. "The Bioresearch Revolution: Our Resource for the Future."
<u>Vital Speeches</u> 48 (15 January 1982): 216–219.

Bodde, Tineke. "Genetic Engineering in Agriculture: Another Green
Revolution?" <u>BioScience</u> 32 (July/August 1982): 572–575.

Cooke, Robert. "Engineering a New Agriculture." <u>Technology Review,</u> May/June
1982: 22–28, 39, 41.

------- <u>Improving on Nature: The Brave New World of Genetic Engineering</u>. New
York: Quadrangle/The New York Times Book Company, 1977.

"Creating Plants that Can Repel." <u>Environment,</u> November 1980: 23.

Epstein, Emanual, et al. "Saline Culture of Crops: A Genetic Approach." <u>Science</u>
210 (24 October 1980): 399–404.

Figure E.2   Sample List of Works Cited

margin and indent each additional line of a citation five spaces to the right.
- Double-space each citation; also double-space between citations.
- When you cite two or more works by the same author, do not repeat the author's name in subsequent citations on your list of works cited. Replace the name with a line of seven dashes. (See sample list of sources in Figure E.2.)
- End each citation with a period.

Specific Citation Forms

1. *Book by one author:*

Williams, Joseph H. <u>Style: Ten Lessons in Clarity and Grace</u>. Glenview, Ill.: Scott
Foresman, 1981.

Notice that the author's name is reversed and followed by a period. The title of the book is underlined and followed by a period. In this citation, the state as well as the city of publication is given because

Glenview is not immediately identifiable as being in a particular state. If the city of publication were New York or Chicago, you would not need to name the state.

2. *Book by two or more authors:*

Leakey, Richard E., and Roger Lewin. People of the Lake. Garden City, N.Y.:

    Doubleday, 1978.

Notice that although the name of the first author has been reversed, the name of the second author appears in normal order. If the book is written by four or more authors, you may use the abbreviation *et al.* ("and others") after the name of the first author.

3. *Chapter or part of a book:*

Fielden, John S. "What Do You Mean I Can't Write?" In Strategies for Business and

    Technical Writing. Ed. Kevin J. Harty. New York: Harcourt Brace Jovanov-

    ich, 1980: 14–28.

Cite a chapter or part of a book only if it is written by someone other than the author or editor of a book, or if it is somehow clearly separate in content from the rest of the work.

4. *Magazine article:*

Menosky, Joe. "Computer Worship." Science 84 May 1984: 40–46.

A magazine is a popular periodical. It usually begins pagination anew with each issue; names of authors are sometimes omitted. If the magazine is issued weekly, cite the date in military fashion: 12 November 1984. Cite inclusive page numbers.

5. *Journal article:*

Pearsall, Thomas E. "University Programs in Technical Communication." Techni-

    cal Communication 20 (First Quarter 1973): 10–12.

A journal is a periodical published by a professional organization. Its pages are usually numbered consecutively throughout an entire volume year. After citing the author, article, and journal, provide the journal's volume number in Arabic numerals and add the date within parentheses. (Journals are not, as a rule, issued weekly. Typical journal dates might be March 1983, Fall 1984, or simply 1985.) After the date, add a colon and inclusive page numbers. If you cite a journal that does <u>not</u> use continuous pagination, add the issue number after the volume number and a *period*, like this: 20.3.

6. *Newspaper Article*

Williams, Winston. "The Shrinking of the Steel Industry." <u>New York Times</u>, 23

September 1984, sec. F:4.

After the title of the newspaper, cite the date, section, and page. Separate the section designation and the page number with a colon. If the name of the newspaper you cite does not include the name of the city in which it is published, add this information in brackets: [St. Louis] <u>Riverfront Times</u>.

7. *Newspaper Article Found through NewsBank*

Mullen, William. "Nurses, Computer Experts: The Warm Feeling of Winners."

<u>Chicago Tribune</u>. 12 February 1982. (Located in NewsBank [microform],

Employment, 1982, 10:EB-10, fiche.)

If you have found a newspaper article through NewsBank, you will not be able to write a standard citation because NewsBank provides only a clipping of the article on microfiche. You cannot find section or page numbers on the clipping. Write the citation following the sample given. After the date, cite the microfiche card number and follow it with a colon. Then cite the column and line numbers that locate the clipping on the microfiche card.

8. *Encyclopedia Article*

"Evolution." <u>World Book Encyclopedia</u>. 1978 ed.

If an author is given, begin the citation with the author's name.

9. *Pamphlet or Brochure*

<u>Architectural/Writer Editor</u>. Series G, Volume 6, No.9. Sauk Centre, MN: Voca-

tional Biographies, 1977.

<u>Technical Writers</u>. Occupational Brief #286. Chicago: Science Research Associates,

1974.

Pamphlets and brochures are often difficult to cite, but treat them as much like books as possible. Provide an author's name when one is given. Underline the title of the pamphlet or brochure, and add any additional information, such as publication number. When dealing with government documents, you will often find that the publisher is the Government Printing Office (GPO). If you cannot find a date of publication, add "n.d." for "no date."

10. *Computer Print-Outs*

> Guidance Information System (GIS). Technical Writers. #239. Houghton Mifflin,
>
> Time Share Corporation Division, 1983.

In general, treat computer print-outs as much like books as possible. Look through each work to find an author, place of publication, publisher, and date. Provide any identifying numbers or codes. If you cannot find a date, use the abbreviation "n.d." for "no date."

11. *Computer Software*

> Roessler, Michael. Regions of the United States. Computer Software. Baldwin, NY:
>
> Daybreak Software, 1983. Apple IIe, 48KB, floppy disk.

Begin the citation as for a book. After the date, add the name of the computer for which the software is intended, the number of kilobytes (KB), and the software format (floppy disk).

12. *Personal Interview or Letter*

> Procter, Charles. Engineer, Union Electric. Personal Interview. St. Louis, Missouri,
>
> 28 November 1985.

Cite the name and title of the person interviewed, as well as the location and date of the interview.

Alternative Methods of Citing Sources

There are other general methods of crediting sources. Because dates of publication are so important in the sciences—as material can rapidly become obsolete—a date is often incorporated into the in-text citation, for easy reference. Most of the systems, however, are similar to the one just described; they require a list of sources at the end of a document and in some way make reference to items on the list within the document.

Three alternative systems of documentation will be described here. For each, the "List of Works Cited" page is typically entitled "References" or "List of References."

Formal In-Text Citation

This system for crediting sources makes use of information in parentheses to identify sources. All elements that would normally be given in a bibliographic citation, along with the number of the page from which the information was taken, are provided. Adding a "References" page is optional.

This kind of documentation is recommended *only* for articles or reports in which very few citations are necessary. When using it, attempt to interrupt the text as little as possible. Work necessary information into the text if you can, and place the remaining information within parentheses. Check the previous guidelines to find out what information to include.

Example

> Robert Pirsig has definite ideas about what is wrong with modern life. On page 66 of his novel Zen and the Art of Motorcycle Maintenance (New York: Bantam Books, 1974) he contrasts the romantic mode, which he says is "primarily inspirational, creative, intuitive" with the classical mode, which "proceeds by reason and by laws--which are themselves underlying forms of thought and behavior." The conflict between these two ways of seeing and behaving, says Pirsig, is the problem faced by contemporary men and women.

Name and Date System

Documentation outside the humanities has long made use of parentheses within the text of a composition. Credits in parentheses, placed at the end of a quotation, paraphrase, or summary, may cite *author and date; author, date, and page; author and title;* or some similar combination. Since direct quotations are used infrequently in reports and scientific articles, the source note most commonly follows a paraphrase or summary.

Example

> An estimated 1.5 billion metric tons of recoverable minerals exist in a 2.5-million-square-kilometer area south of Hawaii (McKelvey 1980, p. 466).

At the end of a document employing this method of crediting sources, add a "List of References" page citing all sources named in the composition, in alphabetical order by author's last name.

If the essay includes information from more than one work written by an author in a single year, the in-text citation must indicate which work is referred to. This is usually accomplished by adding the title of the work, often in a shortened form.

Numbered Bibliography

In some disciplines, each item in the list of references (once it is established) is given a number. The list may be ordered alphabetically or according to the order in which works are cited within a composition. The in-text documentation consists of the work's number on the list of references, a colon, and the number of the page from which the information was taken. Both numbers are placed in parentheses.

Example

> There will be many openings in the 1980s for people with an electronics education. The American Electronics Association estimates that the industry will need some 140,000 technical paraprofessionals by 1985 (1:158). By 1990, as many as 685,000 new jobs are projected in the high technology field (4:166).

A sample numbered list of references is shown in Figure E.3.

LIST OF REFERENCES

1. "California Trains Technicians." Electronics, 28 July 1982: 158.

2. "Engineering." (St. Louis Community College) Career Planning and Placement Newsletter, January–February 1983.

3. Menashian, L. S. "Resources for Electronic-based High Technology R & D Professionals." Educational Technology, November 1981: 11–14.

4. Wheatly, Mary. "High Tech." Ms., August 1982:166–169.

Figure E.3 List of References

Acknowledgments

P. 34, from *The World Book Encyclopedia.* Copyright © 1985 World Book Inc.

Pp. 82–83, M. K. Hamilton, Director (1981–present); S. C. Landis, Director (1975–81), Counseling Center, Southern Illinois University.

Pp. 144–145, from *Science and Survival* by Barry Commoner. Copyright © 1963, 1964, 1966 by Barry Commoner. Reprinted by permission of Viking Penguin, Inc.

P. 231, "Here are tips . . . " courtesy of National Retail Hardware Association.

P. 233, from *Complete Do-It-Yourself Manual.* Copyright © 1973 The Reader's Digest Association, Inc. Used with the permission of the publisher.

P. 240, courtesy of Amana Refrigeration, Inc.

P. 247, from *Complete Do-It-Yourself Manual.* Copyright © 1973 The Reader's Digest Association, Inc. Used with the permission of the publisher.

P. 264, from U.S. Department of Energy, Office of Scientific & Technical Information, Oak Ridge, Tennessee.

P. 265, reprinted with permission from *Criminal Justice Abstracts,* published by Willow Tree Press, Inc., PO Box 249, Monsey, NY 10952.

Pp. 269–270, reprinted by permission of *Science 84* Magazine; copyright the American Association for the Advancement of Science.

P. 277, from U.S. Department of Energy, Office of Scientific & Technical Information, Oak Ridge, Tennessee.

Pp. 279–280, copyright © 1981 Time Inc. All rights reserved. Reprinted by permission from *Time.*

Index

432

434

To the Student

Usually only instructors are asked about the quality of a text; their opinion alone is considered as revisions are planned or as new books are developed. Now, we would like to ask you about *Practical Writing.* Your suggestions will affect the next edition. Please return this questionnaire to the English Editor, College Department, Holt, Rinehart and Winston, 383 Madison Avenue, New York, NY 10017

Name _____ Date _____

School _____ Course title _____

Instructor _____

1. Did you find this book too easy? _____ too difficult? _____

   about right? _____

2. Which chapters did you find the most helpful? Why? _____

   _____

3. Which chapters did you find least helpful? Why? _____

   _____

	Helpful	Not Helpful
INTRODUCTORY PRINCIPLES		
1. An Introduction to Practical Writing	_____	_____
2. The Process of Practical Writing	_____	_____
LETTERS AND MEMOS		
3. Writing a Business Letter	_____	_____
4. Writing Memos and Informal Reports	_____	_____
5. Writing Letters of Application and Résumés	_____	_____
RESOURCES AND TECHNIQUES		
6. Gathering Information—Library Research	_____	_____
7. Gathering Information—Field Research	_____	_____
8. Using Graphics	_____	_____
SPECIAL FORMS		
9. Describing a Mechanism	_____	_____
10. Writing Instructions	_____	_____
11. Writing an Abstract	_____	_____
REPORT FORMS		
12. Writing a Formal Investigative Report	_____	_____
13. Writing a Proposal	_____	_____
14. Giving an Oral Presentation of a Report	_____	_____

4. What changes would you suggest for the next edition?